Bridge to the Gods

Tales from Kyushu

MEMOIRS OF LIFE IN FAR SOUTH JAPAN

ANDREW THOMSON

First published 2018 by Ryan Publishing
PO Box 7680, Melbourne, 3004
Victoria, Australia
Ph: 61 3 9505 6820
Fax: 61 3 9505 6821
Email: books@ryanpub.com
Website: www.ryanpub.com

RYAN PUBLISHING

 A catalogue record for this book is available from the National Library of Australia

Title: *Bridge to the Gods: Tales from Kyushu Memoirs of Life in Far South Japan*

Paperback: 978-1-876498-59-7
Hard Back: 978-1-876498-76-4
eBook: 978-1-876498-77-1

Copyright © 2018. Andrew Thomson.

Apart from any fair dealing for the purposes of private study, research, criticism or review, as permitted under the Copyright Act, no part may be reproduced by any process without written permission. Inquiries should be addressed to the publisher.

Internal and cover design by Luke Harris, Working Type Studio, Victoria, Australia. www.workingtype.com.au

Contents

Map of Japan		iv
Map of Kyushu		v
Glossary of Japanese words		vii
Introduction		xiii
One	After the Earthquake	1
Two	Lawyers	13
Three	In search of the kamikaze	25
Four	Origins	45
Five	Kyushu on the palate	55
Six	Yakuza	67
Seven	Tea	85
Eight	Rice	105
Nine	Shinto — the Way of the Gods	119
Ten	Cousin Kyoko's Orchard	161
Eleven	The Teacher and the Defacing of the Graves	175
Twelve	The Kirishitan Relics	199
Thirteen	Looking for Confucius	213
Fourteen	The Admiral	239
Fifteen	The Earthquake	257
Sixteen	James Bond and the Search for Kissy Suzuki	269
Seventeen	Japan's Gettysburg	289
Eighteen	The Challenge of Air-Conditioning	303
Nineteen	Preparing For War	311
Twenty	Elections	331
Twenty-one	The Stones of Miyazaki	353
Afterword		375

Japan and Northeast Asia

Kyushu

Glossary of Japanese Words

Akibare	fine autumn weather
Ama	diving girl
Anaguma	a badger-like animal
Araa	exclamation of surprise
Basashi	raw horse meat
Bengoshi	lawyer
Beni shōga	pickled red ginger
Bento	boxed lunch
Besso	holiday home
Bonsai	miniature tree
Burakumin	outcast caste
Bushido	samurai code of honour
Biwa cha	loquat leaf tea
Bōryokudan	gangster groups, polite word for yakuza
Champon	Chinese-style noodles from Nagasaki
Chōnaikai	local citizens associations
Daikon	Japanese radish
Daimyo	a samurai lord
Danchiku	a type of bamboo
Dohyō	sumo wrestling ring
Dokudami	herbal tea (*Houttuynia cordata*)
Enoki	a type of mushroom
Gaiben	foreign lawyer
Gaijin	foreigner
Geinojin	a person with artistic talent, celebrity

Genmaicha	green tea flavoured with toasted rice
Gyōji	sumo referee
Gyokuro	highest grade of green tea
Gyoza	dumpling
Hachimaki	traditional headband
Hakko ichi-u	a patriotic slogan
Hakome	a wooden box with a pane of glass used to peer underwater
Hanami	viewing of cherry blossoms
Hanshiren	a Chinese herbal medicine
Harai	Shinto ceremony
Hatsumode	first prayers of the New Year
Hinohikari	famous rice brand from Saga Prefecture
Hinoki	Japanese cedar tree
Hiragana	Japanese phonetic script used for Japanese words
Hōki	Japanese broom
Honden	main building of a Shinto shrine
Honke	original restaurant of a chain
Hora	'Look at that!'
Hoshi gaki	dried persimmon
Inaka	countryside
Inoshishi	wild boar
Iwanori	pulverized nori seaweed paste
Izakaya	a type of Japanese restaurant with a counter
Jidori	Free range chicken
Jinja	Shinto shrine
Jishin	earthquake
Jōnōkin	money paid to yakuza superiors
Jukyō	Confucianism
Juwari soba	pure soba made by hand
Kabosu	a type of citrus fruit
Kaedama	extra helping of noodles
Kaede	a type of maple tree

Kaiseki ryori	classical Japanese cuisine
Kakashi	a type of life-size doll
Kaki	persimmon
Kakure kirishitan	Hidden Christians
Kami	Shinto god
Kamidana	small, indoor Shinto shrine
Kamikaze	suicide pilots in Pacific War
Kanpa	cold wave
Kara age	fried chicken dish famous in Oita Prefecture
Katakana	Japanese phonetic script used for foreign words
Kenri	right, entitlement
Keyaki	Zelkovia tree
Kokusai teki	international
Kombini	convenience store
Kōsa	fine atmospheric yellow sand from China
Koshihikari	High grade rice
Kotatsu	heater table used in Japanese homes
Kirishitan	old term for Christians
Kirisuto-kyō	Christianity
Kitsune odori	fox dance
Kun	suffix denoting a young man
Kusami	stink of food, especially tonkotsu ramen
Kuwa cha	mulberry leaf tea
Maa	exclamation of uncertainty
Madoguchi	window into something
Maguro	tuna
Mai nambaa	'My Number' – citizen registration number
Manju	a type of sweet cake
Manyoshu	ancient Japanese text
Matcha	powdered green tea
Mentaiko	spiced cod roe
Michi no eki	roadside market
Mikan	mandarin orange

Miko	girl serving at a Shinto shrine
Minshuku	Cheap local inn, usually run by a family
Misogi	Shinto ceremony of purification
Mizutori	box for absorbing humidity
Mōsho	severe summer heat
Motsunabe	offal hotpot stew
Nakōdō	matchmaker
Nattō	fermented soya beans
Nigiri	rice ball
Nōkyo	National Agricultural Co-operative (now known as JA)
Nori	edible seaweed
Nōrin Chūkin	Japan's Agricultural Savings Bank
Obaasan	Grandmother
Okaasan	Mother
Okami-san	proprietress
Okonomiyaki	a type of savoury pancake
Onigiri	rice ball
Onsen	hot spring
Otoosan	Father
Ozeki	second-highest rank in sumo wrestling
Ramen	Chinese-style noodles
Remokon	remote control
Rotenburo	outdoor hot spring bath
Ryokan	traditional-style Japanese inn
Saaa	expression of something being considered
Sakaki	sacred tree in Shinto
Sake	Japanese rice wine
Sakura	cherry blossom
Saru	monkey
Satori	sudden enlightenment in Zen Buddhism
Sazae	a type of shellfish
Seinan Sensō	South-Western War

Sencha	plain green tea
Sensei	honorific title for lawyers, doctors, teachers, politicians etc
Sensō	war
Shakai fukki	return to normal society for convicted criminals
Shakai no chouwa	social harmony
Shiatsu	medicinal massage
Shinden	holy sanctuary building within a Shinto shrine
Shochu	white spirit made from barley, potato, or sugar cane
Shōgatsu	New Year
Shukan Bunshun	a weekly news and gossip magazine
Sugi	Japanese cypress tree
Suiseki	ornamental rocks
Takoyaki	octopus balls – a type of fast food from Osaka
Tatami	woven-straw flooring
Tokkōtai	kamikaze pilots
Tonkotsu	Kyushu-style pork-flavoured ramen soup
Torisashi	chicken sashimi
Tororo	grated mountain yam
Tsunami	tidal wave
Tsuyu	rainy season June-July
Udon	thick noodles
Ujigami	tutelary god of the samurai
Umi no kami	gods of the sea
Uni	sea urchin
Wagyu	Japanese beef
Wakame	edible seaweed (*Undaria pinnatifida*)
Yaki soba	fried noodle dish famous in Hita
Yakitori	broiled chicken on a skewer
Yakuza	gangster
Yatai	Outdoor food hawker stall

Yokozuna	highest rank in sumo wrestling
Yomogi	mugwort herbal tea (*Artemisia indictor*)
Yosan	budget
Yuba	soft tofu skin
Yuzu	a type of citrus fruit
Yuzu gosho	citrus-based mustard

Introduction

My father was a professional golfer. Beginning in the 1950s he played tournaments for a living, for a while dominating golf outside the United States and winning the Open Championship five times. The Dunlop company, then British-owned, asked him to visit Japan in 1955 to play an exhibition match. Although it was only a decade since Japan's defeat in the Pacific War – a conflict my father had lived through as a teenager – he found Japan a delightful place, inhabited not by savage samurai types but with courteous, refined people who made him feel warmly welcome. Thus, began his lifelong affection for Japan and its people.

In the 1960s my father made it a habit to invite some of Japan's own professional golfers to come and stay at our house in Australia during our summer and play tournaments. There were few tournaments in Japan and none during their winter. I grew up meeting these men almost every year, and they made a strong impression on me. Some of them cooked *sukiyaki* for us, and my sisters and I enjoyed judo with them on our front lawn after they returned from the golf course. Later, with my father's encouragement, I began studying the Japanese language at school. It became my best subject, my father rewarding my efforts with trips to Japan as a teenager. The more I saw of the country, and the more of its language I mastered, the more I liked it.

Later I went to university in Tokyo, returned there after qualifying as a lawyer in Australia, and worked in Tokyo during the 'Bubble' economy era of the late 1980s and early 1990s. I had the good fortune to fall in love with and marry a girl from the town of Hita in Kyushu, my wife Sayuri. When she and I went to see her parents to seek formal permission to marry my command of Japanese was very good. Yet I could barely understand what her father Noriyuki Sakamoto had to say, such was his Kyushu accent and thick dialect. He asked me a series of questions. Not understanding him I simply answered "Yes" to each one until my wife dug me in the ribs and told me to shut up. After the interrogation was over, and permission to marry granted, I asked Sayuri what my prospective father-in-law had asked me.

"You are a complete idiot," she cried. "He said your parents would reject me because I have bad manners, and you said yes!"

"Oh, sorry."

"And then he said you don't have enough money to support me, and you said yes!"

"Ah, sorry. I couldn't understand him."

"Well just shut up in future and let me do the talking."

I left Japan in 1991, worked in Australia for a while, served in the Federal Parliament, then practised law in Washington DC, Saudi Arabia, and Beijing. Just before the 2011 tsunami and Fukushima nuclear disaster I returned to live in Tokyo. By late 2012, though, I was tired of life in the capital and made the decision to move to Kyushu and open my own law office in Fukuoka.

Since the encounter more than twenty-five years ago, my father-in-law and I have become good friends. When I decided to move from Tokyo to Kyushu he was delighted to have me come and live in his home for a while until I found a house of my own near Fukuoka. Likewise, my mother-in-law Sayoko Sakamoto was overjoyed to have someone young back in her home. As the months passed I gradually understood more and more of their Kyushu dialect. Now, after six years living in Kyushu my friends in Tokyo sometimes laugh at my own Japanese accent, half *gaijin* and half Kyushu.

I settled down and opened my own law office in Fukuoka, my wife Sayuri and children Sara and Cail were all living in Australia by then. This left me alone on weekends. Riding my 900cc Kawasaki Vulcan Classic motorbike I began to explore Kyushu, an island with a population of around ten million people. The more I travelled and the more I read about Kyushu the more I began to understand the importance of its place in Japanese history. The origins of the Japanese people and their Shinto myths are found here. The tragic history of Japan's early Christians are all in Kyushu.

The *kamikaze* pilots who sacrificed themselves in the dying months of the Pacific War all flew off to their deaths from airfields in Kyushu. And Japan's most violent *yakuza* gangsters lurk in great numbers beneath the surface of society in Kyushu.

Indeed, it is this island where the Shinto creation myth has Japan's history beginning: in Takachiho down in Miyazaki Prefecture - Kyushu as the Bridge to The Gods. Shinto is deeply embedded in Kyushu, as is Buddhism and Christianity.

These many aspects of Japan's history are essentially Kyushu stories, yet nobody seems to have taken the time to sum them up in a book for people outside Japan to read. Along with the travel and the research, I had conversations with many local people in fishing villages, mountain hamlets, and around the cities of Kyushu. I visited my parents-in-law most weekends to take them to a hot spring or out to dinner, doing my best to make their days pleasant now that they had retired and closed their kimono shop.

Kyushu is very close to the Korean peninsula and to China. Over the past three years as tensions with Beijing worsened, and as Kim Jong-un began firing missiles to intimidate everyone, it began to look as if war would erupt. Donald Trump was elected president in the United States and I began stockpiling food, fuel, and water at home. Life became bizarre for a few months. Yet the tensions eased, and life returned to normal.

In recent times Japan has suddenly become a popular place to visit for tourists from all over the world. The streets of Ginza, Asakusa, Kyoto, and Hiroshima are full of foreigners, as are the ski slopes of Hokkaido. Every time I fly back to Australia on JAL or Qantas, I meet people who have been to Japan and loved it.

Yet few foreign visitors make it down to Kyushu. Life is different down here, less crowded and with more distinct flavours in the food and drink. It's worth a visit, and if this book prompts a change in someone's original travel plans for Japan, then all the better.

Andrew Thomson
Itoshima, Fukuoka Prefecture

One

After the Earthquake

In late 2010, I was living alone in Beijing, working as a lawyer for an Australian law firm. My wife and two children had stayed in Australia. My wife Sayuri, being Japanese, was wary of life in China where anti-Japanese sentiment was regularly stirred up by the Party. Although she was by no means anti-Chinese herself, Beijing being fascinating, dirty, and scary was asking too much.

Going to distant places to earn a living seemed my destiny. A mere six years after leaving parliamentary life in Australia back in 2001, I began living away from my family. This was not because of marital discord or breakdown. Far from it. Sayuri, looking at things with the practical eye of a country girl from Kyushu, told me I would make the most of my chances in professional life if I gave up trying to earn a living in Australia and used my other languages for the benefit of my clients.

Over the years since my school days and after university in Tokyo, I'd learned to speak, read, and write advanced Japanese, pretty good Mandarin Chinese, and basic Arabic. So, I went to live and practise law in Abu Dhabi, Saudi Arabia, and then China.

I'd been in Beijing for two years. It was stressful, entertaining, and though I had enjoyed it for the first year by making friends and getting my Chinese language skills into very good shape, during the second year it began to wear me down. The Chinese Government began harassing foreign companies and complaining about Western culture "polluting" Chinese youth. The uncensored version of Google was shut down, and the whole internet crackdown began in earnest. The air was getting worse every year.

When I played golf with friends on bad days we couldn't see the flag on the greens when standing on the tees. Finally I decided I'd had enough. I wanted to go back to Tokyo where I'd lived, studied, worked, and married twenty years ago.

When I told my wife I was sick of life in China and planned on moving back to Tokyo after twenty years away she was cautious.

She asked, 'You spend two years alone in Beijing becoming fluent in Chinese and earning a good income as a lawyer, and now you want to give it up?'

You're Japanese, I replied. You can never live in China with me because of the hostility. And neither of us wants to inflict Beijing's air on our children.

Well, maybe I'll come and live in Tokyo if you move there, she said.

I moved to Tokyo in January 2011, eight weeks before Fukushima.

When the earthquake struck at a quarter to three on that Friday afternoon in mid-March 2011, I was standing by my desk in the office I shared in Aoyama, Tokyo's *haute couture* district. It was a small office on the top floor of a new and narrow ten storey building in the street informally known as Kottō Dōri, or 'Antique Street' on account of the antique shops that are almost all gone now. As a freelance lawyer I rented a desk there from my friend Warwick Johnson, who ran a Japanese equity fund from Sydney. His three Japanese staff and I got on well, and I found it a convenient alternative to renting my own office.

The earthquake began as usual with a tiny jolt, but what began to alarm us was that the shaking continued for more than the normal five seconds. As soon as it started, Chisato Tamaki, the lady who kept the books for Warwick in Tokyo, uttered the customary exclamation, '*Jishin desu*,' (It's an earthquake) in a quiet voice. We glanced at each other and smiled nervously. I had a visiting Kiwi lawyer with me, Lloyd Baggott, who was smiling. He'd been in Japan plenty of times and being a Kiwi he knew what earth tremors were all about. Across the room young Takagi-*san*, Warwick's equity analyst, sat at his desk trying to ignore the tremor. When the shaking suddenly increased after five more seconds we knew something was going badly wrong. The building was making loud groans, the windows rattling in their frames. Then it got worse again, and things began to fall off shelves and desks. This was no ordinary *jishin*. This was…..Shit!.....This was The Big One.

As I started moving towards the door to the liftwell the shaking got so bad that I couldn't stand up without clinging on to partitions or chairs. As the filing cabinets toppled over and computers crashed to the floor, I began to think we were all going to get hurt. Yet, the disbelief that comes with the idea of the building cracking up around us somehow kept panic at bay. The violence of the quake was such that you couldn't panic. I ended up on my hands and knees crawling across the carpet trying to reach the men's bathroom where it's supposed to be safest in a big quake. Why? Because the pipes in the walls are said to offer you extra protection from the collapsing structure. Halfway there I saw the umbrella stand had fallen over, and I briefly thought of trying to make it stand upright again. When I reached the lift lobby outside the office the shaking began to fade, and within a minute it had stopped. I got up, went back into the office, and burst into euphoric laughter.

'Hey, we survived!' I shouted. 'We survived!'

Tamaki-*san* and young Takagi surveyed the damage, gasping quietly in disbelief. Lloyd kept muttering something and then said, 'We'd better get out of here.'

The lifts had stopped working so we left the office using the fire escape, a steel staircase on the outside at the rear of the building. Down in the street I was astonished to find no damage whatsoever. There were no broken windows, no cracks in the footpath or road, just a lot of very rattled people standing around looking stunned. Tokyo had survived the quake without a scratch.

Later that evening I got back to the small room I was renting in Hiroo and turned on the television news. That's when the full extent of the disaster became clear. A few minutes after the shockwave of the earthquake had reached Kottō Dōri and the rest of Tokyo the giant *tsunami* had smashed into the coast of Fukushima Prefecture and further northwards along the

Pacific coast. It hit the Fukushima nuclear power station with immense force, shattering the concrete casing around the reactor and destroying the electrical system in the plant. Like a kettle left on a gas stove for too long, the nuclear reactor in No. 1 plant lost its cooling system and began to melt down. Pretty soon clouds of poisonous, raw radiation began spewing into the air like a volcano. In a terrible irony, just like Hiroshima and Nagasaki, Japan had been hit again with a nuclear catastrophe, only this time it was the bewildering violence of Nature that took everyone by surprise.

Eighteen months later, Sayuri and Cail having come to live with me in Tokyo a few months after Fukushima, I left the city and moved to Kyushu, the large island in the far south-west of Japan. It wasn't for fear of radiation from the wrecked Fukushima nuclear power station or a second, devastating quake. Not in the least. The large Australian law firm I had been representing in Japan lost interest in the country, and at the end of that year Cail was due to return to Australia to continue school. What was the point of my staying in Tokyo alone, trying to eke out a living as a single lawyer? Suddenly I decided I might have a chance if I left Tokyo. Sayuri was born and raised in Kyushu, so why not there?

Three months before Sayuri and Cail left Tokyo to return to Australia I left them behind there, taking my much-loved Kawasaki Vulcan Classic motorbike with me. There you have it. A man who takes his motorbike and leaves his family behind in an earthquake-prone city, a mere 250 kilometres from a melted down nuclear power plant, probably has some serious issues, as they say.

Tokyo is a vast city. It works with an efficiency you have to admire, and apart from Nature it boasts pretty much the best of everything a city can have or host. Its restaurants, in number and quality, are way above any competitor. Its public transport system is a work of art. Its urban architecture is generally good on the eye. Its fish market is the world's largest, and its temples and shrines are immaculate. Yet a year after what became known

A view of Mount Fuji over Tokyo's evening skyline in winter. After years living in the city as a university student and later as a lawyer I decided to move to Kyushu in search of a life closer to that of most Japanese people.

as "Fukushima" in English, and the "Great East Kanto Region Disaster" in Japanese, life in Tokyo became an exercise in boredom.

Along the Pacific coast north of Tokyo the fishing villages had been literally wiped out by the *tsunami*. Stories were broadcast of entire schools being swamped with seawater, the students gathered outside on the parade ground all swept away and drowned together with their teachers. Tens of thousands of people in Fukushima and Miyagi Prefectures who survived the tsunami were living in temporary housing up in the mountains. For those people unlucky enough to have homes within a 20 kilometre radius of the nuclear power station, life had changed forever. They can never return to those homes and farms. Their livestock and pet dogs roam wild, their fields overgrown. Their shops in the towns and villages are abandoned, the stock still on the shelves. It was, and still remains, a ghastly and depressing reality.

The one cheerful event around that time was the World Cup victory of Japan's women's soccer team, known as Nadeshiko Japan. Their captain, the redoubtable Miss Homare Sawa, was the only public figure providing the people with any inspiration.

In 1983 I was in my early twenties and a student in Japan, attending Keio University in Tokyo. I had a bit of extra money from part-time work as an interpreter at golf tournaments, and grew to love Tokyo as my friends and I wandered around looking for fun to be had. We explored the older quarters of the city around Asakusa and Ueno which had been destroyed by fire bombing during the war, and we spent plenty of time in the younger more trendy areas of Shibuya and Harajuku where girls were to be found in larger numbers, not that this made much difference to our success rate as Romeos. I came back to live in Tokyo again in 1986 and found work as a lawyer and then as a fund manager for a while, but by then Japan was experiencing what became known as "the Bubble Era" when speculation in everything from stocks, land, and even golf club memberships went berserk. Tokyo lost its post-war innocence and joined the big, bad modern world of high finance.

Now, twenty years later, after the Fukushima disaster the radiation problem was bewildering and very scary for a few weeks as the Tokyo Electric Power Company (TEPCO) did its best to cover up what was happening with the meltdown. The Kan Government floundered around trying to convince everyone it had a grip on the situation, something nobody believed in the slightest. Yet, by around June that year, the worst fears of radiation had faded and Sayuri was preparing to leave Australia and come back to Tokyo. By September, she and I and our eight year-old son Cail had moved into an apartment I'd found in Aoyama. Our daughter Sara remained at boarding school in Australia. I had misgivings about her staying in Australia without us, but she had been to school in Japan as an 11 year-old in my wife's home town of Hita in Kyushu and she wanted to stay with her school friends in Melbourne.

Though generally an ebullient child, Cail was miserable in Tokyo at first, having left his school pals behind and without a single friend in the city. I desperately wanted him to enjoy life in Japan, and it distressed me to see him so morose every day. Had the move to Tokyo for him been a dreadful mistake, I wondered.

One day we were watching the September sumo tournament on television together late in the afternoon.

'Sumo's pretty good, eh?' I said.

'Yeah, they're cool, those guys' he replied. At last something about Japan had cheered him up.

'Which wrestler do you like best?' I asked him.

'I like Baruto,' he replied. Baruto was a tall, blond Estonian who had reached the second-highest rank of *ozeki*. He had a habit of smiling ruefully when he lost a bout, a trait that endeared him to the Japanese fans. He had an obvious humility.

Cail's decision to follow Baruto closely gave me an idea as to how to really cheer him up. I did some searching on the internet and found Baruto's stable and its rather crude website. There was a section for the supporters club one could join.

'We can go and meet Baruto in person,' I told Cail confidently.

'What? Actually meet him?' He was thrilled by the prospect. Life in Japan was suddenly looking a lot better.

It turned out that the fellow who headed up Baruto's stable supporters club lived just around the corner from us there in Aoyama. I called him, half expecting resistance to the idea of a *gaijin* [a foreigner in colloquial Japanese] asking to join, but no, not at all! Iwamoto-*san* met me at a nearby café where I paid him the annual fee of ¥20,000 (around $200) and had a chat. He was in his mid-thirties, with slightly long hair and messy but expensive clothes. He spoke basic but workable English, having lived in Hawaii for a few years 'working in the restaurant business,' he said. When he realised I spoke Japanese with no difficulty he gave up using English. What line of work was he in now? I asked. Ah, in the entertainment business, he replied vaguely, clearly reluctant to go into any detail. Then he suddenly changed his mind and began to elaborate.

'In Tokyo there are lots of TV and movie production companies,' he said. ' I make sure my clients' actors, singers, and *geinojin* (artistic talents) get work.'

Ah, I replied, suddenly aware of the situation. In Japan the *yakuza* gangs, or the three main groups: the Yamaguchi Gumi, the Inagawa Kai, and the Sumiyoshi Rengo, have a lot of influence in the entertainment industry. Among other things they pressure television and movie companies into hiring talent from their captive agencies and take a cut of the earnings. It's all done quietly, and blue chip companies steer well clear of such troublesome business. Indeed, the television broadcasters outsource almost all their content to production companies in order to avoid dealing with the bad boys.

It seemed likely that Iwamoto worked as an intermediary for one of the gangs. That was probably also the reason for his time in Hawaii. As a sideline he worked in the sumo world, or as he explained it, his old friendship with the stablemaster's wife led him to offer to run the supporters club. All this I found a fascinating window on how sumo worked. As Iwamoto explained, he solicited large donations to the club from wealthy sumo fans all over Japan, mostly *pachinko* gambling parlour owners and especially in Kyushu from where the stablemaster and most of his wrestlers hailed. In return, the donors got to have dinner with the *ozeki* Baruto when they came up to Tokyo, so they could boast about it to their friends back home.

For a while a few years ago, sumo was scandalised by match-fixing, yet they cleaned that up with the expulsion of a few wrestlers and corrupt stablemasters. For me, that people such as Iwamoto were involved was no big problem. Sumo needed money, and having dinner with senior wrestlers was a perfectly proper way to bring it in. Cail and I went to Baruto's stable to watch the early morning practice a couple of times. Then Baruto surprised us all by winning the January tournament in 2012. One morning a fortnight after he won we had breakfast with him and his fellow wrestlers at the stable. Cail, with the bold innocence of a child, asked him in English, ' How much money do you get for winning?'

Sitting on the *tatami* floor eating his enormous breakfast the gentle blond giant, son of a dairy farmer, replied in a low growl, 'Not enough!'

I had to laugh. Only for a child could you get such answers in Japan.

Apart from a deteriorating workload, life for the next year was fun as I watched Cail get to know Tokyo. After an unsuccessful term at an expensive international school he ended up at the local primary school in Aoyama and played happily every day with his Japanese classmates. For New Year in 2011, Sara came to Japan from boarding school in Australia for a few weeks and we all went down to Sayuri's hometown in the mountains of Kyushu, the town of Hita in Oita Prefecture.

As we had done for most of the previous twenty years of our marriage, these trips to Hita involved days of visiting local hot springs to sample the waters, going to noteworthy temples and shrines to pray, staying at mountain inns, and eating enormous amounts of Kyushu food such as raw horsemeat, deep-fried chicken, and the best *gyoza* in Japan made in the tiny shop two doors down the street. Sayuri's elderly parents, Mr and Mrs Sakamoto, still ran a kimono rental shop and hairdressing salon near the station in Hita. Not long ago, Sara lived with them for a year when aged eleven, attending school with the local children.

Life in the countryside — *inaka*, a most important Japanese word — is still governed by tradition in every way. Sayuri complained that everyone seemed to know everything about everyone else, or felt they *should* know. It's socially stifling, she declared. Doubtless true for her, having grown up in Hita, yet to me, the foreign outsider or *gaijin*, there were and still are no such irritations.

That trip in 2011 was also the first time we went into the city of Fukuoka to have a look around. The streets were not crowded like Tokyo and were laid out nicely with canopies of trees here and there. Neither did Fukuoka have the boring uniformity of Nagoya or the ugly, messy sprawl of Osaka. The city seemed to express the notion that in Japan you could actually have everything that was good about Tokyo but without the pressures of a huge population. From almost anywhere in the city you can see the nearby mountains, and the edge of the sea lies only a mile from parts of downtown.

It was during this visit that I began to wonder whether I could ever live in a place like Fukuoka, or at least outside Tokyo. Could a *gaijin* like me find enough work to survive, I wondered.

When we were back in Tokyo I raised the subject with Sayuri as delicately as I could. 'I think I want to go and live in Kyushu,' I mentioned in passing.

She was nonplussed, to put it mildly.

'Why would you want to do that?' she said, having left Hita after high school for university in Tokyo and never given the remotest thought to going back to Kyushu.

'Well, it would make sense in a way,' I replied.

'You are mad. How can you be a lawyer in Kyushu?'

'You can be a registered foreign lawyer anywhere in Japan,' I explained.

For some weeks we argued about it. Tokyo is too competitive for lawyers, I complained. The large Australian law firm I represented in Japan was never going to open an office in Tokyo, and without such support, I had no chance of being given any legal work by either a Japanese or foreign client.

'If I go and open my own office in Fukuoka I'll have 13 million people almost to myself,' I argued. Twenty years of marriage had taught Sayuri to be highly sceptical of such ideas, yet something worked to gradually change her mind. Of course she flatly refused to come with me. I tried to persuade her, but to no avail. The final agreement was that I would move down to Kyushu while she and Cail stayed in Tokyo. I would, of course, be back in Tokyo for about a week every month. Family life would hardly suffer. The sooner I launched this effort in Kyushu the sooner we'd know if it was going to work.

In truth I was very keen to experience everyday life in Japan outside Tokyo. After spending a good deal of my early adult life in Tokyo, apart from six months at university in Sapporo up in Hokkaido, I knew how much I *didn't* know about the country outside the capital. Those visits to Hita at New Year for the past twenty years had given me a glimpse of another Japan, and I was intensely curious.

Conflict with China over the Senkaku Islands had exploded after Naoto Kan resigned as prime minister in favour of the decent but hapless Toshihiko Noda. Noda then nationalised the Senkakus to stop Shintaro Ishihara, the maniac governor of Tokyo, from buying them. Suddenly the possibility of war between China, Japan, and probably the Americans seemed quite real, as bizarre as that seems. History, with all its complications and discomfort about culture, past acts of aggression, and responsibility began to occupy my mind every day.

Who are the Japanese? Why are they like they are, and what will they do now that everything has changed in Asia? The answers to all this did not lie in Ginza, Shinjuku, Aoyama, bike rides to Tsukiji to buy fresh fish, or anywhere else in the twenty-three wards of metropolitan Tokyo. I decided they lay in Kyushu, and I decided to discover them for myself.

Two

Lawyers

I went through the expected bureaucratic hoops to register as a foreign lawyer in Japan, a *gaiben* in abbreviated Japanese, and finally joined the Fukuoka Prefecture Bar Association after a brief skirmish with the Japan Bar Association (the Nichibenren), the implacable bastion of protectionism for the nation's legal profession. A tiny spelling error in my writing the Japanese address of a former employer — the *ga* in Kasumigaseki was incorrect — led to the rejection of my application and a three week delay in my being able to formally start work. Welcome to *gaiben* life: on behalf of Japan's lawyers the Nichibenren welcomes you and hates you before they've even met you.

There were around 1500 Japanese lawyers in Fukuoka, and three *gaiben* — Mika Akiyama, Chris Jacobsen, and now myself. Mika, who qualified as an attorney in North Carolina before returning to Japan, became a good friend. Cool, perfectly mannered, a divorced mother of two sons, she worked in a large law firm called Kitahama Partners. Chris was American by birth but grew up in Japan and loathed life in America. Society over there, he told me over a coffee in the Rosarian café in Tenjin when we first met, is fundamentally hostile to the individual. 'I give it ten years, at the most,' he declared, shaking his head. Just what would happen after that he never said, but it wasn't going to be pleasant.

The word for lawyer in Japanese is *bengoshi*. Literally this means 'gentleman who speaks and protects'. Lawyers are habitually given the title *sensei*, meaning 'teacher' or 'master.' For the young *bengoshi* to be called *sensei* seemed ridiculous, but such is the right of a lawyer in Japan no matter their age. In my experience the women lawyers in Japan were far, far ahead of the men in every way. Sure, there are some men *bengoshi* who are masters of their craft, but there are also plenty of others who are vain and incompetent. Women *bengoshi* get the work done in a far better fashion, which is usually the case in almost every aspect of life in Japan except sumo.

I did the polite thing by visiting most of the major law firms in Fukuoka to introduce myself and, I hoped, pick up some work. In two weeks of such meetings I learned the reality of life in Kyushu for a *gaiben*: there were a good number of large companies in Kyushu that did a lot of business overseas, but if they had any serious foreign legal problems they always referred such matters to the five major law firms in Tokyo that could handle such work. The presence of three *gaiben* here in Fukuoka made no difference to this age-old habit, and no manager in a large company was likely to risk his career by giving work to Mika, Chris, or me just because we worked in Kyushu. At first this depressed me, but some of the *bengoshi* I'd befriended cheered me up by pointing out that there were plenty of small or medium-sized companies in Kyushu who did business overseas, or aspired to do so, and these were the ones likely to engage me for advice. The trick was getting the word out that I was there in Fukuoka available for consultation.

As the months passed there was some such work, but not much. I had other work outside Japan which sustained me, but I was disappointed that the innate caution of Japanese companies, or their aversion to doing business by careful drafting of contracts denied me the professional pleasure of helping them.

Tamayo Misumi, a robust woman from Hita whose parents ran the town's best sushi restaurant, was a divorce lawyer in Fukuoka. That said, she brought me my first actual matter — advising a funicular railway maker on how to exclude liability for product defects in an English-language contract — and took the time over dinner in Akasaka to spell out for me how things work.

'First, we have an awful education system in Japan. Everyone is forced to study all night, get into a good university, and then try like mad to get a job with a blue chip company. Kyushu Electric Power, Fukuoka Bank, Nishitetsu Railway, JR Kyushu, etcetera. In the end, whatever job you get you're not going to risk your precious career and get demoted or fired. If that happened you'd have to apologise to your parents, to your whole family, even to your dead ancestors! Nobody takes risks if they can avoid it. Not for anything. The only way a *gaiben* is going to get work in Kyushu is if a company thinks it's too risky *not* to consult you. And that isn't going to happen very often.'

Divorce lawyers are usually this blunt.

She explained that Japanese companies see legal issues as a threat to their reputation. If they get embroiled in litigation — no matter that they're in the right — they soon acquire a bad reputation, and that makes it difficult to find new customers or recruit good staff. Or worse, it means banks will be wary of supplying credit. Lawyers carry that stigma as if we habitually nurse leprosy patients. And to many Japanese companies we *gaiben* represented foreign leprosy. Could anything be worse?

The *bengoshi* I found easiest to get on with were those who wanted to improve their English skills. Why they wanted to do this was a mystery to them as much as it was to me. However, I was soon persuaded to give a series of lectures in the evenings on common law and legal English. Mika agreed to help, though she warned me that this had been tried in her own law firm.

'The young *bengoshi* were told they had to attend,' she said, ' but it only lasted a couple of sessions. They were too tired from working overtime, and it was all too difficult. We gave up.'

What I found interesting was the attitude of the young *bengoshi* to the law and its role in Japan. When we studied controversial cases in the lectures, such as the US Supreme Court decision on same-sex marriage, I asked the class of about ten whether the Japanese Supreme Court would ever bring down such a ruling. 'No way', said Hiroshi Hamada with a quick laugh. He was a tough, knockabout lawyer with an advertisement for his practice on the wall in Hakata Station. He spoke some English, and I had the feeling that he represented clients who got themselves into serious trouble, possibly even some *yakuza* gangster types. But he was a solid fellow and I trusted his judgement.

Noriko Uchida was a woman *bengoshi* in my class who lived for the day when she could represent refugees *pro bono*. Sadly for her there were very few, if any, such clients in Fukuoka, but she never gave up hoping for someone to seek asylum. She said the rights in Japan's Constitution were quite explicit, having been put there by the Americans who drafted it under General MacArthur's reign in the late 1940s. But she agreed with Hiroshi that, most unfortunately for everyone, the Japanese courts were very conservative and interpreted written legal rights as narrowly as possible.

'Is it the European legal tradition that Japan follows, or is it fear of disturbing the harmony of society?' I asked the class.

'Exactly!' they chorused. '*Shakai no chouwa* (social harmony) is the aim of Japanese law', someone said.

This, coming from the lawyers, rings very true in everyday life in Japan. In the daily public discourse through the media or in any official text one very rarely hears the word *kenri*, meaning a legal entitlement or right. If uttered, it's usually about something outside Japan. Citizens of Hong Kong are in the streets demanding their *kenri* to choose who governs them. Ukranians want the *kenri* to be closer to Europe than to Russia. Black Americans are apparently denied all sorts of basic *kenri*. The Chinese have very few *kenri* at all.

After the classes we often went out and ate dinner at one of Fukuoka's many *yatai*, a kind of hawker stall on wheels where you can sit on a wooden bench at the counter and eat *yakitori*, *ramen*, and drink beer, *shochu*, or *sake*. In their hatred of disorder, most Japanese cities have banned *yatai*. Yet, to its eternal credit, the city of Fukuoka promotes and regulates *yatai* as both an integral part of urban life and as a tourist attraction. People in Kyushu actually like a touch of informality.

Sitting there on the hot summer nights drinking deliciously cold *sake* and eating *yakitori* with the young *bengoshi*, I developed a strong sympathy for them. They had to put an immense effort into passing the bar examination, and life as a young lawyer in the office was often a punishing regime of extraordinary long hours of overtime doing menial, semi-clerical tasks for the senior *bengoshi*. Feudal, they told me in strict confidence after a few drinks.

I received emails from some of them sent at 2am asking follow-up questions after my lectures. It gave me a feeling of pride that because of what I showed them about the cases being fought in the highest courts of the UK, Europe, and the US they might be wondering whether they could ever fight a constitutional rights case on behalf of a client in Japan. That was a key reason why I kept going with the lectures.

I noticed, too, when the next general election came along that a lot of the candidates for the Japan Communist Party were *bengoshi*, many of them women. In fact, *bengoshi* seem to be the backbone of the Japan Communist Party, the party of protest. When you consider how conservative and male-dominated Japanese society remains today, this isn't all that surprising. These *bengoshi* are, in a sense, breaking down the old Confucian culture in which loyalty to clan, village, emperor, and country is supreme.

One of my favourite *bengoshi* was Koichi Abe, a shrewd man who has been in practice in Fukuoka for decades, a man who has seen the worst of individual behaviour during his long professional career. Abe-*sensei* remained a cheerful, almost optimistic fellow. He took an instant liking to me because his wife came from Hita as mine did. The one case he loved talking about, the subject of a chapter in a book he wrote about his career, concerned a man who appeared in his office one day after being charged with the arson of a hotel in a hot springs resort. The police had evidence pinning the crime on Abe's client (whom we'll call Tanaka for the sake of the story). But as Abe said, nobody could figure out a motive for the act, and Tanaka steadfastly refused to explain why he set fire to the hotel. His life until then had been unblemished. He was self-employed and not in debt or short of money.

'The answer', Abe wrote, 'emerged from a more thorough investigation of Tanaka's personal life.' It turned out that he had a mistress. Worse, she claimed that Tanaka had promised to marry her so that he could continue to have sex with her regularly. The only trouble was, he failed to tell her he was already married. He had to book the hotel for the wedding and the reception to maintain the fiction and and continue the carnal pleasure.

As the months passed and the terrible day loomed closer he grew desperate. To admit that he was married would both end the sex and cause him a disastrous loss of face for having lived a lie. Finally he decided that burning down the hotel was the only way to postpone the wedding while a suitable alternative venue could be secured. Sadly for Tanaka his car was seen close to the hotel shortly before the fire, and the kerosene in the trunk gave him away. Divorced now and in prison, Tanaka hasn't a *kenri* left in the world. And Abe-*sensei* is still there in his office above Akasaka subway station defending Fukuoka's misunderstood citizens with the same cheerful expression on his face.

Life as a *gaiben* in Fukuoka was tranquil. Almost all the work I had was nothing to do with my being a member of the Fukuoka Bar Association, the Fukubenren in Japanese. Despite this lack of purely legal work it did, however, seem to be worthwhile to have the status of a *gaiben* when dealing with Japanese companies in commercial matters on behalf of foreign clients. It gave me an importance I didn't deserve, but it was useful. One thing, though, began to irritate me about the Fukubenren. Our monthly dues as members were ¥55,000, or around $600. This struck me as absurdly expensive, being around what you'd pay for an entire year's membership in Australia, the US, or the UK. Why did the Fukubenren charge so much for membership?

'Oh, it's always been that much,' said Hiroshi Hamada when I asked him. 'It's set by the Nichibenren. No prefectural bar association can set its own fees.'

'So the members of the Fukubenren, that's us, we *bengoshi* and *gaiben*..... we can't decide our own fees?'

'No. The Nichibenren does it.' He laughed.

I was not surprised to hear this. Ironclad central control of such things is one of Japan's modern curses, and there's little resistance to this trend as the population gets older and more timid. I discussed the matter with Mika Akiyama over one of our regular lunches, arguing that because we *gaiben* received so little work as Fukubenren members we ought to petition for a lower monthly fee.

'Oooh,' she sighed, smiling broadly and shaking her elegant head. 'That's been brought up before. Shikichi-*sensei* [her managing partner] put a proposal to the committee for a lower *gaiben* fee, but they refused him.'

'Why? It's hardly fair to charge us the same fee as the *bengoshi* pay.'

'Well, ask him about it,' she chuckled. 'He told me that the Nichibenren is not all that friendly towards *gaiben*.'

'That's for sure.'

'…..and the Fukubenren is too, well, scared of the Nichibenren to suggest any change so the *gaiben* fees can be lowered.'

'Scared of them? How so?'

'Well, as I understand things, the senior *bengoshi* in the Fukubenren want to be elected to Nichibenren committees to give them national status here in Kyushu. So the last thing they're going to do is act in some rebellious way, especially over us *gaiben*.'

'But they're always going on about Asia and about Fukuoka being more international, blah blah blah. Yet they won't lift a finger to help us, the foreign lawyers who've forsaken the big world of Tokyo and set up practice here in Fukuoka.'

Mika smiled again. 'Oh, they do want to be more international as a bar association, but I don't think that involves we *gaiben*.'

'Then what does being "international" mean to the Fukubenren?'

'Well, things like more overseas trips for some committee members. You know, like they go to Korea, Taiwan, Thailand, and Myanmar to have meetings with local lawyers.'

'And play golf.'

'Sure. But that's internationalisation for Fukubenren members.'

'No wonder we pay so much every month.'

The level of our fees was not going to change. That was certain. But what was it all being spent on? I went to the Fukubenren office behind the District Court building and took the matter up with Mrs Ishii, one of the clerical staff who sat at the desks behind the counter. A patient, sometimes almost comatose middle-aged lady, she always dealt with the *gaiben*. I didn't want to become known as a problem in the profession in Fukuoka. That sort of reputation could hinder my chances of getting referrals from senior *bengoshi*, but the fee issue just had to be clarified.

'I'm concerned that we don't seem to have any transparency about the expenditures of the Fukubenren,' I said, standing at the counter. Mrs Ishii's answer was a confusing series of mumbles, ending with mention of the annual report.

'So the breakdown of the expenditure is in the Fukubenren annual report. Is that correct?' I asked.

'Oh. Ah. Hmm…..Well, there's an annual report with information in it,' she replied.

'May I have a copy, please?'

'Oh. Ah, it's on the website. Please download it from there.'

'Don't you have a copy here in the office?'

'Ah, no. We are very sorry.'

'Okay. Who is the current treasurer of the Fukubenren?'

'Oh, ah…..it's in the annual report.'

'But surely you know who he or she is, Ishii-*san*. I'd like to have a talk to him or her about the use of our monthly fees.'

This prospect clearly rattled her. I could see the other staff were listening to what I was saying while pretending to do other things. The thought of a bolshie *gaiben* daring to actually inquire into the spending habits of the Fukubenren was too painful to bear. I could see the anguish in Mrs Ishii's face and felt embarrassed. She was never all that helpful, but she wasn't a bad person.

'Look,' I said, 'it's not a formal complaint or anything. I simply have some suggestions for the Fukubenren to enhance our international reputation.

That's all. Obviously one must begin with knowing whether there's any room in the budget for new initiatives.'

Mention of the word "budget" (*yosan* in Japanese) brought her back to a safer place. Every organisation in Japan has a *yosan*. Now that this dangerous *gaiben* was speaking in a more normal vocabulary the threat seemed to have diminished.

'Oh. Ah. Hmm….Well, the Finance Committee chairman would…..ah, you could write to him.'

'And he is…?'

'Oh. Ah. Hmm…..There's been an election recently. You'll need to confirm the name. To be quite sure.'

Mrs Ishii's bureaucratic stonewalling was irritating, but hardly unexpected. Was it that difficult to take responsibility for steering me towards the finance committee chairman? If the chairman were to complain later that the *gaiben*'s approach was unpleasant or troublesome would she have to take the blame? Welcome to modern Japan. In any other country the staff would've simply given me the chairman's name and let me loose on the poor man or woman.

The quickest way to get the truth about the monthly fees was to talk to one of the senior *bengoshi* directly. I was friendly with Hitoshi Katsu who had done a masters degree in London. He sat on various Fukubenren committees and knew his way around.

' I don't mean to upset anyone,' I said, ' but please understand my curiosity.'

'Of course,' said Hitoshi. 'It's a fair question. Actually, the money raised in monthly fees is spent on three main things. First, operating expenses for the Fukubenren. Staff salaries, rent, overheads, all that. Second, some goes to the committees to pay for their activities.'

'Like trips to Korea and Myanmar.'

'Yes, and many, many trips to Tokyo. I don't go on those trips.'

'I see.'

'The third item is legal aid. There's a big budget for paying legal fees for poor people. It's part of our social obligation as lawyers to provide enough free or low-cost legal advice.'

'Really? Isn't it done *pro bono* by individual lawyers? Or doesn't the prefecture provide the budget?'

'Ah, well, it's not like in the UK or the US or maybe Australia. The government doesn't provide any legal aid budget. We *bengoshi* do.'

'So we Fukubenren members, we pay certain other members to act as lawyers for poor people.'

'Yes, that's correct.'

'Who are these lucky *bengoshi* who get all this work?'

'Members of the relevant committee, mostly. But it's not great work.'

'I'm not asking for any. It's not within a *gaiben*'s competence or licence.'

I thanked him for explaining the reality of the *yosan* in the Fukubenren. While it was disappointing to learn that as a matter of culture the situation was not going to change — that the mass of ordinary lawyers in Fukuoka were forced to pay money every month to support a system that funneled that money to the activist and politically ambitious lawyers — everyone was part of a hierarchy. The hierarchy was in charge. But there was another element to it that was particularly relevant to Kyushu.

'You must understand that there's competition among the prefectures in Kyushu,' said Hitoshi. 'All the prefectures compete against each other for favours from Tokyo.'

'You mean there's no sense of solidarity in Kyushu? No, Kyushu versus Tokyo?'

'Oh, no. It's the opposite. Originally all the prefectures had different cultures.'

'Like going back to the feudal times?'

'Yes, and remember that we had a civil war here in Kyushu.'

'Well, yes, I suppose so. The Satsuma Rebellion.'

'Correct. People from Kagoshima, Oita, Kumamoto…..they don't really like Fukuoka.'

I agreed it was the same in the UK and America.

'So you as a foreigner see Kyushu as one region, but the people in Kyushu don't really agree with that.'

After two years as a *gaiben* member of the Fukubenren I decided I'd had enough. It was time to resign.

'But isn't it a waste of what you've done so far?' Sayuri complained. 'You went to all the trouble of joining, and now after only two years you're giving it all away!'

I explained that the income I earned as a lawyer in Fukuoka was unlikely ever to exceed the monthly fees I paid the Fukubenren. This fact prompted her to reconsider, agreeing that there was no point in wasting money any further. I'm only being realistic, I said. I can earn the same income as a former *gaiben*, or a retired *gaiben*, without filling the coffers of the Fukubenren every month.

I went to the Fukubenren office and told Mrs Ishii I proposed to resign.

'Oh. Ah. Well, you'll have to fill in all the required forms,' she said severely, sucking her teeth in concern.

'Fine. Please give me the forms and I'll fill them out now.'

'Oh. Ah….They're on the website. Please download them. And…. ah, you'll need a reason for the resignation in order for it to be properly accepted.'

'A reason? What would you recommend?'

Mrs Ishii looked grave. ' Oh. Ah. We can't recommend a reason. It's up to you.'

'Really? Well, what reasons have others used in the past?'

'Ah…..There's never been a *gaiben* resignation.'

'So I'm the first. How about that? What reasons do the *bengoshi* give when they resign?'

'Ah, various reasons. It depends on each case.'

'Would resignation on health grounds suffice?'

Mrs Ishii looked puzzled. ' Health grounds? Ah…Oh….'

'Sure. Maybe my poor health won't allow me to continue as a *gaiben*. There are grave questions of liability here. If, as a *gaiben*, my poor health caused me to give negligent legal advice, then there might be a complaint or a claim made against the Fukubenren.'

'Oooh….Well, in that case…..'

'Some would say that protecting the reputation of the Fukubenren should be our highest priority, but if health grounds are not sufficient…..'

'Oh, no, health grounds would be fine,' Mrs Ishii said quickly.

'I wonder, do you have any copies of the resignation forms here in the office?'

'Oh. Ah….Well, maybe we do. Just a moment.'

Sure enough, the forms materialised and were quickly handed to me over the counter. Monthly fees were important to safeguard, but a sick *gaiben* dispensing negligent legal advice was another matter entirely. Mrs Ishii was suddenly eager to see the last of me.

Within a month I had changed my website, given up the lease on my office in downtown Fukuoka, and was thereafter happy to be working from my house in Funakoshi. I was now an ex-*gaiben* and glad to be so. And, despite the reason given on my resignation form, I was in very good health.

'I'm sorry you resigned,' said Mika over another lunch.

'Well, it made sense.'

'I know, but now there's only two *gaiben* in the whole of Kyushu.'

'That's true, but I don't think you'll see anyone complaining about it. I'm not disappearing. You can always call me for informal advice if you need it, not that I'm much use as a lawyer.'

'No, no. You're way overqualified to work down here. You should be a partner in some big law firm.'

'Ah, but I chose to live in Fukuoka, didn't I? I have to accept the limits of that. Anyway, I'm okay for income. I can survive, and I love living in Kyushu.'

'But how can you work from out there in Funakoshi? You'll be bored to death.'

I shrugged. 'I guess I'll figure out something,' I said.

Three

In search of the kamikaze

If, like me, you are blessed with the luck of being married to a Japanese spouse, inevitably the subject of past military conflict will come up at some point. This is no simple thing, let me tell you. Forget your John Wayne movies. It's Clint Eastwood, with his Iwojima stories, who is more on the money. A lot of people died: men, women, and children. Also, a lot of men who served their nation with courage died a long way from Japan, their bones never recovered and repatriated to their towns and villages. When you think of all those young Japanese men who willingly gave their lives, the word *kamikaze* is hard to avoid. Yet all is not so melancholy.

Kyushu is home of the *kamikaze*. This may not sound such a felicitous phrase. Yet, in Japanese the term *kamikaze* has a variety of associations, some good, some not so good. In the beginning the word *kamikaze*, which literally means "divine wind", was coined to celebrate the defeat of the Mongol invasion of Japan in 1281, marking the first time the Japanese people acted together as one nation. Seven centuries later the young suicide pilots who flew in the Pacific War, attacking the American navy as it approached Japan's mainland, became known in the West as kamikaze pilots. In Japanese they are always called *tokkōtai*, meaning "special attack squad".

Feelings about the Pacific War and its outcome are mixed in Japan. Probably a majority of people quietly regard it as a terrible mistake, though this view is tempered with a certain historical resentment at the lack of respect for Japan by the British, French, Americans, and other Western colonial powers at the time. On the other hand a small but politically powerful minority don't really accept that Japan lost the war. Their peculiar interpretation is that Japan's work to properly civilise Asia and its people, China and Korea in particular, suffered merely a rude and unfair interruption in 1945. In any case, feelings about the young *tokkōtai* pilots are an emotional mixture of heartfelt pity for young lives thrown away and a deep admiration for their courage and patriotism. I came to understand that Kyushu was the last piece of ground in Japan the *tokkōtai* boys walked upon before making the ultimate sacrifice for Emperor and country.

So how to find the *kamikaze*?

The first *kamikaze* was not a group of people, but a typhoon. It destroyed the Mongol invasion fleet on the sea around the island of Takashima, on the northern ocean border of present day Saga and Nagasaki Prefectures, not so far from my home in Funakoshi. The Mongols and their Korean and Chinese troops took shelter in the calm waters of Imari Bay, but it was there that the great typhoon found them, smashing their ships against the shores of the various islands in the bay, Takashima in particular. As recently as 2014 archaeological exploration under the sea along these shores recovered the remains of the Mongol ships, together with loads of Chinese pottery, coins, and weapons. Large numbers of Mongol troops who landed on Takashima before the typhoon hit were slaughtered or taken prisoner by the samurai forces.

On Takashima itself there are plenty of stone memorials to the samurai figures who defeated the Mongol troops. The Mongols themselves, alas, are remembered on Takashima with only a meagre theme park called Mongol Village, located on the far tip of the island facing the ocean. This grassy hilltop boasts a dozen Mongol yurts, all available for overnight accommodation for those intent on living the Mongol steppe life on an island in Kyushu.

On the lovely, sunny spring day I visited the place I found that interest in Mongol life was definitely in need of a revival. There were just three bemused Japanese families wandering around amid soothing Mongol music being played from loudspeakers every few yards. One family of parents, two small daughters, and two weary grandparents were inspecting a motionless pony and some excitable goats penned up in wooden yards near the edge of the cliff overlooking the ocean. The two little girls had picked some long grass and were feeding the animals. As I greeted their mother, one of the girls called out, 'Mummy, where are the Mongolian people?'

Her mother looked blank and glanced at me for advice. I shrugged, agreeing with the little girl that a few Mongolians would be helpful in giving the village a sense of excitement. Even a few Japanese dressed up and pretending to be Mongolians would've been helpful. 'They're away somewhere', the mother replied.

'Where've they gone?' the little girl persisted.

'To the sumo tournament', I muttered. The mother giggled but said no more.

On the way out the cheerful man who tended the ticket counter at the entrance to the Village told me with great pride that the sumo grand champion, the unbeatable Mongolian *yokozuna* Hakuhō, had actually visited the Village last November, 'with his family!'

I called in at the Koton Café down the road, which advertised *ramen* on a flag outside. There was a sign in English in a window that read "Sorry, Closed", yet the Japanese sign on the door of the café read "Open". Was this an attempt to discourage foreigners, in the island's tradition of repelling Mongols? Probably not a lot of Mongolians can read English or have the time or inclination to visit Takashima, the site of their ancestors' mass drowning. I knocked on the door and found two women inside. 'Yes, we're open', they cried. 'Come on in!' I asked for the *ramen*, but the older lady who was running the café, whose name was Toshiko, said only *champon* noodles were available. 'No problem, I prefer *champon*', I said, so that was settled.

'You speak excellent Japanese', Toshiko said. She looked particularly weary. I wondered if she was in poor health.

'I do my best', I replied as humbly as possible.

'How about the Mongol ships?' I asked. 'Where exactly were they wrecked on the shore?'

This question puzzled both women. It seemed the events of 1281 were not exactly daily conversation for the townsfolk of Takashima. 'You'd better ask at the museum', they said. 'They're the people who know all about that stuff. Anyway, how come you speak Japanese so well?'

'I was fortunate to study Japanese as a schoolboy', I said. 'In Australia.'

'Really? Amazing!' they told each other, marveling that people in a place so far away would go to such a length to show friendship and respect for Japan. The woman who wasn't serving me was sitting at the tiny counter near the door. She answered her mobile phone, listened for a while, then said in a loud voice, 'I'll be drinking *here* tonight, not at the inn. Come over!'

Who was she talking to? Was it an ageing island Romeo chasing some mature skirt, I wondered. Or was it another Takashima wife or widow looking for like company on a boring Monday night?

The *champon* was as good as I had eaten anywhere, on a par with the *champon* served at the Takaraya restaurant in the station square in Hita. The soup stock was brownish rather than the usual cream colour. I asked the lady what it was made from. Pork knuckles, she said. I prepare them for a long time. This was different from the Hita *champon* which uses chicken as the base for the soup.

As I left I politely drew Toshiko's attention to the misleading English sign in the window. She was most embarrassed, and would only let me go once I had pledged to come back sometime. 'And remember to ask at the museum!' she called out as I walked to my car.

I drove over to the museum only to find it was closed on Mondays, and today was a Monday. So much for the first *kamikaze*.

Two days later the weather turned freezing cold as a large cold front came over from the Asian mainland. A light snow started falling along the coast as I headed off in search of the other *kamikaze* story, that of the *tokkōtai* pilots. The old airfield site and the Tachiarai Peace Museum sat among small factories, tiny farms, and new housing estates forty minutes drive inland on the outer urban edge of Fukuoka. The area was a maze of narrow local roads crowded with trucks and lined with chain stores, factories, the usual giant Aeon shopping mall, gas stations, and *ramen* restaurants. A

The champion Mongolian sumo wrestler Hakuhō, whose ancestors attempted to invade Japan and were destroyed by a typhoon in Imari Bay. The Japanese called the typhoon the 'divine wind' or kamikaze.

Kirin brewery, with its "Beer Farm Restaurant," loomed over everything. This was boring, low down Japan where life is not much fun. Nobody makes any decent money, except perhaps the local doctors and dentists.

I hurried inside from the carpark, the air freezing and more snow on the way. In the car on the way there NHK radio was reporting with great excitement on the progress of the cold front. Gale warnings had been issued for all coastal areas in northern Kyushu and all the way along the Sea of Japan coast to Hokkaido, where the usual heavy snowfalls and blizzards were coming to punish the island and its hardy inhabitants. The announcer was delighted to tell us that over at Omuta, an industrial rustbelt town on the way south to Kumamoto, the winds would be the strongest since 1997!

Thinking of the pilots who flew from the Tachiarai Airfield both before and during the war having to deal with all aspects of Kyushu's weather, I entered the museum, bought my ¥500 ticket, and was immediately taken in hand by a guide, a pleasant gentleman named Kawanami. He lead me to a space with a huge aerial map on the floor where with the aid of a torch he pointed out the geography of what used to be here.

Here is the grass runway. Here is the airfield terminal. Here are the factories that manufactured aircraft. That's the station: it used to see 20,000 people a day go through it at the peak of production.

Before it was used for *kamikaze* squadrons during the Pacific War, the Tachiarai Airfield was the third and final stop in Japan on the first international air route, which started in 1931: Tokyo — Osaka — Tachiarai — Ulsan (in Korea) — Seoul — Pyongyang — Dalian. Those were the days, Korea and Manchuria being firmly under Japan's control.

'And I understand the airfield suffered some bombing', I ventured.

Kawanami-*san* nodded enthusiastically and produced a black-and-white laminated aerial photograph. 'This was actually taken from one of the American B-29 bombers,' he explained. 'You can see the smoke beside the runway from the aircraft on fire. They came across here from Hita.'

'Hita? My wife is from Hita', I exclaimed.

'Well, they started from the American air bases on Saipan and then

Iwojima, and they flew up here to cross the coastline at Oita, then continued to Hita, and then to here. It was to attack the airfield and the factories.'

'Was there not another airfield from where the *tokkōtai* operated during the war?' I asked.

'Ah, Chiran,' said Kawanami-*san*. 'It's down in Kagoshima. But you have to understand, Chiran was just a branch of the air corps headquartered here at Tachiarai. Just a branch.'

I wonder how the Americans knew about the factories, I remarked.

'Oh, we were making aircraft here well before the war started. It was famous for that.' He went on, 'the Americans destroyed Tachiarai a week before they landed on Okinawa so our planes couldn't attack them.'

'Did they succeed? I thought the *tokkōtai* continued to fly up until the end of the war.'

'Quite right. The B-29s didn't get all the Japanese planes. And the *tokkōtai* didn't just attack ships. They also fought the B-29s in the sky,' Kawanami-*san* said proudly.

Given the tone of his commentary, it was hard to pin down the purpose of the museum. Like many historical matters in Japan one should not approach these things with a Westerner's thirst for exactitude. Japan is a living contradiction in so many ways, and the Peace Museum was no exception. Beyond doubt the official educative message is anti-war, yet the displays speak of the superb engineering skills of the early aircraft industry, the stoicism and suffering of the local people during the B-29 bombing raids, and most of all they exult the bravery and heroism of the young pilots.

On two walls in a corner of the museum I walked past large photographs of dead pilots, their faces tender and innocent in their uniforms, the pale furry collars, leather helmets, and huge goggles pushed up above their faces. Some were smiling broadly, some wore expressions of the utmost seriousness and commitment. Takaro Adachi, 18 years old; Morio Kishida, 21 years old; Shigeru Yoshimori, 20 years old; Tetsuzo Kawashima, 18 years old. Beside each photo was a handwritten message to their families, written before their final flight. I noticed a few Japanese visitors to the museum reading these letters with intense concentration. The tender age

18 year-old kamikaze pilot Takarou Adachi, born in Tottori Prefecture, who flew to his death from the Tachiarai Airfield in Fukuoka.

A group of young kamikaze pilots before they flew to attack the approaching U.S. Navy.

Mr Ryutaro Hanamichi on video recalling how he returned to the Tachiarai Airfield after failing in his suicide mission expecting to be severely punished. Instead he found his squadron commander weeping with joy that he had returned alive. He is quoted at the bottom of the screen as saying, 'You know, we just couldn't sleep before a mission.'

of these *tokkōtai* boys brought home the tragedy of the whole thing in a very confronting way.

The exhibit that meant the most to me was a video of a cheerful old man, Mr Hanamichi, recalling his failed suicide attack. He explained how the *tokkōtai* squadron commander had wept as he bade farewell to his pilots before they took off on their last mission. 'My father was poor, just a farmer,' Hanamichi-*san* said in a matter-of-fact way. 'All I wanted to do was help him somehow. I didn't want to die, not at all.' As it happened, his squad of pilots struck heavy rain as they flew south over Kyushu at the beginning of August 1945 and they got lost when the leading aircraft disappeared in the clouds. Hanamichi-*san* eventually ran short of fuel and so turned back, landing at Tachiarai and expecting to be severely punished for failing to attack the Americans. 'Instead the deputy commander rushed over to greet me and said, "Welcome back! You can try again when the weather clears up." He too was weeping as he spoke to me.'

As I left the museum I thanked Kawanami-*san* and asked about an incident in which some schoolchildren were killed in the bombing. Yes, he said with no emotion. It's only a couple of kilometers away from here, at a place called Tonta Forest. The children were sheltering with their teachers in the small forest which stood right beside the elementary school when a B-29 bomber accidentally released a bomb too early, well before it reached the airfield and the factories. The bomb hit the forest, and all 31 pupils and their teachers were killed.

The story of the children in Tonta Forest sounded very like the story of the school in Fukushima where all the students were assembled on the playground after the earthquake. Instead of climbing the hillside immediately behind the school the teachers made them wait where they stood. When the *tsunami* rolled in a few minutes later it was too late to scramble up the hill, and all of them were drowned. Their parents were still battling in the courts trying to get a formal verdict that the local education board was responsible for the children's deaths. The board had refused to acknowledge that the failure to include evacuation to higher areas in the school's earthquake procedure was what led to the tragedy.

After the museum I had to visit Hita to pay my residents tax, so I decided to visit the Tonta Forest on the way. My own son was in elementary school, and I loved going to collect him after classes and seeing him play with his classmates. The elementary school where the dead children studied is still in the same place, though now very large and surrounded by new houses. I looked at the map on my mobile phone to get my bearings. Then I realised what had happened. The forest was gone, its site now occupied by a large, pale brown hospital. I drove around the narrow streets looking for a memorial sign, but there was nothing visible. I passed a restaurant serving whale meat and grilled *jidori* chicken, the latter a Kyushu specialty. The children that lived through the bombing of Tachiarai would be around 80 years old now, the same age as Sayuri's parents in Hita. I wondered whether they remember as small children seeing those B-29s come over on the way to Tachiarai. Or would they ever forget it?

Three weeks later in warmer weather I went back to the island of Takashima to have another try at understanding in more detail what had happened to the Mongols. Having been unable to see the museum that Toshiko in the Koton Café recommended on my last visit, I felt my effort was incomplete. This time I went on a Sunday, taking with me Tom Yates, the Australian Consul-General in Fukuoka, a man of rare diplomatic achievement, and his wife Susan. The three of us drove west from Fukuoka on a bright April morning with the cherry blossoms close to full bloom.

Toshiko was right. The people in the Takashima Historical Museum really knew their stuff. Or at least for a drab, unassuming building clearly not endowed with a fat budget, the place was a genuine surprise. There was something particularly impressive about seeing pieces of a seven hundred year-old wooden ship right before your eyes. Stranger still was that the dozens of pieces of wood, recovered only months ago from the seabed a hundred metres offshore, were sitting in plastic tanks of fresh water on the floor of a large room in the museum where you could wander around and actually handle them if so minded. The usual museum signs saying "Do Not Touch" were nowhere to be seen.

Elsewhere in the museum amid the static displays there were paintings of the battles between the Mongol soldiers rushing ashore from their boats to fight the waiting samurai, the scenes depicted in a realistic fashion. One painting showed a grieving woman bent over the body of a dead man, her husband or lover. Her kimono was disheveled, revealing the edges of her breasts.

Just like at the Mongol Village at the other end of the island, in the lobby of the museum beside the ticket counter there were two photos of Hakuhō, the Mongolian *sumo* champion, hanging on the wall. The great man had actually come twice to see for himself what happened when his ancestors arrived to attempt their conquest of Japan.

One thing that struck me about the museum was that the underwater archaeological work on the Mongol wrecks was being done not by any university here in Kyushu, or any important national scientific body from Tokyo, but by staff of the University of the Ryukyus, the main university in Okinawa. Maybe it was because, coming from a warm, tropical area with plenty of coral reefs, they were the real diving experts among universities in Japan.

Okinawans are racially different from mainland Japanese, with a distinct group of languages, too. And it's fair to say that for a host of reasons these days tensions between the Okinawans and the rest of Japan are as bad as ever. Firstly, there's the presence of the US military forces on the islands today. Then there's the memories of the awful mistreatment of Okinawan civilians by the Japanese military in the closing weeks of the Pacific War, something for which an apology or acknowledgement has never really been accepted by the Okinawans. Maybe even the original annexation of the Ryukyu Kingdom by Meiji Japan in the 1880s and the forced exile of the indigenous royal family still rankles.

'You know,' I said to Tom in the car as we headed back towards the port of Aoura, 'it's weird that it's an Okinawan university doing the research here.'

One of Tom's tasks as a trade diplomat was to pitch Australian universities as places to study abroad for Japanese students. He prided himself on his knowledge of Japanese universities. 'Oh, well, they know all about diving,' he said with certainty.

'But don't you think it's ironic that it's these Okinawan university researchers doing the work to discover and preserve the relics of the Mongol invaders?'

'Okinawans and Mongols…..I suppose it's an odd combination. But it's the diving,' he insisted.

Whatever they might have thought about the Mongols and Japan the team from Okinawa had certainly done a brilliant job of finding and preserving the pieces of the wrecks and the pottery, coins, cannon balls, and other objects buried under the seabed.

Then another thought struck me.

'The collection in that museum is extraordinary,' I continued. 'Those sorts of historical artifacts should be on display at the big museums in Fukuoka.'

'Mmm. It's a bit tricky to take it up with the governor,' Tom said.

'Seven hundred year-old pieces of a ship! They're almost hidden in a half-forgotten museum on an island way off the beaten track. Nobody seems to give a damn about them.'

'You're right. But I can't go bothering the governor about one of his own museums.'

'It's weird. There's nothing to be ashamed of, after all, the Mongols lost.' I said.

The Sangenya floating restaurant sat on the water in the small harbour at Aoura Port, the biggest harbour on the island. We stopped there for lunch at the same time as a group of motorbike riders in their leathers and T-shirts. All of us sat at wooden tables on a balcony overlooking the clear, jade-green waters of the harbour in the warmth of the midday sun. We sat waiting for the food, gazing out at the fishing boats, warehouses, and the houses that made up the town climbing the hill behind.

In another corner of the restaurant a few metres away from us a family with two small children were peering into a tank of running water that contained dozens of live squid. The little boy was trying to touch the squid, but much to his frustration they kept flitting away at the last moment. His mother gently scolded him, while his father encouraged him to keep trying.

Across the other side of the harbour, perhaps two hundred metres away, the staff of the Sojitz blue-fin tuna farm were loading huge chunks of dried fish food into a barge where it was mixed with water in tanks on the deck, ready to be spray pumped into the tuna pens out beyond the harbour walls. In the air a few sea eagles lazily floated on high, keeping an eye on what everyone was up to at sea level. No seagulls were visible, which struck Susan as odd for a fishing port.

After we finished our lunch we stopped to talk to the Sojitz staff. I struck up a conversation with a young man named Hideki Yamaoka dressed in bright blue plastic overalls and a red shirt, doubtless the company uniform.

'How's the tuna farm going?' I started by asking.

'It's tough,' he replied, his face suitably worried. 'The cost of food is so high now.'

Like the beef farmers, Tom suggested. Hideki nodded gravely.

'But the tuna are growing okay?' I asked.

'Of course. Well, yeah, they're growing. We do that okay. Some are 80 kilograms. We harvest them every week. Customers want different sizes.'

'How about the Mongol ships, the *kamikaze* thing?'

Hideki looked puzzled, almost offended. Changing subjects mid-conversation was one of those crazy *gaijin* habits, his face seemed to say.

'Well, I suppose.....they're out there somewhere. One was discovered last year, I heard.'

We drove a short distance beyond the port to a lovely, empty beach where Tom and I decided to have a quick swim. I put on a mask and snorkel and had a look beneath the water. It was perfectly clear, but there were no Mongol relics visible, only plenty of *wakame* seaweed and a few rocks. Tom had an energetic diplomatic swim and declared the water temperature cold enough never to forget.

We dried ourselves in the warm sunshine on the concrete concourse above the sand. There were freshwater showers at a pavilion, but it was closed and local officials had gone to the extent of removing the tap handles to make sure nobody stole a shower outside the official swimming months of July and August. I thought of taking a tool from my car and forcing the shower on just to hit back at this sort of idiocy, but Tom was keen to avoid a diplomatic incident over the matter.

We dressed again, hair a bit tousled, and drove over to the Koton Café. Toshiko was there alone, looking as weary as ever. She welcomed us with a warm smile, immediately remembering me from my previous visit. We sat down inside the tiny café and ordered coffee which she set about brewing in a huge glass container over a flame.

I felt good meeting her again, my only acquaintance on the island. 'How are things', I asked.

Her daughter was away travelling, she complained. In Bali this week.

'She works for a few months and then goes off travelling somewhere on her own. I used to worry about her, but these days I don't so much. She knows what she's doing, I suppose.'

'Does your daughter help out in the café?'

'Sometimes, but she's always looking around for jobs with the best pay, then she works until she saves enough to go away again. When will it end, I ask myself.'

'When she gets married?'

'No, that's not likely,' Toshiko said with a sigh.

'And you yourself, were you born on Takashima?'

'No, I came as a bride, all the way from Kitakyushu. In those days it was a huge journey. We didn't have any expressways, just local roads through the mountains. And no bridge, of course. We had to use the ferry to reach the mainland.'

Along the roadsides on Takashima we had noticed a few signs promoting locally grown tobacco. One sign read "Local tobacco! Have a puff today!" We mentioned this to Toshiko as we sipped our coffees.

She shook her head sadly. 'It's terrible. Seventeen tobacco farmers have given up in the past year alone. The prices have gone down and down. How can that happen? People are still smoking cigarettes. Something's not right about it.'

Ever the enterprising trade promotion man, Tom suggested the locals take to making cigars from their locally grown tobacco. It would be a unique product.

Toshiko looked intrigued for a moment, but lapsed back into her usual resignation to the facts of life on Takashima, saying, 'Ah, but we Japanese have lost the habit of smoking cigars. Who would buy them?'

I agreed with Tom, telling her that foreigners would buy everything they made. It would be an export success. Beyond doubt. A unique product.

Toshiko considered this suggestion for a while, her head slightly inclined in contemplation. Maybe there was something in it. Then she looked at me directly and said, 'You know, my niece married a *gaijin*, a Scottish fellow. They live in Kitakyushu, where I came from. He runs an English conversation school there,' she added with approval. Was she suggesting something in the context of her yet-to-be-married daughter? I wondered. No further questions, Your Honour.

Long gone the Mongols, I thought as we drove across the bridge back to the mainland. Time passes, and things change.

To finally satisfy my curiosity about the *tokkōtai* I drove to Chiran, a small town in the mountains of south-western Kagoshima Prefecture, way down the bottom of Kyushu. It is known for two things: green tea and a museum commemorating the *tokkōtai* efforts in the final stages of the Pacific War. The museum sits on the site of the old Chiran aerodrome from which many of the young kamikaze pilots took off to go to their deaths attacking the American naval fleet then approaching Okinawa. I went to visit the museum on a fine spring day, finding it a confronting experience as a foreign resident of Japan. Like the museum at Tachiarai the most uncomfortable aspect for the visitor was the age of the pilots whose photographs adorn the walls of the exhibits. Most of them were between eighteen and twenty-one years old when they flew and died.

I spent a half hour inspecting the exhibits, the sole foreigner among a lot of Japanese visitors. Nobody said a word to me as I read the hundreds of letters the pilots wrote to their families. Almost all were addressed to their mothers and I was surprised that in the pre-war times people used a lot of *katakana* script rather than *hiragana*. Such was the style of the times. These days katakana is used only for foreign words such as *rajio* (radio), *terebi* (television), or *kompyūtā* (computer). There were plenty of aircraft on display both inside the museum and outside in the grounds. It's a fact that the Mitsubishi Zero was an amazing fighter plane at the time, and the Japanese are proud of their military aircraft. At the front counter I bought an English-language booklet called *The Mind of The Kamikaze* about the *tokkōtai* pilots. For the most part it was badly written, but the individual stories about some of the pilots were compelling reading. One passage in particular caught my attention. It told of how the guards in the barracks at Chiran sometimes found young pilots weeping under their bedclothes during the night.

To me this was the only really significant revelation in the booklet. On the surface the peer pressure on the pilots to die for a cause that was already lost in military terms was overwhelming. Yet under the surface, in the still watches of the night, some of the pilots were terrified of the death that lay ahead of them. Many had probably lost their fathers. They knew their mothers and younger siblings, or their wives, had nobody to support them once the *kamikaze* mission was set in train. Yet there was no way out of it. There they were in the barracks at Chiran trying to sleep the night before they knew they were going to die.

I went off to have a bowl of *soba* for lunch at one of the restaurants beside the car park and thought about this in the context of Japan post-war and Japan these days. Unpalatable as it may seem, there is a certain dignity in the fact of self-sacrifice in war. You might call it the ultimate dignity. The fact of history wherein a large cohort of young Japanese men believed so strongly in their culture that they willingly killed themselves in the hope of saving it does not simply disappear with the passage of time. It remains, and it buttresses the faith in that culture for those in later generations.

These days that culture is peaceful. During the 1930s and 1940s it became malevolent, inflicting immense harm on both other Asian peoples and a lot of innocent, patriotic Japanese people at home. There is a multitude of experience in the whole issue of the Pacific War. As you tour the Chiran museum you ask yourself why were the *kamikaze* pilots so young? Because there was no one else left to fly the planes? Perhaps so.

The war, as Admiral Yamamoto predicted before Pearl Harbour, had gone so disastrously wrong that Japan simply ran out of able-bodied men to fight in the last stages. As much as for the war crimes committed against other Asians, it's for that appalling result too that the wartime military leaders of Japan should have been prosecuted after the war. What they did to their own people was perhaps their ultimate crime against humanity.

A few days later I was back in Hita at the home of my parents-in-law. By the entrance to their kimono shop above the small counter there was a calendar on the wall from the Yasukuni Shrine. Each month's page had a colour photograph of a Shinto shrine, often the Yasukuni Shrine itself, and below it a small black-and-white photo of a deceased soldier, sailor, or airman together with a script explaining his heroics.

That month, just days after my visit to Chiran, I noticed the hero of the month was a *tokkōtai* pilot called Uemura Masajiro. He was from Akita Prefecture in the cold, far north of Honshu, and he died on 21 March 1945, aged twenty-six. The accompanying text said he was decorated for his efforts in bombing raids in Szechuan Province in China, fought in the Battle of Midway where he was shot down and rescued, and later served in one of the first *kamikaze* squadrons. He was killed in action on the way to attack an American battleship.

Uemura had married a girl called Kikuchi Ryo and was blessed with one child before he died. His last letter to his wife read as follows:

> "I have caused you nothing but pain until now, always being headstrong myself, never giving you any pleasure, nor taking you anywhere nice any time, and leaving you poor, but I thank you for trying so hard nevertheless. Now, I believe I will not be returning, so please look after the little one. Please get on well with my sister and consult her when the need arises. I

think you know me well enough. If I were to see you I would burn up and tears would flow.

 Good-bye.
 Your husband."

Four

Origins

It had been three months since I moved into Sayuri's parents' home above their kimono shop in Hita, and the eighty minute commute to my office in Fukuoka by highway bus had become a real trial. To avoid the long bus ride twice a day I began staying in a cheap but clean business hotel in Fukuoka on weeknights, a short bike ride from downtown Tenjin where I had my office in Meiji Dori street, right beside the Suikyo Shrine.

When I announced I wanted to find a house of my own, my mother-in-law Mrs Sakamoto was disappointed.

'But where will you live?' she cried. It was the first time in almost thirty years she had anyone living in the house apart from her husband, and she doted on me day-in-day-out.

'I'll have to find somewhere in Fukuoka,' I replied.

'Oh, dear,' she moaned. 'Fukuoka?'

'Well, that's where I work.'

'Oh, dear,' she said, shaking her head.

'I'll come back to Hita on weekends. Anyway, it'll take a good while to find a place in Fukuoka,' I said. This cheered her up slightly.

On weekends when I wasn't riding the Vulcan around Kyushu somewhere, I would usually accompany my in-laws to one of the local hot springs before dinner. My father-in-law was a terrible driver, terrifying in fact, so on these short car trips, much to his chagrin, I used to grab his car keys while he was getting ready and insist on driving.

During those first three months in Kyushu I had no friends with whom to spend weekends. I tried to entice one or two of the *bengoshi* I'd become acquainted with to come travelling somewhere or go fishing, but they politely declined, pleading the burdens of work or family. As a result I found myself riding the Vulcan around parts of rural Kyushu exploring mountains and coast entirely on my own.

The beauty of these places is hard to convey. In the mountains you find little valleys here and there, the mountain slopes covered in cedar and cypress forests, the valley floors decorated with rice fields, small orchards, and clusters of traditional style farmhouses. Likewise, there are dozens if not hundreds of small fishing ports along the coastline with their standard concrete harbours to protect the fishing vessels from typhoons and wooden houses lined up along the streets around the wharf. Riding a motorbike along local roads, up into the forests and over the ridges was a pleasure I had never experienced in Japan before. I kept a small towel in the rear saddlebag in order to stop occasionally at a local *onsen* late in the afternoon and bathe in the hot spring water.

I stayed overnight at various *minshuku*, a kind of B&B where you get a simple but decent breakfast and dinner, a bath, and a sleep on a futon in a *tatami* room in someone's home. The standard price for a *minshuku* for one person is ¥8000 to ¥10,000 depending on the popularity of the destination and the quality of the food served. I avoided the popular destinations such as the famous *onsen* towns, instead exploring the backblocks of Kyushu where to my eye the scenery was just as pretty and one is more likely to find solitude.

One weekend I decided to visit the island of Hirado on the far north-western tip of Kyushu. I was intrigued by the history of the so-called Hidden Christians who had gone underground with their religion for some two hundred years when the Shogun banned it. I called a *minshuku* by the name of Tobi-Uo (flying fish in Japanese) in the main port and found myself talking to a Mrs Hayashi. She didn't seem too pleased to be on the phone with a *gaijin*.

'Well, we only serve fish here,' she said as if that would put an end to my enquiry. 'You probably won't like that.'

'I love eating fish', I replied. May I stay on Saturday night?

'There's nothing but fish here. Even for breakfast. It's only fish.'

That's one reason I want to visit Hirado, for the fish.

'Really? Well, if you insist. It'll be ¥8000 for the night. And there's only fish. We don't serve anything else.'

Mrs Hayashi's husband turned out to be a fisherman, hence the lack of anything else to eat for dinner or breakfast. The fish she served was magnificent in its freshness and flavours, better than anything you'd find in a Fukuoka restaurant. Both she and Mr Hayashi ate dinner with me that night, Mr Hayashi pouring me glass after glass of cheap *shochu*. He spoke in a thick Kyushu dialect and declared himself against the Mongolian *sumo* wrestlers. *Ore skan da*, he said, which in the dialect means, 'I bloody hate 'em.'

The next day I rode the Vulcan around the roads of Hirado in bright sunshine. After eating a *bento* box lunch bought at a shop halfway down the island I found a stunningly beautiful beach with pure white sand and azure blue water. With not a soul in sight I parked the Vulcan on a patch of grass beside the road just above the beach, walked down onto the sand with my towel, and stripped off stark naked before plunging into the chill water. I frolicked around for a few minutes in the water before drying myself off and dressing again, right there on the beach. I was utterly alone.

Later that day I learned that the beach, in the village of Neshiko on the western side of the island, had been the execution ground for dozens of Japanese Christians three centuries ago. On the orders of the Shogun Hideyoshi the local samurai had rounded up the Christian villagers and ordered them to renounce their religion by stepping on a painting of the Virgin Mary. Those who refused to do so were beheaded there on the beach one by one. Nobody, including the children of the village, was spared.

That such an awful thing should have taken place at one of Kyushu's most beautiful spots was unfortunate, to say the least. Would I swim again at Neshiko? Maybe, after saying a prayer for the martyred villagers, I might. In fact if I knew the anniversary of their slaughter I might do so every year so they aren't forgotten.

I started looking at houses for sale in the Itoshima district, which is a peninsula jutting out into the Genkai Nada Sea about thirty kilometers west of Fukuoka City. Its beaches are among the best in Japan, all golden sand and not dark grey volcanic ash like Honshu's beaches. Inland from these beaches and the five fishing ports of Itoshima I found acres and acres of rice and vegetable fields. A good few *gaijin* residents of Fukuoka lived out there for the lifestyle, such as Humphrey Smith, an Englishman I'd met through some British friends in Tokyo. Humphrey, a former apprentice gunsmith in Britain, was emphatic, as he was about pretty much everything: 'Mate, you *have* to live in Itoshima. There's no other choice. Believe me, this place is the *best* in Japan.'

And he was right. The only issue I faced was that almost all the houses

The beach at Neshiko on Hirado Island. Acting on the orders of the Shogun, the local samurai slaughtered dozens of Japanese Christians on this beach for refusing to forsake their Christianity. The campaign to eradicate the foreign religion led to thousands of Japanese Christians going underground for two centuries. Known as the Hidden Christians or kakure kirishitan, they often disguised their Christian worship by using Buddhist icons to fool the authorities. When Christianity became legal again in the 1880s many Hidden Christians refused to return to the Catholic Church, preferring instead to follow their secret liturgy.

for sale were either lonely, abandoned farmhouses in the traditional wooden style or weekender holiday houses. On a real estate website I found what looked like a decent house on a large plot of land, but I was puzzled by its extraordinarily low price. Ayumi Ihara, a cool-mannered lady real estate agent I knew, agreed to show it to me. She and I drove over to the fishing port of Funakoshi, and at the far end of the harbour we found a gated community of holiday homes (*besso* in Japanese) called Lauben Kolonie. Yes, a German name for some strange reason. After gaining permission to enter the grounds and inspect the house we drove up to the top of the hill of what is a small peninsula in itself to find a rundown 1970s *besso* sitting in a heavily overgrown garden. It was barely visible from the road below and had been long abandoned by its owners.

'You can't buy this,' said Ayumi. 'It's filthy dirty. There are other clean *besso* for sale. You'd get sick living here. Definitely.'

We fought our way through the bushes blocking the stone steps up to the house and went inside to find the place very dirty, cobwebs everywhere, dust on every surface, and the windows filthy. The garden was a mass of waist-high weeds and wild bushes. Ayumi spotted some animal dung and cried out, ' See, wild boars live here! And viper snakes.' Yet looking out through the trees from the filthy windows of the main room I caught a glimpse of the ocean.

I can clean this up, I said.

Ayumi rolled her eyes. 'You'd have to destroy it and rebuild it. Please, let's find a *clean* house.'

Never underestimate the Japanese love of purity, nor the predictable lunacy of a *gaijin*.

'No, in Australia we renovate old houses', I replied. The price being asked for the abandoned *besso*, with nearly a hectare of land and a decent garage, was around four million yen or $40,000. This was the cheapest dwelling with an ocean view in the civilized world, I decided.

As Humphrey explained later, no Japanese buyer looking for a *besso* would dream of buying and renovating a dirty, abandoned one. Such a place is deeply stigmatized. So in essence houses such as this one had no prospective buyers at all. The price asked was about the cost of demolishing the existing structure so as to build a completely new *besso*. Hence the real transaction was that a nice piece of land was on sale for $40,000, plus another $40,000 in demolition costs, so $80,000 all up. A further $250,000 would get you a simple but new holiday house good for about twenty years of use. That's the Japanese way of evaluating the deal.

But I was a *gaijin* buyer.

Much to Ayumi's disgust and disappointment I bought the place in June, and after a month's hard work during the sweltering heat and humidity of July I had shed five kilograms of weight repairing the house. I fixed up the damaged exterior, painted the steel supports under the balcony with grey ship's paint, and with the courageous help of Humphrey's teenage son, Tarquin, we lopped off enough tree branches in front of the house to create a broad view of the ocean. From the living room I could see now the island of Himeshima a few kilometers out to sea, and even on clear days Iki Island forty kilometers beyond it.

The fishing boats from Funakoshi chugged out to sea across the waters in front of Himeshima, the sound of their diesel engines distantly audible early every morning and again in the evenings when they returned with the day's catch. I had never dreamed that one could live in Japan in such a beautiful place.

To go to the main train station in Itoshima, called Chikuzen-Maebaru, I had to drive through the port of Funakoshi as soon as I left the gates of Lauben Kolonie. The harbour and its fishing industry intrigued me. The fishermen, called *ryoshi* in Japanese, are tough, hardy people, and not friendly to outsiders. In recent years it's been difficult to make a living from commercial fishing because fuel costs have risen as the yen has weakened and the wild catch has gradually diminished under pressure from the Chinese and Korean fishing fleets. To my eye at least half of the fishing vessels in Funakoshi never went to sea, and the same was the case in the other fishing ports of Kyushu.

Facing the ocean and the Korean Peninsula beyond the horizon, it slowly dawned on me that these beaches, little bays, and villages are among the oldest inhabited places in Japan, or at least settled by the people who came across to Japan from the Asian mainland. Living in Itoshima now I asked myself: who actually came to Japan? As a student of Japanese language in my teens I had been taught the simple story that the hairy Ainu were Japan's aboriginal people, now driven way north to Hokkaido and almost gone. It's a bit more complicated than that, but the real question is who was it that came to Japan to do battle with the Ainu?

Looking for more clues as to the origins of Japan's people, I began to think of the languages spoken in prehistoric and ancient times. All this talk of crossing oceans is fine, but how on earth did people communicate with each other once they arrived? This is one thing not covered in any museum, but it's something close to my own heart. I was not born with much mathematical skill, something I regret, but I do have a gift for languages. I mastered Japanese and Chinese at school and university. Later I made a serious effort to learn Scots Gaelic and Arabic. In my idle days working at the World Bank in Washington DC for a year I studied Hindi and then Uighur, the language spoken by the Muslim minority who inhabit China's far western province of Xinjiang, a largely desert region that forms a part of the ancient Silk Road stretching from Persia to China.

The other forum for amateur reflection and observation of Japan's ethnic origins is sumo wrestling. To those who have spent years studying and writing about anthropology at university, this may come as a professional insult. But let me plead my amateur status and let fly with what I have seen. The longer I lived in Kyushu the more I looked at sumo through Kyushu eyes, but for now let's acknowledge that Mongolian wrestlers dominate modern sumo. These men come from a tradition of Mongolian wrestling that is similar to Japanese sumo. The two combatants face each other, and like sumo the first to put a hand, elbow, or knee to the ground loses. The coincidence is impossible to ignore. It speaks volumes about the Mongol tribes who gave Japan its chief ethnic basis, yet the connection between the two styles of wrestling goes almost unremarked. Certainly, while the

Japanese sumo wrestlers are unable to dislodge the Mongolians from the top ranks of the sport this is unlikely to change.

Starting with Hakuhō, the senior Mongolian *yokozuna* grand champion, who seems certain to break all Japanese records for tournament victories, the Mongolians are physically little different from their Japanese competitors. There is a slight wideness in their facial features, but like the Japanese their bodies are hairless. The Mongolians tend to avoid putting on excessive weight. Instead they rely on muscular strength, speed of movement, and a hungry agility in the sacred ring, the *dohyō*, that marked the Japanese champions until the 1980s.

The dominance of the Mongolians, it must be said, sent the sport into something of a decline in recent years, though this loss of popularity can be attributed to a match-fixing scandal as well as the dominance of the foreign wrestlers. Things are looking better now that three Japanese wrestlers in the tough-as-nails Goeido from Osaka, the young and handsome

Mud volleyball being played on Iki Island, which lies between Kyushu and the Korean Peninsula. Iki was one of the islands that the immigrants from Mongolia and Siberia used to cross over to the Japanese Archipelago in prehistoric times.

Endo, and the new *yokozuna* Kiseinosato are beginning to climb the senior ranks. But to the average sumo fan this does not really matter. Two men confront each other on the *dohyō*, watched over by the *gyōji*, the referee, in his gorgeous traditional silk costume. The test is one of strength, agility, and sheer technique. The Mongolians usually prevail because of an extra ounce of competitive hunger. One might call it a will to win.

Though a further observation, which may be dismissed as crude and fanciful, is that to some people in Japan, the success of Mongolian sumo wrestlers resembles that of Japan's military machine in the 1930s. This notion came up during a conversation I had with a delightful and very left-wing *bengoshi* I got to know in Fukuoka. I shall call him Norio Takahashi because he pleaded with me not to use his real name in writing about him and his opinion.

'I should not be so racist,' Norio said as we talked about Japan over some *motsunabe*, Fukuoka's celebrated offal hotpot stew. 'But the Mongolians look to me like a throwback to something like our samurai culture. I don't for a moment say they are capable of atrocities or cruelty, and they behave very well in sumo. They even have Japanese wives, and they speak perfect Japanese. But they remind me of Japan's military culture from before the war.'

Five

Kyushu on the palate

One of the benefits of my moving to live in Kyushu was the larger role of food in daily life. It's true that in Tokyo, Osaka, and elsewhere people pay great attention to food, and Kyoto's ancient court life, when the emperor and his family lived there for centuries in virtual seclusion, led to the creation of classical Japanese cuisine, called *kaiseki ryori*. But in Kyushu there is something of an obsession with local cuisine, especially its noodle dishes.

Ramen, with its thin noodles served in an oily, savoury soup, is at the top of the ladder here. Kyushu's specialty is *tonkotsu* ramen. The *tonkotsu* soup which hosts the noodles (boiled separately in water) is made from pork bones simmered at great length at high heat and the resulting broth carefully spiced. The website Rameniac describes the result of this process as follows:

"Such a method of cooking releases the bone marrow into the broth and gives the soup its characteristic richness. *Tonkotsu* soup is creamy, spiced with a hint of garlic and ginger, and quite unlike the *miso*-flavoured soup used in ramen from Hokkaido and around Tokyo."

Tonkotsu ramen originated in the cities of Kurume and Kumamoto in central Kyushu and spread to Fukuoka where the ramen stalls outside the fish market of Nagahama developed what they called Hakata ramen. This version of *tonkotsu* ramen has a roasted sesame topping to it, along with shreds of pickled red ginger called *beni shōga*.

Some *tonkotsu* ramen restaurants pride themselves on their unfiltered, lightly spiced soup which has an unforgettable stink, or *kusami* in Japanese. Rather than using plenty of spices and filtering techniques to remove the natural odour of the boiled pork bones, mainly pig heads to be frank, the *kusami tonkotsu* restaurants give you the full, unrefined version. Only true devotees of *tonkotsu* ramen can bear to enter these places. Much to my wife Sayuri's amusement I made the mistake of doing this one day at the ramen restaurant in the station square in Hita, only to stagger back out into the street. The smell was truly overpowering. There I was, the pathetic *gaijin* who couldn't hack the true *tonkotsu* experience.

After opening my office in Fukuoka I was excited to have a brief professional association with the *tonkotsu* ramen business. Mark Nishizawa, a friend from the trading company Sojitz, asked me to help his company export frozen *tonkotsu* soup from Miyazaki Prefecture in southern Kyushu to Australia. This was to supply the largest of Kyushu's *tonkotsu* ramen chains, Ippudo, which had decided to open a restaurant in Sydney as part of their global expansion. Naturally they wanted to use their own soup in the ramen to provide something truly authentic.

But the Australian food import quarantine rules are notoriously strict. When I learned that in preparing the *tonkotsu* soup it was mainly the heads of pigs that the manufacturers use to make the soup I was delighted. This would be a quarantine nightmare. Think of the objections! These sort of complicated situations are usually excellent news for lawyers because they give rise to long and detailed arguments with authorities and hence generate plenty of fees. Unfortunately for me, though, the Sojitz people and Ippudo were realistic about the challenge and soon gave up on the idea of exporting the frozen soup from Kyushu. They decided instead to do the pig head boiling in Australia using local animals, bringing to an end of my dream of adding *"tonkotsu* soup export advice" to my professional curriculum vitae.

Another aspect of Kyushu ramen is the thinness of the noodles. This means they can be cooked very quickly, because Kyushu people are said to be impatient diners. The servings are smaller than ramen served elsewhere in Japan, but the other side of this coin is a system unique to Kyushu called *kaedama*, in which for an extra hundred yen (about a dollar) you can order a further serving of noodles alone, to be dumped into your remaining soup once you've eaten the first lot of noodles.

There are a few well-written blogs in English about ramen. In Japanese the number of ramen blogs is beyond counting, with people travelling all over the country to sample regional ramen types. When searching this material for information on the origins of *tonkotsu* ramen, I found constant reference to the city of Kurume, an industrial centre that sits at the foot of the mountains a forty minute drive south from Fukuoka.

Kurume is Mecca for those who revere *tonkotsu* ramen. This dish is said to have originated in Kyushu at a yatai stall called Nanking Senryo in 1937, now a small ramen restaurant near Kurume Station. I decided to go and have a look at it, more so because a food blog said the restaurant had moved to new premises. It was mid winter, and the Great Cold Wave or *kanpa* had struck Kyushu a few days before bringing more snow than anyone could remember. The new location of what was the *honke* or "home restaurant" of Nanking Senryo (it had four other branches) was on a busy road a couple of miles away from Kurume Nishitetsu Station. It sat opposite a pachinko parlour that had a slogan in English on the front window that few, if any of its patrons understood:

"Happiness is when what one does, what one says, and what one thinks, are all in harmony."

Terrific. Just what this slogan had to do with wasting one's money gambling on pachinko was anyone's guess. Maybe that's why it was written in English.

Opposite the pachinko parlour the new Nanking Senryo *honke* was two doors down from another ramen restaurant called Marukyu. This rival was much newer, cleaner, and had a carpark for ten cars. Nanking Senryo had maybe one car parking space outside. Never mind, the pachinko parlour opposite had a huge carpark.

Inside everything was old-fashioned. The walls were decorated with a tired bamboo strip façade. The tables and the counter were all well used, and there were plastic flowers in baskets. Clearly, the move to the new premises had not involved new furniture or a new interior. It looked very much as if the old restaurant had been stripped bare and transplanted

Snow on the beach at Itoshima. Kyushu faces the Korean Peninsula across the Genkai Nada Sea, and sometimes suffers a kanpa or "cold wave" bringing snowstorms with it. Japan's media goes into overdrive when such weather phenomena strike, issuing frenzied warnings of danger.

here. Maybe that was done on purpose to preserve a sense of history. I had expected a strong, pungent *kusami* smell from the *tonkotsu* soup, but such was not the case. The smell inside was mild. Soft piano music played as I sat down at a table. Although it was lunchtime only two other men were there eating, one at the counter and one at another table. Nobody looked up at me. An old lady serving customers greeted me with a soft '*Irasshaimase*' and gave me a stiff, single page menu to browse and a glass of water. She didn't seem at all surprised that I was a *gaijin*.

I ordered a plain *tonkotsu* ramen with *gyoza* dumplings and started looking around the room. Near the front door there was a glass-fronted cabinet full of memorabilia: ancient black-and-white photos of the founder and inventor of *tonkotsu* ramen, Miyamoto Tokio, various toy dragons and Buddhas, a photo of former Prime Minister Koizumi with a round-faced man, and half a dozen golf trophies.

Both the other customers ate their ramen quickly and were soon gone, replaced by only one other man. Sure, it was a cold day, but the snow had melted and you would expect people to go out and eat. Things at the home of *tonkotsu* ramen were not exactly flourishing. I finished my lunch and went to pay the bill. The old lady emerged from the kitchen to accept my money. She seemed to be on her own, though I'd noticed an old man in there when I ordered.

'May I ask you,' I said, 'I see in the glass cabinet over there a lot of golf trophies. Was Miyamoto-*san* the founder of this restaurant a good golfer?'

'Oh, no. They're my husband's.'

'Your husband? I see. And you're the Miyamoto family?'

'He's the founder's son. They didn't play golf when this place was started.'

'Ah, I suppose not,' I said. There was actually a bit of golf played in the 1930s in Japan, but not by men running ramen stands at night. 'May I introduce myself to your husband? It would be an honour to meet him.'

'Of course. He's out the back somewhere. I'll fetch him. Stay here.'

Soon the younger Miyamoto-*san* emerged, a man in his seventies wearing a baseball cap and an apron. His wife had given him my business card, and he brought his own, smiling broadly.

'I hear you've come especially to Nanking Senryo,' he said cheerfully. 'Sit down. Have a coffee with me.' He removed the baseball cap to reveal receding hair dyed black in streaks. I liked him immediately.

'Thank you. I came here from Hita. Your restautant is the home of *tonkotsu* ramen, after all.'

'Well, yes, that's us. But Hita? Really? My son married a girl from Hita. Fancy that. They run one of our branches.'

We spoke about golf and the spread of *tonkotsu* ramen overseas, the success of Ippudo and Ichiran. He seemed very pleased with this, and showed no sense of having missed out on the chance himself. I asked him about the photo of former Prime Minister Koizumi.

'Oh, that was when he visited the Nansei Hospital just behind here. The owner, Doctor Nozawa, he supported me a lot over the years, so I displayed that photo of him with Koizumi. He's dead now.'

'Did Koizumi eat here?'

'Well, he was very busy that day. So Hita, eh? I played golf there a lot. The president of Hita Kokusai Golf Club was my friend. He's dead now.'

'I see. And tell me, has the price of your raw materials gone up much?'

'Oh, it did a while back. But it's okay. We get by.'

'You have four branches in Kurume, I understand.'

'Yes,' he said, suddenly serious. 'But only two of them are allowed to use my trademark. Here, the *honke*, and my son. The other branches only use the name Nanking Senryo, not the official trademark.'

'Are they franchises?'

'Ah, in a way. Brothers.'

So that was it. There had been a split in the family, and the sons of the founder had all opened their own Nanking Senryo ramen restaurants, but only the eldest son (and *his* son, who had married the girl from Hita) was allowed to use the family trademark. That's why the brand had not spread.

I thanked him for the coffee and said time was pressing, promising to come back again.

'Actually, I've been studying English conversation,' said Miyamoto-*san* as he saw me out into the street.

'Really? Well, next time I come we should speak English,' I said, still in Japanese.

'Oh, I'm no good. It's just a hobby. Be careful on the roads.'

Three other dishes that Kyushu calls its own are worth special mention: *motsu nabe*, offal hotpot, *mentaiko*, spiced cod roe, and *basashi*, raw horsemeat. The first two have their beginnings outside Japan, again Kyushu as the gateway, while *motsu nabe* was eaten in Fukuoka for a few decades before becoming popular in Tokyo and elsewhere in Japan only in the early 1990s.

Around 1992 the Japanese economy fell into a deep recession after the collapse of the stock market and a crash in real estate values. This pushed thousands of companies into bankruptcy. A number of Japan's largest banks found themselves insolvent, and across the nation hundreds of thousands of people lost their jobs. The collapse of the "Bubble Economy," as the frenzy of speculation that began in the late 1980s was later christened, was the biggest shock the Japanese people had suffered since defeat in the Pacific War.

During this time of economic misery, somebody opened a Fukuoka-style *motsu nabe* restaurant in Tokyo, and the fashion of eating offal as a gesture of frugality really took off. People in Tokyo and elsewhere loved the rich flavour of the stock, the fresh vegetables, and the offal in the hotpot itself as much as the idea of eating frugally. More of these restaurants sprang up in Tokyo, Nagoya, and Osaka. Processed food companies made retort packet *motsu nabe* products for sale in supermarkets so you could cook it at home, if you could buy the offal, which wasn't easy to find. Finally, in the annual survey the national broadcaster NHK runs at the end of every year to choose the most popular words used in media discourse the winner for 1992 was, yes, motsu nabe. It summed up the year perfectly: Japan had hit rock bottom, and eating offal was the way to go.

If an offal stew of sorts was common food for the imported Korean labour in Kyushu's coal mines, the innovator or originator of motsunabe as a restaurant dish for Fukuoka's people is generally acknowledged to have been a lady named Hatsuko Matsusumi, whose family lived in a village at the foot of the mountains just inland from Fukuoka. Her restaurant, originally a sweets shop, was called Manjuya.

When I discovered that Manjuya was still going, though in a new location not far from the original shop in the rear suburbs of Fukuoka, I had to go and see it for myself. Manjuya was presided over by Mrs Matsusumi's daughter Sachiko, now in her eighties, who still welcomed customers and manned the cash register with her own daughter.

'You see,' she said when recalling her early life, 'Mum used to serve our *motsu nabe* in aluminum bowls, one per customer. I used to help her every day as a young girl. I washed the guts endlessly so everyone knew our food was absolutely clean. We tried using iron pots, but they ruined the soup by boiling it too much, so we switched to stone pots. The ones we use now are made in Korea.'

I asked about the different style of *motsu nabe* in the coal district of Tagawa and over in the port of Shimonoseki where many Koreans used to live around the turn of the century. Sachiko looked blank. 'Oh, I wouldn't know anything about that,' she muttered.

The recipe of Hatsuko Matsusumi's *motsu nabe* had hardly changed since 1943. It was an unusual combination of sweet and spicy flavours, coming from the Korean chili and a mixture of soy sauce and perhaps some *sake*, the underlying *umami* flavour no doubt from the traditional bonito flake/*konbu* stock. The *motsu* or offal pieces themselves were either soft tripe or the more chewy intestines.

If Mrs Matsusumi's invention sprang from the necessity of eating frugally during wartime, I wondered how frugal one could be by eating *motsu nabe* these days?

The one thing a traveler in Japan will almost never see is a horse. To do so you have to go to a racetrack, or to one of the very few horse riding attractions for tourists. The almost total absence of pasture land makes it impossible to own and ride a horse such as is common in rural America, Britain, Australia, or many parts of Europe. But in Kyushu, especially in Kumamoto and Oita Prefectures, one does regularly encounter horse in another form, as *sashimi*. This is not as terrible as it sounds.

From the day I married a girl from Hita, in the northern part of Oita, my father-in-law made a point of buying fresh horse *sashimi*, called *basashi*, from his favourite *basashi* butcher almost every time I visited and stayed for dinner. Such is still the case today. Like many things in Japan there is a polite alternative word for horse *sashimi*: *sakura niku*, or 'cherry blossom meat.' In Tokyo there are a few *basashi* restaurants that cater for homesick Kyushu folk enduring life in the capital, but down here in Kyushu people are typically straightforward about what they're eating, and *basashi* is the word they use.

The meat is lean and a deep red colour, without the odour that *kujira* (whale meat) sometimes exudes. *Basashi* is eaten in small slices, dipped in the heavier, sweeter soy sauce that Kyushu people prefer, infused not with

Five   Kyushu on the palate

Basashi or horse sashimi. A specialty of Kumamoto in Kyushu, *basashi* and other horse meat dishes are thought to have originated with the early Christian missionaries who, unlike Buddhists, allowed their followers to eat meat.

wasabi but with a touch of ground garlic and *yuzu gosho*, the spicy, citrus-based mustard-like condiment that people in Kyushu use instead of *wasabi*. You wouldn't eat a full meal of *basashi*, but as a starter it's fine, and it goes down well not so much with *sake* but with *shochu*, the clear grain, or potato-based spirit, that Kyushu drinkers prefer.

Why is *basashi* a specialty of Kumamoto Prefecture? I found various opinions on this subject. One official tourist website, welcomekyushu.

com, is unusually frank about the origins of this cuisine: "Most people in Kumamoto started eating horse meat after the Second World War, with the exception of some farmers who had eaten it previously. It is said that the 6th Infantry Division had war-horses on a large piece of grazing land located in Aso. After the war ended and the animals' duties ceased, they were used as a substitute for beef and pork, due to lack of food."

Other opinion has it that the early Christian missionaries around Kumamoto were happy for their flock to eat meat, which the Buddhist priests forbade, and this was so popular with the peasants that they thought becoming a Christian would lead to a more satisfying diet. At the time the missionaries were in fierce competition with the Buddhists to recruit followers. Maybe it made sense to offer something enticing to recruit greater numbers.

Which is true? Certainly, driving around Kumamoto Prefecture these days you don't see any horses grazing peacefully awaiting their journey to the restaurants and butcher shops. Where do these *basashi* restaurants and butchers get their inventory?

The answer came to me in one such restaurant in Kumamoto City on a Saturday night in early spring. I'd been down in Kagoshima inspecting the *kamikaze* museum at Chiran on the Saturday and was wondering whether I ought to drive the four or five hours back to Itoshima in one go, or stop somewhere on the way to spend the night. Suddenly it struck me: why not go to Kumamoto to eat some horsemeat for dinner? It was halfway back to Itoshima. Using my iPhone I reserved myself a room at a hotel near Kumamoto Castle while sitting in my car in the museum carpark and set out. By seven o'clock that night I was seated at the counter of a horsemeat restaurant in the Hanabatacho district ordering various dishes from the menu, along with a large glass of cold *sake*. When it came I noticed the *basashi* was different from the lean, cherry-red horsemeat that my father-in-law usually bought. It was heavily marbled.

'How do you like it?' the chef on the other side of the counter asked me when he saw me start on it. He seemed particularly interested in what I, a *gaijin*, thought about the dish. He wasn't asking any of the Japanese guests what they thought.

'Fine,' I replied, chewing the raw meat. 'It's good. My wife comes from Hita in Oita prefecture. The *basashi* we buy there isn't so marbled as this.'

'Oh, that's because the local people who eat it won't pay so much for the expensive *basashi*,' he said. 'This is the best.'

'I see. I'm sure it is.'

'We don't see too many foreign visitors here. Why did you come?'

This was somewhat blunt language, but I didn't mind. The chef was being friendly. 'Well, I've eaten a lot of *basashi* in Hita, but until tonight I've never come to Kumamoto to eat it,' I replied. 'I was in Kagoshima this morning, so I thought I'd drive up here and stay in Kumamoto. After all, horsemeat is the city's famous dish.'

This impressed him. 'Correct. And you drove here especially to eat *basashi*?'

'Yes. I'm on my way back to Fukuoka.'

'*Ara*! Where do you come from?'

'Well, I live in Fukuoka, but I grew up in Australia.'

'*Haaa*. What a wonderful country.'

'You've been there?' I asked.

He shook his head. 'No, but my friends have. Maybe one day I'll go.'

I said I hoped he would make the trip soon. 'May I ask you, this horse meat.....are the horses from Kumamoto Prefecture?'

'No. From Canada. '

'Canada?'

'Sure. They're good quality.'

'Ah, may I ask, are they slaughtered here in Kumamoto, or does the meat come from Canada frozen?'

'They're slaughtered here,' the chef said as if I'd uttered a mild insult. 'It's fresh.'

'Well, it certainly tastes good,' I hastened to add.

'It's the best,' he said.

Six

Yakuza

Japan's organised criminal gangs are known colloquially as the *yakuza*, which has a better ring to it than the more formal term for the gangs, *bōryokudan*, meaning "violent groups." For historical reasons Kyushu has more *yakuza* gangs than anywhere else in Japan. Some say this is because of the heavy industry in northern Kyushu, which attracted large numbers of unskilled labourers, including Koreans, a century ago when the island's coal mines were industrialised. Others say it was Kyushu's distance from Kyoto and Tokyo and its proximity to Korea, as well as its natural tendency to rebel against authority, that gave fertile ground to the gangs.

In the past and still these days the *yakuza* are romanticised in movies and comics for their supposed code of honour and fierce loyalty. This is unlikely ever to have been quite true, and these days it's a morbid joke. The truth is the *yakuza* gangsters are predatory scum who, over the decades, have wormed their way into Japanese society, finding dark places to ply their trades of prostitution, gambling, pornography, drug trafficking, and plain old-fashioned extortion. They control large chunks of the entertainment industry, including movie-making, talent agencies and television production, as well as parts of the construction and transport industries and labour-broking.

Modern Japan is highly regulated and sometimes rigid, but after the trauma of the war and the brutality that preceded it, there is a strong social priority to avoid all forms of violence. People are polite, courteous to each other, and gentle in their public manners. The *yakuza* exploit this gentility by their willingness to use violence against vulnerable individuals to make money. They rob, cheat, and intimidate elderly people, taking advantage of the ageing population and the epidemic of dementia. The Japanese movie director Beat Takeshi's modern *yakuza* movies, *Outrage*, and *Outrage Beyond*, rightly dwell on the commonplace treachery and betrayal among the gangsters.

In Kyushu it's hard to ignore the *yakuza*. When I was pressing the Ministry of Economy, Trade, and Industry (METI) for help in locating likely places for an underground coal gasification (UCG) project, one of the two areas containing old coal mines was the Chikuho District around the towns of Tagawa and Iizuka, an hour's drive from the city of Fukuoka. I was looking for deep coal seams uneconomic for mining, but which might be drilled into and gasified using UCG technology from Australia, which produces a crude but flammable gas. Because Japan is devoid of any domestic energy source, the project attracted METI's keen interest, until I mentioned the coal seams of the Chikuho District.

Why don't you try Omuta, said the METI Bureau in Fukuoka. There's plenty of coal underground there.

'But it's under the sea', I replied, 'and the seaweed farmers will object to anything that might damage their image'. Like it or not, gasifying coal seams under the seabed is not something that will enhance the appeal of the seaweed grown there. 'What about Tagawa?' I asked.

The METI team in the meeting looked uncomfortable. It's difficult over there, they said. Too many houses these days. People would complain.

'But the industrial estates sit on top of the old coalfields', I countered. 'Drilling under a few factories isn't going to attract any opposition. A UCG plant could be sited inside such a zone and not threaten any residential area. More than that, the local residents would get cheap gas for their homes.'

A symphony of pained grunting greeted this appeal. 'It would be very difficult to build,' said Mr Mukai, the METI team leader, 'and no Japanese partner would be happy operating there.'

'Why?' I asked. There was more shuffling from the METI boys. 'Social conditions are unfavourable', they said.

I was mystified, but needing METI's help I let the matter drop and agreed to look closely at the town of Omuta on the edge of the Ariake Sea on the way to Kumamoto. After the meeting Hiro Kato from the Australian Trade Office who was accompanying me to these meetings explained everything.

'It's the *yakuza* gangs,' he said. 'They would interfere in a construction project in Chikuho. It's their local area. A Japanese company would be scared to operate there. The gangsters would visit the company managers at home if necessary. You have to forget it.'

So even the mighty METI shies away from any confrontation, even indirect, with the *yakuza*. Why? Because the gangs have a habit of seeking out individuals, bankers and the like, or even local politicians, and quietly but effectively threatening them at home. In Japan, despite the many local police boxes and general tight control of society, the *yakuza* usually get their way if they operate up close and personal. If you resist them you will suffer, as some fishermen in Kitakyushu found out.

A mere 2000 or so gangsters among a population of around twelve million people may not seem such a big deal, but in a society where violence is extremely rare the effect of these 2000 *yakuza* thugs is significant. Every medium size town in Japan has a night quarter of hostess bars, *karaoke* joints, and small bars called *snakku*. The *yakuza* collect protection money from these small enterprises without hindrance. Companies in the construction industry likewise pay protection money, as do logistics companies serving the ports. All of this is based on actual violence or the threat of it.

Among the Kyushu gangs three stand out for their history of violence and disregard for the normal *yakuza* decorum: the Dōjinkai in Kurume, the Seidōkai in Omuta, and the most noteworthy of all, the Kudōkai of Kitakyushu. The Fukuhaku Kai gang based in Fukuoka City is headed by a Japanese man of Korean descent, as was the Seidōkai.

The Kudōkai has attracted the most publicity because of the arrest in April 2015 of its top two members on murder charges going back sixteen years. This arose from a feud between the gang and the Wakinoura Fishing Co-operative of Kitakyushu City. In 1997 a former chairman of the Co-op, 70 year-old Mr Kunihiro Kajiwara, was chairman of a local company that supplied gravel to the major construction companies in Kitakyushu. The Hibiki Container Terminal project, involving almost twenty years of sea reclamation, was a huge business because of the amount of gravel needed to create acres of stable, reclaimed land from where the sea had once been. Around 7pm in the evening of 18 February just as he was about to enter his favourite drinking bar, two men approached Kajiwara and shot him four times in the head and chest, killing him instantly. Someone was sending a message.

Because the Hibiki Container Terminal project was taking place within the fishing rights area of the Co-op, the board of the Co-op was able to negotiate compensation payments amounting to around $100 million equivalent. Although some sort of settlement is normal in Japan, where the fishing and agricultural co-operatives have the absolute support of the Liberal Democratic Party, this sum clearly outweighed the loss of fish and was way above the normal quantum of compensation. Strangely the mainstream media had nothing to say about this unusual settlement.

At that time the Kudōkai was under the command of Hideo Mizoshita, with the slight, bespectacled but vicious Satoru Nomura as head of the Tanaka Gang, a sub-organisation within the Kudōkai. Mizoshita demanded a share of the compensation from the Co-op, as well as a share of the gravel business profits. Kajiwara and his family, fishermen as well as gravel merchants, were stubborn people. They refused to comply, arguing that the money belonged to the Co-op members and no one else. As one magazine blog put it years later, "They were the kind of guys who wouldn't hand over what shouldn't be handed over."

Police strongly suspected that Mizoshita delegated the task of persuading the Co-op to comply with Nomura, who then personally murdered Kajiwara as his first measure.

Nothing happened for some years, and the construction companies completed the Hibiki Container Terminal project. Satoru Nomura became head of the Kudōkai in 2000 when Mizoshita retired, and in 2011 Nomura himself retired, handing the day-to-day management of the gang to his deputy, Fumio Tanoue.

Then early in the morning of 20 December 2013 the then chairman of the Wakinoura Fishing Co-operative, 70 year-old Mr Tadayoshi Ueno, was shot dead at point blank range as he was putting out the garbage. Despite having a different surname, Ueno was the younger brother of Kunihiro Kajiwara. It turned out that Ueno's family had been suffering harassment from the Kudōkai for years, with bullets fired into their cars and houses, and indeed Ueno himself had narrowly escaped death when a gunman took a shot at him in 1998 and missed. Then in May 2014 a dentist was attacked one night and stabbed repeatedly in the head and stomach. The dentist was the son-in-law of Tadayoshi Ueno.

This looks like a typical case of a *yakuza* gang preying on civilians, which is usually what they do. But such is not the case here. The major newspapers and magazines did not publish what their own journalists knew, doubtless out of fear of personal retribution. According to a blogger called Black Cat Momotaro who writes on the Ameba blog platform, the Wakinoura Fishing Co-operative was itself infested with *yakuza*. In particular, the blogger claims that Kunihiro Kajiwara and Tadayoshi Ueno were members of the old Kajiwara Gang, one that fought with the Kudōkai over a long period and in 1950 assassinated the son of Takaaki Kusano, one of the Kudōkai's senior figures. The murders over the money from the container terminal project were just more incidents in a decades long war between these gangs.

The 2007 assassination of the mayor of Nagasaki was a national scandal. But once again reporting of the incident in the mainstream media does not tell the whole story.

Mr Itcho Ito was a three-term mayor of Nagasaki, and a member of the conservative Liberal Democratic Party. As is expected of any mayor of Nagasaki, Ito campaigned against the use of nuclear weapons on the international stage, making a speech at the International Court of Justice in The Hague in 1995 where he argued that their use is a violation of international law.

Like all Japanese politicians campaigning for re-election, Mayor Ito spent time outside the main railway station giving speeches and greeting passer-by

Black sesame ice cream on sale outside the coal museum at Tagawa in the Chikuho District of Fukuoka Prefecture. The town was once a major coal-mining centre and is still home to the Taishu Kai yakuza gang formed in 1954 by a coal miner named Ohta Suharu. One explanation for the large number of yakuza gangsters operating in Kyushu is the island's many coal mines, all of which are now closed. The tradition of elaborate body tattoos worn by sworn yakuza men and women is said to come from the feudal-era coal miners who wore tattoos so their bodies could be properly identified after death in mine accidents.

voters. At 7pm in the evening on Tuesday 17 April 2007 he was walking to his campaign office just up the street from the railway station when he was approached from behind by a man who shot him twice in the back with a pistol. The assassin, a man named Tetsuya Shirō, was immediately detained by Ito's campaign staff and arrested by the police. Shirō was the underboss of a yakuza gang in Nagasaki called the Suishinkai, affiliated with the Yamaguchi Gumi.

All the reporting of the incident has it that Shirō shot the mayor as a result of a personal grudge and not on the orders of the Yamaguchi Gumi senior bosses. A couple of years before the shooting Shirō had damaged his car when driving over a large pothole near some footpath construction. He complained to the city government that the damage was its responsibility and demanded compensation. This sounds very much like a contrived grievance: a yakuza gangster demanding money from a city government has the definite ring of extortion about it. But the city officials refused to pay anything, as did Shirō's vehicle insurer. Apparently Shirō was so upset by this knockback that he decided to shoot the mayor in revenge. Really?

Other reports had it that Shirō was furious that the city had also denied a construction company under his gang's control a large public works contract. This sounds more plausible, but the mystery is why Shirō would sacrifice himself over such a trivial matter? As deputy boss of the most powerful yakuza gang in Nagasaki he was one of the most influential people in the city. Of course he wanted the city government to push construction work his way to maintain the Suishinkai's income, but at the expense of going to prison for life or worse?

The news and blog website, Naver Matome, discusses Shirō's motives as follows:

"[Shiroo] started life as a gangster in 1965 and was seen as the next boss, but in 2002 he was effectively demoted and his position within the gang became uncertain. In January of that year he used a construction company that generated cash for the gang and applied to the city's small business financial support scheme. This was simply a method of obtaining free money — borrowing public funds and never repaying the loan. The company could not obtain clearance from the credit guarantee association and so could not qualify under the city's scheme. A year later Shirō damaged his car at a footpath construction site and failed to receive compensation.

"He became depressed after failing to secure either income from his gangster activity nor any compensation, and his pride as a yakuza was injured when the city refused his improper demands. It is presumed that he wanted to assert his position as a gangster and shake up society by perpetrating such a major crime [shooting the mayor]."

This suggests Shirō was so depressed by his failures as a *yakuza* that he risked the death penalty by publicly shooting the mayor and allowing himself to be immediately arrested. While, as usual, the mainstream media left the motive thus, some bloggers suggested there was more to it. Writing in May 2007 on the website, Our Age, a blogger named Itsuki Kaoru sketched a larger political motive:

"Why did the Nagasaki mayor have to be so viciously murdered?....Dare it be said that, in the context of major changes in defence policy being pushed forward, such as the relocation of US forces in Japan and ballistic missile defence, certain political forces felt a sense of crisis over Mayor Ito's advocacy of nuclear weapons abolition and pacificism. So there's a possibility that they put the easily manipulated *yakuza* up to it and brought about this violent crime. As a conservative politician from the site of an atom bomb attack, his thoughts and words were the symbol of the broad anti-nuclear movement and were a true threat to the post-war age of the destruction of the Left."

The same blog linked Ito's assassination to the murder of a Democratic Party of Japan Diet member, Kohki Ishii, who was stabbed to death in October 2002 by a Yamaguchi Gumi gangster who surrendered to police after escaping from the murder scene. Ishii, a former communist with a Russian wife, had a record in the Diet of investigating scandals in government procurement and construction projects and was on his way to the Diet to make a speech on "something terrible" he had discovered. The media criticized the police investigation of Ishii's murder as wholly inadequate.

Among other things Ishii's diary and briefcase contents were mysteriously stolen the day after his murder.

In the very real context of links between the *yakuza*, the ultra-nationalists, and the ultra-conservative wing of the LDP, the real motive behind or reason for Tetsuya Shirō's murder of Mayor Ito remained a mystery tinged with suspicion. The present crackdown on the *yakuza*, forced on the LDP by the banks and the business world, would always be hampered by the *yakuza*-nationalist-politician axis.

It struck me during a visit to New York, in the late spring of 2015, why the Kyushu *yakuza* gangs are more independent, that is, less likely to be influenced by the national umbrella groups. It's the proximity of North Korea and China, and the trafficking of illegal drugs and their precursor chemicals. The Kyushu gangsters have a great business of their own and don't need any help from Kobe or Tokyo.

While in New York I fancied the idea of going to visit the Fulton Street Fish Market to see how it compared to Tokyo's Tsukiji Fish Market, the biggest in the world. A search on the web revealed the sad news that the Fulton Street market had gone, moved to the Bronx somewhere, just like Tsukiji market is scheduled to move out to a boring expanse of reclaimed land at Toyosu soon.

Another item on the Google search results page caught my eye, something about mob activity in the New York fish market and the Genovese crime family. I read the article, and then kept reading more articles about the New York organised crime scene. It was fascinating stuff. I was struck by the similarities to the *yakuza*, how the American mafia made money from gambling and extortion, but also how like the *yakuza* they are deeply embedded in the transportation industry, especially the docks. This means access to smuggling channels, and that means illegal drugs.

On a grim, overcast Monday afternoon at the start of *tsuyu*, the official rainy season that begins in Kyushu around the second week of June each year, I stopped in Kurume on the way back to Itoshima from a visit to Hita where I caught up on my unpaid taxes and stayed a night with my parents-in-law to check on their well being. Kurume looked its drab, industrial worst in the incessant rain. People trudged down the streets under umbrellas, and cars waited impatiently as the traffic got slower and slower.

I headed towards the expressway that would take me back to Fukuoka and lapsed into a Big Mac combo lunch instead of the ramen. While sitting in my car in the McDonalds carpark eating my hamburger and French fries, I decided the miserable day would be improved by a visit to the official headquarters of the Dōjinkai. I found the address on the Wikiyakuza website and entered it into my car navigation system, surprised to see that it was very close to Kurume's Shinkansen station.

The station has a main entrance on the east side and a quiet, lesser gate on the west side. A new block of apartments dominated the area around the west gate with its carefully landscaped car park and gardens. What struck me as odd was the total lack of any shops. It was an empty, sterile, rather lonely place.

Following the navigation system I drove down a very narrow street behind the apartment building and found a factory, the Tanaka Dye Works (Kurume is famous for its indigo dyeing industry), and a large, multi-storey pachinko parlour called Wonderland. In the ground floor car park of Wonderland I noticed two or three *yakuza* vehicles, white sedans with elaborate bright aluminum wheel caps. Just around the corner down another narrow street I found what I was looking for — a squat, pale orange building perhaps two storeys high with no windows and a large CCTV camera above a solitary door, the fortress of the feared Dōjinkai. On the wall just outside the door was a large plaque bearing the name of the resident of the building, Matsuo. Usually gang headquarters proudly display the gang name and crest, but not this time. Just Matsuo.

Around the corner of the house I noticed a two-vehicle carpark containing another yakuza vehicle — again, white sedan with elaborate wheel caps — and a clothes line. Did the Dōjinkai gangsters hang their washing out to dry here after a hard day's work extorting protection money, trafficking drugs, or pimping girls in Kurume's hostess bars? Did Mrs Matsuo do their washing for them?

Having seen off the Seidōkai in the war between the two gangs the Dōjinkai was still active in pursuit of various criminal enterprises around northern Kyushu. A glance at the recent media reports on the Asahi Shimbun newspaper website gave me an idea of what they are up to these days:

"A Dōjinkai gangster, Kojiro Mizoguchi was arrested in April 2015 by the Fukuoka Police on suspicion of violating the Copyright Law by making numerous copies of DVD movies. Mizoguchi pleaded not guilty, saying he was doing it to give the DVDs to friends and to watch them himself. Police seized 849 copied DVDs and a notebook computer from the Dōjinkai office in Kurume. Among the illegally copied DVDs was *Amazing Spiderman*."

"In March 2015, a Fukuoka judge acquitted a Dōjinkai gangster, one Masataka Mikasa, of a charge of conspiracy to defraud the government of unemployment insurance training subsidies. The judge said the possibility of the investigating police having fabricated a confession could not be ruled out in this case."

In mid June 2015, Satoru Nomura, boss of the Kudōkai, suffered his "Al Capone moment" when the Fukuoka Prefectural Police "rearrested" him on charges of criminal tax evasion. Quite how Nomura was "rearrested" when he was already detained in custody pending trial on charges of ordering the murder of the Wakinoura Fishing Co-op chairman was a mystery. Did the police burst into his prison cell, grab his arms, handcuff him, and announce the new charges? Hardly. It was merely an administrative procedure, announced for PR purposes.

The new charges were something of a revolutionary step, though not without difficulty for the police and prosecutors. The evening news bulletin on NHK explained the problem as follows. Nomura, as boss of the gang, received money every month from his gang members. Each gangster had a fixed sum he had to pay. This money was called *jōnōkin* or 'money paid upwards' within an organization for the purposes of operating the organization. Bear in mind that the Kudōkai gang was an unincorporated non-profit voluntary organization under the law. It existed, in theory, for the purpose of fraternal association. As NHK explained, this is no different from the thousands of small neighbourhood associations (*chōnaikai*), which run local festivals, or even school PTAs.

When the police charged Nomura with tax evasion they did so alleging that he used the contributions from his gang members not for the purposes of running the gang, which would leave the money untaxable, but for private purposes. Hence the money became taxable. Spending the money on restaurant meals, travel, entertainment such as golf, and on buying a motor vehicle, was now declared to be a private purpose.

Dear, oh dear, said NHK. That's pretty much what a lot of neighbourhood associations and PTAs do with their money — spend it on entertaining their members. How could this be distinguished from the Kudōkai spending? If the *chōnaikai* and the PTAs were to be taxed then Japanese society would be shaken to the core. The whole thing was "laudable but terribly risky."

The police also maintained that Nomura had deposited around ¥20 million (around $2.2 million) in his relatives' bank accounts, thus converting it to private funds and making it taxable. This struck me as most unlikely. Why would Kyushu's most senior gangster do anything but keep the money in cash? Japan is a cash society. It's still suffering deflation. Even if Nomura cared about preserving the value of his money, what interest would be earned in a bank account? Maybe 0.01%.

Japanese people love hoarding cash and transacting business in cash. I bought my house in Itoshima by handing over four million yen in cash. It's an indelible national habit, and the story from the police was next to impossible to believe. Was Satoru Nomura and his CFO so careless as to bank the money?

Nomura's lawyer was quoted on the news as asking simply, 'And why is this tax evasion?'

Superintendent Yoshida of the Fukuoka Police said in his press conference, 'We will get to the bottom of this "money paid upwards", which is the lifeblood of this gang. This investigation is another step towards destroying the Kudōkai entirely.'

Jun Mizoguchi, an author who writes about the *yakuza*, was interviewed on the late evening news bulletin. He was astonished at what the police had done. 'This is a ground-breaking step. If the same investigation is made of other *yakuza* gangs, well…..there's going to be a lot of trouble.'

For Satoru Nomura, boss of the Kudōkai gang, things went from bad, to worse, and then to very embarrassing. In early 2015, he was arrested on various charges, including involvement in the attempted stabbing murder of the dentist son-in-law of the chairman of the Wakinoura Fishing Co-operative. The underling gangster who actually wielded the knife, one Kazuto Wada, denied in court that Nomura had ordered the attack. The judge rejected Wada's evidence entirely, finding that he had indeed attacked the dentist with intent to murder and that Nomura had ordered him to carry out the crime. Wada was sentenced to eighteen years in prison for the attack and for a series of other violent crimes.

Further to Nomura's woes was the incident in which a nurse was stabbed outside her home in Fukuoka one night. This crime gave rise to some salacious media comment when it turned out that the nurse worked at a cosmetic surgery clinic that had treated Nomura. According to the prosecutors, who had indicted a junior Kudōkai gangster named Nakada Yoshinobu for the stabbing, Nomura has undergone surgery at the clinic to enlarge his penis and remove much of his pubic hair. After the operation he was dissatisfied with the results, complaining that his private parts were "rotting", and worse, that the nurse had treated him in an unbecoming manner. Oddest of all was that Nomura went back to the clinic two days after the nurse was stabbed. Noting that she was absent from work he remarked, 'She was stabbed, that one. Well, I guess such things can't be helped, eh?'

The court found that, just as with the dentist, Nomura had ordered the attack on the nurse.

If you ask people 'What's in Kitakyushu?' you'll probably get an answer along the lines of 'industry and *yakuza*.' While this is unfair to the many artistically talented and decent people who live in Kyushu's second biggest city, it's also an accurate reply. The city is home to the Yahata Steelworks, a massive, rusty-brown complex that was Japan's first major industrial plant. It was also the original target for Fat Man, Harry Truman's second atom bomb, yet bad weather on 9 August 1945 caused a change of plan that led to Nagasaki being the eventual victim. Yet Kitakyushu these days is also home to some highly sophisticated industries making, among other things, the industrial robots that have over the years created a revolution in manufacturing.

But the second part of the standard reply is also true. There is an inordinate number of gangsters in Kitakyushu. Moreover, they are, by reputation, crude and more than usually violent.

Satoru Nomura (in white), boss of the Kudo Kai yakuza gang in Kitakyushu, being arrested on murder charges. Nomura, one of Kyushu's most vicious gangsters, was convicted of several murders and is now languishing in prison. He also ordered the stabbing of a nurse who he felt treated him with disrespect at a clinic he attended for penis enlargement surgery.

Six   Yakuza

One evening, I watched a program on television about a small group of former *yakuza* gangsters who, after being released from prison, decided to make a clean break from gang life and go straight. They opened an *udon* noodle restaurant in the middle of Kitakyushu. The program showed the senior man, one Nakatomo-*san*, talking about the futility of trying to find normal work as an ex-*yakuza* just out of prison.

'We had no choice,' he said to the interviewer. 'It was either *udon* or back to the old ways, and back inside again. None of us want to do that, so we're going into the restaurant business instead. *Yomogi udon*.' As an ardent observer of *yakuza* activity I was instantly intrigued.

It took me some months to get up to Kitakyushu to start a friendship with this man. The city was an hour's drive from my house in Itoshima, and I had no other reason to go there, no business and no friends there apart from some lawyers I'd met a few years back. Later I went to northern China to speak at a conference in the city of Qiqihar, way up near the Russian border in what was once Japan's colony of Manchukuo. Looking around the bleak, flat landscape it struck me just how ambitious had the Japanese military government been during the 1930s, and how stupid. Had they decided to stop there and not invade the entirety of China, Pearl Harbour may never have happened, and what a different world it would be today.

Returning to Kyushu after the Qiqihar visit I found beautiful spring weather, a mass of flowers blooming in Lauben Kolonie, and not much to do for the weekend. I'd promised to go and visit my parents-in-law in Hita, who reports from family members suggested were in a declining mental state, so it came about that I decided to drive to Hita via Kitakyushu to eat lunch at the *yomogi udon* restaurant run by the group of former *yakuza*.

The restaurant was in a bright and clean covered shopping arcade close to Kokura Station where the Shinkansen train stops before it leaves Kyushu and crosses over to Honshu on the way to Hiroshima, Osaka, and Tokyo. The giant steelworks across the river dominated this central part of Kitakyushu. I walked down the arcade and found a corridor with a low ceiling off to one side, the Tarumaya *yomogi* undon restaurant way down the end, as if hidden out of shame.

Nakatomo-san, the 27-year veteran of a yakuza gang in Kitakyushu who now runs an udon restaurant after resolving to turn his back on the life of a gangster. ' You start from minus,' he said, referring to post-prison life. ' Our position in society is a difficult one.....sensitive, you know. So it takes a while to get from minus back up to zero.'

It was already mid-afternoon. Entering the place I saw only one other customer, a young girl sitting at a counter slurping her *udon*. It was small inside by any standard, two counters on either side of the room and a black, wooden table with six seats in the centre. An older woman with hair dyed light brown emerged from the kitchen and smiled at me. This was both pleasant and disappointing, yet where were the heavily-tatooed ex-*yakuza*?

'*Konnichi wa*,' I replied. 'You're famous for the *niku udon*, right?'

Niku udon means "meat *udon*" in Japanese, almost always beef.

'Indeed,' said the woman.

'I'll definitely have that, then.'

She returned to the kitchen and repeated the order aloud. I was encouraged to hear a man's voice reply.

Soon she brought a steaming bowl out to me full of dark, clear soup filled with pale green noodles and pieces of stewed beef, garnished with a brace of chopped shallots. 'Here, try this on top,' she said, handing me a small plastic box of pulverised ginger.

First I took a plastic spoon and tried the soup. It was excellent, not too salty as is too often the case. The noodles, flavoured with the herb *yomogi*, were soft to chew and tasted better than the normal white *udon* noodles. The best thing of all was the stewed beef. It had an unusual flavor, something like rosemary. Slowly I finished the bowl of *udon*, drank some chilled water, and got up to pay my bill. The woman and the man were in the kitchen, obscured by a hanging curtain. Carefully I poked my head in and said, 'That was delicious. May I have the bill, please?'

Inside the kitchen I saw a man whom I recognised from the television program. He wore a black, collarless shirt with long sleeves, no doubt to cover his tattooed arms. His glasses were of a fashionable style, and his upper body was well muscled and carrying no excess fat. This, beyond doubt, was Nakatomo. He came straight up to me and extended a hand to shake mine. No bowing, just a handshake.

'Really? You liked it?' he asked.

'Sure. It has an unusual flavor, better than the usual *udon*,' I replied. 'I've had *yomogi* tea before, but I've never had it in *udon*. How do you get the flavour into the noodles?'

'Powder. We mix it with the flour and make the noodles that way,' Nakatomo replied seriously, a chef discussing his major dish.

'I saw your restaurant on television last year,' I said. 'That's why I came. When did you open?'

'Last year in June. The owner of this arcade, he's a good guy, powerful around here. He encouraged us.'

The television program had discussed *shakai fukki*, meaning a return to normal society for convicted criminals. I told him I was writing a book about Kyushu, and that I'd like to include something in the chapter about food featuring his *yomogi udon*.

'Thanks,' he exclaimed. 'We could use the publicity.'

'Maybe a few foreigners might come for the *udon*.'

'Great. Anyone's welcome. The more the better.' I got the impression that business wasn't so good. 'You're writing a book, eh? I've got a book coming out in September,' he said with a touch of pride.

'Please invite me to the launch,' I said.

He looked confused. 'What's that?'

'A book launch. You invite a whole lot of people, media especially, you make a speech, and hopefully people start buying the book. It's a PR campaign.'

Nakatomo looked skeptical. 'A guy like me......*Maaa......*'

'Well, you need to promote the book.'

'Maybe,' he said, laughing quietly. Ex-*yakuza* have to be modest. *Shakai fukki* isn't the easiest path to tread in Japan.

That night I watched the TV program again on YouTube.

'I was twenty-seven years in the gang, right?' Nakatomo said, wearing a wry expression. 'Starting again after prison means starting from a minus position. To most people you'll always be a *yakuza*. It's not like starting from zero. You start from minus. Our position in society is a difficult one, sensitive, you know. So it takes a while to get from minus back up to zero.'

Seven

Tea

At 6.15am I ventured out into the streets of Upper Midtown in New York, hopelessly jet-lagged and utterly unable to sleep. It was mid-May and the weather was clear, the air cool and fresh on my face and arms and the sky a bright blue above the buildings. In Seventh Avenue two blocks south of Central Park a few people were walking, shuffling along, or standing around waiting for something or someone. I paused, taking it all in while a young, dark Hispanic man walked past shaking his head and talking to himself furiously, '….fuckin' nobody, fuckin' nobody, fuckin' nobody….' Across the street two platinum blonde women who looked like tourists were giving coffee to a derelict black man sitting on the footpath outside a Starbucks. They were having some trouble getting him to accept it. I bought a newspaper and walked north towards Central Park, the pungent odour of horse manure in my nostrils when I stopped at the kerb waiting for the lights to change.

In twenty-four hours I would be back in Kyushu from New York, I told myself. I'd come all the way here to meet some lawyers on behalf of my client Pie Face, whose American partner, soon to be former partner, was suing the company for fraud, misrepresentation, and sundry other alleged villainies over the failure of the Pie Face stores in New York to make a profit. Things were not looking good. One of the lawyers for the angry partner, a supremely confident woman from Florida, had won cases before the United States Supreme Court, so to her dealing with a small Australian company like Pie Face would be like squashing a bug. Clearly we were legally outgunned. I went to the meetings with my friend John Nicolis, a director of Pie Face and a friend from my university days in Melbourne and from the years in Tokyo where we both worked, chased women together, and had a lot of fun when we were younger.

I walked around the park watching the joggers and the cyclists and the dog walkers. No mad people or homeless bums seemed to be around. It was a beautiful scene. John had said some Russians were paying $100 million for penthouses around the park. Could you make $100 million in Japan? Possibly, but not easy.

Central Park was the brainchild of a Democrat New York politician called Dan Sickles who later became a famous Union general in the Civil War. Sickles was the first person in the common law world to be acquitted using the defence of temporary insanity, dreamt up by his Irish-American lawyer, after shooting dead his wife's lover in 1859 in Washington DC, just across the street from the White House.

I walked out of the park looking for a café for breakfast. A bull-headed man driving an expensive black Lexus SUV and smoking a big cigar rolled by. Is he a mobster, I wondered, Tony Soprano out early for something nefarious? The Lexus had New Jersey plates. Maybe he really was a mob guy.

I chose a foreign, organic food café a block back from the park. Feeling homesick for Japan I wished I could have a simple Japanese breakfast of plain boiled rice, *nori* seaweed, and a raw egg, maybe with a small piece of grilled fish, and of course a few cups of hot green tea made not with some ghastly tea bag but with loose *sencha* leaves in a pot. But no, my breakfast must be the very ordinary coffee served in America and either a bagel, a croissant, or some sort of granola. Somewhere in Manhattan there must be a café serving a simple Japanese breakfast. Perhaps it's down in SoHo or the Village where Bob Dylan, Robert De Niro, and Sting or Bono probably live. Looking at the huge apartment buildings on the Upper West side of the park I wondered what Yoko Ono has for breakfast these days. Surely she has *ocha*.

Ocha is tea in Japanese. There are many kinds of Japanese tea, from plain *sencha*, to the *matcha* used in the tea ceremony, to the fragrant *genmaicha* with its toasted rice hulls, and finally the rare, exquisite, and very expensive *gyokuro*. Green tea is said to help keep your weight down, yet the tea farmer I got to know best in Kyushu was fat, no question about it. A more cheerful person you would not meet in Japan, where, unless you are Prime Minister Abe or an idiot TV celebrity, being cautious, pessimistic and gloomy is the national mood these days. But Yuji Kurihara was definitely not gaining the weight control benefit of the tea his family grew.

The usual way to meet people in a business setting in Japan is by formal introduction, but I had no such thing with Yuji. It all began when someone in Fukuoka suggested I use my foreign legal skills to help Kyushu's farmers develop the intellectual property around their products. In other words, branding, so that they might begin to export. I could be hired to arrange registration of trademarks and the building of English-language websites. This was the theory at least. There were various agricultural products to choose from: *wagyu* beef, *shochu* liquor, some unusual fruits, and green tea. I decided to start with Kyushu's tea.

Tea is grown in three main districts in Kyushu: Yame, in Fukuoka Prefecture; Ureshino, in Saga Prefecture; and down in Kagoshima Prefecture at Chiran and around Mount Kirishima. Yame is only a forty minute drive inland from Fukuoka, and not far off the route to Hita. Before going there I had a meeting with some officials of the Fukuoka Prefectural Government Economic Promotion Bureau who were enthusiastic about the idea of agricultural exports.

'This is exactly our policy,' they said. 'Kyushu's farmers must boost their exports in order to survive for the long term. Being an international lawyer you are just the person to assist and advise on this.'

'Indeed,' I replied. 'I am more than happy to do such work, and I have some ideas about how it should begin. The only question is, who will retain me?'

The question of payment for services brought on an awkward moment for the two men. They started grunting and emitting mild groans of mental anguish.

'Ahh…..we…ahhh….don't retain lawyers for this sort of work,' they said. 'It isn't in our budget. Someone else must do so.'

'You mean JA?' I said. The national agricultural co-operative was, as a matter of pure theory, the ideal hirer of an intellectual property lawyer, but they had never done this before. 'Perhaps the prefectural government could provide a budget to JA who could then hire me,' I suggested.

More groans of anguish ensued. 'This has never been done before,' they said gravely.

'Well, that's why there aren't any agricultural exports to speak of, because nobody has bothered to develop any English-language intellectual property. Once a brand exists you can go out and sell it,' I countered.

'Mmm…..aahhh. This could be true,' the officials allowed. 'But there is no precedent for engaging a foreign advisor, not by the prefecture. Perhaps if a brand was developed and a delegation of producers attended an international exhibition then the prefecture could reimburse the costs of the travel and the booth.'

'What about my professional fees?'

'Ah, that would be difficult,' they said. 'But if you attend the exhibition as advisor, maybe you could be paid from the proceeds of sales.'

They looked very pleased with this neat bureaucratic solution. That way no public money could be used on the unprecedented notion of a foreign advisor, even though we were talking about selling Kyushu products in foreign markets, and the farmers wouldn't have to pay anything either. Barter trade, in other words.

This was an exasperating business, but I had to accept their logic. If no bureaucrat, let alone a farmer or JA co-operative officer, was going to pay me then I would have to invest my own time and effort as capital. I could reap a dividend when sales were made, and perhaps even negotiate an ongoing royalty arrangement, which might prove more lucrative in the long run. Such dreams come easy when you're struggling to launch a new venture.

I decided to avoid approaching JA in Yame, anticipating the same sort of frustrating exchange as I had with the prefectural officials. Instead, I looked for Yame tea growers directly on the internet. In English there were various websites selling Yame tea, but none of them were actually located in Yame. In Japanese it was better. I clicked on a few websites until I came across the cheerful round face of Yuji Kurihara at his website, www.e-yame-cha.com. The website was entirely in Japanese, which was what I wanted, and the Kurihara family were real tea growers, not just merchants. They even had a Facebook page.

I telephoned and got through to Yuji, introducing myself as an Australian from Fukuoka interested in exporting Yame tea. I didn't say I was a lawyer nor mention anything about intellectual property. That would have complicated everything. Yuji said their farm was located in the village of Yabe, way up in the mountains at the very back of the Yame District. No problem, I said. Driving from Hita it's over the mountains beyond the Nakatsue hot springs.

We got on well the first time I sat down in the small office at the side of the Kurihara's family home, a traditional style farmhouse located up a narrow side road from the main village of Yabe. Up so high in the mountains the air is fresh and the valleys are tranquil. Forests of dark green cedar and cypress cover the steep sides of the ridges. Right in front of the Kurihara's house is a 150 year-old tea tree marked with a small white sign.

Inside the office the walls were decorated with framed photographs of prize giving ceremonies for tea tasting events, posters of Kyushu's natural scenery, and a glorious photo of the sumo wrestler Kotoshogiku, who hails from Yanagawa in Fukuoka Prefecture, with an infant child on his knee and the child's family clustered behind him.

'Does Kotoshogiku drink your tea?' I asked, most impressed.

'Ah, well, I think so,' said Yuji as he carefully made me a sample of his best *sencha*. 'Actually the baby is my brother's boy. It's good luck for an infant boy to be cuddled by a sumo wrestler. Gives him strength.'

'Of course. So you donate tea to Kotoshogiku's stable?'

'No. Tea makes you pee a lot. Not easy for a wrestler.'

I laughed. The tight loincloth-like garment the wrestlers wear might well make it awkward to pee often. 'They drink plenty of beer, don't they? Anyway, I hope Kotoshogiku wins a tournament sometime,' I added.

'It won't be easy,' said Yuji. ' I just hope he tries hard.'

His *sencha* was fresh such that the fragrance in the cup when I sniffed

Yuji Kurihara, tea grower at Yabe Village in the mountains about Yame City. The Kurihara Tea Farm is one of the highest by altitude in Japan and grows very high quality green tea, including traditional gyokuro tea, grown underneath straw mats to reduce the exposure to sunlight. In 1191 tea was brought to Japan from China by the Buddhist monk Eisai, founder of the Rinzai Sect of Zen Buddhism. Working with Yuji I developed a new blend of tea using wakame seaweed and genmai or toasted rice.

it was so strong your nose remembers it for days. He explained that the Kurihara Tea Farm was one of the largest family-run farms in Yame District, and that its tea was grown at among the highest elevations in Japan. Because of that it grew slowly and gained more flavour than lowland teas. Also, because there were fewer insects at such an elevation they used very little insecticide.

They had won second and third prize in the national competition for *gyokuro* tea in recent years. His brother Akio ran the farm while he, Yuji, managed sales and promotions.

'Sometimes we have enquiries from overseas, but we can't do business in English. Your help would be much appreciated,' he said.

We talked about my being a lawyer and about trademarks and so forth. Yuji agreed that nobody would pay me to do legal work. I was welcome to act as an agent of some sort. That was how things worked in Japan. We tossed around various ideas, and I promised to return with a specific proposal.

I was unsure how to proceed. In essence everyone was asking me to sell Kyushu tea overseas when all I wanted to do was help establish a brand of tea using legal intellectual property. How on earth could I sell tea to the world starting from scratch?

Tea in Japan is usually, but not always, green tea. There are dozens of herbal teas, most of which have some medicinal use according to *kampo* or Chinese traditional medicine, which is still very popular in Japan. My mother-in-law always kept a plastic jug of mulberry leaf tea (*kuwa cha*) in the refrigerator. Every night at dinner she would pour us a glass, declaring it to be very good for one's health and that people with diabetes drink it. Sometimes, for the improvement of one's mood, she mixed a little *kuwa cha* instead of water with *shochu*, Kyushu's favourite alcoholic beverage.

I looked up mulberry tea on the internet and found plenty of material confirming her view about its medicinal properties. *Morus alba*, as it's known in Latin, has plenty of material online about its medicinal effects. An article on the American Diabetes Association website said it can be used to treat diabetes, something my mother-in-law had often told me. When I lived in Hita for those first few weeks in Kyushu after leaving

Tokyo I spent the weekends riding the Vulcan around the northern part of Oita Prefecture cruising the local roads that wind their way through the little valleys and over the mountains. One of the common places I would stop for a rest were the *michi no eki* or roadside markets. These are not a group of stalls under tent cover, but proper buildings where you find a wide spectrum of local farm products for sale, including herbal teas. I began looking for these herbal teas at every *michi no eki* I could find. Around Hita the most common herbal tea on sale was *dokudami*. This herb *Houttuynia cordata* in Latin, is used as a sort of general cure for colds in traditional medicine. It tastes something like lemongrass. *Dokudami* in Japanese means "stop poison" and the herb is said to be efficacious as an anti-inflammatory and anti-viral agent. What intrigued me the most was that it was widely used by Chinese doctors in the SARS virus epidemic in 2005. Later on I mixed *dokudami* with another herb called *yomogi* (*Artemisia indicor* or Japanese mugwort) to make a powerful hangover cure. It worked so well I christened it "The Hammer" because it could hammer a headache to death.

During this month or so of fascination with Japan's medicinal teas, I gradually came to the conclusion that it would make sense to combine Yuji Kurihara's superior green tea with a selection of Japanese herbal teas and offer it to the world. Thus was born the venture we called Teas of Kyushu. I added *biwa cha*, a tea made from the leaves of the Japanese loquat tree which is good for the skin, as well as a rare tea from Okinawa called *kwanso cha* which is used to treat insomnia and anxiety conditions. Yuji introduced me to a company in Yame called Takara Pack that processed tea into tea bags, and we were ready to tackle the global tea market.

One of the first promotional events we attended was a business forum held in Fukuoka for European companies and their trade consuls in Japan, called the Nishi Nippon Business Forum. We set up a stall outside the main meeting room in the Fukuoka Convention Center and offered free tea to the conference delegates. I did the translating for Yuji as he took questions from the French consul, the Dutch consul, and various Italians, Swiss, and others. While sipping our teas one of the delegates mentioned Fukushima, saying the nuclear disaster was a problem for any food products from Japan.

Yuji and I were puzzled. 'But Fukushima is way north of Tokyo. We have no radiation down here in Kyushu,' we said.

Ah, but to sell your tea in Europe you will have to *prove* to consumers you are not anywhere near Fukushima, he said. And that will not be easy. How many people in Europe are familiar with Japan's geography?

This was quite a shock. Although I was highly irritated at first, it was obvious that the man meant well, and I had an idea he was right. No matter the reality that Kyushu suffered no radioactive fallout from the Fukushima nuclear disaster in 2011, we would have to do something to prove this was the case.

Tea, of course, originated in China. As with other elements of Chinese culture that enriched Japan in ancient times it was the Buddhist monk-priests who brought the first tea back from China, in particular a monk of stubborn, independent mind named Eisai, who also introduced Zen Buddhism to Japan. Eisai planted the first tea bushes at the Ryosenji temple on Mount Sefuri in 1191, high in the mountains between Fukuoka and Saga Prefectures, not so far from where I lived in Itoshima.

On a Saturday morning I went down to see Toya-*san* in the Lauben Kolonie office to pay my monthly co-op dues.

'Have you heard about Japan's first tea bushes over at Mount Sefuri?' I asked.

He looked blank. 'Tea bushes?'

'Yes. The first ones ever planted in Japan. They're over on Mount Sefuri. Surely this is well known in Fukuoka.'

'Never heard of it.'

'I'm sure it's true. I'm going over there now to see them.'

Toya-*san* accepted my money for the montly dues and shook his head. 'You do the strangest things,' he muttered.

I drove up to Mount Sefuri to see Eisai's tea bushes some 824 years after he planted them in 1191. That month, it being 2015, the world was fretting about a vicious war on foot in Syria and Iraq. In 1191, during the Third

Crusade, the city of Acre in what is now northern Israel fell to the forces of Richard the Lionheart, who later defeated Saladin at Arsfur in southern Palestine. As I drove my car the NHK radio news was reporting the result of the G7 Summit held in Bavaria. The leaders were wringing their hands about Russian and Chinese aggression. President Obama was promising to do more in Iraq to stop the relentless march of Islamic militants who seemed to defeat everyone in their path. These modern-day Saladins seemed in no fear of Obama's threats to launch a crusade to wipe them out.

Driving up the mountain from Itoshima on the way to Mount Sefuri I found myself in thick fog as I navigated the sharp bends in the road, my car lights on high beam in case an elderly farmer came at me from the opposite direction in one of those ubiquitous light pickup trucks that infest rural Japan. Then suddenly the fog was gone as I crested the pass, emerged from the dark forest, and began the descent into an upland plateau of lushly green, newly planted rice fields. I continued on for an hour or so across the plateau until close to Mount Sefuri.

Then the road began descending again down towards the Saga plain in a series of bends. I emerged from another dark forest and was excited to see the first tea farm, a row of perfectly shaved tea bushes on a tiny terrace between hairpin bends. Down I went past more miniature tea farms. These were nothing like the size of the Kurihara or other tea farms over in Yame.

Still it puzzled me. Why did the monk Eisai come all the way over here to plant the first tea bushes? From where he landed when returning from China, probably somewhere around Itoshima, it was a very long journey for a man on foot. Why didn't he plant the seeds in Itoshima or Hakata?

Descending almost to the foot of the mountain I saw a huge sign pointing the way to the Tom Sawyer Forest, one of those well meaning but useless theme parks usually paid for by a prefecture's taxpayers as a way of attracting tourists. NHK Radio was now playing foreign music from the 1960s. I heard The Beatles song *Revolution No. 9*. — Number nine.... number nine.....number nine.....with music being played backwards. A panel of guest commentators speculated on Yoko Ono's influence in this unusual recording, gravely agreeing that she must have had a hand in it somehow.

Next it was Simon and Garfunkel's, *The 7 O'Clock News,* with the panel expressing shock as they discussed the newsreader in the song saying that Vice President Richard Nixon had called for a greater effort in the Vietnam War. More war? What a horror, they agreed.

There were no signs at all indicating the location of Eisai's historic tea bushes. This seemed odd for such a significant site. Tom Sawyer got a huge sign, but then again the prefecture had money at stake there. I drove up towards the tunnel that goes through Mount Sefuri back to Fukuoka and stopped at the Sazanka Senbōkan (Thousand Monk Residence) Roadside Market, one of thousands of such markets, called *michi no eki* in Japanese, that make country driving such a pleasure. A tourist sign in the car park carried a map of the area with major attractions marked on it, and at last I found the location of Eisai's tea bushes at the ruins of the Ryosenji temple. It was up a side road across a deep valley from the *michi no eki.*

I had a quick peek inside at what was for sale — carp sashimi (not recommended), fresh chicken legs, Saga's famous *hinohikari* rice, said to be the best in Kyushu, and hooray, "Eisai tea." I felt obliged to buy a small packet, along with a plastic tray of plums.

Out the front they were selling all sorts of plants for your garden: vegetables, fruits, flowers, and some other plants. I asked a moon-faced lady at the cash register whether they sold tea bushes.

'You have to be a farmer,' she declared, deftly dismissing such an impertinent question. I felt like arguing the point with her but decided it would be a waste of time. A *gaijin* could not, by definition, be a farmer.

At the turnoff to the forest road that led up to the temple ruins there was no sign mentioning either the temple or the tea bushes, only that the road led to the Sakamoto Pass. Again, poor old Eisai gets blithely ignored by the Saga Prefecture authorities.

I parked my car and walked up a well-constructed path through a forest with perfect steps and posts along the way carrying what looked like Zen sayings written in vertical Japanese script. I stopped to examine a small and ancient stone pillar inscribed with the Sanskrit character, *ah.* It was moss-covered and to my amateur eye looked as old as what you see at Angkor Wat.

Finally after climbing for another five minutes I stood at the bottom of a steep, cleared slope about an acre in size containing a plantation of perhaps a hundred untended tea bushes. Looking carefully at the bushes I could see they had not been harvested. The tiny new leaves on the end of each stem were still there, nobody having bothered to pick them. What about the so-called "Eisai tea" I had bought at the *michi no eki*? No doubt it came not from Eisai's own tea bushes but from the local tea farms. Would the famous monk have tolerated such a trick?

The remains of the temple must be above the tea bushes, I thought. I climbed the steps to one side of the plantation, and when I reached the top I experienced a *satori*, a sudden enlightenment. Now I understood why Eisai chose this site. It had one of the best views in Kyushu. From the front of the small wooden building that houses a Buddhist altar you can look out majestically over the Saga plain, and out over the Ariake Sea beyond it to the peak of Mount Unzen way over in Nagasaki Prefecture.

In a word, it was magnificent, and the incredible effort the monks and pilgrims made in ancient times climbing all the way up there to worship the Buddha gave me a sense of what it was all about. It's hard these days to understand, but to them the significance of religion in a world with almost no mental stimuli must have been immense, even life-changing. Eisai had decided to plant his tea seeds at the top of the highest mountain around, because it was a sacred place.

By now it was well past noon. I thought of trying to uproot a small tea bush and take it home as a souvenir, but that seemed a sacrilege. I was not a vandal, just interested in Japanese history. I walked back to my car and drove back across the mountains looking for somewhere interesting to eat a late lunch. In the little town of Mitsuse I saw some banners on the side of the road advertising *juwari* soba. The restaurant was called Matsugen and was housed in a traditional style house. Just as I approached the front door the apron-clad proprietress came rushing out and said, 'I'm terribly sorry but we've run out of soba. The master is making some more and it could take quite a while.'

I laughed. 'You mean he's making it by hand, right now?'

She nodded. 'I'm terribly sorry. It'll take at least ten minutes.' She seemed to expect me to storm off in anger.

'I'm coming in. Fresh soba is just what I want. There's nothing more tasty.'

Delighted with this response she showed me in and I removed my shoes in the tiny foyer before being ushered to a table with a sunken floor where I sat down and started reading a Japanese newspaper.

'Ah, you read the paper!' the proprietress exclaimed. 'Then you'll be able to read our menu. It's only in Japanese.' By this time it was nearly two o'clock and I was the only customer in the restaurant.

When the soba came, together with a basket of beautifully cooked *tempura* of vegetables, chicken pieces, and fish, it was truly perfect, strong of flavour and chewy in my mouth. *Juwari* soba is pure soba, made by hand with only buckwheat flour, unadulterated with other cheaper ingredients. That's what makes it sticky.

The cup of warm tea that came with the meal was *soba cha*, a tea made from toasted buckwheat. No surprise there. I asked the proprietress what she knew about Eisai's original tea bushes at Mount Sefuri. She looked puzzled.

'Ah…..I think there's something over there….' she said with uncertainty, glancing back at her husband behind the counter.

'It's at the ruins of the Ryosenji temple,' I said. 'I've just been there, and I saw the first tea bushes ever planted in Japan.'

'Oh, yes. I think that's right.'

'It is. I saw it myself.'

'Really? Wonderful! You speak Japanese so well. May I ask how long you've been in Japan?'

'Since the Showa Era,' I replied.

On the way back to Itoshima I noticed an abandoned rice field with a white crane standing next to a faded election campaign poster of Prime Minister Shinzo Abe. He was wearing an expression of infinite tranquility as he gazed at some aspect of his country, maybe its rice fields. Did Eisai see the same thing? I wondered. Or did he sip his green tea and look inwards?

Before I had been back to him with a specific proposal for marketing his tea outside Japan, Yuji suddenly called me to say that the Kurihara Tea Farm *benkyokai* or "study meeting" was being held two Saturdays hence and would I like to come? Before I could reply he added that it was essential that I come, absolutely necessary, in fact.

Of course I'll come, I said. I liked Yuji and wanted to help him in whatever way I could.

Excellent. There are some important people in the Kyushu tea world coming and I want to show them how Kurihara Tea has become "international".

Ah, our old friend *kokusai-teki*, the adjective "international" in Japanese. All my life in Japan since coming here as a teenager I've heard this phrase when I'm around. Being *kokusai-teki* is to be a cut above the average in Japan, but these days it has a tired air of the 1970s about it.

Sure, I'll be glad to add some *kokusai-teki*ness to the study meeting on that Saturday, I promised.

Great. By the way, it'll be ¥5000 per person, he said.

Ah, the Japanese farmer, I thought. He will give you gifts of what he grows, but money is money. I help you improve the brand of your tea, and I pay you ¥5000 for the privilege.

It was a Saturday in early August and even at that elevation the weather was very hot. A group of around twenty tea enthusiasts met at the Kurihara's processing factory just up the little valley from the main family home and office. To my delight, almost all the participants were women, one or two of them quite attractive. As we introduced ourselves I learned that they ran tea salons, tea shops, or wrote blogs and even magazine articles on tea and Japanese cuisine. The tea study meeting was one big Kurihara PR exercise.

A microbus arrived and drove us up the mountain to a large tea field where Yuji explained we would pick our own tea leaves and then later process them at the factory so as to learn more about how tea is made, in essence a hands-on experience. He gave us baskets and sent us out into the tea bushes to pick the tiny green leaves on the end of each branch. Some of the women in our group donned elaborate bonnets to shield their faces from the sunlight. I used a towel over my exposed neck and a battered Panama hat.

Once everyone had a decent load of fresh tea leaves in their basket we were driven back to the factory. There Yuji's brother Akio took charge. He showed us how to roll the leaves by hand so as to gradually crush them, letting the fermenting process begin after we spread out the crushed leaves in our baskets and left them in the shade for an hour. The fragrance of the crushed leaves was like jasmine. An hour later we were divided into two groups: one to make black tea, the other to make oolong tea, the latter requiring only a light toasting of the fermented leaves.

Everyone received a *bento* lunch from Yuji's mother and sister who were in charge of things now. By this time about a dozen local people had arrived to join in the fun and were eating from *bento* boxes and drinking the fresh *sencha* on offer. The ladies from our tea study group were talking in a learned fashion about all sorts of tea-related things. I was left a bit on my own until one of the locals, an old man in his eighties, face brown from years in the sun and slightly bent over, took a sudden interest in me.

'You're English, I hear,' he said, looking up at me and nodding.

'No, actually Australian,' I replied as politely as I could.

'Oh? Well, the English love tea. It's well known.'

'Indeed, that's right. It's part of British life. No doubt about it.'

'Queen Elizabeth has black tea every morning,' he declared.

'Quite probably she does.'

'Are you sure you're not English? We heard that an Englishman was helping Yuji-*kun* to sell his tea to Queen Elizabeth. I heard it at the post office.'

'Ah, no, I'm not English, but I've been there often.'

He nodded as if this was expected of every *gaijin*. 'How are you going to sell Kurihara tea to Queen Elizabeth?'

'Well, in fact Yuji and I discussed offering the tea to the Queen of Holland, not England.'

'Holland? No, England is better. Much bigger. Holland's too small. If Queen Elizabeth changes from black tea to green tea we'd all be better off.

Green tea is better for your health. Tell that to the Queen. Japanese live longer than English people. It's because of our green tea.'

In fact I had suggested to Yuji that because KLM flew directly to Amsterdam from Fukuoka three days a week we should try to get the Dutch ambassador to agree to our presenting a gift of the Kurihara's prize-winning *gyokuro* tea to Queen Beatrix. It would help promote friendship between Kyushu and The Netherlands and might feature in KLM's marketing and promotional activities in Japan. We were hoping that KLM would then start buying *sencha* from us. Thus, had the story got around Yabe Village in mistaken form that the *gyokuro* would be going to Buckingham Palace in London.

'I'll mention it to the ambassador," I said.

'*Un*,' the old man grunted. 'You tell him.'

Following Eisai's progress from Mount Sefuri to Hakata it was logical to next visit the Shofukuji, Japan's first Zen temple. Many times in the past I had been down to the Gion area near Hakata Station to visit the Fukuoka Chamber of Commerce, a half mile up the broad boulevard called Taihaku Street from the station. The cluster of temples across Taihaku Street from the Chamber had never interested me before. In fact, for some odd reason the large copper roof and pagoda of the Tochoji Temple that fronted the street seemed all too prominent to me, a sort of irritating intrusion into the city.

But now it was different. I came back to the office buildings and the streets of Fukuoka with a new attitude. Once you've been all the way up to the Ryosenji Temple ruins atop Mount Sefuri and seen the tea bushes and the vista over to Mount Unzen life changes for you in a subtle way. It's something to celebrate that a cluster of ancient temples and their gardens survive within the glass-and-concrete of the inner city, sitting there surrounded by multi-storied office buildings.

I went there on a day of early summer heat and humidity. Emerging from the No. 1 exit of the Gion subway station I donned my battered

Panama hat and strolled down Taihaku Street past the Tochoji Temple, a huge stone plinth with gold lettering declared that the temple was Japan's "first sacred ground". Quite a claim, I thought. This was pure Buddhist arrogance. The native Shinto cult was well established centuries before Buddhism came to Japan.

It was late morning, and turning down a little side street just past the Tochoji Temple I passed a man putting out a sign carrying a menu for a soba restaurant. I greeted him and promised to return for lunch after visiting the Shofukuji, which I found at the end of the street beyond a mud wall topped with traditional tiles.

Inside the wall the temple grounds were suddenly quiet. Everything was green. Dozens of old zelkovia trees, *keyaki* in Japanese, provided a near-seamless canopy of shade, the ground underneath covered with a carpet of emerald green moss. The wooden temple buildings stood across the other side of the grounds. This was tranquility itself, but without the exclusive perfection of the Kyoto temples. In one corner a Buddhist statue stood separately in a grove of bamboo enclosed by a simple bamboo fence. I crossed a stone bridge over a pond and approached its roofed gate. Entering the area I found a woman sitting on a bench surrounded by a dozen cats.

'Lots of cats,' I said. 'They live here, do they?'

'They do,' she said. 'It's safe inside the temple.' She was well groomed, maybe forty, and wore a black lace blouse. 'You speak Japanese very well,' she added.

'I study every day if I can,' I replied, which is the reply I always use. It satisfies everyone to know that the language is hard enough that a *gaijin* has to keep at it the whole time. 'And this Buddha,' I said, pointing to the statue, 'is it part of the Zen temple here?'

'No, it's different. This is the Takasago League.'

'Really?' It was too hot to enter into a discussion of whatever Buddhist sect this Takasago League was. The lady in black lace and her cats were better left alone.

I excused myself and wandered over to the main building of the Shofukuji. A group of school children were lounging around on the wooden platform in front of the altar laughing and chatting as they wrote in notebooks. I asked their lady teacher what they were doing.

'It's a history project,' she said. ' History of Fukuoka.'

One of the schoolgirls looked at me and said 'Hello! Hello!' The other children waited to hear what I would say in reply.

I nodded and muttered the same greeting back. They seemed satisfied and went back to their giggling and writing. The teacher then ordered them to pack up and go to the next stop on the excursion. They lined up for group photographs in front of the building, jostling and shouting. When they were gone I peered into the dark interior of the building. Three large Buddhas, each glittering and golden, sat there in majestic repose. Two of them wore headdresses of vibrant cobalt blue, irresistibly attractive to the eye. A young man quietly walked up beside me, tossed a coin into the votive box in front of the altar, and clapped twice before praying briefly. He departed immediately.

I looked around for an office to ask about the temple but found none. This was not your normal Buddhist temple with a monk or nun at a counter selling amulets and incense. It was utterly unmanned. Maybe that's the essence of Zen, I thought. Out the back of the grounds I noticed a traditional style gate with a wooden sign indicating the office of the Rinzai Sect Zen Temple. I was about to walk in to ask something about Eisai when I saw another sign that said "No visitors allowed".

Well, okay then. Hardly the sort of welcome a pilgrim expects. Surely Eisai would've tolerated a stranger coming in burdened with a curiosity about Zen. Not so at the Shofukuji. Apparently an introduction is required.

On the way back to the subway station I felt hungry and, feeling calm and peaceful after walking around the oasis of tranquility, a bowl of cold soba seemed perfect, just like the *juwari* soba I ate at Mitsuse a few days ago. I stopped at the soba restaurant, called Nakada, took my boots off in the tiny lobby and climbed the stairs to the second floor. The owner greeted me with a smile, his elderly wife making an immediate fuss over me. There was a counter with four seats and a small room with two tables overlooking the shaded grounds of the Tochiji Temple.

I sat at the counter alone and ordered the cold *tororo* soba. Grated mountain yam is mixed with *wasabi* and a raw egg, all on top of a pile of cold soba noodles. The chopsticks were carved from bamboo. This restaurant was a quiet and peaceful mixture of Japan and the West. In the background I could hear cello music playing softly as I ate the soba. Black ink etchings of Japanese houses and small oil paintings in a Western style adorned the walls. Clearly this was a place of artistic taste and culinary excellence.

After what was the perfect post-Shofukiji lunch I ordered a bowl of warm *matcha* tea and some sweets to follow. In the kitchen behind the counter there was a large antique *tansu* cabinet in which the owner kept the ceramic bowls used to serve the soba. The top of the *tansu* was crowded with a collection of things including a *kamidana* or indoor Shinto shrine, a series of Shinto amulets large and small, and a row of souvenir *shochu* and beer bottles. One of the *shochu* bottles bore the crest of the Hanshin Tigers baseball team from Osaka. Tigers fans are known throughout Japan for their ferocious loyalty.

I thought of striking up a conversation with the owner and his wife about Eisai and Zen and so forth. It seemed the right thing to do with a bowl of warm, frothy *matcha* in hand given Eisai's historical contribution to life in Japan. But just then another customer came in. He sat down at the counter with an audible sigh. It seemed awkward for me to start talking about Eisai and Zen. The man, who had the air of a regular customer, ordered a bowl of sesame soba, paused for a moment, and said to the owner's wife in an incredulous tone, 'You know, they're sending the Crown Prince and Princess Masako to Tonga!'

'Tonga?'

'Yes, Tonga. Why would they go to Tonga? It's meaningless.'

'Dear me,' said the owner's wife. 'There must be *some* reason.'

'Tonga has a king,' said the owner from the stove. 'That'll be why they're sending the Crown Prince. To see the King of Tonga.'

'Well,' said the man in mild disgust, 'there must be more useful places to go than Tonga. Surely….'

'Saaa…' said the owner's wife, a Japanese non-expression that means something like either 'What a mystery' or 'Surely they'll do something to fix that.'

Listening to this exchange I suddenly realised something: Princess Masako's decade-long depressive illness was said to be gradually improving, and as consort to the next emperor it was vital to help her ease back into attending public events. She had been doing this in Japan for the past year or so, but overseas trips were a problem. The previous year she had pulled out of a visit to The Netherlands at the last minute due to her fragile state of mind. Perhaps an easy visit to Tonga was part of the rehabilitation program: no intrusive local media, no politics, just a sleepy little island nation. That would restore her confidence. I felt sorry for her. The Imperial Household Agency had treated her with obvious cruelty in the first year or so of her marriage, which led to the chronic depression. I wanted to say something in the restaurant about her, but it just wasn't the correct decorum for a *gaijin* stranger to be commenting on the Imperial Family and its struggles with modern life.

Eight

Rice

Rice, or *kome* in Japanese, is the most sacred of things in Japan. But just why are the Japanese so obsessed with rice? Why does it play such a key role in the Shinto cult? Most other Asian countries use rice as a staple food, yet it's only in Japan that the grain has such religious and cultural significance. I set out to find the answer to these questions in Kyushu.

At the end of July, Japan is baking hot and very humid. After the rainy season, which the Japanese call *tsuyu,* the country is assailed for about a fortnight with high temperatures and little wind. A heat mist envelopes the mountains, the sea is flat and hot, and everyone does what they can to avoid going out. In the qualifying games for the annual high school baseball championship in Osaka, which is played in August, the young, crew-cut competitors slog it out in perilously hot weather. Everyone admires their guts for persevering in such conditions.

But in the rice fields of Japan the deep, emerald-green stalks of young rice sit in muddy water and absorb all the sun they can get. Some say that a hot summer and a cold winter produce the most flavoursome rice.

In search of more antiquity in Kyushu, I went looking for what is said to be the first rice field in Japanese history, pretty sure that it was over near Fukuoka Airport in a place called Itazuke. My friend Peter Bruce, husband of Australia's senior trade commissioner Leonie Muldoon, had once visited it. I tried to find the address by asking my internet browser for "Japan's first rice field". To my surprise the answer suggested that this was not near the airport in Fukuoka but in the small city of Karatsu, just along the northern coast of Kyushu from Itoshima where I lived. Indeed, from my balcony I could see parts of the city across what is called Karatsu Bay looking south-westwards. According to the Karatsu Toursism Association a museum called the Matsurokan houses the site of Japan's first cultivated rice, a site they call the Nabatake Ruins.

In a strange way because of the heat I felt an urge to visit the site immediately. Why wait until the weather cools down? If it really is so significant a place, I thought, then it deserves a visit as soon as possible.

Writing in the Japan Times in March 2014, journalist Winifred Bird tells the story of how in the 1970s a group of local archaeologists took advantage of a road construction project in Karatsu City to excavate and sift through some soil in an area they suspected had been inhabited during the Jomon Era, around 2,500 years ago. In doing so they discovered some carbonized rice grains, the remains of a cooking pot. Soon they discovered a small plot of cultivated rice in terraced fields. This, they declared, was Japan's earliest example of rice cultivation. The discovery caused a frenzy of excitement for a time because it proved that rice cultivation had begun in Japan not in the Yayoi Era but earlier than that, towards the end of the Jomon Era.

Today the Nabatake Ruins are far from the centre of attention. The Matsurokan is a small, two-storey museum sitting in a large garden, fenced by wooden posts, each with a two-inch gap between them, and surrounded by houses. In the first century AD, during the bloody Three Kingdoms Period, the Chinese authorities called the Karatsu area *mò lú* (末盧), pronounced *matsuro* in Japanese. Thus did Karatsu City give the museum its historical name.

I parked my car in a shady place in a backstreet behind the museum and hurried inside to escape the heat. The cool air was a welcome relief. Inside everything was utterly quiet. I approached a small window at the reception to buy a ticket. A man with a small silver beard and scholarly spectacles came over from a desk in the office beyond the window and greeted me politely. Entry would cost me ¥200, he said. I paid up and asked him whether he was Mr Ryuta Tajima from Winifred Bird's article. He gladly confessed to being the very same and then emerged from the office to exchange cards with me.

He pointed upstairs to the museum exhibit and said, 'It's terribly hot up there, so please take a fan with you.'

I accepted the fan and went upstairs. Just as Tajima-*san* said, the air grew very hot and stuffy at the top of the stairs. I fanned myself hard and started looking at the exhibits. Like the museum on Takashima Island dealing with the Mongol fleet invasion of 1281, the Matsurokan has a collection of surprising antiquity. I saw bronze spearheads, bracelets, and best of all some original wooden tools used to cut and thresh the rice those original immigrants cultivated there. A table top model display showed tiny villagers doing all sorts of things: farming rice, hunting wild boar in the nearby forests, spearing a whale from boats in the bay, and gathered together to worship at an altar decorated with rice and boars' heads. Not entirely different from things these days in a rural village.

On the wall I saw a large map stretching from central China to include Korea and Japan. The title read " Transmission of Rice Cultivation". It showed lines and arrows leading from the Yangtze Valley to the Shandong

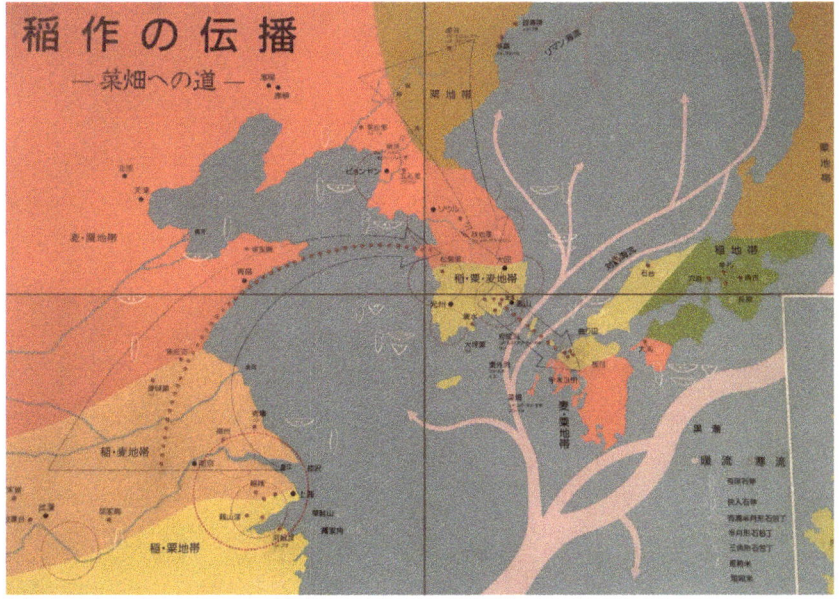

Transmission of Rice Cultivation - the map on the wall of the Matsurokan Museum in Karatsu showing how rice cultivation made it way from the Yangtze Valley in China to Japan, via the Korean Peninsula.

Peninsula and then across to Korea, thereafter island-hopping via Tsushima and Iki Islands to Kyushu. There was no specific mention of the immigrants from Korea who brought the skills with them, only "transmission" of the skills. This way, I thought, nobody can be offended. Still, it seemed odd to say nothing about the people involved.

I returned downstairs to the cool, air-conditioned comfort zone and put the fan back into its holder on a desk. Tajima-*san* came to the window to greet me. I congratulated him on the exhibits and expressed my surprise that the two big museums in Fukuoka and Dazaifu did not even mention the Nabatake Ruins and Kyushu's first rice cultivation.

'Their displays seem to ignore this completely. Why is this?' I asked.

'*Saaa*,' said Tajima-*san* with a wry smile.

'Is there some reason for this neglect? Maybe the ultra-nationalists object to such history being on public display.'

Tajima-*san* laughed, moved his head sideways and then up and down in a very Japanese way that indicated reluctant agreement, but said no more. One could hardly expect him to open up on such a sensitive subject at the first meeting with an unknown *gaijin*. I wondered what he would say after a few cups of *sake*.

'Well, I think your museum is terrific,' I said.

He thanked me sincerely and suggested that despite the fierce heat I go outside and inspect the "model rice fields". The original location of the rice fields is under the gate, he added.

Buried?

'Yes', he said, in a matter-of-fact tone. 'We've reconstructed the plots in the garden to make it easier to understand.'

So the city authorities had concreted over the original rice field. I was astonished.

The garden had green lawns and various trees which provided the villagers with all sorts of nuts and fruits. A small creek had been created, carefully built with sides of rock so water could be diverted into the small plots or paddies terraced into the ground on each side. In each plot stalks of rice were growing in neat rows, planted by hand in May, Tajima-*san* had said.

Eight Rice

Kyushu farmers hanging freshly harvested rice out to dry in the traditional way, known as hoshi ine. This kind of rice attracts a premium for being dried naturally. Farming in Japan is suffering from the relentless decline in rural populations, and in distant parts of Kyushu more and more rice fields lie abandoned.

Looking at this I saw the knowledge the settlers from the mainland had brought with them, a knowledge that the hunter-gatherer Jomon people did not possess. Channel the water, create the paddies, and divert the water to inundate the paddies so the seeds grow.

Over the wooden post fence at the back of the garden I heard some children splashing about in an inflatable pool. I called out to them in Japanese, freezing their loud, happy conversation.

'Hey, what are you guys doing?' I asked.

'Ooh,' said one boy. He and his friends looked to be about ten years old.

'You're swimming?'

'Yeah. We're swimming,' the boy replied.

It's a *gaijin*, said another boy to the group.

'Are you guys learning English at school?' I asked.

'Yeah, we are. It's really difficult.'

'So speak some.'

They laughed. ' No. It's too difficult,' a boy shouted back.

'*My name is……*' I said in English to encourage them.

This did the trick. 'My…name…is…Soma,' said the main boy in standard Japanese schoolboy English.

'Well done,' I said in Japanese. 'You know these old rice fields in here, they're the oldest in Japan. Have you been in here to see them?'

'Yeah, lots of times.'

'Did you plant the rice?'

'Ah…..sometimes.'

I think he's an English teacher, said one of the boys.

Nah, he's just an ordinary *gaijin*, said another.

I went back inside the museum to thank Tajima-*san*, keen to get more out of him about the Jomon vs Yayoi issue.

'It's true that the Jomon people were quite different,' he agreed. 'They came from the other side of Kyushu, and from up in Hokkaido.'

I remarked that Saigō Takamori, samurai hero from Kagoshima, actually looked different from most Japanese men.

This got Tajima-*san* excited. 'Indeed,' he said. 'If you look at the Mohri clan people from Honshu, Prime Minister Abe's ancestors in fact, you see they have long, straight faces, whereas Saigō had a round face with heavy eyebrows. That's the difference. The Yayoi people gradually pushed the Jomon people out of most of Japan except Hokkaido and Okinawa, but some of their blood remains. '

The office Tajima-*san* occupied was spacious and full of files, boasting maybe six desks for one man and a lady assistant. Just why they needed such resources to run a museum that few people visited was a mystery, but good luck to him, I thought. The municipal authorities of Karatsu pay for the museum, and it is listed on the local tourism association website as a significant local attraction. But, despite the sanctity of rice in Japanese life, surrounded by houses and well inland from the present day seashore, I got the sense that Japan had turned its back on the true story of how rice cultivation reached the country.

When I walked to my car parked in the shade behind the museum the children behind the back fence noticed me. Young Soma, bold and without fear, came out to the front of the house to have a closer look. Like the other boys he was wearing a dark swimsuit and a cap.

'It's very hot,' I said.

'Yeah, it is.'

'Is this your house?'

'Yeah.'

I noticed there was no car in the driveway of the house. 'Are your parents out at work or something?'

'Yeah, they're not here.'

'Well, good-bye then,' I said.

'Good-bye.'

Despite the slaughtering heat I was glad I came. In Japan, or at least in Karatsu, you can safely leave your kids at home to play on a hot summer's day.

One Sunday, a few days after visiting the Nabatake Ruins at Karatsu, I drove over to Saga in the post-*tsuyu* heat to visit the Shimomura Farm. It was still very hot, the temperature around 35 degrees Celsius. Leaving the expressway I drove for a few miles through flat land dotted with houses and fields. The whole Saga Plain is flat, and frankly boring. Arriving at the Shimomura Farm, not marked with any signs, I found a small, rather lonely stall selling organic vegetables. Nobody was present in the office to one side of the stall, but after enquiring at a large farmhouse across the road a friendly older lady appeared and announced herself as Shimomura-*san*'s elder sister.

'He's gone somewhere,' she announced sadly, as if this was the typical sort of insult a younger brother could inflict on visitors.

'It's terribly hot,' I said. 'Maybe he's gone to the beach to swim. Today's a Sunday after all.'

'Oh, no. He runs the farm by himself. No wife. He should be here.'

I asked whether I might buy some of the organically-grown rice, prefacing my request with the suggestion that it being so late in the year they probably had no inventory left from last year.

to innocent Japanese consumers. (Such fanatics do exist in Japan, but they tend to spend their energy railing against China, Korea, and Russia for territorial sins, or Koreans for daring to live in Japan). It's more because of the danger of online campaigns targeting retailers as being unpatriotic.

No doubt because of the peculiar position of rice in Japanese society and the rural economy, trade friction over rice imports became a constant in Japan's economic relationship with the United States and some other countries. Until 1999 Japan maintained a strict ban on the import of any foreign rice. This led to some noteworthy incidents, such as the day in 1991 when at a food exhibition in Tokyo the US Rice Council and US Rice Millers Association put on display a bag of Californian-grown koshi hikari rice. Incensed by this violation of Japan's sovereignty, the Ministry of Agriculture immediately sought help from the police to confiscate the American rice and presumably arrest and deport the Americans who criminally imported it. As the New York Times gleefully reported:

"Each day, Japanese Government agents arrived at the Foodex international exhibition here and, with a perfunctory bow and the look of highway patrolmen who had a speeder where they wanted him, studied the contraband: a few sealed bags of American rice and some plastic containers containing samples of different American varieties.

"Not only was the rice in plain view, but the United States Rice Council was also handing out bumper stickers that said, "Have a Rice Day".

"Each day the agents from Japan's Food Agency demanded that the Americans remove the rice. Each day, the Rice Council listened politely and ignored them."

The US Embassy's agricultural counsellor asked the Food Agency to explain where in the Food Control Law it was made unlawful for Japanese people to look at foreign rice in Japan, but no such explanation was ever given. Eventually, having made their point and under pressure from the American Embassy, the American rice growers reluctantly removed the rice.

Despite this hardline stance Japan's impenetrable wall finally crumbled, though not quite as happily as the American and other foreign rice growers had been hoping. As part of the Uruguay Round trade agreement, in 1999 Japan scrapped the outright ban on imports and replaced it with a system called a tariff rate quota. Under this new system Japan would import around 682,000 tons of milled rice a year. But who bought it? Why, the Ministry of Agriculture, Fisheries, and Forestry, of course. The entire amount of imported rice went into government stocks and was released occasionally, but only as long as it didn't reach the table of any consumer in Japan. It was sold to food processors after a 700% tariff was levied, or was re-exported as food aid to starving Africans or refugees.

Two days after visiting Karatsu, I felt obliged to have a look at its rival, the Itazuke Ruins, less than a mile from Fukuoka Airport. This site also claimed to be Japan's oldest discovered rice field. Compared to the Nabatake Ruins, Itazuke had the budget and the scale to prove its case. It had a museum full of pottery, replica wooden tools, replica woven clothing, and outside it had a full replica Yayoi village complete with circular moat. This was the full symphony, the comprehensive experience.

Fair enough, one might say. Fukuoka has ten times the revenue of Karatsu, so naturally *its* original rice field had to outshine anything else in Kyushu. But putting aside this rivalry, the museum at the Itazuke Ruins had a few things that make it well worth visiting.

As I was slowly browsing the exhibits I came face to face with an old man dressed in outdoor work clothing and clutching an old broad-brimmed straw hat. Outside it was very hot and this maintenance man or garden worker ought to stay indoors, I thought, especially at his age. I murmured a greeting and moved past him. Five minutes later I ran into him again as he emerged from the museum office. He looked at me and smiled. Not knowing what to do I asked whether I might question him about the exhibits, fully expecting him to call for one of the museum staff to help.

Far from being one of the outdoor staff he turned out to be the museum

'Oh, no, we've got plenty,' she said, and vanished into a small shed next to the stall. I followed her inside where she opened a large airproof cabinet and lugged out a 5kg bag of rice in an attractive brown paper package. 'It'll be ¥2300.'

I paid for the rice and thanked her.

'Let me call him,' she said. 'He's around here somewhere. He should come and see you himself.'

I insisted that I'd be back sometime soon and that her younger brother ought not be dragged back just to see a curious *gaijin* like me on a Sunday. We exchanged bows and I left a business card before retreating from the heat to my car with the bag of rice.

The Buddhist canon of mercy as applied in Japan forbade the slaughter of animals for human consumption. Because of this the Japanese diet for many centuries was limited to fish and vegetables along with rice (though plenty of farmers and mountain dwellers ate wild pork and venison). That's history. In Japan today eating meat is almost as common as taking a daily bath. The point is that when Westerners began to arrive in Japan and actually live there, some clear point of cultural difference simply had to be established, and rice, as usual, was at the centre of this effort.

Symbols, of course, matter for everyone, not just the Japanese. And with rice, the Japanese go to great lengths to point out how their own rice is short-grain whereas Chinese rice is long-grain. Short-grain rice grown in California is more of a problem. In blind taste tests it is virtually impossible to tell the difference between *koshi hikari* grown in California and the same variety grown in, say, Niigata or Chiba. But it's the symbol that counts.

Throughout Japan one can hardly pass a day without noticing the signs in restaurants, especially chain restaurants, saying "This place uses domestically-grown rice". This is not because the restaurant chains live in fear of a crazed *uyoku* rightwing fanatic bursting through the door brandishing a samurai sword and denouncing the chain for serving polluted foreign rice

Korea. Archaeology in Japan seems honest about these things. Being a science of sorts it does not, or should not, lend itself to religious or nationalist myth-making.

I went outside to have a look at the reconstructed rice paddy and the reconstructed Yayoi village and moat. In the intense heat of the late morning, two small boys were squatting by the paddy catching tadpoles by hand in the water amid the stalks of rice. I strolled over to join the fun. Their mother, sheltering from the sun under an umbrella, chided them for getting too close to the water. Clearly she had never tried to catch a tadpole.

'Are you learning English at school?' I asked the boys.

'That's in fourth grade,' one of them replied with force.

I walked on and saw that the village and moat sat across a narrow street from the main grounds of the museum, which looked little more than a small municipal park with some lawns and ponds outside the simple museum building. Dragonflies buzzed above the rice paddy in the heat. Old men and ladies slowly cycled through the grounds on a gravel pathway that bisected the grounds, connecting the public housing estate to the north with the houses to the south. The boys' mother lost all patience and approached them, chastising them in ever more severe language. One of the boys lunged after a tadpole and fell into the paddy bottom-first.

'Ahh!' cried the mother. 'Now you're all dirty!'

The boy pulled himself out and was marched off towards home, his shorts covered in dark grey mud. His brother carried the plastic bottle containing the captured tadpoles.

I crossed the street and kept in the shade of some trees as I walked to the entrance to the reconstructed village. Looking up into the branches of the trees I suddenly noticed acorns growing. Yet the leaves of these trees, no doubt a species of oak, or *quercus*, were completely unlike English, French, or American oaks. They were shiny, oval, and had no lobes on them. Another tree was sprouting what looked like small chestnuts.

So this was what the Jomon people lived on, in addition to the fish they caught and the deer and boar they hunted. No surprise that they were of short stature. When rice became available with the arrival of the Yayoi director, Yamaguchi-*san*. Meet Japan's ageing Indiana Jones. After politely dismissing Karatsu's claim to have the *oldest* ancient rice field in Japan he told me a few things that surprised me.

First, archaeological work in Japan has established that around 100 BC the average height of an adult male grew from 160cm to 170cm over the period of a century. Thereafter it shrank back to 160cm until the Edo Period some 1600 years later. The cause of this spurt of growth and regression is unknown, he said.

'It must've been because of the rice that the people grew taller,' I said.

'*Saaa*,' said Yamaguchi-*san*. 'We don't really know. There's not enough evidence.'

Second, on one wall was a series of photographs of people in a mountain village in Cangleng County, Yunnan Province, in China. These were clearly ethnic minority people, Dai or Miao by the look of them. The design of their thatched houses was very similar to that of Yayoi Era Japan.

'So there's a connection here?' I asked. This was an exciting revelation.

'Well, it's only a theory,' said Yamaguchi-*san*, sounding sceptical. 'People have all sorts of ideas about such things.'

'But you've got all these photographs on display here. Surely the theory has validity if you're showing the photos of these ethnic minority people in Yunnan.'

'*Saaa*,' he said again, the favourite reply of a museum director in Kyushu. 'You see, the city paid for the delegation that visited Yunnan. That's why the photographs are on display.'

'Well, the houses do look similar.'

'Actually, there's more to it than that. There's an oak tree that's native to Yunnan that also grows around here. It provided food for the people in the village here.'

'An oak tree?' I was puzzled by this, never having seen an oak tree in Kyushu.

I resisted the temptation to engage this kindly man in a discussion about the sensitive subject of Japan's ethnic origins. The museum made no bones about the rice culture having come to Kyushu from China via people it must have been a huge change to daily life. Little wonder the Japanese revere rice as a semi-religious item. It changed life here. It made Japan a nation.

That the importance of Itazuke and Nabatake goes largely unheralded these days is as much a pity as a mystery. This is where Japan really began. But it's the people that matter, not the rice, and the whole Shinto creation myth with the Sun Goddess and the great shrines at Izumo and Ise can only treat these maps on the museum walls as an unwelcome contradiction. Myth will always defeat science, and Japan is hardly alone in finding comfort in this.

Nine

Shinto — the Way of the Gods

In early October 2015, I made a trip to Korea with my parents. It was my second visit of the year, this time to watch an international golf tournament called The President's Cup. My father had been captain of the International Team twice, the only captain ever to defeat the Americans, a triumph that happened in 1998. The event was played at Incheon, on the west coast of the Korean Peninsula. Having read and thought about the beginnings of Japan and the immigration of people from the Asian mainland across to Kyushu, while there in Incheon I couldn't help thinking about those people who in prehistoric times came down from the Mongolian and Siberian steppes in search of a better life, of a place where they could secure a safer existence.

Did these families walk down this coast, hearing stories of an even better place further south and across the seas? The landscape in Korea is generally hard on the eye. It struck me that with its poor soil this place could not have supported large numbers of people who had to grow what they needed to survive. Maybe this was how eventual emigration to Japan happened for these people.

A week later I was back in Kyushu. The days were sunny and mild, that pleasant autumn weather called *akibare* in Japanese. One evening, after meetings in Fukuoka, I drove home to Itoshima just before sunset, quickly changing into a T-shirt and swimming shorts then hurrying down to the beach at the bottom of the hill with a can of cold beer and a towel. I sat on a bench in the pavilion in the fading light of dusk at the beach sipping the beer, watching the pink-orange sky on the horizon slowly disappear into semi-darkness. The air was perfectly still, the surface of the sea glassy calm. I could see the fishing boats motoring back to port in my village of Funakoshi, the *rrmm-rrmm* of their diesel engines the only audible sound. Such tranquil moments are precious. Whoever thought one could live in Japan like this?

How different this was from the harshness of Korea and the Asian mainland, I thought. Surely this was why the immigrants from over there were in such awe of nature's beauty in Japan. It was a paradise compared to the landscape of their origin. The beginning of Japanese nature worship, of gods in nature, of Shinto, must have been born of this kind of evening.

I finished my beer and padded down across the sand to the edge of the still water. Then I stripped naked in the dark and walked into the cold sea. If anyone knows a better way to praise and appreciate the *umi no kami* or gods of the sea, I await your advice.

Having married a Japanese woman I had made plenty of visits to Shinto shrines, known as *jinja* in Japanese, over the years. Every New Year in Hita we visited the Ohara Jinja as a family for *hatsumode*, the important first prayer of the year. On these occasions I would stand in front of the main shrine building and bow my head to pray, not knowing much at all about Shinto as a religion, not really knowing to whom I was praying. Now that I lived in what was essentially a country village there were *jinja* everywhere, most of them small local ones. Though I was living apart from my wife most of the time I wanted to be a decent husband, so with time on my hands it made sense, even after twenty years of marriage, to learn more about Shinto.

On a warm autumn morning in mid-October I left home to visit two of the local *jinja*. One was across the bay from where I lived in Funakoshi, at the tiny fishing port of Kafuri, and one was right there just behind Funakoshi's own fishing port. These two Shinto shrines were nothing more than local places of worship, far removed from the august Shinto of the Imperial Family and the great shrines at Ise and Izumo.

I usually bought my morning newspaper and a cup of coffee from the Family Mart convenience store at Kafuri. It was on the main road to

Maebaru Station where I went if I took a train to Fukuoka, and also on the way to the expressway if I decided to drive into the city. The *café latte* from the Family Mart machine cost only ¥150 and had a very ordinary taste, but from behind the counter young Miss Shojima, daughter of the lady who owned the franchise, always enjoyed a chat about wine sales, Japanese soccer, or the state of the weather forecast. The morning customers at the store were a mixture of tradesmen working on local building sites, truck drivers stopping on the way to Fukuoka, some carrying light goods and some live fish, and a smattering of local people young and mostly old. The Kafuri Shrine was just down the street from the Shojimas' convenience store, past the Nakamura Fishing Tackle Shop. I had driven past the shrine's entrance plenty of times but never bothered to go in and visit.

That morning I pulled up and parked my car in the street below the shrine, which sat on a hillside overlooking the port and the houses around it. From a decrepit wooden shed across the street I heard a cock crowing loudly. An old man sitting by a small truck eyed me warily but said nothing. Just another *gaijin*, suspicious by his very presence but not actually inflicting obvious harm on anyone yet. I nodded a greeting to him before walking over to the curved stone *torii* arch and the stone steps leading up to the shrine.

Halfway up the steps I found a terrace with a sumo ring under the usual large roof canopy supported by four large pillars. Many *jinja* in Kyushu have sumo rings, used for an annual tournament by local men and boys.

At the top of the steps I found an open space made of brown gravel with the wooden shrine building opposite. The place was utterly silent, nobody there but me. I approached the shrine and bowed slightly, a habit I'd picked up from years of visiting such shrines with my wife's family in Hita. Even with nobody there it always seemed the right thing to do. To one side of the shrine building I saw some more stone steps leading up into the dark green forest that covered the hill. Maybe there was something significant up there, I thought, but a quick walk up the steps revealed only a grove of bamboo. Some of the trunks were much thicker than a wine bottle. The light within the grove was dim and mysterious. In places I saw where someone had cut lengths of bamboo.

Back in front of the shrine I read an inscription on a big stone tablet written in what looked like classical Chinese. The text seemed to suggest the shrine was dedicated to the rice harvest and to fishing. Nothing so surprising in that. Another set of characters written vertically on a stone pillar indicated that the current shrine was "built with good fortune in the ninth year of the Emperor Showa", meaning in 1935. What sort of place was Kafuri in 1935? Not so different from now in most respects as people fished or farmed for a living, growing rice and vegetables, maybe raising some chickens or cows, and between Japan and China there was a lot of trouble.

Okay, so this was all fine. But there didn't seem to be anything particularly religious about the shrine. Gods of the harvest and fishing was terrific stuff, I thought. What about the worshippers? Did they feel spiritually refreshed after praying there? What did it mean to them?

Just then an old lady walked past the *torii* stone arch at the bottom of the entrance steps. I hurried down and asked her about the shrine.

'It's the Kafuri Shrine,' she said vaguely. 'Tenmangu.'

'Indeed it is,' I agreed. 'Do people come here every day to pray?'

She looked puzzled by the question. 'Well, maybe some do. I don't know. There's the festival in summer, of course.'

I didn't know what more to ask her without seeming rude or overly inquisitive, so I thanked her and watched her hobble away. In the street the old man with the small truck had gone, and the cock was silent.

Step one of the journey of Shinto discovery now achieved, I got into my car and drove slowly back across the river estuary to Funakoshi. Because we hadn't had strong winds for more than a week or more the air was full of mist, particulate pollution from China. At the close of the typhoon season western Japan is calm and still. Instead of heading straight home I turned off at the entrance to Funakoshi village and cruised slowly along the street that runs along the inner bay, at the end of which there is a small grove of trees below the thickly forested hill. The Watasumi Shrine sat on a ledge above this grove. I walked into the shade of the trees and read a sign explaining the shrine's significance. It included something about praying for horses, an odd notion in a fishing port. In fact there were three shrines there. Two small ones either side of the Watasumi Shrine. An old man with hair dyed jet black was quietly sweeping the sandy grounds with a traditional broom made of long twigs.

'May I ask you about this shrine?' I began.

'Please,' he replied, happy to be involved in a conversation with this curious *gaijin*.

'There are three shrines here, I think.'

'Yes. Watasumi in the middle, then Ebisu for the fishermen, and the Yaku Shrine for illness.'

'I see. And this place seems famous for some historical things, too.'

'Indeed, it is very famous. The Shogun Hideyoshi assembled a lot of horses here for the invasion of Korea.'

'Ah. That's why they prayed for the horses, I suppose.'

'Yes. And for cattle.'

'Cattle?'

'Sure. Cattle. Beef, you know. It was their food.'

'I see. And did Hideyoshi actually invade Korea?'

'Ah….I don't think so. Maybe the bad weather stopped it. But you should ask the priest. He comes here to offer prayers at 11am on the first day of each month. At 11am. Don't miss him. And you should also ask Nakada-*san*, the head of the village. He knows all the history of this place. It's famous, you know.'

'Where is the priest usually?'

'Oh, at the shrine near the village hall at Kuka.'

'I see. You've been very kind to explain all this. Many thanks.'

'And of course this bay was an airbase during the war, you know,' he added with authority. 'There's a sign in front of the ossuary in the port.'

'I've seen that, yes. Amphibious planes, right?'

'Exactly.'

'They flew down to Okinawa to attack the Americans, right?'

'They did, yes. From here,' he said, gesturing at the placid surface of the inner bay. 'Lots of them, actually.'

'Did you see them?'

'Ahhh, I was a boy then. Very small.' He laughed.

I thanked him, bowed, and wandered back into the grove of trees. Another sign carried the legend and map of a voyage to Korea made in AD 736 by an emissary named Abeno Tsugumaro, who set off from present-day Osaka by boat. En route to Korea, stormy weather forced him to seek shelter at Funakoshi before crossing to the islands between Kyushu and the Korean Peninsula. This trip is recorded in the *Manyoshu*, an ancient Japanese text, making our village quite special.

Again, the same thought struck me: what benefit did one get from praying at the Watasumi Shrine?

At the petrol station the next morning I mentioned this to Miss Kanae Kuwano. She was a cheerful girl, born and raised in Funakoshi. She and I had become friendly over the past three years, discussing a variety of issues including gasoline quality, the cost of fuel for the local fishing fleets, and sometimes her plight as a mother of two working six days a week.

Did you know that Funakoshi is mentioned in the *Manyoshu*, I asked her.

'The *Manyoshu*? I never knew,' she said as she put the nozzle of the petrol pump into my car.

'It's true. There's a sign at the Watasumi Shrine.'

She smiled, a radiant sight if there ever was one.

'You….You're always saying things like that,' she said with a laugh.

'Maybe. I suppose so. Do you got to a shrine sometimes?'

Kana-*san* frowned slightly. This was a serious question. 'Oh, well, you know…..for New Year's prayers. That's all really.'

For the foreigner, the journey getting to know and understand Shinto often begins with the language. After a few months learning Japanese your vocabulary expands to include words for what you might see when wandering around in Japan. You learn the basics of nature: mountain (*yama*), river (*kawa*), sea (*umi*), sky (*sora*), rain (*ame*). Then you progress to inanimate objects, and this is where you first encounter religion in the form of the two places of worship seen all over Japan — the Shinto shrine (*jinja*) and the Buddhist temple (*o-tera*). The trouble is, nobody tells you much about the difference between the two. As you get to know Japan you learn to distinguish between the two religions, and you learn that Japanese people are happy observing both.

The first time I came across a Shinto shrine was in Kyoto on my first visit as a young teenager. Though the memory is faint, I vaguely recall an impression of how lovely was the wood in the structures. All Shinto shrines, and most Buddhist temples, are built of wood, with all but the small ones having a copper roof. The wood ages well, giving the *jinja* a welcoming feel. As the years passed and I travelled more widely in Japan I took a closer interest in *jinja*. They seemed the key to understanding what was mysterious about Japan. The simplicity of this religion and its lack of an identifiable deity — there is no Buddha, Jesus, God, or Allah — gave it a mystic feel.

As I made more Japanese friends I sometimes asked them about Shinto. Most could not explain it at all, or at least refrained from explaining it to me. This was not because I was a *gaijin* and should not be allowed to hear about Shinto on account of it being some sort of national secret, but probably because in fact they knew little about it themselves. More years passed and occasionally I read more myself, finally grasping where Shinto fits in with Buddhism and Confucian beliefs in Japanese history.

The early noble families of Japan claimed descent from the gods that everyone worshipped, this eventually became the cult of the Sun Goddess and the establishment of the imperial line therefrom. It's worth a detour to understand Japan's original creation myth, a part of which took place in the south of Kyushu. The stories of the beginnings of Japan are first recorded in two ancient texts, the Nihon shoki and the Kojiki (Record of Ancient Events). These texts were written in the seventh century AD. As records of ancient myths they present quite a challenge.

Some foreign scholars, it must be said, are deeply sceptical of this myth. They maintain that it was manufactured to serve a political purpose, that of keeping the Imperial Family and its allies at the top. The divine status of the emperors throughout the ages as direct descendants of the Sun Goddess rests on the veracity of texts whose description of the original gods was written probably a thousand years after Yamato Japan came into being as a self-identifying entity. The texts are, on any reasonable reading, full of bizarre exaggerations about these gods. But far from troubling modern Japan, the creation myth provides great comfort, much as the notion of the virgin birth in the Bible comforts millions of Christians.

A week or so later on a Sunday morning Toya-*san*, the manager of the estate where I lived, hailed me over as I was driving through the front gate. I held Toya-*san* in some affection. Like me he enjoyed riding motorbikes and always had a ready smile and a sense of humor, unlike the dour grounds manager Yamashita-*san* who liked nothing better than to lecture me about my breaking some rule of the estate. Yamashita was a natural police sergeant, whereas Toya was more like a sympathetic local doctor or shopkeeper.

The estate management committee's monthly meeting is at two o'clock this afternoon, said Toya-*san* with a grin. He knew I hated attending these meetings. You're expected to come, he added.

These meetings were torture. They went on for as long as three hours on a Sunday afternoon, the kindly chairman Dr Kohno going out of his way to be fair and polite to everyone and never able to stop the committee members babbling on about trivia. Because I had missed so many of the meetings I felt trapped. Then Toya-*san* said, 'They're going to debate the *inoshishi* problem.'

'Well, I'll definitely be attending,' I replied. The wild boar — *inoshishi* — in the forests of the estate were out of control, and the dour Yamashita and his two assistants had failed to capture more than a few in their ancient cage traps. The mature *inoshishi* were too smart for that.

At two o'clock the committee meeting began with a talk by a young man named Tsuru, apparently an *inoshishi* removal contractor from

Nine Shinto — the Way of the Gods

Shika-no-shima, a district east of Fukuoka City. He gave us nearly an hour on our problem, including maps of the places where the *inoshishi* slept, ate, and moved around. This was Japanese analysis of the highest quality. One of our key problems was that the *inoshishi* love eating small crabs of the sort that infested the rocks along our foreshore, plus the many buried mountain yams, chestnuts, and the fallen fruit from all the persimmon trees. My own lawn, planted with ryegrass seed specially smuggled in from Australia, had been twice devastated, the entire area vigorously rooted up by the *inoshishi* while I was away overseas or asleep in the house. It was a rough, dug-up mess now because I hadn't bothered to repair the damage. When I complained to Yamashita-*san* he dismissed the problem by blithely suggesting I buy an electric fence to surround the property.

What would that cost? I asked him.

Oh, you should put aside a budget of, say, ¥50,000.

$600!

That seems an awful lot, I replied.

Well, you have a long boundary up there. They'll get in if you leave part of it unprotected.

Great. ¥50,000 for peace of mind and an intact lawn.

When Tsuru concluded his lecture I decided to play the unruly *gaijin* and ask a blunt question. 'Tsuru-*san*, many thanks for your detailed explanation of this problem. I have some experience of hunting wild pigs in my own country, and I must say they are very tough animals. Very tough indeed. In the case of our estate, I think the object must be to reduce the numbers of *inoshishi*. Simply that. May I seek your assurance that you will actually kill our *inoshishi*? Anything less seems a waste of time and money. Unless you kill them the number of *inoshishi* will not be reduced.'

The question caused an audible gasp among the aged committee members. *Kill* the *inoshishi*? What an extraordinary suggestion!

'Well, there is the question of the estate's reputation in the local area,' said Dr Kohno with a pained expression.

I was about to protest when Tsuru stepped in quickly and said, 'Those *inoshishi* I catch in my snare traps will be removed from the estate completely. No question about that. Their numbers will fall.'

I was going to press the point and demand an assurance that Tsuru would actually kill the beasts but decided instead to let him continue. Japan does not welcome stridency.

'I should get about thirty of them here. But you're main problem is that the estate border with Funakoshi Village's forest is unprotected. There are a lot of *inoshishi* in that forest, particularly near the two shrines on the hill. Unless you seal off that border with a very stout fence more of them will find their way into the estate. There's too much food here for them to resist.'

My ears pricked up at the mention of shrines.

'You mean the Watasumi Shrine?' I asked.

'No, the two small shrines on the hill behind the houses, immediately above the fishing port.'

This was news to me. I had driven through the village hundreds of times over the past three years and never known of two other shrines. While the committee debated the cost of Tsuru's proposal to trap the *inoshishi* and remove them, I quietly checked the map on my cellphone. Sure enough, it showed two small shrines just where Tsuru had said they were up, in the forest on the hill behind the fishermen's houses. One was called the Wakamiya Shrine and the other the Hikizu Shrine.

A couple of days later I found the time to go looking for these two shrines. It was hot and sunny in the late morning, and I wore my golf cap and sunglasses. The streets were deserted, everyone out fishing or harvesting oysters for the oyster hut restaurants that the villagers operated. I walked back towards the hill and found a long stone staircase leading upwards to the Hikizu Shrine. Fifty yards further on an old man was wrestling with some wire mesh, no doubt an anti-*inoshishi* measure. I climbed up to the top of the steps, which ended halfway up the hill, and found the shrine. It was dedicated to Ebisu, the god of the sea, and looked out over the port and the bay inland toward Mount Raizan and the rest of the mountains. Every fishing village in Japan has an Ebisu *jinja* somewhere nearby. The salt air had given the wooden structure of this one a pale, worn look, unlike the darker wood of the inland shrines around Hita. I prayed briefly then wandered into the forest at the rear. Further up the hill I saw a bamboo forest like the one behind the Kafuri Shrine. The ground beneath the trees was heavily disturbed by the *inoshishi*. Tsuru was right, this place was alive with the beasts.

Coming down the stone staircase I went looking for a path to the Wakamiya Shrine but couldn't find anything, just a few houses on the edge of the forest. I noticed a dam up a small gully, its front edge engulfed in thick *danchiku* bamboo. Walking along a path that ran alongside a vegetable patch heavily protected with wire mesh, I approached the *danchiku* and found every square inch of the ground uprooted. This was Inoshishi City. Fearful that any moment now a huge sow or boar would come charging out at me, I beat a noisy retreat back to the road.

The situation for our estate was hopeless. No matter what we did, the *inoshishi* from this hillside would continue to invade our own forests. That was obvious. Only a major campaign with guns or hunting dogs and sharp knives would reduce their numbers, and that was an impossibility given the sensitivity about our estate's local reputation. The Funakoshi villagers were too busy fishing and operating their lucrative oyster huts to care.

Reading a book on the history of Shinto I came across a story that gave me an idea about our *inoshishi* problem at Funakoshi and how we might tackle it. When the people in Hitachi, an area north of present-day Tokyo, attempted to cultivate some new rice fields a group of what they called *yato-no-kami* that had "the bodies of snakes and horns on their heads" gathered together and stopped the people from going ahead with their task. A local chieftain named Matachi of the Yahazu clan came to their aid and attacked the *yato-no-kami* with a spear, killing some of them and driving the rest away. He confronted the remaining *kami* and offered them a bargain. They could have the forest land above the rice fields as their own, and he would become a priest and worship them forever. He founded a shrine right there and worshipped them as promised, his descendants doing likewise afterwards for years to come.

These *kami* may well have been *inoshishi* given the vagaries of translation way back then. As unlikely as it seemed, if it worked for Yahazu Matachi and his people then maybe it would work for our estate at Funakoshi.

I went to our local GooDay store — a kind of hardware and homewares store like Walmart — and looked at the small, portable Shinto shrines called *kamidana* on sale. They were not cheap. People usually erected them inside a private house high on a wall with votive offerings of rice, *sake*, and a *mikan* orange. I went to see Toya-*san* in the estate office and explained my plan. He laughed aloud.

'A *kamidana*? Are my ears deceiving me?'

'No,' I insisted, 'you Japanese men have to take charge of this. A *gaijin* would not attract the favour of the *inoshishi* god, Okkoto-Nushi.'

'What?'

'Yes, Okkoto-Nushi. That's the name of the *inoshishi* god, at least according to the internet.'

'Well, I've never heard of that, but if you say so......'

'I do. But you'll recall that last Sunday I advocated the slaughter of these creatures, so I don't think I'm the right one to put up the shrine.'

'That's probably true,' he conceded. 'What did you say the god was called?'

'Okkoto-Nushi, the wild boar god. They appear in Miyazaki Hayato's animation movie, the one called Princess Mononoke, as good guys, actually. My children used to watch it over and over again. '

'Mmm, as you say, then. But I thought you wanted to kill them,' Toya-*san* said.

'Well, maybe there's another measure we could take. I'm not so sure about killing them now, not entirely. In Japan, as you know, for every problem there are always a few different ways of solving it.'

'That is quite so,' said a suddenly serious Toya-*san*. As the manager of a residential estate, problem-solving was his highest professional priority.

For me, doing this sort of thing carried obvious risks. It might even get into the local papers: demented *gaijin* insists on erecting a mini-*jinja* to placate predatory *inoshishi*. Going native and cooking Japanese food or writing a book about Kyushu was one thing, but becoming a Shinto adherent?

This was too bizarre for words, a good way to earn a reputation for having an incurable mental disorder. Well, maybe so, but the thousands of people who attend Shinto shrines every day can't all be mad.

As George Sansom wrote in the 1930s they are there to praise the *kami*, to appreciate them. After all, I thought, what exactly is a religious belief? It's certainly not something that comes with positive evidence of a god's existence. People believe in…..what they think they *should* believe in.

My own interpretation, for what it's worth, sat comfortably with Sansom's view of praise and appreciation: the *inoshishi* were admirable creatures, and although they had wrecked my garden I had to admit they deserved respect for their efforts in doing what came naturally to them, even if I had advocated their slaughter. Such is the way one starts to think when living in a heavily forested estate in rural Japan. When you enter the village, you respect its customs, as the old Japanese proverb goes. In other words, when in Rome…..

On a Halloween Eve Friday, I drove to Hita and had dinner with my parents-in-law. NHK's evening news bulletin made a great fuss about the crowds of young people expected in Tokyo's Shibuya Station square on Saturday night to celebrate Halloween, something relatively new to Japan. The whole thing left my mother-in-law utterly confused.

'What's this all about?' she exclaimed at the news. 'Never seen anything like it. It's not even New Year!'

'I haven't a clue,' said my father-in-law as he carefully poured a beer for me at the kitchen table. We sat on the floor on tatami around a *kotatsu* table. From their distant perspective such baffling things from Tokyo and abroad were common and always merited a good bout of sceptical comment.

'Well, it's really an American festival,' I said.

'American?' she said.

'Oh, yes. It's something about driving away witches and demons.'

'Witches? And demons? Dear me.'

'Children go from house to house asking for sweets,' I said. 'If they don't get them they threaten mischief.'

'Ah, I've heard of that,' she allowed. 'There's something over at the supermarket about it.'

Japan's retail industry and coffee shop chains had seized on Halloween as a means of boosting sales, staging the usual frenzy and offering all sorts of food, drinks, costumes and decorations for people to waste their incomes on.

'I think the tradition is to carve out a large pumpkin, put a candle in it, and carve a demon's face into it,' I said.

'How could you carry a pumpkin on the train? Ridiculous,' said my father-in-law. Nothing pleased him like pouring scorn on a modern event. He set about unwrapping the chicken *sashimi* bought from the supermarket. 'Here, you're drinking beer, right?' he said to me. 'Want some *shochu* instead? Go on, whatever you fancy. Drink up now.'

I thanked him and drank some of the beer.

One of the reasons I came to Hita that night was because he wanted me to go with him to the Ohara Shrine the next day to organize a *harai* for my son Cail who was coming to Kyushu with my wife Sayuri in December. He said it was vital to invoke the gods' protection so that Cail didn't get injured with all the soccer he was playing. 'After all, if he's good enough to play professionally one day we'd better make sure he doesn't injure himself. That'd wreck everything.'

I said I was sure that Sayuri, a soccer fanatic in the true Japanese sense, would welcome this measure.

Ohara Hachimangu Shrine is the dominant *jinja* in the Hita district. It's dedicated to the god Hachiman, the god of archery and war and the *ujigami* or tutelary god of the samurai. There are said to be 25,000 *jinja* in Japan dedicated to Hachiman, the chief of which is the Great Shrine of Usa, not far from Hita in western Oita Prefecture. Cail was given the usual *harai* as an infant at Ohara Hachimangu, as was his older sister Sara, so it seemed appropriate to go back there for another one to ward off injury, especially given his samurai-like approach on the soccer pitch.

On the Saturday morning I drove my parents-in-law over to the Ohara *jinja* which sat high on a hill. Before we even started out my father-in-law announced that I had to drive up the hill to the carpark because his sore back would not allow him to climb the long stone staircase up there. When we arrived at the *jinja* we noticed a family entering the main building with a priest and an infant for a *harai*, and another priest blessing a new car in a corner of the shrine grounds. I loved this place, its tall trees, ancient stone lanterns, and aged wooden shrine buildings with their traditional architecture. We walked over to the shrine office where my father-in-law addressed a young assistant priest through the reception window in his country dialect.

'Look, it's like this. It's my grandson…..Ah, he plays soccer a lot. Needs a *harai*.' He indicated me standing behind him. 'This is my daughter's husband. The boy is in Australia…..can you give him a *harai* here, to, ah….. to stop the injuries?'

The young assistant priest looked puzzled.

'Well, yes, anyone can receive a *harai*, but he's in Australia? I don't know about that…..Is it today? I'm not sure we can.'

'No, no, he's in Australia. Australia. But he's coming here, in December. Can you do it then?'

The assistant priest frowned. 'Well……'

I stepped in and explained the situation, asking whether we needed to make a specific appointment for a *harai*.

'Oh, I understand. At the end of the year we're pretty busy going out and performing various prayers and rites, but if you call up two or three days in advance it can be done.'

'And the donation?' my father-in-law asked. 'How much is that?'

'Oh. Well, you must consult Chief Priest Hashimoto about that. I can't handle such money matters, I'm afraid. He's busy now over there with the child's *harai*, but you can telephone him later on.'

We left the conversation there and with my parents-in-law I went to the various small shrines behind the main building, throwing our coins in the votive boxes and praying at each one. Some of the shrines were dedicated to the rice harvest, some to relieving illness, and one to commercial success. The god Hachiman was enshrined in the main building, but I was happy to leave my prayers for martial and archery success until another time. I had done this for the past twenty-five years or so and despite being a Christian

I felt no embarrassment or discomfort praying at a Shinto shrine. To be honest I believed in the *kami* and was grateful for any help I could get from any god that would hear my prayers. That this contradicts the Christian insistence on one God Almighty is obvious, but I'd been living in Japan too long to obey that commandment.

As we returned to the car park we ran into a group of a dozen or so men dressed in dark suits, some with black mourning neckties and some tieless. They didn't look like business people, being slightly rough of face and most of them tanned. Nor did they have the stocky appearance of farmers. Just then the assistant priest came hurrying out of the *jinja* to greet them. He stopped for a moment near us, so I greeted him and asked him who the men were.

'They're the police,' he said.

'Police? At the shrine? Is it a funeral or something?'

'No. Across there....' He pointed at a stone monument in the forest over beyond the car park. '... is a memorial for an ancestor of the local police. Every year they come to pray there. After that they come into the shrine for more prayers.'

I thanked him for the explanation and asked him his name.

'I'm Nagase. But you have to call Chief Priest Hashimoto about the *harai* donation.'

The next morning, a holiday Tuesday, the early mist covering Hita turned to a fine day by shortly after breakfast, bright sunshine illuminating the town. While my mother-in-law and I were preparing breakfast — a combination of toast, muesli, sliced banana for the toast, and weak coffee — my father-in-law appeared from upstairs complaining about a sore back and an uncomfortable stomach. Such is the way a day begins with elderly cohabitants. He sat down on the *tatami* floor at the table over the *kotatsu* foot warmer, glanced at the television news, and began reading the morning newspaper.

After a decent interval I retreated upstairs to the guest bedroom where I stayed when visiting their home and set about answering the overnight email traffic. The news from the outside world was not encouraging, but the human condition requires that younger family members battle on regardless of the obstacles in our path to success and freedom from the razor blades of commercial life. By ten o'clock that morning my in-laws suddenly appeared dressed for the outing to Usa Jingu Shrine I had promised them the night before. An indolent day at home was no way to spend one's time, I agreed. Let's get going. *Otoosan* (my father-in-law) could stretch out in the back seat to give his painful spine and hips some rest.

I drove down the road past the turnoff to the village of Onta, central Kyushu's pottery village of dreams. My mother-in-law made a series of observations about the cheerful purple colour of the cosmos flowers along the roadside and the lamentable lack of autumn colours in the trees on the steep hillsides each side of the road.

'Ten days from now it'll be perfect,' she remarked.

'More like three more weeks,' came the commentary from my father-in-law in the rear.

The district's rice fields lay there half-harvested. The bright orange blobs of fruit hanging from the persimmon trees would soon be dangling on strings from the eaves of the farmhouses to dry. *Hoshi gaki*, or dried persimmon, is a delicacy we enjoyed every winter in Japan. I often ate it chopped up in yoghurt for dessert or breakfast.

We drove down the long and winding road that ran along the river valley down to the town of Nakatsu and then on to Usa, a journey that reminded me of the time I did it alone on the Vulcan two years back. The trick was to find the roads with the least number of traffic lights and other urban obstacles to our destination, the mighty Usa Jingu Shrine, home of the god Hachiman, tutelary god of the samurai, impatient motorbike riders, and other such travellers in a hurry.

Usa Jingu is by far the most decorated *jinja* in Kyushu, many of its flat wooden surfaces painted in bright vermillion. The walls of the Kure Bridge at the western entrance were just the start of this expanse of arresting colour. The bridge had a thatched roof to protect the pilgrims from rain and storm, its shelter across the moat interrupted by a closed door on the inward side. My father-in-law struggled up the steps of another bridge across the moat a hundred yards downstream. The three of us thus made slow progress to the *temizu* font at the bottom of the worshippers' pathway that led up through the forest to the Upper and Lower Shrines, these being the key objects of the pilgrims. Families with small children dressed in ornate *kimono* passed us by.

'I can't make it any further,' my father-in-law announced when we reached the font. 'Back is too sore to go on.'

'Well, you just stay here on that bench,' said my mother-in-law. 'Andrew and I will go up and pray. We'll be back down here soon. Wait here.'

'I'll do that,' he sighed. ' You two go on up.'

Each side of the worshippers' path was lined every few metres with moss-covered stone lanterns, interspersed at intervals with wooden lanterns on tall posts painted bright vermillion. As my mother-in-law and I walked slowly up the steps through the dappled light under the forest canopy I imagined the progress of a samurai man and his family in ages past. The shrine was founded around 1,300 years ago. No doubt a man my age or younger had done the same thing before. In troubled times the average life of a samurai was not so long. They frequently died in battle or in sword fights along local roads, cut to pieces with *katana* swords or pierced through their armour by an enemy's spear. The walk reminded me of time spent strolling along the broad path into the Meiji Jingu Shrine in Tokyo. At the top of the steps we stopped in front of the main gate, its middle panel conspicuously adorned with three Imperial chrysanthemum crests. We bowed once and proceeded through the right-hand opening in the gate.

Immediately inside the gate I had the sense of being within a very holy place. There were three signs on posts celebrating the Emperor's gracious gifts of cloth and rice cakes on the occasion of the three *matsuri* festivals the shrine had offered to the gods so far that year. I approached the amulet shop and began talking with the *miko* girl serving behind the counter about the signs.

'Is this shrine owned by the Imperial Family?' I asked

'No, it's not their property. They just send gifts and envoys,' she replied.

'Envoys?'

'That's right. They don't come themselves.'

'Really? Why not? It's such a beautiful place.'

'Well, others come instead. Not the actual Imperial Family members.'

'Forgive me, but that seems odd given their close connection with this shrine.'

The girl was not going to continue this debate. 'Your purchase will be ¥1800,' she said sternly as she gathered the amulets I had chosen and put them into a white paper envelope that bore the crest of the shrine.

'As you say,' I replied, paying with two thousand-yen notes. My amulets were for health-and-long life, and for car safety.

My mother-in-law and I stood together and prayed at each of the three altars that led into the inner sanctum of the *jinja* proper where, during the daytime, the god Hachiman resides. At night he retreats back into the inner-inner sanctum. The sign outside the altars demanded four claps from a worshipper rather than the usual two. I delivered the claps slowly and bowed my head to pray. Afterwards I was struck by the irony that my golf cap carried the image of St Andrew on its front. So Hachiman, meet the tutelary god of golf.

Worshipping at such a grand shrine seemed to carry more meaning than doing so at the little local shrines. The god Hachiman at least had a name, and being regarded with such awe and reverence gave me a sense of humility standing there. But still, to my Western mind it all seemed a bit short, even shallow. I couldn't say I felt my soul was enriched by the moment. But the ceremony of it all was satisfying. I had, I supposed, communed with the mighty Hachiman by coming to the Usa Jingu, though to what effect I couldn't say. As my mother-in-law and I slowly descended the stone staircase through the forest after praying I asked her what she thought of Usa Jingu.

'Oh, it was wonderful. I haven't been here in years,' she replied, grasping the metal rail to steady herself as she took the steps one by one.

'Is the god here a special one?'

'Oh, yes. Well, it's an important shrine.'

Maybe that was enough, I thought. She was happy that we'd been there to pray.

On the way out at the western car park we found three young boys casting lures into the moat upstream from the Kure Bridge. I went to take a photograph of them and asked them what they were after.

'Black bass,' replied the oldest boy who, unlike his companions, had not waded into the shallow stream.

'Any luck so far?'

'Not yet.'

'Maybe you guys should go and pray. Then you'll catch some fish.'

The boys laughed. Crazy *gaijin* makes ludicrous suggestion.

My father-in-law settled himself into the back seat again and declared that we did not need lunch. 'Late breakfast. We've had enough for now. Let's get going. Are you hungry or something? Want something to eat?'

'No, no,' I replied. 'Late breakfast. No need at all. Not yet.'

Then I made my own declaration: rather than return to Hita by the same route we would take the expressway right through the mountains and stop to bathe in the hot springs at Amagase.

'That's a great idea,' said my father-in-law.

'Maybe some tea would be good,' said my mother-in-law.

'The hot water will ease *Otoosan*'s discomfort,' I said. 'We'll stop on the way at Kusu to get some tea, maybe some of that anti-cancer *hanshiren* tea.'

'Let's go,' said the rear commander. 'They'll shut the car park on us if we delay any longer.'

'*Otoosan*, what are you talking about? It's only one o'clock in the afternoon,' said my mother-in-law.

'They do those things, you know. You never know what they'll do in a place like this. Big shrine…..they can do anything they like.'

What was the connection between Shinto and the Pacific War? This question had been bothering me for a while. Beyond doubt, from the 1920s Japan's military extremists and radical nationalist politicians had perverted worship of the Emperor into a cult-like movement to justify their foreign aggression. According to the creation myth of Japan, the Emperor was at the top of the Shinto hierarchy. Yet this misuse of Shinto seemed a long way removed from the nature worship type of Shinto I saw at the local shrines in the countryside. That said, the Yasukuni Shrine in Tokyo where the souls of Japan's war dead are enshrined has a special place in the nation's heart. As much as I thought the invasion of China in the 1930s and the Pacific War had been a horrible disaster, I couldn't help feeling something for the young Japanese men who served in the war.

A night or two later I was back home in Lauben Kolonie writing up my notes from the trip to Usa Jingu. Staring at me from across the room as I wrote was the pale, round, becapped face of one Hironomi Yasuda, the featured soul-of-the-month on the Yasukuni Shrine calendar that my mother-in-law gave me before I left Hita. Born in Ibaraki Prefecture, the 24 year-old corporal died at Mount Kangipotto in the north-west of Leyte Island on 1 July 1945. On 25 December 1944, the commanding officer of General Tomoyuki Yamashita's 14th Army had ordered all remaining infantry forces to "fight on independently on your own," and the final battle for these Japanese soldiers left on Leyte occurred here. Brave young Yasuda perished somewhere on the mountain with his fellow soldiers. He wrote a will to his parents that read:

"Dear Parents, thank you for my life of over twenty years. As a foundation stone of the Great East Asia Project, I now give up my life for my country. Please forgive my failure to remain filial and the many disloyal things I've done. But, as I throw away my life for military success, I'm sure you've prepared for this day.

Dear Parents, do not weep for my passing. You know that in life there are many such things. And please take good care of [the girls] Masako and Etsuko…..Please believe that my life has not been wasted. So, with the cherry blossoms at the Yasukuni Shrine in full bloom in my heart, I go to lay down my life for my country.

Yours ever, Hiro."

What did this young man do for a living before the war? I wondered. Who paid him the wage with which he fed and schooled his daughters; or was it his sisters? Did he work in a restaurant, a factory, a petrol station, or

139

was he a railway man or a coal miner? Japanese authorities kept meticulous records of such things, so somewhere the answer to these questions doubtless lies in some dust-laden archive. But the answer to the key question — why did he think his precious life was worth sacrificing for his country's leaders? — can be found only in his belief in Japan's destiny as a great nation. In his last moments did he remain silent, or did he cry out in horror at what was about to happen to him and his colleagues? Maybe, I told myself, it's best to leave Corporal Yasuda to his private thoughts as he imagined the cherry blossoms in full bloom at Yasukuni and stood to meet his end.

Did anybody go back to the scene of Yasuda's last stand to collect his bones and those of his colleagues for repatriation and burial in Japan? Probably not.

On Monday nights in Japan NHK broadcasts a travel program hosted by a comedian and television actor named Shofukutei Tsurube, which is a traditional comic stage name. This Tsurube is a rambunctious, rough-talking Osaka man who travels around small towns all over Japan talking to local people and celebrating their family lives for the program. I had grown addicted to watching his travels and despaired when work commitments forced me to miss the program on a Monday night.

One Monday recently I was surprised and delighted to see him and his fellow actor guest visit Yoshiimachi, a small town where my mother-in-law grew up, not far downriver from Hita. The program showed him doing the usual thing by accosting old people in the mostly empty streets and demanding, in a friendly fashion, to know all about their lives. One scene in particular caught my attention. Tsurube and his companion went to a shrine called the *Mizu Jinja* or Water Shrine. It was raining, and they made jokes about rain and the shrine's name. They walked in, prayed, remarked on a large statue in the grounds, and then hurried off back to the main street of Yoshiimachi to accost more of the locals.

I was intrigued by this scene. Yoshiimachi is more or less on the way from Itoshima to Hita, if you leave the expressway at Haki-Ukiha. I decided that my quest to understand Shinto would not be fulfilled unless I, too, went to the *Mizu Jinja*. The twin towns of Haki and Ukiha sat either side of the Chikugo River, but was that enough to have a shrine devoted to the worship of water?

I left home in Itoshima after lunch on the Friday, stopping at the local petrol station but disappointed to find both Kana-*chan* the other girl Kyon-*chan* off duty. I drove onto the expressway at Maebaru and headed southeast through Fukuoka and then on towards Oita Prefecture. When I got to the Haki-Ukiha exit I felt a vague sense of stupidity. What did I, a lonely *gaijin*, think I was doing heading off to another Shinto shrine by myself? Surely this was a sign of creeping depression or insanity. I had been down this path before a few years back, and the symptoms were familiar. Or maybe it was the act of a curious, enterprising amateur scribbler trying to find and record what's left of old, rural Japanese culture.

Despite these misgivings I kept following the navigation computer in my car whose destination was set to the shrine, stopping once at a convenience store to buy a yoghurt drink, and driving further down a narrow country road taking care to avoid a collision with the oncoming trucks. To drive in rural Japan is to learn the skills necessary for navigating very narrow roads. There was no sign of water anywhere until suddenly beside the road a small canal appeared brim full, the water flowing strongly. Then a larger watercourse appeared, a tributary of the Chikugo River. In a grove of trees on the other side I saw the shrine. It was actually called the Nagano Mizu Jinja and had a small, neat car park and a public toilet out the front. I parked the Toyota, got out in the sunshine, and walked up to the large stone *torii* arch at the entrance, removing my St Andrews golf cap before I walked under it.

Inside there was a large statue, just like on the NHK program: one Inatomi Takato, a revered local politician since passed away. Later research revealed he was a Socialist Party Diet Member devoted to the interests of small farmers in the Kurume-Yoshiimachi district. Elected to the Diet in 1946, he was purged from public office by the Occupation authorities on political grounds, later returning to the legislature as a right-wing faction Socialist.

The grounds of the Nagano Mizu Jinja boasted plenty of trees. Stone monuments said the shrine was 350 years old. At the *shinden* or main sanctuary I found a middle-aged lady slowly sweeping the earth outside with a small straw broom. I offered to help her, but she laughed. I introduced myself and asked her name.

'Kumadaki,' she replied. Literally speaking, this sounded as if it meant either boiling-a-bear or hugging-a-bear. 'You know, bear…and hug,' she added, making a pretence of hugging something. So that was it. Neither boiling nor hugging bears is common in Japan.

'Ah, my name is Thomson,' I repeated, not knowing what else to say. 'Would you mind if I prayed at the shrine?'

'Of course. Go ahead.'

I approached the *shinden*, threw in some coins, clapped twice, and said my prayer before bowing to the altar. Inside the *shinden* I noticed an old black-and-white photograph on the wall above the altar. It showed an august Japanese man wearing a uniform and a sash, with some sort of decoration pinned to his left breast.

I retreated from in front of the *shinden* and asked Mrs Kumadaki about the photograph.

'It's Sumitsuin,' she said.

'Sumitsuin-*san*?'

'Ah, maybe. I'm not so sure. Sumitsuin. You'd better ask the priest.'

'Is he here today?'

'No, he's in hospital. His son is doing the work for him. And he's away.'

The name Sumitsuin sounded a very odd one, but maybe it was one of those rare, classical names that Japanese statesmen seemed to have before the war, like Prince Konoye. I thanked her and walked away, happy that I'd now seen and prayed at the Water Shrine like Tsurube had. I realised later that I'd forgotten to ask her about the water, but the canal was probably what it was all about. A day or so later I read more about the shrine on a Shinto website. Far from being dedicated to the canal, it was founded for the purpose of worshipping a god called Mizu Hameno, born of the original god Izanagi and designated as the god of water, as the word *mizu* suggests. The canal was built well after the local people founded the shrine. They probably decided to worship Mizu Hameno to guard against flooding of the Chikugo River.

Heading back towards Hita on the local roads rather than the expressway I passed the big Ukiha *michi no eki* roadside market, then passed a worn out love hotel called Hotel Touch in English before stopping at a small tofu store called Tobitaro to buy some *yuba* and soft tofu for dinner with my parents-in-law. In Japan it's a courtesy to bring with you some sort of delicacy if going to visit or stay with someone. I had stopped here once before. Its tofu, made over in Haki, is as good as the best in Japan. The lady at the store put a plastic bag of ice in with the tofu and *yuba* to keep it cool.

I drove on to the Kanpo Inn hot springs, an establishment owned and operated by the Post Office insurance company. The company had just gone public on the Tokyo Stock Exchange, and the share price had done well after the listing. I bought a ticket from the vending machine at the entrance and had myself a very decent bath. The hot water at Kanpo has such a heavy mineral content that it leaves your skin slippery. The feeling you have after drying yourself and leaving the changing room is one of utter physical perfection and mental tranquility. For ¥600 this is an absolute bargain.

In the shop inside Kanpo I bought my usual cold drink, a can of *kabosu* fruit drink with bits of the fruit floating in it, and asked the lady serving there about the company's float and share price.

'Share price? I wouldn't know about that,' she said, puzzled by the question.

'But you work for Kanpo. Surely you own some shares in it. Don't they give you shares as part of your bonus?'

'Oh, no. I'm only a casual employee. Like most of us here. We never got any shares.'

'I'm sorry to hear that. Sounds a bit unfair.'

'*Saa*. Anyway, who'd know anything about shares around here. I wouldn't know what to do with them.'

My parents-in-law and I had dinner at the coffee shop-restaurant next door to their kimono shop. I had never been in there before, though I was friendly with the owner, Hiyoshi-*san*, who I sometimes met outside in the street. He had the common Japanese habit of watering the footpath and road outside his shop every morning no matter what the season, rainy days excepted. As usual my father-in-law drank too much *shochu* and became loud. We hurried our meals so my mother-in-law and I could hustle him out of the place before the other customers complained. Hiyoshi-*san* looked relieved as we left. While we were eating and chatting an ageing tradesman sitting at the counter overheard my description of the Nagano Mizu Jinja and suddenly remarked, 'That shrine is hard to find. But I know where it is. I'm from Haki.'

This prompted a lively but friendly exchange between him and my in-laws, during which I heard my mother-in-law say, 'You know, I think my father worshipped at that shrine sometimes.'

After this conversation we retreated to their home above the shop and watched television for a while. I stayed up to watch the preview of the Kyushu sumo tournament, which was to start on Sunday afternoon. Then I went upstairs to the guest bedroom to write up more notes on the visit to Yoshiimachi. Before I went to sleep my mother-in-law gently knocked on the door and poked her head in. She often did this to check whether I was warm enough in winter.

'Are you really warm enough in here?' she asked. 'Don't you think you need another *futon*? It gets very cold overnight.'

'No, thank you. I'm fine as it is. Really. I don't think it'll get very cold tonight.'

'Well, if you need another one…..'

'Not for the moment. I'm okay, truly.'

'Well, that's good. Ah, Andrew, would it be possible to visit that shrine, maybe tomorrow? I'm sure my father went to the Mizu Jinja a few times. I'd love to see it. Haven't been there for a long, long time.'

How could a filial son-in-law refuse? 'Of course we can go. We'll use my car. Let's head off mid-morning. We can have lunch somewhere over that way.'

'Thank you. Thank you. I haven't been over there for years,' she said.

I knew my mother-in-law had grown up in Yoshiimachi, but, for reasons I found out later the next day, she had never said anything much about it in my presence. I'm not even sure how much Sayuri knew about her mother's childhood. We set off on the Saturday morning in the usual fashion, my mother-in-law sitting in the front passenger seat and my father-in-law ensconced in the rear with pillows and other paraphernalia for his painful back and hips. We drove along the old road to Kurume on the south-west side of the Mikuma River, back past the Tobitaro tofu shop and the Hotel Touch, past the Ukiha roadside market and then down some narrow local roads in the direction of the Nagano Mizu Jinja.

Suddenly my mother-in-law said, 'Ah, I think my old house was around here somewhere.' The area was a flat expanse of farm houses and small factories separated by rice fields and vegetable patches.

'Really?' I asked. 'Whereabouts? Right in this area?'

'Ah, I think it's over there where the river is. You'd better turn right.'

'No, no, it's on the left,' said my father-in-law.

'No, the right,' she insisted. 'Turn here.'

I did what she asked, and we started down an even narrower road. In a small car park I saw a flatbed truck with a company name on its side: the Ishii Sawmill. Ishii was her maiden name, and her father had owned a sawmill.

'That truck, it's your family company's truck, isn't it?'

'Well…..in a way. In fact it was my uncle who took over the sawmill.'

'But it is your family's sawmill, right? The Ishii Sawmill.'

'Well, yes, I suppose so. Keep going straight. The house is down here somewhere.'

We continued down a gentle slope towards the river. At a tiny intersection amid some houses and a small shop two old men were talking to each other by a light pickup truck parked outside the shop. It was so narrow that I had to slow down to a crawl to get past them. One of the men, a small

My mother-in-law, Mrs Sayoko Sakamoto, outside her childhood home near the town of Yoshii, Fukuoka Prefecture. This visit was the first time she had been back in fifty years. The old communal bath was gone, but she remembered a great deal about life as a child in the village, including hearing the American bombs falling on the city of Kurume not so far away.

fellow wearing a baseball cap and the clothes of a farmer, glanced at our car as we stopped to pass him carefully.

'Hey, he's my old classmate,' cried my mother-in-law. She opened the passenger side window and hailed him. '*Oi*, it's me, Sayoko. From school, remember?'

'*Oiii*, Sayoko? It *is* you,' said the man with a big smile. 'Haven't seen you around here for a while, eh?'

'Ahh, it's been maybe fifty years, I think,' she replied. 'How are you?'

'Oh, so-so, you know. What brings you back here?'

'We came to see my old home. My husband's in the back. And this is my daughter's husband,' she added, indicating me. I nodded to the man and greeted him in polite Japanese.

'He's from Australia,' she added.

'Australia? *Maa*, how about that, eh? Someone went down there once, I think,' said the old man.

'It's a lovely place,' said my mother-in-law. 'We've been there three times.'

'They drink wine there, don't they? Not *shochu*.'

'And lots of beer,' said my father-in-law.

'They mentioned Australia at the TPP meeting we had down at the JA office the other day,' said the man.

'Ah, I think the house is further down this road, right?' I said quickly, knowing a touchy subject when I heard one.

'Yes, it is, as far as I can remember,' said the old man. 'But you'd all know better than I would. *Maa*, Sayoko, fancy meeting you again!'

'I haven't been here for fifty years. Maybe sixty.'

'Is it that long?'

'Let's go,' said my father-in-law. 'It's down here somewhere.'

'When did *you* ever come here?' my mother-in-law said. 'Keep going,' she said to me. 'We can come back here later.'

I drove on very slowly, and we came to the end of the houses above a flat area of land that sloped down to become the river bank. There was a small shrine down near the edge of the water beyond some vegetable patches. I parked the car and we got out, my mother-in-law beaming brightly. I had rarely seen her so buoyant. She pointed at the house on the corner behind us, above the vegetable patches. 'That's it, I think.'

'You think?' said my father-in-law. 'Don't you know? It was your house, wasn't it?'

'Yes, I *think* that's it,' she said slowly. 'And this *jinja*…..'

My father-in-law, Mr Noriyuki Sakamoto. After getting over the shock of his daughter marrying a foreigner in 1991, he became very fond of his Australian son-in-law over the years and enjoyed serving me horse sashimi whenever I visited. In his later years his driving became so dangerous that his son, Hidenori, forced the sale of his car, leaving me as the family's sole chauffeur.

I walked to the front of the shrine and read the stone tablet attached to the *torii* arch: the Mizu Jinja. 'Well, this is another Mizu Jinja,' I said. 'Maybe it's a branch of the Nagano Mizu Jinja.'

'Must be,' said my father-in-law. 'No doubt about it.'

'Ah, look at the river,' said my mother-in-law in wonder. 'We used to swim there. We jumped in from a rock somewhere here. In those days the river bank wasn't like this. It was flatter back then. Looks like it's higher now.'

We walked along the river's edge, now effectively a dyke the local authorities had built to keep out the flood waters, and sure enough, there was the rock, a two-metre high pyramid-shaped thing that sat right on the edge of the water.

'It's deep just there,' said my mother-in-law. 'We used to climb up the rock and jump in, all of us. It was so much fun.'

I suggested we go up to the house and see who lived there. My father-in-law declined because of his sore back, declaring that he would stay in the car, so my mother-in-law and I walked back up the road to the house. Just below the house I noticed a series of drains whose walls were reinforced with round river rocks set in concrete.

My mother-in-law pointed at the drains and said, 'That's the spring we had. It provided water for the communal bath over there.' A grove of bamboo sat in front of the houses further along.

'That was the communal bath?' I asked.

'Oh, yes. Over there beyond the bamboo. The spring fed it with water. We all used to bathe together, everyone in the hamlet. Men and women together.'

At the house we called out from the front yard and a middle-aged man emerged, not looking terribly happy.

'Ah, sorry to bother you, but I grew up in this house,' said my mother-in-law. 'Do you mind if I have a look around?'

' I have to go out, so you can't really come inside,' the man said. 'Have a look outside if you must,' he added, then got into a small white van with a sign on it reading "Police Assistance PATROL". He drove off down the road and left us there. We had a look around and then walked back to the spring. There was a path along the edge of the drains to the bamboo. I started down the path, my mother-in-law muttering about her brothers and sisters as she followed me.

'We used to run naked from the bath down to the river and back. It was great fun, but Father objected. He said it was forbidden, but we did it anyway.'

On the other side of the bamboo I found a patch of bare ground surrounded by a concrete wall now buried up to its top. 'This was it,' she said. 'The bath was right here. I suppose they've filled it in. Looks like the spring stopped, too. Almost.' There was nothing but a thin trickle of water in the drain. She stared at it, possessed by the childhood memory of it all. Of all the moments over the twenty years I'd had with Sayuri and her parents this was perhaps the most touching one I had experienced. Me, the foreign son-in-law, giving an elderly Japanese woman a sudden glimpse of her own childhood.

We continued on back to the river's edge. I looked across the other side where there was a small hamlet of houses. 'Did you ever swim across?' I asked. 'Surely there were other children over there. You must have played with them sometimes.'

My mother-in-law's expression changed to one of concern. 'Yes,' she said slowly, 'but they were different, maybe not normal Japanese people.'

'Were they Koreans?'

'No, sort of different in another way. Mother wouldn't let them into our house, not at all. She was very strict about that. They weren't allowed in. I wanted to give them tea in our house but she absolutely refused to allow it. Wouldn't even let them cross the threshold of the front door and sit down. Some came with meat for us.'

'Meat? Were they....what you call *burakumin*?'

'Yes, that's it,' she said, a trifle sadly. 'They had a slaughterhouse for animals over there somewhere. That's why Mother wouldn't let them in.'

So they were *burakumin*, Japan's old caste of untouchables who worked in the meat and leather industry dealing with the unclean business of slaughtering animals and tanning hides. The discrimination against these people

My parents-in-law outside the Ohara Jinja Shinto shrine in Hita. Our family always offered New Year prayers or hatsu mode at the Ohara jinja. Set on a hill overlooking Hita, the surrounding garden is a beautiful sight during the cherry blossom season or during the autumn colours. Shinto as a religion is an essential part of Japanese life.

continues today, though in a much more subtle way. Nobody uses the term *burakumin* any more.

We said a prayer at the small Mizu Jinja and then drove away towards the bigger Nagano Mizu Jinja. Before we left I filled a half-litre plastic bottle with water from the small stream that the spring fed near the old communal bath site. It tasted soft.

We drove further downriver. At the Nagano Mizu Jinja there was nobody around, which was the usual state of things in my experience. My father-in-law stayed sitting on a stone wall near the car, so my mother-in-law and I walked around the back of the shrine to a house. I pressed the bell and the same Mrs Kumadaki emerged. Apparently she was the priest's wife. She recognized me and smiled. 'So you're back again?'

'I am. It's such a nice shrine. I brought my wife's parents with me. This is my wife's mother, Mrs Sayoko Sakamoto.'

The two women bowed and introduced themselves.

'I did not realize you are the priest's wife,' I said.

'Yes, I am. He's in hospital these days. My son does the work, but he's out somewhere. Come and we'll show Sakamoto-*san* the *shinden*. You can both come inside with me if you want.'

Inside the wooden *shinden* I had another good look at the old photograph on the wall. The Sumitsuin was Japan's Privy Council, a body that sat above the Cabinet in the constitutional hierarchy in Meiji times to advise the Emperor on matters of state. According to Mrs Kumadaki the man in the photograph was named Kuradomi Yuzaburo. He looked like General Nogi, but with a rounder, fatter face. Later on I looked him up on the internet. He was a local aristocrat who had a tumultuous political career, much of which was spent in Korea and Manchuria. He was afflicted with some sort of lethargy complaint and spent a lot of time resting.

'This shrine is three hundred and fifty years old,' said Mrs Kumadaki.

'*Maa*, that old?' said my mother-in-law.

'What about the other smaller Mizu Jinja over near the West Nagase Hamlet?' I asked.

'I grew up there,' said my mother-in-law. 'In West Nagase. My family prayed there.'

'Did you really?' replied Mrs Kumadaki. 'Well, that one was originally a branch of this shrine, but I think it sort of separated itself at some point. There are two shrines over there, I think.'

'That's right,' said my mother-in-law. 'The East Nagase Hamlet had their own *jinja* with its own festival in summer. It wasn't like ours.'

'That's often the case around here. Everyone has their own *matsuri*,' said Mrs Kumadaki.

We thanked her again, remarking on the beauty of the white flowers on the *sazanka* tree outside the shrine office. I asked her whether the shrine had its own sacred *sakaki* tree.

'Of course, right there,' she said, pointing to another evergreen tree.

The pathway through the first leading up to the mighty Usa Jingu Shinto shrine near Nakatsu. Usa Jingu is held to be the third most important shrine in Japan after Ise Jingu and Izumo Taisha.

'The seeds of the *sakaki* tree don't sprout unless they've been digested and excreted by a bird. Only then do they sprout. That's how this tree started. You can't just collect the seeds and plant them. Amazing, isn't it?'

On the way out my mother-in-law and I stopped at the statue of Inatomi Takato. She looked up at the great man and laughed loudly.

'His wife was one of the clients at the hair salon where I was apprenticed, in Yoshiimachi main street. The owner of the salon used to help in Inatomi-*sensei*'s election campaign. Imagine that! A Socialist! Who'd have ever thought…..?'

When we left the car park it was time for lunch. A young boy at a Seven-Eleven convenience store suggested we try a *soba* restaurant back across the river between Haki and Hita. 'It's the best one around here. They make their own *soba*. Highly recommended. And there's a hot spring there, too. You can take a bath after lunch if you want,' he said.

'Well, we'll think about it,' said my father-in-law. It was unlike him to show any hesitation about taking a bath in a hot spring, but he was fussy about the quality of the water.

At the Wasada Soba Restaurant we sat on *tatami* and ate a simple but delicious lunch. Through the windows we could see a few maple trees in the garden showing their autumn colours. I raised the topic of a bath across the road.

'No, I don't think so,' said my father-in-law. 'Don't know about the water there. Still, Sayoko's elder sister's house is only a half mile from here. And their grape orchard.'

'That's right,' said my mother-in-law. 'Dear Tsugika. Sad to say, but she's in hospital these days. Maybe we should go and visit her instead of having a bath.'

We drove over to the Haruzuru Hot Springs Hospital a few miles downriver. I didn't feel like going in and seeing my wife's Aunt Tsugika in what was sure to be a very poor condition. I liked her a lot, but I thought it would hurt her dignity for me to turn up at her bedside. I waited outside and wrote some notes about the day's events while my parents-in-law went in to see her.

Day almost became night as a sudden squall hit us on the way home, the road ahead one minute bone dry and the next awash with swirling water. I slowed down and gripped the steering wheel tightly, steering the Toyota as carefully as I could. Cars and trucks came at us out of the gloom and the driving rain. Somehow I avoided hitting them head on by swerving at the last instant.

'My, what heavy rain,' said my mother-in-law, more than a trace of concern in her voice.

'It's okay,' I said. 'We're safe on the left-hand side.'

'Don't hesitate to stop somewhere if you have to. We're not in a hurry.'

'We'll be fine,' I said. 'Just a lot of water, that's all.'

The flood of rain got her talking in the same fashion.

'You know, I was kicked out of my home when I was young,' she began.

'Really? I've never heard you say that before.' More swerving as the trucks came at us at us out of the rain ahead.

'Well, I was. Father's family objected strongly to my becoming a hairdresser. They said it wasn't the sort of thing a girl in my position should do. They owned a local business, so it was important that I didn't have to go out and work for a living. That reflected badly on them, and they said I'd have to leave if I persisted.'

'So what did you do?'

'Oh, I persisted. I'd wanted to be a hairdresser since middle school. I thought everyone who wanted to look good should be able to do so.'

'And that was such a radical idea for them?'

'Oh, indeed. It was a terrible stigma. They said I might be dragged away by some *yakuza* people or something. So they loaded up a car with my clothes and a *futon* and drove me out into the countryside somewhere. They left me on a road near some shops or buildings. I can't remember much about it now, but I recall looking at a bank and standing outside. Someone took me and my things to the salon in Yoshiimachi and I stayed there, or maybe in an empty house close by. I don't think I went home again because everyone was so angry with me.'

'That seems pretty harsh.'

'Well, it was how they thought in those days. I worked hard and became a good hairdresser. People came to the salon so that I would do their hair. The family that owned the place begged me to take over its running, but I had my eyes on a place near the old cinema in Haki, near the bus terminal. There were a lot of people there, and I was sure it would be a success. But I couldn't persuade the owner of my salon to move over to Haki. Instead, I agreed to get married and move to Hita. My husband and I were acquainted because one of my aunts had married into his family and recommended me as a wife. They insisted I open my own salon near Hita Station, and they paid for it.

'I kept money aside to pay for more study. I knew I had to be good at more than just perms. I had to be able to do weddings, dressing the brides in special *kimono*, and doing the wigs that they wear. That took some doing! My teacher had to come to Hita all the way from Fukuoka, and I had to pay for her! She taught me the skills I needed. Sayuri was just a baby, and because the teacher and her husband had no children of their own they doted on her while I learned the craft.'

'What did *Otoosan* do at that time?'

'Oh, I don't know. This and that. He looked after the books and bought the inventory we needed for our salon and *kimono* rental business. That sort of thing. He went to all the local committee meetings to build our reputation as good people. Someone had to do that while I studied. It attracted customers. And he drove the customers all over the place. That was also important in those days.'

When we drove past the old *burakumin* hamlet she stared out the

The pilots who flew the Zuiun seaplane bombers from the air base at Funakoshi. Unlike the kamikaze pilots these remarkably young men sought to return alive from their missions attacking the approaching Allied fleet around Okinawa. These days the fishing village of Funakoshi has a few discreet monuments to the men who served at the air base. When I asked at the local museum why the Japanese military had used seaplanes as bombers I was told it was because the Americans weren't able to destroy the runway with their own bombers.

window and said, 'There. In there. That's where they lived…..' She wore a fearful look as if the ghosts of the children who were not allowed in her house had reappeared.

'I'm curious about the communal bath,' I said.

'Well, there's a couple of them on the river bank at Amagase, mixed bathing, you know. Everyone naked as the day they were born. You can go anytime you want.'

'No, what intrigues me is how you heated the water,' I said.

'Oh. Well, we had a stove underneath the bath. It was fed from the spring.'

'Underneath? Didn't that mean that people burnt their backsides or feet if they touched the bottom of the bath?'

'No, there was a wooden platform at the bottom to stop that happening. The main problem was that each family had to take turns bringing wood for the stove and tending the fire. It happened about every twenty-one days, I think. Our family had the sawmill so we had plenty of wood offcuts. We had an old cart on two bicycle wheels, and it was my job and my brothers and sisters to push it from the mill down to the bath, all full of wood. When the river flooded and bits of wood washed up on the bank it was much easier. My father and his brothers would cut the wood right there.

'What was the most fun was sneaking into the changing room and hiding the adults' clothes so they couldn't get dressed and walk home. We had great fun doing that. Everyone in the hamlet bathed together.'

'All at the same time?'

'Well, no. There was a rough order to who got to have a bath at what time. It was usually the adults first. Or maybe it was whichever family was on duty to heat the water. I forget. But we children used to get in with the adults and then run down to the river naked. The people in East Nagase didn't have a spring like we did, so they didn't have a communal bath. I can't remember what they did to stay clean.'

'What happened during wartime? Was the wood scarce or rationed?'

'I can't remember wood being rationed, but maybe it was. A lot of wood from the forest was used to make charcoal for heating and cooking. That's what everyone used for fuel in those days. Oil was scarce, that's for sure.

We ate a lot of whale meat. It was cheap. There was a lot of it around after the war, too, when no one had much food. Dear me, we ate a lot of it.'

'And the air raids? What about that?'

'Oh, yes. I remember when the Americans bombed Kurume, which wasn't far away. We children rushed outside and we could see the plumes of smoke from the fires. I think we heard the bombs falling, or the explosions… Booom!.....Booom!..... And the black smoke in the air. Mother and Father got cross with us for standing outside. But no bombs fell on Yoshiimachi. We didn't have anything the Americans wanted to bomb, I suppose.'

'Not the sawmill?'

'No, they didn't go after that sort of thing. Just the big factories where aircraft were made. That's what they bombed. Kurume had lots of factories. Rubber mainly.'

'It's still the hometown of the Bridgestone tyre people, I think,' I said.

'Sure is,' said my father-in-law. 'Ishibashi is their name. Big factory over there.'

'And I heard that *tonkotsu ramen* was invented in Kurume.'

'I'm not sure about that,' he said. 'Lots of people say they invented it. It could be Kumamoto…..or maybe Nagahama, the Fukuoka fish market….'

'That's where the whale meat came from,' said my mother-in-law.

A week later I drove back to Hita to pay another tax bill at the city office and look in on my in-laws. When passing Haki on the expressway I noticed a large persimmon tree just before Aunt Tsugika's grape orchard which was heavy with fruit, the *kaki* as bright orange as ever. Nobody had harvested any of them. They just hung there on the tree in their hundreds. Were all the local farmers in hospital?

When I reached my in-laws' home I found my mother-in-law semi-comatose on the *tatami* floor of the kitchen under a blanket. My father-in-law was watching the sumo on television. I expressed alarm straight away.

'No, she's okay,' said my father-in-law. 'She went to the neurology hospital and got an intravenous drip. That fixed her up. She wasn't eating anything.'

'Dear me,' I said. 'And has she started eating since then?'

'Not really. But she's okay. She goes up and down all the time. Hey, want to eat out tonight again? Sayoko won't be cooking anything, that's for sure. Let's go to Takara-ya and have *champon*.'

'Well, I'm more worried about *okaasan*, I think. Maybe we should stay here, get some takeaway.'

'No, no, you go out,' said my mother-in-law in a weak voice. 'I'll help myself to something here. There's some toast left over from this morning. I can't eat much.'

'Shouldn't we take you to the hospital again? You don't look at all well.'

'No, I'll stay here. I'm fine. I just need some rest.'

I called Sayuri in Australia, who urged me to call my sister-in-law, Katsumi. She came to Hita once a week to clean their house and keep an eye on things. Katsumi said she'd been there on Tuesday and all was well. Mother-in-law fell sick the next day, it seemed. I said all was calm now, but I'd make a decision the next morning based on my mother-in-law's appetite for breakfast. By 6pm she was more chirpy, still lying down under the blanket on the *tatami*, but offering comments on the sumo bouts as they happened. The situation looked okay, so when the sumo finished I took my father-in-law to a *yakitori* restaurant around the corner. Sixty years living in Hita and he had never been there.

It was the normal smoky atmosphere inside. We ordered various sticks of *yakitori* and some *shochu* with hot water. I expressed my concerns about my mother-in-law's condition.

'Nah, she's fine. She goes up and down like this all the time. It's her brain, the doctor said. She forgets things all the time. So do I, but not like her. One minute she can be running around doing things, the next she'll just keel over. I've seen it before…..happens regularly. Then she recovers and goes back to normal again.'

When we got home my mother-in-law was sitting up watching the television and sipping a cold cup of coffee. She smiled wanly. At least she looked better. All the sleeping had done her good. I was vastly relieved and sent my wife and sister-in-law text messages saying all seemed okay, pending the morning's appetite check.

Ten

Cousin Kyoko's Orchard

It rained all day that Saturday. I was up early to find NHK television reporting a major terrorist attack in Paris. I stood in my mother-in-law's kitchen watching the television while trying to organise some toast and coffee.

'This is terrible,' I said.

'Dear me,' muttered my mother-in-law. Such incidents outside Japan were common these days. She fussed about the kitchen pulling plates out from shelves and going about the many mysterious tasks that constituted her breakfast preparations.

It all looked ghastly on the television. Sayuri, Cail and I had stayed in a hotel just down the street from the Charlie Hebdo office only four months ago, and the streets where the various massacres took place were right where we went out every night. Our daughter Sara stayed in the same area only a month later.

The news from Paris got worse as the minutes passed. After breakfast I went upstairs, answered some emails, walked over to the new Lawson convenience store to buy a newspaper, and generally wasted the morning. I went to Takara-ya on the station square and had yet another meal of Japan's best *champon* noodles for lunch. Walking back to my in-laws' home after the meal I ran into Kamei-*san*, the man who operated the camera and printing shop a few doors down the street from us. He and I had become friendly some years back. He admired an oilskin winter jacket I sometimes wore in winter, always mentioning that Barbour was a brand much in vogue around the world. My jacket was not a Barbour, but it was close enough for him to be pleased to see me wearing it every winter.

'*Oi*, Kamei-*san*!' I greeted him. 'This weekend is the Sennen Akari festival here in Hita, right? You'll get plenty of business from people wanting to print out the photos they take of the lights.'

'Well, yes, but actually, you know, there's a similar festival down in Usuki. Down there they don't just light up a river with bamboo lanterns like here in Hita. They light up the whole town. Every shop. It's incredible. You know I come from Usuki, don't you?'

'I didn't know that. Usuki…..?'

'It's the next town from Oita City, on the way to Saiki.'

'Ah, that's where the sumo wrestler Yoshikaze comes from.'

'Well, Usuki is the place, I tell you. There's more culture down there in the southern part of Oita Prefecture. Hita isn't bad, but Usuki is better. There's a National Treasure there, the stone Buddhas. And the town, it's got a castle and a samurai residence. You should go and see it.'

'Oh, I will. I will go, no doubt. I hope you get plenty of photo printing business from this weekend's festival.'

'We'll see.'

I went home and enjoyed a brief siesta before heading off by car for Itoshima. That Saturday night I had promised to attend a dinner meeting of the Japan Agricultural University's local alumni chapter to be held in Itoshima, at a restaurant near Maebaru. My tea-growing friend Yuji Kurihara had organised it and for weeks had implored me to attend. He was such an enthusiastic, decent fellow I could not refuse.

As the day wore on something odd happened. The more I thought about the terrorist attack in Paris the more energy I felt within me. The terrible nature of what had happened spurred me into action. I drove at speed back to Itoshima and set about cleaning my house with an unusual fervour.

The dinner with Yuji's friends was pleasant enough with lots of talk of agriculture and what Japan could do better, but I was bored by it.

The next morning, I rose early and walked down the hill to the beach. The feeling of both sadness and frustration over the Paris attack had turned to something like a determination to *do something*. For some reason a swim in the cold sea seemed appropriate. Without warming up, I walked into the water and spent a minute or so swimming in the shallows. After the customary shower of cold water onshore to wash off the salt I dried myself and walked back uphill to my house where I changed into shirt and trousers. A half hour later my lower back began to ache.

I drove back to Hita after lunch to photograph the Sennen Akari festival on the Kagestu River in Mameda-machi after dark, keen for the respite of the mountains and my in-laws' home again. Truth be told, I was not in the best shape in my head, either. There had been a lot of difficulties in Australia with my key client Pie Face. When I got out of my car in the car park behind the kimono shop the pain in my lower back was worse. Something was definitely not right down there. It was an effort to mount my father-in-law's bicycle.

In the evening darkness before dinner, using a camera and tripod, I took a few dozen photos of the mass of bamboo and *washi* paper lanterns that decorated the riverbanks. I had a drink at Setoguchi-*san*'s bar alone amid the crowds of people attending the festival, then rode back to my in-laws' home somewhat unsteadily after the drink and with a still aching lower back. Sitting at the *kotatsu* table on the tatami in their tiny kitchen with them I ate a very decent meal of *yuba* tofu and chicken sashimi, dipping the little slices of chicken heart and pieces of breast meat in heavy, sweet soy sauce and the homemade *yuzu gosho* mustard we used instead of wasabi. This was Kyushu home food at its best. My mother-in-law fussed over my painful lower back and issued me with some *shōchu* and hot water to dull the pain.

'I wonder, could you recommend a *shiatsu* or acupuncture clinic nearby?' I asked my in-laws. Japan has lots of such clinics.

They conferred immediately and with the pleasure that elderly people enjoy when discussing a younger person's medical troubles. Before long they lapsed into a squabble about which clinic would be best, arguing the merits of this and that doctor. Meanwhile I searched on my cellphone's internet browser.

'The doctor that rents one of the apartments I own is a really good guy,' said my father-in-law. 'They say he can cure anything. He fixes all sorts of ailments. Everyone talks about him.'

'Nonsense, *Otoosan*. We don't even know him,' cried my mother-in-law. 'He just pays the rent every month by direct deposit. I can't even remember his name.'

More squabbling went on while I ate the *yuba* and raw chicken. This stuff was magnificent. I had another *shōchu* and hot water to wash it down. Then I went to bed early for the second night in a row.

The following morning the lower back pain was still bad. I ate a quick breakfast and went back upstairs to do some work on my laptop. Around 9am I called one of the *shiatsu* clinics I'd found on my internet search. No answer. Still too early for patients. I went down the street to Kamei-*san*'s camera shop to print out some of the previous night's photographs and asked him about local clinics for sore backs. He referred the question to his wife who immediately said, 'Try Nakashima-*san*. He's the blind man with the place behind the bus terminal.'

I walked over across the station square towards the bus terminal. Suddenly my father-in-law appeared beside me on his bicycle. '*Oi*, I've remembered where that doctor has his clinic. It's behind the bus terminal. I'll show you. He'll fix your back. No problem. Follow me.'

I did as he asked, walking behind while he slowly rode ahead. Across the other side of the narrow street behind the bus terminal there were a few four-storey buildings. One had a sign outside listing its tenants, the fourth-floor one being a place called the *Mentaru Kuriniku*.

My father-in-law pointed up at the sign. 'That's it,' he announced. 'In there. That's his clinic. Go up there and you'll be in good hands.'

Mentaru kuriniku: in English "Mental Clinic." It was a psychiatry practice. In Japan to avoid the stigma of mental illness these days they use this foreign expression.

'Ah, it's a clinic for mental conditions, not sore backs,' I said.

'Oh? Not sore backs? Everyone says he can cure anything.'

'Well, no, it's not really what I need. But thanks anyway.'

Beyond the *Mentaru Kuriniku* I noticed another building, this one a freestanding residence. Outside it had a sign saying "Nakashima Acupuncture Clinic" in Japanese.

'Okay, I'll be fine, *Otoosan*,' I said. 'I'll try Nakashima-*san*.'

'Oh, well, as you wish. Good idea, probably. You do that. He'll fix you up,' he said and rode away on his errand muttering about the confusion of modern life in which people used too many foreign words on their signs.

An hour later and a mere ¥3,000 spent, the blind, 82-year-old Nakashima-*sensei* and his needles had banished the back pain.

'When I heard you speaking when you came in here, I thought you were Japanese,' he said. 'I can't see, you know. Amazing the way you speak.'

'Well, if you spend your weekends with elderly people here in Hita you don't encounter a lot of English,' I replied. 'Maybe that's why.'

'Yes, yes, you speak like an old Japanese person. Amazing. I've never come across that before. Very rare.'

In Kyushu, as all over Japan, local fruits form part of the food culture and are very important in farming. Japanese cuisine does serve desserts that use plenty of sugar, but sugar-growing was never a big part of Japanese agriculture, being mostly done in Okinawa. Thus, natural sugars from fruits are more common, and a small plate of fruit after a Japanese meal is more in line with tradition.

Southern Kyushu, including our own Oita Prefecture, has an abundance of citrus fruits, the most common being the *yuzu*. The *kabosu* is less bitter, but *yuzu* is the true essence of Oita. It tastes like a mild lemon.

I came back from Tokyo on a Friday. It had been a long week up there, the hotels full of Chinese tourists who had driven up the prices and forced me into an unpleasant little hotel in Akasaka. I went over to Shibuya by subway every day to observe the preparations for the opening of the flagship Pie Face store. As a young student many years ago, I spent a lot of time in Shibuya. It was full of cheap restaurants and bars in those days, which is still the case today. The streets are full of young people, some of them men with ponytails and earrings, and a lot of young Japanese women dressed as dolls. Shibuya Ward was Japan's first to hand out marriage licences to gay couples.

Our partner in Japan, the Duskin company, had secured an excellent location for the first Pie Face store. People began to line up before the store opened at 9am to be among the first to taste the pies. The store opened, and the customers began buying pies by the half-dozen to take home. The queue stretched out, taking forty minutes to get to the counter. As the hours passed the average age fell. Shibuya is an afternoon and evening place for young people, and the pies kept selling. Plainly it was a huge success. Our partner company executives stood around smiling and telling us that it would take three months to judge whether the brand would survive Tokyo's high rents and fickle consumer tastes.

I stayed another day and went down to Kawasaki to visit another store our partner had opened without any publicity three weeks earlier. It was in a food court within a giant new mall on the west side of the station. People were queueing there too, and a lady in the queue told me that she'd heard the pies were especially tasty, so she'd come a way to try them. Her daughter had been to Australia and came home praising meat pies.

After seeing the store, I took a train for Haneda Airport to catch my flight back to Kyushu. I couldn't wait to escape Tokyo. I still had a few friends living there but being among the crowds and the density of everything was a form of slow suffocation. Life in Kyushu had changed me forever. As I walked through the departure lounges at the airport I noticed a huge advertisement for JA Bank, which used to be known as *Nōrin Chūkin*, or the Japan Agricultural Savings Fund. How things change. The poster showed a row of happy Japanese people standing in a field of ripened rice ready for harvest. The group included some children in formal kimono, elderly people, mothers, and a couple of farmers beaming with delight at their good luck for being able to deposit money in, or maybe borrow some, from the JA Bank. I thought of Aunt Tsugika and her husband Hiyoshi-*san*, both hospitalised. They were not so lucky these days.

When the flight from Tokyo arrived in mid-afternoon I drove out of Fukuoka Airport and headed inland for Hita. I got there in time to watch the last couple of sumo bouts in which the two senior Mongolians clashed: Harumafuji deafeated Hakuhō to set up a real contest for the tournament

Ten   Cousin Kyoko's Orchard

instead of Hakuhō winning as usual. Our man Yoshikaze from Oita went down in his bout to stand at a 7/6 win-loss record, thus risking demotion if he couldn't win at least one of the two remaining bouts.

The television news had a story about a smash-and-grab robbery at the Harry Winston jewellery store in Omotesando, not that far from the Pie Face store in Shibuya. It sounded very unlike the *yakuza* to carry out such a disturbing crime. Maybe it was Russians, I thought.

After a meal of the best *gyoza* in Kyuhsu — from Yano-*san*'s tiny restaurant Ippinshan two doors down from us — I went to bed exhausted from the travel.

The next morning, a Saturday, the Nikkei newspaper was reporting Prime Minister Abe as pledging to Obama that he would send Japan's Self-Defense Force to help with the confrontation in the South China Sea. This struck me as a bad but inevitable portent of the future. The ASEAN countries were hopelessly divided in facing up to the Chinese, too weak or too timid to defend the sea lanes. The US defence budget was being cut. So, Japan had to step up and help. Sending Japanese naval vessels into the South China Sea on active service was one very big and controversial step to take. The Nikkei carried a small commentary piece saying that whatever Abe's ambitions — and they were not small in the defence area — Japan couldn't spare any vessels from their task protecting the Senkaku Islands in the East China Sea without leaving that area vulnerable to Chinese aggression. So, what's Abe going to do? I wondered.

Hidenori, my wife's younger brother, arrived from Okinawa. He and I used to go fishing together in my canoe in summer before his company transferred him to Okinawa. We were close friends, and I always appreciated his sense of humor and moderation about everything. His wife Katsumi didn't come with him that day. After a rest and some tea, it was announced that we had to go and pick *yuzu* for my mother-in-law to make jam and *yuzu gosho* mustard.

'Where will we go?' I asked.

'Kyoko's land,' was the reply.

'Kyoko?'

'You know, Kyoko,' said my father-in-law. 'My niece.'

'The *enoki*,' said Hidenori. 'Over near Onta.'

Ah, *that* Kyoko — Sayuri's cousin, whose father was my father-in-law's older brother, the *nakōdō* or official matchmaker at our wedding twenty-four years ago. Kyoko married a fellow named Tanaka who grew *enoki* mushrooms in a factory on the road to Onta.

We set off in my four-wheel drive car for Kyoko's *yuzu* grove. On the way my father-in-law talked in grave tones about the difficulties of getting to the *yuzu* that grew on the topmost branches of the trees.

'It's almost impossible to pick them,' he said, sitting in the back seat of the Toyota. 'I don't know how we'll reach up that high.'

'There's plenty of *yuzu* on the low branches,' said my mother-in-law. 'We're not going to pick all that many. Just enough for some jam and *yuzu gosho*.'

'Maybe we could…..Well, if there's a bamboo pole around I'll hit them high up.'

'Or perhaps we could use the roof of this car,' I said. 'Stand on top and pick them.'

'*You* could, maybe,' said my father-in-law. 'You think we old people are going to stand on the roof of a car? '

'I've heard you say more ridiculous things than that,' my mother-in-law said.

'When? I've never said that,' he replied.

Kyoko was in the *enoki* factory when we arrived. She emerged wearing a paper hair covering and a dark blue smock. After remonstrating with my father-in-law over something, she got into a light pickup truck and led us up the road towards Onta. This was the Ono River valley, one of my favourite places in Japan for its flowering trees, its little farms, and its sheer beauty all year round. Kyoko pulled over on the side of the road past Ono Village where a bridge spanned the river. She told me to leave my car there. We gathered our gloves and boxes and put them into the back of her small truck. Then she drove the truck across the bridge with my father-in-law sitting in the tray at the back smiling under his cloth hat. At one point he stood up, gripping the back of the cabin, as Kyoko drove down a mushy, grassy track that followed the river past some terraced rice fields into the *yuzu* grove. Hidenori and I walked behind.

Once inside the grove she parked the truck and we went about preparing to pick the *yuzu*. The ground beneath the trees was moist and covered with dark green moss. I took a wicker basket and a pair of clippers, choosing a tree heavily laden with *yuzu* where I started harvesting the low-hanging fruit, trying to cut the stem as close as possible to the fruit and then catch it before it hit the ground. It was difficult to reach them without getting pricked by the many thorns on the branches. Soon my father-in-law appeared with a long bamboo pole. He looked around and announced that my tree had the best *yuzu* up high. Standing to one side he hefted the pole and began poking and shaking the upper branches. A few moments later a dozen *yuzu* came raining down on my head and back as I was tackling the lower branches.

Picking yuzu fruit in Aunt Kyoko's orchard with my brother-in-law Hidenori. My father-in-law (standing in the truck) took charge, shaking the trees and gleefully raining the fruit down onto my head.

'*Otoosan!*' cried my mother-in-law. 'The *yuzu* are hitting Andrew! What the hell are you doing?'

'He's okay,' said my father-in-law. 'He's down low. It's no problem.'

Kyoko observed all this without comment, carefully moving away from my father-in-law's vigorous work with the bamboo pole.

'They're hitting him, right now. I saw it,' my mother-in-law said angrily.

'He's fine. Just a few *yuzu*. I'll get some more.'

'Maybe you'd better move,' said Hidenori.

'Sure. I'll try another tree,' I said.

'Hey, don't forget those ones that've fallen,' said my father-in-law. 'Pick them up. They're good. And you won't get any thorns in you if you wait for them to fall.'

I did as he asked, amused by the incident. More *yuzu* fell around me into the moss and the mud. At another tree I soon filled my wicker basket. And then another. Soon we had filled the cardboard box we brought as well as a large, reinforced paper bag. Both were loaded into the back of Kyoko's pickup truck. She executed a neat U-turn within the grove while I took artistic photographs of some *yuzu* I'd placed on a rock near a tiny stream.

We transferred the box and bag of *yuzu* to my car back on the side of the road. A man had appeared close by digging in a vegetable patch behind a deer-proof fence. My father-in-law began talking to him, so I greeted him too.

'Damn good vegetables you've got there,' said my father-in-law.

'Lots of them,' said the man as he dug, squatting down.

'This fence is very strong,' I said. 'It keeps the deer out, I suppose.'

'*Maa, ne.*' Which meant "perhaps" in this context.

'Are there many deer around here?'

'Too many. They're everywhere up in the forest.'

'I suppose they come down at night.'

'Daytime, too. In the daytime you see them.'

'*Maa*, that's terrible,' I said.

We bid Kyoko good-bye at the roadside and drove back to Hita, stopping at the Sofuren *yaki soba* restaurant for lunch. The meal was as good

The bamboo candles at the Sennen Akari festival on the Kagestu River in Hita. This festival is one of three held every year in Hita.

as ever. On the wall of the restaurant I noticed a couple of posters. One of them announced an event entitled "Hita-Kon — *kapuringu paatii*." Coupling party. In other words a singles night for unmarried Hita men and women, sponsored by the Hita Chamber of Commerce. "Lady participants warmly welcome!"

The tag line on the poster read, "Will you find your Santa?" Just what Santa and marriage had to do with each other in Hita was left to the imagination. In my experience, not many single men in Hita looked like Santa.

The other poster carried a long Chinese poem that was the origin of the name Sofuren, which means roughly "The Love of Couples Together" in Chinese.

Over lunch I asked Hidenori about all the political trouble in Okinawa, the struggle between Governor Onaga and the Japanese Government over the new US base to be built on reclaimed land at a place called Henoko. Okinawa Prefecture and the Government in Tokyo were heading to court about the Governor's purported cancellation of the construction permit for the sea reclamation, and there had been the usual citizens protests in Okinawa.

'There's always some sort of trouble going on,' said Hidenori as he ate his *yaki soba*.

'This time it seems quite serious,' I said. 'They're going to court about it.'

'Well, it doesn't affect us in our office,' he said.

'That's good.'

'Okinawans are always arguing about things,' said my father-in-law, who had been down there once some decades ago. 'They like arguing.'

'They'd rather live without the fights, I think,' said Hidenori.

'Well, what can we do, then? They're part of Japan!' said my father-in-law.

Yes, they are, I thought, but not a hundred percent so in their minds any more.

By evening my mother-in-law had gone to great lengths washing each of the *yuzu* in the tiny bathroom on the same floor as the kitchen. A short time later she was squatting down on the floor in the kitchen diligently slicing the *yuzu* one by one and squeezing them with both hands so that the juice collected in an aluminum bowl. She put the squeezed halves into a big plastic bag for the next step.

'Let me do some of that squeezing,' said my father-in-law from where he lay on his side by the *kotatsu* table watching the sumo broadcast on the television.

'Quiet! Don't interfere,' said my mother-in-law.

'Hey, let's go out and get something to eat,' he said.

'There's lots of food left over from last night,' I said. 'Surely we can eat that here at home.'

'No,' he declared, 'I'll go out and buy some sashimi. Later I'll go. Got to watch the sumo.'

In the kitchen there was an overpowering smell of *yuzu*. Hidenori was busy by the sink washing the plastic trays from the refrigerator. The sumo broadcast was turned up very loud because of my father-in-law's poor hearing. My own hearing was damaged from careless conduct at clay target shooting a year ago, and the ambient noise was torture. I watched as Yoshikaze and Gōeidō lined up for a bout. They clashed, and a violent exchange of *tsuppari* thrusting and slapping erupted. Yoshikaze went berserk and gradually pushed Gōeidō backwards until he'd got him out of the ring. *Kachikoshi* for our Oita man — a majority of wins over losses. Thank the gods for that.

Former *yokozuna* Chiyonofuji — now called Stablemaster Kokonoe — appeared in the commentary box with the NHK presenter mourning the great *yokozuna* Kitanoumi who had died the previous day of bowel cancer. The tournament atmosphere had changed. Kitanoumi, Chiyonofuji, and the younger Takahanada were the last of the Japanese Grand Champions before the Pacific Islanders and Mongolians took over the top ranks.

Eleven

The Teacher and the Defacing of the Graves

Winter came again to Kyushu. At first the skies were generally clear, winter being the dry season in Japan. Without much wind the sea was crystal clear along the edge of the beach. I swam again at dawn and in the evenings, the water now very cold. Coming out of the sea my lower legs ached, but the shock to the body was delicious, the whole effort worth the pain.

After the harvest many of the rice fields had been left fallow as the days got colder. Now a bright green carpet of grass covered these fields while others were planted with a winter crop of barley or wheat. Around Funakoshi the fishermen and farmers wore hats and coats to keep warm as they walked, cycled, rode their ageing scooters, or drove their small pickup trucks here and there. The oyster hut restaurants in the port were in full swing now, the carpark choked with cars on weekends and busy on weekdays. The fishing families of Funakoshi were making good money again. With the international oil price way down fuel was cheaper than ever, and those fishermen not involved with the oyster huts were out every day in their vessels hauling in the winter catch. It is an article of faith among Japanese people that fish tastes better in winter.

I had come back to Kyushu on Boxing Day after spending a month in the heat of the early Australian summer, enjoying my days and nights there seeing friends, spending time with my parents and with Sayuri, Sara, and Cail. Sara, now nineteen, had become an admirable young adult. I worried about her future as fathers always do, but she seemed to have enough street sense to remain in charge of her destiny. My parents were ageing, especially my father, and they got a lot of pleasure from my being back there and around to help with various tasks and share meals with them. I loved family life, both with my wife and children and with my parents and sisters. Yet the comfort and excitement of life in Japan — the safety, the sense of public courtesy, and the scale of the threats from North Korea and China — was easy to miss.

Once Christmas was over I flew back to Japan. Sayuri and Cail had already gone there a few days ahead of me. Sara stayed in Australia to pass the summer with her friends. This was no great surprise or disappointment. It would be a test of her maturity and sense of responsibility to look after our house in Melbourne with its garden, the cat and the dog. Children must learn the burdens of adulthood somehow.

As soon as I arrived in Fukuoka, where Sayuri and Cail met me at the airport, we drove to Hita to spend a few days with Sayuri's parents.

'Oi, Andrew!' my father-in-law greeted me cheerfully. 'Are you okay?'

It was his habit to express a degree of amazement that anyone who travelled outside Japan could come back in good shape. For a man who rarely left Hita the outside world was a fearful ordeal.

'Thanks, I'm fine. It's pretty cold here now, eh?'

'Oh, it's cold. It's really cold. Winter, you know.'

'It's actually a warm winter so far,' Sayuri chimed in. She and her parents had a generally tense relationship, a stark difference from my own relationship with them. Unlike me she had a hard time tolerating their dotage. Where I rather enjoyed the mild confusion and fuss inherent in the way they lived — a wonderful antidote to the pressures of modern life in the urban and international world with its emails, traffic, and multifarious threats — she grew annoyed by almost everything they said and did. There was nothing I could do about this. I was the son-in-law, the outsider whom they treated with affection. She was their daughter, and she had firm — nay, unshakeable — views about how they should live.

If truth be told, she could see things about their steadily declining health and lifestyle that I could not see, or that I just overlooked and accepted as part of their life in Hita. I thought they were happy as they were, but with Sayuri there in their home I began to doubt my own judgement. All I knew was that my in-laws and I enjoyed each other's company and that they had nobody but me to buoy them up and entertain them when their son and daughter were away, which was usually the case. Like a great many, if not most elderly people in Japan, they lived quite apart from their children.

While staying in Hita we spent the days exploring by car, something we had always done every year when we went back there after getting married twenty-five years ago. In the past we usually took my parents-in-law with us and travelled across Kyushu to an *onsen* to take the waters and enjoy a night in a traditional *ryokan* with its elaborate Japanese meals and perfectly clean *tatami* rooms. But this time we didn't have the energy to travel far. And besides, Sayuri declared that her parents would be coming to stay in the house at Funakoshi after New Year. So, we decided to concentrate on staying local and searching for new *onsen*, restaurants, and whatever else looked interesting. A winter holiday around Hita is not a stimulating world full of wonder, but it has its own slow pace and can be entertaining enough if you go off the main roads in search of something new.

Sayuri's instinct for a good bath took us to Harazuru Onsen where Aunt Tsugika was lying in hospital, unlikely to return home to her grape orchard. This place was only twenty kilometres down river from Hita, not far past my mother-in-law's childhood home and just across the Chikugo River from the Mizu Jinja. After visiting Aunt Tsugika in her hospital, for a bath we chose a modern hotel called the Hanamizuki in what was a very small town — really a collection of mostly ageing inns and hotels all with their own hot spring — and received a delightful surprise once settled in the bath. The water was so mineral-rich it made your skin slippery, and it had a mild but distinct smell of sulphur. At ¥800 per adult the price of the bath was not cheap by local standards, but the hotel was an upmarket one and there were no fewer than six hotel staff members between the front door and the entrance to the bath to bow and wish us a warm welcome. The comfort and luxury of such service is what you enjoy paying for in Japan.

Cail and I and my father-in-law lay in the men's bath for a while soaking up the minerals and the sulphur. It was our habit to emerge from an *onsen* a good twenty minutes before Sayuri finished. When we had dried ourselves and dressed in warm winter clothes we went outside to the half-empty carpark and began playing cricket with a rubber ball and a remarkably well-made cricket bat Cail had fashioned from pieces of wood, nails, and a few screws. It seemed he had a talent for making things. I bowled slow off breaks while he batted, using a back wheel of our car as the wicket. An old man walked past and stared at us for a while.

'*Konnichi wa*,' I said, and offered a quick bow.

He replied with a similar bow and a quick '*Ooh*' grunt. I noticed he wore a fedora hat against the cold, similar to the Minister of Finance, Taro Aso.

'*Kuriketto desu*,' I said. It's cricket. I knew this wouldn't mean anything to him, but it seemed polite to offer some explanation of what we were doing.

'Baseball?' he replied.

'Ah, similar. But different. It's from England, and Australia.'

Cail was looking both nervous and impatient, keen to keep playing but wary of our being scolded for doing what nobody would dare do except some *gaijin* — using a carpark for playing ball sports.

'*Ooh*,' the man grunted again and continued on his way. The young man from the Hanamizuki hotel staff who had been standing outside the front door when we arrived had vanished inside. We were safe, and I started bowling again. Sayuri emerged from the hotel with her parents in due course and said nothing about the cricket. She strongly approved of ball sports and, provided nothing was being damaged saw nothing wrong with using a mostly empty carpark for some post-*onsen* practice.

At night in Hita we usually ate at home around the *kotatsu*, whose warmth on the feet and calves was a necessity given the single-digit temperature in my in-laws' home. What I didn't realise was that in their old age they had begun to lose their sense of temperature. For some reason the heating in their home had been disconnected during the summer and they hadn't got around to having it reconnected. I was a bit shocked to discover this. Sayuri took it as a timely opportunity to chide me for thinking I knew all that was going on in their lives.

In Hita, like most country towns in Japan, you can go out and buy an extraordinary range of things to eat for dinner. Because Sayuri and Cail were there we extended the shopping spectrum for food beyond the norm. Besides the usual treats of *gyoza* from the small, eight-seat restaurant Ippinshan next door, dark red *basashi* (horse sashimi), *kara-age* deep-fried chicken, and *torisashi* (chicken sashimi), we ate some delicacies the family had received as gifts. One such item, a gift from Sayuri's sister-in-law Katsumi's parents who lived in Hiroshima, was a jar of mashed crabmeat and *uni* sea urchin, made in Hokkaido. Although intended to be eaten with a bowl of rice, we ate it on its own in tiny amounts with chopsticks and washed it down with a premium *sake* called Shinzui (which means "essence, mystery") from the Saijoutsuru Brewing Company of East Hiroshima served chilled in a glass. As a winter pre-dinner starter this was the tastiest thing I had eaten in a long time.

A week later we went to Tokyo. Both Sayuri and Cail were to fly to Spain in a few days for a soccer camp and matches against Real Madrid and other Spanish football clubs, and they both wanted a few days in Tokyo to catch up with old friends (Sayuri) and former school pals and soccer team mates (Cail). I had Pie Face business to do there, though I went alone by Shinkansen via Osaka to present New Year greetings to Pie Face's Japanese partner Duskin, whose head office was in Osaka. In Tokyo we stayed with friends who lived between Shibuya and Minami Aoyama, where we'd lived until three years ago. I spent one day alone with Cail visiting the Pie Face shop in Shibuya and having lunch there. Because Duskin had decided against providing tomato sauce in the shop to go with the pies we, as Australians will do, bought our own tomato sauce beforehand and used it on the pies we bought. We shared it with an Australian family who came to eat there while we were seated, much to their delight.

'A pie without tomato sauce is like sushi without soy sauce,' said the mother.

I left Tokyo before Sayuri and Cail flew to Spain. I felt especially sad to part after having such fun in Kyushu together. I took the Shinkansen back to Osaka to sign some tax documents at Duskin's office. On the next leg from Osaka to Fukuoka I noticed that none of the rice fields were planted with a crop of winter grain or grass until we were well past Hiroshima. Such is the difference in local climates, I thought. Once back in Kyushu I spent a cold night alone in Itoshima before loneliness made me decide to go back to Hita to spend time again with Sayuri's parents. Spending the weekend alone in Itoshima was too much to bear. With wife and son suddenly gone my mental resilience was at a low.

The next morning, a Saturday, I packed a bag of clothes and headed out as usual to the expressway. The Shojimas' Family Mart convenience store was closed, a new one under construction immediately next door. A big sign said it would open again in a month. I wondered what my friend Miss Shojima was doing in the meantime.

Heading back to Hita the lure of the waters at the Harazuru Onsen was too great to resist, and there was the memory of playing cricket with Cail in the carpark. I left the expressway at the Haki-Ukiha exit and drove straight to the Hanamizuki hotel for a bath. It wasn't the same without Cail in the bath with me, but I did my best to enjoy it. Afterwards in the carpark I noticed something odd on the mountain east of the town. There was a large building that looked like a Swiss chalet with a large sign that read *Ohru Goru* and a huge coloured statute of what looked like a Madonna, doubtless a Buddhist Kannon or Goddess of Mercy. I hadn't seen this before now. Being alone there was no reason to hang around, so I drove off towards Hita, stopping on the way at Tobitaro to buy some *yuba* tofu for my parents-in-law and a *sofuto kuriimu* ice cream for myself.

One of the best things that happened that winter in an intellectual sense was the delivery of a book I'd ordered a few weeks ago, a biography of Fukuzawa Yukichi, a native of the nearby town of Nakatsu and the founder of Keio University. Fukuzawa, whose face is featured on the ¥10,000 note, is famous as one of the first figures in Japan to open a school for Western-style education, which still survives today as Keio University. What really made Fukuzawa's character was being born into a family near the bottom of the samurai ranks. This class system was almost inviolable. Once born into a place in the hierarchy you could never rise, except perhaps during wartime, when particularly skilled samurai could occasionally be promoted through good fighting and swordsmanship. But in peaceful times you were stuck and Fukuzawa hated this. As he wrote in a passage entitled *My revolt against feudalism*:

> "The thing that made me most unhappy in Nakatsu was the restriction of rank and position. Not only on official occasions, but in private intercourse, and even among children, the distinctions between high and low were clearly defined. Children of lower samurai families like ours were obliged to use a respectful manner of address in speaking to the children of high samurai families, while these children invariably used an arrogant form of address to us. Then what fun was there in playing together?.....I was sure I was no inferior, not even in physical power. In all this I could not free myself from discontent though I was still a child."

In 1983, I attended Keio University for a year as an exchange student from the University of Melbourne where I was studying law, together with Japanese and Mandarin Chinese for an arts degree. I was a lot better at the languages than in my studies of the law. At my school, Geelong Grammar, there had been little emphasis on formal scholarship — writing with footnotes and logical construction — the emphasis being placed on character-building, boldness, and adventure. Thus, I was unprepared for the mental method necessary for being a good lawyer. But the boldness and risk-taking needed to master a foreign language was right up my alley. The Japanese teachers at the university recognized this and chose me to attend Keio as that year's exchange student.

When I got to Keio I attended classes in Japanese language and culture at the main campus in Mita, an area of Tokyo south-east of the Tokyo Tower. This campus was the original one and there was an old wooden building painted white close to our classroom. I remember being told that it was once Fukuzawa's house. I never paid Fukuzawa any attention then or afterwards until the day I took my parents-in-law to the Usa Jingu Shrine and the thought came to me of visiting Nakatsu to see Fukuzawa's family home.

Who was this man? The best summary comes in the first three sentences of the foreword to the 1991 reprint of the 1899 edition of his autobiography, entitled *Fukuō Jiden* or *Autobiography of Aged Fukuzawa*, written by Albert Craig, the distinguished Harvard historian and Fukuzawa scholar:

> "Few historical transformations match in scope or drama that of Japan during the second half of the nineteenth century. Rarer still are instances when one can point to a single figure and say, here is the man who more than any other provided the intellectual impetus for the change. Fukuzawa Yukichi was such a man. His *Autobiography* gives us an inside view of the formation of a new Japan."

What I discovered from reading the autobiography was that modern Japan — that of the Meiji Restoration in 1868 and the rapid adoption of Western technology and institutions thereafter — came about from two revolts. The first came from three samurai domains that rose up and overthrew the feudal shogunate government in Edo (now Tokyo) and restored the emperor to a position of power at the top of a new, Cabinet-style government. Those domains were Satsuma at the bottom of Kyushu, Choshu at the bottom of Honshu where it meets Kyushu, and Tosa on the Pacific Ocean side of Shikoku.

The second revolt was a social and intellectual revolt against the stifling samurai ranking system, the classical Chinese education system, and the class system that placed the samurai at the top and the merchants at the bottom. Fukuzawa, through his prodigious translations of foreign technical, legal, and philosophical books and his own polemical writing, was the leader of pro-Western, modern thought in Japan at the time. If he hadn't made those efforts in providing the Western texts in Japanese, Japan would not have modernised as quickly and effectively as it did. History would have taken a different course.

By mid-January, having read almost half of the biography, I decided the logical next step was to visit Fukuzawa's ancestral home and the museum dedicated to his memory in Nakatsu. My parents-in-law agreed to come with me. They had become used to these weekend excursions by now, seemed to enjoy them and it was only a little over an hour from Hita by car, not an overly taxing journey. I'd never been to Nakatsu before, hardly surprising given that the town has little else of interest, to put it politely. Oita Prefecture is very mountainous, and the major towns such as Hita and Nakatsu are isolated from each other.

In the space between the museum building and Fukuzawa's ancestral home, a mud-walled, thatched roof structure, we found small pine trees planted to commemorate the visit of Emperor Hirohito in the 1950s. A few elderly visitors were wandering around touching the mud walls and murmuring about the place in the cold air. It began to rain, so I guided my parents-in-law to the car. Every minute or so my mother-in-law asked whether we were going to the castle, prompting a rebuke from my father-in-law.

'He told you we're going there. Get in the car.'

'But…..the castle….'

'Yes, to the castle. Get in the back.'

I helped her into the back seat where I'd placed a sheepskin seat cover for warmth. This constantly asking for reassurance about things was something I'd begun to notice recently about my mother-in-law. Was it because I was a *gaijin* and prone to doing odd things suddenly and without warning? Maybe. The standard definition of a *gaijin* for elderly Japanese is pretty much exactly that, and I had plenty of form in that regard. Or was it because she was outside home and hence nervous about her safety? Probably the latter. If I'd answered her question by suddenly declaring that we were going not to the castle but to Tokyo or Osaka or Beijing I suspect she would have only mildly protested.

At the castle, which required a bit of a climb, I expected my father-in-law to start moaning about his sore back. But not so. He climbed up the front steps without the usual protest. In fact, he had been twice to Dr Nakashima for acupuncture after I got such a good result there, and the beneficial effect was now plain. Inside the castle grounds we wandered into a small exhibition room to read wall displays about the castle and about Kuroda Kanbei. A lady on duty at the exhibition, wearing a purple rainproof jacket though standing inside, urged us to take a guide into the castle. 'It's free,' she said in an urgent tone as if Nakatsu Castle was the last bastion of such visitor-friendly treatment. But I demurred, knowing this would prolong the visit beyond what we wanted. At the ticket booth just beside the exhibition room the guide stood waiting for us in ambush. He was a large man with only one tooth visible and a superior smirk, talking loudly to the young girl inside the ticket booth. We ignored him and accepted tiny paper cups of some sort of herbal tea from the ticket girl.

'It's eye medicine,' she said with force. 'The lord of the castle had an eye disease, and this cured it. It's for sale,' she added, indicating a basket full of packets of the tea.

We sipped the tea in silence. It tasted woody but not unpleasant.

'*Otoosan*, you've got an eye problem, right?' I said.

'*Saa*, a bit,' he replied, wary of the question. In the past I had driven him all the way to the Hayashi Eye Clinic next to Hakata Station in Fukuoka for examinations. Yet he didn't wear glasses and as far as I knew had excellent eyesight for a man his age.

'Maybe we should buy the tea for you.'

'Ah, ooh, well…..I don't know that I need it.'

'Good idea,' said my mother-in-law who loved a good traditional remedy.

It was expensive stuff at ¥1300 for a packet of ten large tea bags, but I bought it anyway, being curious about such things. On the back of the packet the label said it was made not in Nakatsu, not even in Kyushu, but in Ibaraki Prefecture north of Tokyo! And there was nothing about what herb it was made from. I felt cheated, a rare experience in Japan.

'What is this herb?' I asked the ticket girl.

'It's from that tree there,' she replied, pointing to a small sapling in a pot plant to the left of the ticket booth. A sign stuck into the soil of the pot read "*Kaede.*" A maple.

'So it's a *kaede?*' I said.

'Ah, that's the tree it comes from. The leaves and the bark are mixed up,' she said. 'It cured the lord's eye disease, really it did.'

'*Maa* ' said my father-in-law as he finished the tiny cup of tea. He was something of a sceptic when it came to herbal remedies, preferring a good dose of Western medicine which was very heavily subsidised by the government. Later on, I read some internet material explaining that maple has long been used in traditional medicine to stimulate the eye nerves.

The castle was four storeys high and full of samurai armour belonging to Lord Okuhira and his descendants. The Okuhira clan had taken over the castle after the Kurodas. I had seen this sort of exhibition many times before and was not particularly taken by it, but my mother-in-law suddenly became excited while standing in front of one of the displays.

'Look at that red stuff,' she said, pointing inside a pair of metal shin and foot guards. 'That red colour came from their socks. It means the armour was actually used. And see the dents, the damage to that metal. That shows it was actually used in a battle. *Maa.*'

It was true. Despite her increasing lack of awareness of things, she was sometimes sharply observant. The metal had been obviously damaged. This probably meant that Lord Okuhira had himself been involved in the fighting. Why the damage to his shin and foot guards? Senior samurai rode horses into battle. His opponents on foot would have slashed at his legs with swords or spears. This was the real thing. Impressed, out of respect for Lord Okuhira I climbed the remaining three storeys to the top of the castle to survey the town.

On the way out of the castle grounds we stopped at the ticket booth to shelter from what was now serious rain. The fat, one-toothed guide was still standing there waiting for someone to engage him. I felt sorry for him now. If he had gone to the trouble of studying up about the castle it was a pity to let that knowledge go to waste. So I asked him about the boats that used to sail from Nakatsu to Sakai. Where was the port from where they took on passengers?

'There's a landing on the riverside,' he replied. 'That's where the boats took on passengers. They left the river according to the tides.'

'That's right,' said my father-in-law suddenly. 'The tides.' I got the feeling that he thought *he* should have asked the question rather than me.

'It took only three days to reach Osaka,' the guide said with pride. Again, the unattractive smirk appeared. 'Just three days.'

'*Maa*,' said my mother-in-law.

For lunch we drove around Nakatsu for a while in the rain, eventually finding an *udon* chain restaurant called Marukame Noodlemaking. I recalled seeing a branch of the chain in Hita opposite the McDonalds on the prefectural main road. I chose the spiced *mentaiko* and raw egg *udon*. The combination of these two ingredients (you whisk the raw egg lightly with chopsticks to blend it in with the *mentaiko*) with the soup stock and the *udon* was magnificent, so much so that I made my own version at home the next night. In Nakatsu I added a deep-fried *renkon* or lotus root to go with it, my favourite vegetable at that time.

On the way home, I suggested we stop for a bath at the *onsen* in Yamakuni, ten kilometres short of Hita. I had been to that *onsen* before after riding the Vulcan to the Mount Hiko shrine and climbing halfway up the mountain and back. But despite my father-in-law claiming to 'know this area very well,' he scotched the idea and insisted we should go to Kanpo back in Hita for a bath. I liked Kanpo, so I didn't protest. One thing about bathing at Kanpo was the *kabosu* juice in a can you could buy afterwards for ¥130. And Kanpo always had the television on in the foyer showing a broadcast of sumo during the tournaments.

But when we had our bath there my mother-in-law took an extraordinarily long time to finish, such that my father-in-law and I grew worried that something bad had happened. When she did finally emerge, she couldn't find her shoes in the shoe lockers, insisting that she had not taken a locker key. This sounded odd to me. We searched the lockers but found nothing, assuming another absent-minded old lady had taken the shoes in error. We decided I would bring the car to the front door and that my mother-in-law would go home in the slippers that Kanpo provided everyone once your shoes were in a locker. When I returned with the car I found my parents-in-law at the front counter, my mother-in-law beaming with delight. She had found a locker key in her bag after all and the shoes were retrieved. Her deteriorating short-term memory was on full display. This was not the first time recently that she had forgotten a key.

After the visit to Nakatsu to see Fukuzawa Yukichi's ancestral home I returned to Fukuoka and Itoshima for work. NHK was forecasting terrible winter weather for the next Tuesday, snow and gales and something they called a *kanpa*. When I heard it on the radio in the car I thought it was some sort of drought — *kan* usually means 'dry' in Japanese, as in *kanpai!* Or "Dry your glass!" as a toast — but that seemed odd when snowstorms were on their way. Once I saw it on television written in Chinese characters I understood — *kanpa* means 'cold wave'.

NHK and the Japan Meteorological Agency have a tendency to overdramatise weather events, which some say could possibly be related to their quest for bigger budgets, but this *kanpa* thing sounded more than the usual snowstorm in winter. Just in case the warnings were accurate I bought more kerosene for my heating stove. By Monday the temperature inside my house at Funakoshi fell to around 5°C and despite the stove and heat from the electric heater/air conditioner high on the wall I couldn't get it higher than 12°C. The ceilings of what was really a summer house were too high. I wore two cashmere sweaters and a hat while inside, along with ski tights under my trousers, uncomfortable but enough to keep warm. That night I made dinner from spreading spiced *mentaiko* mashed and mixed with sesame oil on two pieces of toast, washed down with a cheap but very adequate South African red wine.

Overnight the wind increased to around 40 knots, pretty much what you get at the beginning of a typhoon. I slept with an extra futon and blanket, enjoying the excitement of it all. The late evening news was a frenzy of cold weather warnings, mainly aimed at Hokkaido where serious blizzards were forecast to hit. Hokkaido has a Siberian climate, so this was no great surprise, but really heavy snow can be fatal. I recalled from the previous February a tragic story on the news of a mother and her two children who froze to death in their car after it slid off a road during a blizzard.

In early January, the local Oita NHK bureau had broadcast a news story about someone vandalising the grave of Lord Ōtomo Sōrin, famous as the first samurai to convert to Christianity. Over the New Year holiday period the vandals had sprayed the grave with black paint. The television showed a Christian crucifix on the grave covered with the spray paint, which looked to me identical to that which had been sprayed on some Korean slave labourers' graves at Omuta a year ago. It was probably the same person or group involved; or maybe a copycat action. But why attack this man's grave? Was it because he was a Christian convert? That smacked of real ultra-nationalism. If the Korean slave labourers in the coal mines got it, and then Lord Ōtomo Sōrin got it, who would be next? Something weird seemed afoot in Kyushu. Despite the impending bad weather, I was intrigued enough by the story to want to visit the grave and see for myself what had happened.

In snowy weather the expressways are either shut or traffic is heavily restricted. Despite all the media warnings about the snow, I completely forgot to pack tyre chains. The snow came in bursts from the sea the next morning, blown sideways by the gale. Out on the ocean the waves were ferocious. There would be no fishing for at least a couple of days and retrieving the oysters from their beds in the shallow bay at Funakoshi would be very difficult in such violent seas. I assumed the oyster hut people had stocked up on extra inventory ahead of the storm.

Sick of the cold I headed off to Hita again, partly on the pretext that my parents-in-law would need help in case of electricity blackouts, yet also keen to attempt the trip down to Usuki in southern Oita to visit Ōtomo Sōrin's grave. By the time I reached Asakura, just over halfway to Hita, the snow was fully covering the fields and occasionally falling heavily enough to reduce the traffic to 50 kph, which was the official speed limit for bad weather. It was too cold to stop for a bath in an *onsen*. I could have a hot shower in my parents-in-law's bathroom at home which they hardly ever used, always going out to a local *onsen* for a bath.

When I reached Hita I found only light snow had fallen in the town. Both my parents-in-law were excited about it. Unusual weather is something they are always proud of, lecturing me about how terribly vulnerable Japan is to such things, the unspoken implication being that the Japanese people are stoic enough to take anything, especially people in country areas such as Hita. Laughing at the difficulties of the soft people in Tokyo who slip over in snow or get drenched in torrential rain is always a pleasure. My father-in-law rushed out clad in a heavy coat and woollen hat to the nearby Sun Live supermarket (which they pronounced *san reevu*) to celebrate my arrival with some red snapper *sashimi* and chicken *torisashi*. I noticed that Yano-*san* had not bothered to open his *gyoza* restaurant that night.

'No one'll come. It's too cold,' said my father-in-law with certainty.

Maybe. I thought differently. I would have loved a plate of hot *gyoza* to go with the *sashimi*, but my mother-in-law began heating up a saucepan of *mizutaki*, a Fukuoka specialty in which chunks of chicken are cooked with vegetables in a strong chicken broth. It was very good, and I had a second bowl as we sat eating around the *kotatsu*.

'Are you really going to Usuki tomorrow?' my father-in-law asked, laughing at the idea. 'You'll never get there. They'll close the expressway on you.'

'Well, I'd like to try and go,' I replied.

'Nah. It's impossible. They're talking about *heavy* snow. It'll be terrible out there. You'll never make it.'

'What time will you leave?' my mother-in-law asked. 'Will you have a shower first?'

My showering in the mornings in addition to having a bath at night in the *onsen* was a regular source of amusement for her. You had to turn on the hot water boiler and wait five minutes before it was ready to have a hot shower. Then the hot water that came out of the tap in the bathroom was near boiling, and several times in the past I had suffered a sudden scalding before adjusting the temperature. Quite how they had no heating system anymore but still had a powerful hot water boiler on the roof was a mystery.

'I'll go around 9.30am,' I replied.

'*Saa*,' said my father-in-law, excited and sceptical of the whole idea.

On the news that night we watched a story of rare delight. In Akita, far to the north of Tokyo near the top of Honshu, snowbound in winter and famous for its tuna, apples, and manual labourers who come south in winter working on road construction projects south of the snowbelt, a two-year-old boy fell into the opening of a road drain outside his house. A man nearby heard the child's cries and instantly figured out what had happened. Cleverly, he hurried down the street and opened the next covering of the drain. Sure enough, the little boy came floating downhill with the flow of the freezing water and the man — one Yoshida-*san* — reached down into the drain and rescued him. The child had no serious injuries, just a few light abrasions and one hell of a chill. He was returned to his parents immediately, put into a hot bath, and survived without a problem.

'Well, we're just local people,' Yoshida-*san* said to the television reporters. 'I suppose it pays to have neighbours close by.'

After the bus crash near Karuizawa in Nagano Prefecture that killed twenty university students on the way to a ski weekend a few days ago, this story restored our sense of equilibrium. Japan was being squeezed by its population decline in many obvious ways, but the bus crash revealed a further aspect of this disaster. There was such a shortage of young drivers for buses that the bus companies were recruiting aged drivers and not bothering to train them properly. Thus, the Karuizawa crash saw an aged, inexperienced driver kill twenty young people whose dwindling numbers made them even more precious. Demand for bus tours had soared with the wave of foreign tourists coming to Japan, most of them Chinese tourists who were submissive enough to endure bus tours. Everyone wanted the tourists' money, but the reality was that the shortage of drivers was now a threat to Japanese lives. This left everyone dumbfounded. An Opposition legislator even asked Prime Minister Abe a pointed question about this in the Diet.

Eleven   The Teacher and the Defacing of the Graves

At least the little boy in Akita survived.

As more light snow fell that evening my father-in-law grew more excited.

'Open the curtains!' he ordered my mother-in-law who was peering out the window into the carpark at the snow. She drew the curtains aside to reveal a light covering of snow on the *bonsai* they kept on the balcony. 'Leave them open!' he continued.

'But it's cold,' my mother-in-law protested.

'No, no, we don't get snow that often, not like the old days,' he said to me, rubbing his hands. 'Look. It's starting to pile up.'

The next morning I went down to the kitchen carrying the electric heater and looked outside, expecting a solid covering of snow everywhere. In fact, there was very little, just a small dusting on the roof of my car, parked next to the fence beside the railway line. I had breakfast and over my father-in-law's protests set off for the trip to Usuki, promising to be back before dark. I got up onto the expressway heading in the Oita direction, noticing a few piles of snow on the side of the road. The traffic was sparse. When I reached the Kusu exit there was a roadblock. Only cars with special winter tyres or tyre chains could proceed further. Everyone else had to leave the expressway and use the narrow local roads. I tried to persuade the young man on duty that by using four-wheel drive I would be fine, but he refused my entreaties. Rules are rules. This was Japan, not some lawless foreign domain. I ended up on the local road, travelling slowly but not unhappy. You see more of the country this way. Expressways are boring anywhere in the world, even in Kyushu.

An internet search had revealed that Lord Ōtomo Sōrin's grave was not in Usuki where he had his castle but in a much smaller town called Tsukumi another ten kilometers or so along the coast. I reached the site of the grave by around half past eleven that morning. It was in a tiny wooded valley behind a lot of houses a mile or so back from the fishing port. I parked the Toyota and walked up a few steps to a grove of tall *sugi* cypress trees, the edge of a forest that led up the slopes of the valley. There were dozens of cherry blossom trees on one side of the hill. On a flat area of ground at the top of the steps I found two graves and a crew-cut young man wearing work clothes staring at them. One grave was made of pale marble and bore a large crucifix. The other was a Buddhist grave of dark stone inscribed with Chinese characters beneath its own special wooden roof. The ground in front of both graves was covered with fallen twigs from the cypress trees.

I greeted the young man and began a friendly conversation.

'These are the two graves,' he said. 'One Christian and one Buddhist. He's actually in that one,' he added, pointing to the Buddhist grave.

'Why two graves?' I asked.

He shrugged his shoulders. 'History, I suppose. I think his descendants argued about which one was correct, so they built two of them.'

Just then two old ladies came struggling up the steps, one of them moaning loudly about the effort it took. The older one, who was making this noise, was dressed in a quilted coat and warm trousers, wearing a black headband of sorts. She waddled past me without saying a thing and stood before the Buddhist grave where she began reciting prayers. The other lady smiled at me. She and the young man exchanged a few words and then each began sweeping up the cypress twigs with a *hōki*, the traditional Japanese broom made of thin bamboo twigs bound to a stout bamboo handle. The older lady finished her prayers and then took another broom from a cabinet and joined in the twig sweeping. Feeling embarrassed I saw another *hōki* in the cabinet, so I grabbed it and added my own efforts to the task. The young man nodded with approval.

'Do you have *hōki* brooms in Australia?' he asked.

'Not *hōki*. Only Western-style brooms. These are much better,' I said, which was true.

'That's right,' he said. 'Japanese *hōki* are very good.' It struck me that he might disapprove of the Christian grave, but I dismissed the thought as silly paranoia. He had been friendly since the moment we began talking.

I turned to the old lady who had smiled at me. 'Do you come up here regularly?' I asked.

'*Haa*,' she replied, but couldn't seem to say anything more. Maybe it was all too much being asked a question by a *gaijin*.

'Are you a descendant of Lord Ōtomo Sōrin, by any chance?'

She laughed. 'Oh, no. We just come up here for something to do now and then. We live close by. You've got to have something to do every day, you know.'

'That's true. Is there a formal association of some sort that looks after the graves?'

'There is, indeed. It's called the Sōrin Club. They come and put the *sakaki* and the flowers on the graves.'

I noticed then that both graves were decorated with *sakaki* branches which are sacred in the Shinto tradition.

'Why *sakaki* leaves?' I asked her. 'You see them at Shinto shrines. Yet this is a Christian grave, and a Buddhist one.'

'*Saa*,' she said, smiling. Only a *gaijin* could ask such a question.

'And plenty of local people come here?' I continued.

'No, not many. But it's famous. Tourists come.'

Just then a distant siren sounded. I asked the young man whether it was a *tsunami* warning.

'No, no,' he said, laughing. 'It's just the quarry up on the hill. They're blasting today. The siren is a warning, that's all.'

'It's cement,' said the old lady sweeping with me. 'It's a really big plant, you know. The biggest in Japan.'

The siren continued to wail. I gave up sweeping and took some photographs though the light was too dim for good results. I climbed the hill among the cherry blossom trees, their branches bare in mid-winter. It would be a wonderful sight when they were in full bloom. Just then a distant explosion sounded. They had indeed blasted the limestone or whatever rock it was for the cement plant. A second *boom* happened a half minute later.

I returned to the graves and thanked the young man, giving him my business card as a gesture of friendship and respect. I asked his name.

'I am Watanabe,' he said. 'Actually I'm a policeman investigating the vandalism of the graves. They sprayed both graves, you know.'

'Really? Even the Buddhist grave?'

'Yes, that one too.'

I expressed my disgust and wished him the best in finding the perpetrators. It was quite something to hear that the attackers had hit the Buddhist grave, too. They must have really hated Ōtomo Sōrin. Maybe it was his traditional enemies the Shimazu from Kagoshima who did it, though that sort of five-hundred-year-old grudge seemed unlikely. Or maybe it was the sort of ultra-nationalists who loathe even Buddhism as a foreign religion, as well as Christianity. Hard to believe, perhaps, but there were such people around. They would have cause to deface both graves.

'And you're a tourist?' asked Constable Watanabe, all business now.

'Yes, I came from Hita today, despite the snow.'

'Hita? What do you do there for a living?'

'I'm a retired lawyer.'

'Oh, I see. Well, take care then. The weather's pretty bad. And where are you going now?'

'To have lunch. What's good to eat around here? There must be a local specialty.'

'*Maguro*,' chimed in my old lady friend. 'It's the best in Japan. They catch it out at sea from our port. And remember to go and see the dolphin park.'

I thought of asking about dolphin *sashimi* but kept quiet. Bowing to all three of them I left the graves and walked to my car.

I had the *maguro sashimi-don* for lunch at a restaurant down at the port. It sat above a shop that sold all sorts of fish and vegetables, including packets of vacuum-packed fatty tuna belly, the sort of thing that fetched top price in a sushi restaurant. My lunch cost ¥1100, more than I'd expected for a meal in such an out-of-the-way place, but it was worth the money for the fresh *maguro sashimi,* and the portion was very generous. In the shop downstairs I found a group of high school students all dressed in work clothes instead of school uniforms. It looked like a work experience excursion. They seemed anything but interested in the fishing industry, the girls giggling and chatting to each other, the boys horsing around in the restrained way that Japanese schoolboys generally do.

After seeing the Ōtomo Sōrin graves at Tsukumi it remained to see his castle in the bigger town of Usuki. I drove there on local roads and

The grave of the Christian samurai Lord Ōtomo Sōrin at Tsunami, in the southern part of Oita Prefecture. Ōtomo is said to have converted to Christianity in order to marry a beautiful woman who nursed him back to health. After his death his first wife, a Buddhist, got revenge by having his bones buried in a Buddhist grave which lies beside the Christian grave. In 2015 Ōtomo's Christian grave was defaced with spray paint, presumably by an ultra-nationalist who felt a samurai should not adopt a foreign religion.

found the place near the sea in the town. It was a huge fortified mound surrounded by supermarkets and offices with plenty of car parking space that gave the place a fresh, open sort of feel. The castle itself did not have a keep or tower on it, just massive stone walls and a moat full of ducks.

Disappointed by the lack of any structure to explore, I looked around for a while but there didn't seem to be much else other than two ancient bronze cannons. As I was walking out of the grounds I passed a roofed wooden platform that served as a minor shrine. On the outside wall I noticed two pamphlets suspended from strings, plainly there for passers-by to browse. I stopped to look at them and saw one bore the title "Iwojima Battle Memorial Society". Inside were pages about the battle on Iwojima.

Lord Ōtomo Sōrin's Buddhist grave in which his bones lie.

The other pamphlet was a tribute to the life of General Tadamichi Kuribayashi, commander of the Japanese garrison on Iwojima. Portrayed so well in Clint Eastwood's film *Letters from Iwojima* by the actor Watanabe Ken, heir to Takakura Ken's tradition of manly cinematic performances, Kuribayashi was very much what the film conveyed: a literate Japanese gentleman with detailed experience of life in America, a humane and skillful military commander, and a man convinced of the lunacy of taking on the industrial might of America. That, some say, is why his enemies in the Tōjō Government decided to send Kuribayashi on what was essentially a suicide mission to defend Iwojima.

Why was this pamphlet about him here in Usuki? For inspiration? Perhaps many of the men on Iwojima were from Oita Prefecture. Or maybe some were from Usuki itself. There was nobody around to ask about this, the shrine office being closed and uninhabited that cold day. I left the pamphlets on their strings and walked out of the castle in a sombre frame of mind.

All restrictions on the expressway had been lifted by late that afternoon. I sped all the way back to Hita and got there in time to watch the last half hour of the sumo tournament on television. Kyushu's — and Japan's — hero of the moment, the chunky wrestler Kotoshogiku who came from Yanagawa City in Fukuoka Prefecture at the mouth of the Chikugo River, managed to overcome the hitherto unbeatable Mongolian grand champion, Hakuhō, to take the lead in the tournament. The prospect of a Japanese wrestler winning a sumo tournament for the first time in ten years suddenly became a possibility.

Three days later, having vanquished the Mongolians and all others, Kotoshogiku stood smiling and a bit tearful on the sacred *dohyō* mound to receive the Emperor's Cup as tournament champion. Japan was back in the business of winning again.

Lord Ōtomo Sōrin

Twelve

The Kirishitan Relics

A few days later the cold wave was still with us and struck Kyushu with a serious snowstorm. I was back in Itoshima and the temperature inside the house fell to 3°C. This was now painful, and I wore a hat and three cashmere sweaters while waiting for the kerosene stove and the wall heater to remedy the situation. After an hour the temperature rose to 5°, then 8°. It was so cold I lost my appetite and had only a piece of toast for dinner. Overnight the pipes froze, and no water flowed from the taps in the morning. Fortunately, I had not emptied the bath from two nights ago, so there was water by the bucket available for ablutions and for boiling. But in such cold, and without running water, it was pretty well impossible to do emails and work, let alone have a bath and cook properly.

I visited a client's office in Fukuoka for a meeting, conscious of not having had a bath or shower for more than a day. My work for this client required me to go to the Fukuoka Bank to arrange a small transfer of funds to China to buy some lubricant oil samples from a company in Qingdao. I went to the local branch but was told I needed my *mai nambaa*, a national identification number that had just been introduced for the purposes of well.... whatever problems the government wanted to solve by tracking our every major transaction: tax avoidance, welfare fraud, you name it. I had received my *mai nambaa* card a month ago and of course had lost it. Silly me. The only solution was to go to the Hita City Office and get another *mai nambaa* card issued. The woman at the bank branch nodded and said no money could possibly be transferred overseas without it. It was a *ruuru*, you see: a rule or regulation in modern, Japanese officialese.

I drove to Hita on the local roads, the expressway being shut because of the snow, the chains on my rear wheels making a violent jarring all the way. It took four hours, but I got there in time and applied for a new *mai nambaa* card. While I was waiting for the card I noticed a man reading the local Oita Godo Shimbun newspaper which carried a front-page story with a colour photograph headlined:

KIRISHITAN RELICS DENIED
Survey by Kunisaki City Education Committee Specialist Team
Doubts About Probable Period of Making

I was instantly intrigued. The next morning I went to the Hita branch of the Fukuoka Bank to resume the battle to send the money to China. Fortunately, they still had a copy of the previous day's Oita Godo Shimbun, so while waiting for the transaction to be reluctantly processed I read the article. Inside the bank a slow version of the Tennessee Waltz was playing.

According to the article, Kunisaki Town's Education Committee had engaged a committee of specialist archaeologists to determine matters surrounding some unusual stone carvings found in sixteen places around the Kunisaki Peninsula, including the town of Kunimi. The stone carvings had previously been recognised as Kirishitan relics. Kirishitan was the old word for Edo Period Christian things, now the modern term is *kirisuto-kyō*. The committee of specialists had shocked everyone by announcing a finding that the carvings "could not be recognised as Kirishitan relics". This was because of doubts about the probable time the carvings were made and because certain Buddhist and Shinto-like motifs were included in the carvings.

Worse still, the committee said the carving was probably done around the beginning of the 18th century, well after Christianity had been officially banned, making it very unlikely that anyone would dare to make such a thing. Kunimi was the town where the Catholic martyr Petro Kasui (1578-1639) was born. Kunisaki Town had joined forces with five other towns and hamlets around the Kunisaki Peninsula to promote these Kirishitan relics and was preparing to apply for them to be registered as National Cultural Assets.

Naturally, local officials were outraged by the committee's conclusions. They went to great lengths to promote tourism to their area. The mayor of Kunisaki, Mr Akashi Mikawa, was quoted as saying, "Petro of Kibe's existence is an undeniable fact, and this [the specialist committee's report] will have no effect on our honouring his memory."

Well said, Mr Mayor, I thought.

I loved these sort of stories, as much for imagining the consternation among the locals at the specialist committee having trashed their tourism strategy. Somehow it was good news that Nagasaki did not have a monopoly on Hidden Christian history, as is commonly thought these days. Especially amusing was the revelation that the chairman of the specialist committee — one Ōishi Kazuhisa — was from none other than Nagasaki, and what's more was an employee of the Nagasaki Museum of History and Culture! Obviously, there was a conspiracy here somewhere. A man from Nagasaki — a history official, no less — had come over to Oita to badmouth our relics! One can only imagine Mayor Mikawa in the city council chamber lamenting his bad luck at this outrage.

A few days later I went into Fukuoka to resume the battle with the Fukuoka Bank over the unpatriotic issue of transferring funds overseas, this time to Australia. My plan was to make the transfer using the bank's website to avoid further frustration by the bank. I armed myself with every possible document I could find: the company's seal, its official certificate of incorporation, my own personal seal, the company's bank passbook, and even my own bank passbook. The bank clerk, a pleasant lady named Akiko Mori, took a good half hour to register the company for a transaction using the website, clucking and sighing over my scrupulously careful filling in of the relevant form. Under her supervision I applied the company seal four times on the form.

Then she adopted an apologetic expression and said, 'Well, I must inform you that before any such transfer can be made from the company's account using the bank's website you need to wait for the temporary password to arrive in the mail. That will take around ten days.'

'But I've just chosen a PIN number for the website,' I protested.

'Ah, yes, indeed, thank you very much. But you'll need another password [*paasu waado*] to go with the PIN number. The bank will provide it to you, but only by mail.'

'So I can't do the transfer until the *paasu waado* arrives?'

'Not using the website. You'll have to come back here in person.'

'Well, that's a terrible inconvenience.'

'I know,' she said. 'But we have bank procedures to follow. There is no excuse for this, but…'

'It's obvious that the Fukuoka Bank is opposed to overseas transfers of depositors' funds,' I said with defiance. 'It's my money in the account, but you won't let me transfer it.'

'Well, no, no.'

'You see, it's necessary for us business people to do these things from time to time. But this bank is making all possible efforts to frustrate my transaction. I guess it's because the bank doesn't like seeing any money leave Japan. Isn't that really the case here?' I knew this was needlessly rude, but I had to say it.

'Not at all. Let me explain the fee structure to you.'

'I don't care about the fees. I'm sure they're high.'

'We will waive all fees for the first six months.'

'I'm glad to hear that, Mori-*san*, but the transaction itself isn't possible. You said I can't do it until the mail comes in ten days' time. Yet I plan to leave Japan next Monday for an overseas trip.'

'An overseas trip? Oh, dear.'

'And why does it take ten days to send me the *paasu waado*? I live only thirty kilometres from here. Ten days? Really?'

'Maaa…..'

There was no point in arguing any further. I left the bank frustrated and depressed and headed back to the car park. These kinds of defeats at the hands of officialdom or banks are the bane of life in Japan.

As I was walking along I noticed a new café in Showa Dori street called the Kunisaki Peninsula Café. This was too much of a coincidence to ignore. Immediately I went inside and found a display of local foods and crafts from Kunisaki along with a Vito's gelati and coffee kiosk. I looked around for a while and found among the items on display a book of photographs about an unusual local festival in Kunimi involving "good devils". The book said it was a rare festival, called the *Shujō Onie* or Devil Alteration Meeting, in which local Buddhist monks appeared in the form of devils wearing masks and woven ropes around their bodies. Local legend had it that both Shinto *kami* spirits and Buddhist spirits appeared in the form of wild devils whose beating on the backs and shoulders of believers would ward off sickness for a year. The book noted that the whole area around the Usa Jingu Shrine — meaning chiefly the Kunisaki Peninsula — was famous for its tradition of syncretism between Buddhism and Shinto, in other words the reconciliation of religions.

If this was the case, then the conclusion of the specialist committee about the Kunisaki Kirishitan relics was misleading. The people of the area had often mixed up various religions, and if the Christian martyr Petro Kasui was around in the era of the carvings — or before they were made — it was no surprise that Shinto or Buddhist motifs were used in what was perhaps a Christian-inspired carving. If anything, this was entirely the local tradition.

Such a revelation had only one consequence — I had to go to Kunisaki myself.

It's a fair hike over to the east side of Kyushu where the Kunisaki Peninsula sticks out into the Inland Sea, with the old eastern road from Satsuma and Bungo to Nakatsu running past it on the inland side where the Usa Jingu sits in all its glory. Kunisaki never had any port. That's why it was left alone over the ages. I set off from Hita early on a Saturday morning, buying breakfast from Miss Tanaka in our local Lawson store and taking the local road, Route 212 to Nakatsu, instead of the expressway. The road was surprisingly empty for a Saturday. I drove on through the drab townscape of outer Nakatsu and Usa, past the great shrine, not really happy until I hit the first tiny fishing port where the peninsula began.

I was heading for Kunimi, eager to see the INRI Prayer Stone Altar, with the clipping from the newspaper lying on the passenger seat beside me in the car together with a brochure from the café in Showa Dori and a book I bought on the various temples around Kunisaki. The coast of the peninsula was a series of very small inlets, each with its own fishing port and a few small boats. The interior was a landscape of heavily forested mountains of different heights, two of them particularly high. Hence the name Futago Temple — *futago* means twins.

Along the coast road there were plenty of *jinja*, common around farming and fishing hamlets, but few Buddhist temples. They were all up in the mountains, part of what they call the *Rokugō Manzan* Culture — All Mountains of the Six Villages — where an ascetic pilgrimage takes place every year, the adherents walking from the Futago Temple all the way to the Usa Jingu Shrine dressed in white costumes and wearing straw sandals praying as they go. The book in the café had plenty of photographs of the pilgrimage, and the English translation at the back of the author's text was unusually clear:

> "I had read about the time-honoured tradition of syncretism of Shinto and Buddhism in Japan where *kami* and the Buddha coexist, but by physically experiencing this syncretism first-hand, my view of the land became ever the more deep. The Shujō Onie festival that embodies Kunisaki is a perfect example of this, and when it rose before my eyes, it became the door that opened the world of Kunisaki to me."

This unusual religious tradition — something I had heard of elsewhere in Japan — pre-dated the Christian presence in Kunisaki by only about a century or two. Perhaps, I thought, that's why this part of Oita Prefecture had an active Christian community before the Shogun banned it. Or maybe it was due to one man, Petro Kasui, the first Japanese Catholic priest and most likely the first Japanese to set foot in Europe.

Reaching Kibe Village in Kunimi in late morning, I found a museum dedicated to Petro Kasui along with a few statues in a roadside park by a small hill. There was a neat Catholic church there too, one that instantly reminded me of Catholic churches in small Australian country towns. Say what you like about Catholics and Christians, but they've spread a lot further than any other religion. I went into the Japanese restaurant beside the museum and showed my newspaper clipping of the INRI Prayer Stone Altar to the lady in charge. It was cold outside, and the place was empty. She recognised the photo in the clipping and said we had to ask about it in the museum.

'Kimura-*san*!' she called out at the museum door. I expected an old man to emerge, but instead a pretty young girl came out. She greeted me and examined the cutting.

'Oh, yes. It's not that far away. Just down the road towards the *michi-no-eki*. Did you pass that on your way here? I'm sure you did. It's near there. It's been on television recently, in the media I mean. Quite a fuss, really. I've got a map of its location. Ah, but I must apologise, it's actually for sale. There's no excuse for this, but….'

I said I'd be delighted to buy the map. 'You need the income,' I added.

'It's four-hundred yen.'

The map was not much use, in fact, being of the entire peninsula and drawn on too large a scale. Kimura-*san* gave me detailed directions instead.

'And tell me, do you get many visitors here?' I asked. 'It's too cold now, of course.'

'Well, believers come from some distance, like Kitakyushu and Kumamoto. They do a pilgrimage around here.'

'To Petro Kasui?'

'Yes, and the relics. There's a church here, too.'

'I saw that. Do they say Mass every Sunday?'

'Oh, no. Not often.'

'Every month, maybe?'

'Maybe. It's popular with tourists.'

Driving to the location of the INRI Prayer Stone Altar, I found it a sad mixture of broken-down and abandoned wooden houses, interspersed with a few large and prosperous farmhouses. All over the place I noticed rusty, discarded vehicles, a few rice fields totally overgrown with rushes, and plenty of long neglected hothouses with only rusty ribs left. I had rarely seen such a poor, pitiful place in Japan.

It didn't take much to find the relic. Above some abandoned wooden houses past an ancient wooden shed full of rusty equipment the stone altar suddenly appeared, about a metre high with a sign next to it.

The carving on the face of the stone was barely visible, but it looked like a fish. The sign read:

"The word INRI is carved into this stone, meaning 'Jesus Our Lord of Nazareth.' And the fish motif comes from the Greek word 'iktos' which was used to mean 'Jesus Christ, Son of God, Our Lord Saviour.'"

I stood before the stone and removed my cap. The carving really did look like a fish. If the Japanese Christians did carve it then it deserved a bit more respectful treatment than it was getting now. I closed my eyes and prayed, or thought: how was it that the story of Jesus of Nazareth got this far? In many ways it was an astonishing thing. I stayed that way for a good while, and felt a strange warmth come over me. Was this a religious rapture of some sort? It felt indescribably good, as if everything would be okay. I remembered my own trip to Jordan and Israel a few years ago, but I had felt nothing like this when visiting places in the Holy Land. It was a profound few moments. Jesus' message of love for one's fellow human beings was more powerful than I'd ever thought. Japan in the 17th century was a cruel, brutal place. Maybe that's why some Japanese people so readily appreciated what the Portuguese Jesuit priests explained to them. It certainly took hold of Petro Kasui of Kibe.

As I was walking back to my car through the fallow rice fields the local government boomed out through loudspeakers the noontime music — Eidelweiss in this case. An odd smell wafted through the still air. It was garlic. Someone in one of the houses was frying up garlic.

Inland from the INRI stone relic the mountains were steep and dark, the valleys between them heavily forested. I drove up there and had cold *oroshi soba* for lunch, eating alone in an empty restaurant. The ladies on duty

Twelve   The Kirishitan Relics

The Hidden Christian rock relic at Kunimi on the Kunisaki Peninsula, Oita Prefecture. Below the square-cut hollow there is an outline of a fish with stripes on its middle. The local authorities regard this rock as having been carved by Christians, sometime after the seventeenth century. It sits in a forest on a hillside behind a small hamlet called Nishihama.

made it with grated *daikon* radish — the *oroshi* — leaving small chunks of the *daikon* that tasted slightly pungent. It was a very decent lunch, and I bought a *matcha*-flavoured *sofuto kuriimu* to take back to the car. Driving back down towards the coast I stopped at the *onsen* at Akane to sample the waters. As Sayuri had taught me, never let an opportunity to try a new *onsen* go by. The signs outside proclaimed proudly that it was a natural, unheated hot spring; the water was naturally so hot that it didn't need artificial heat. The indoor bath was small and full with three old men lying in it, so I went outside to the *rotenburo* outdoor bath. The water there was so hot that I had to slowly ease into it. In any other country there would have been warning signs everywhere.

'Really hot, eh?' said a cheerful old man who came outside to join me.

I agreed it was much hotter than normal *onsen*. Maybe 45°.

'More. It's the hottest bath in the whole district. Anyway, where are *you* from?'

'Hita. I came on a day trip.'

'Hita? But you're a *gaijin*. What's your country?'

'Australia.'

'Oh! Hey, I saw some Australians on the television this morning. They were tourists, said they'd come to Japan because we're friendly and we don't have guns. How about that?'

I chuckled. 'No terrorist attacks here.'

'That's right.'

'Immigrants are scarce in Japan.'

'That's right.'

Another old man came out to join us. He slipped into the hot bath without complaint. The first old man introduced me as 'a Japanese-Australian from Hita!' I said I'd come to look at the local temples and religious relics.

'Japanese religion comes from India,' said the second old man. He was a serious fellow without needless bonhomie. 'The Buddhism we have here came via Dunhuang in China. It's different from the Buddhism in South East Asia. It's called Daijō Buddhism. In South East Asia it's called Shōjō Buddhism.'

'Why are there so many Buddhist temples here in Kunisaki?' I asked. The first old man had gone inside, leaving the two of us lying naked in the bath. It was a very pleasant and civilised way to enjoy a cultural conversation.

'Oh, the Buddhists were always dividing into different factions.'

'Like the LDP.'

He smiled for the first time. 'Religion and politics…..similar, but they shouldn't be mixed up. I think it was the Tendai sect who built all these temples around here. They fought with the big sects in Kyoto, so maybe they came down here to escape.'

'And the Christians? There's been quite a fuss recently about the Christian relics.'

'Petro? Really? I didn't know. They were here, too.'

The Kifune cafe at Kunimi, where motorbike enthusiasts gather every weekend. The owner of the cafe said he had grown up in the area and never heard of any Christian relics until the local authorities began making a fuss over some obscure rock carvings found down the road.

After the bath the old men and I ended up in the changing room at the same time. I dried myself and dressed in silence. Then as I was about to leave I turned to them and bowed formally, thanking them for the opportunity to bathe together. Half dressed, they all bowed back and acknowledged my gratitude. It was a lovely moment.

I drove down to the coast road and went back to Kibe where that morning I'd noticed a café painted an attractive bright blue, close to the Petro Kasui museum. I walked in and found a group of middle-aged men having a loud and happy conversation, bottles of whisky and *shochu* on a table full of half-eaten food. Everyone looked at me in surprise, but said nothing. I told a lady behind the counter that I was on my own and wanted just a coffee.

'Ah, coffee?' she said nervously.

'Yes. Any coffee will do.'

'Ah. Yes. Well, please sit down.'

I took a seat on a sofa. The coffee came in due course. Another man who seemed to be working there — he wore an apron and a baseball cap — smiled at me and said to the others, 'Oooh, he's a *gaijin*.' I smiled and acknowledged the obvious.

When I finished the coffee and went to pay, the man in the apron and baseball cap said, 'Actually, we don't open for business until next Tuesday. Today's just a test run with our friends. But don't worry. That makes you our first real customer.'

This announcement was greeted by all present as a matter of enormous joy, more so perhaps because I wasn't Japanese. An astonishing turn of events: a café opens in an obscure, distant hamlet in Oita, and the first customer is a *gaijin*! What could this mean? Something good, beyond doubt. We fell to talking. They were a group of motorcycling friends. I told them about the Vulcan. Hooray! You must ride it here next time you come, they cried. Imagine that — a *gaijin* riding a Kawasaki, not a Harley!

When I said I'd come to Kibe to inspect the Christian relics that were in doubt, one of the men said, 'You know, I grew up here, and when I was a kid we never knew a thing about all that. They just put it on the shelf in those days.'

'Do you think they're genuine Christian relics?' I asked him.

'*Saaa*,' he said, inclining his head to one side.

'Of course they are,' said the café proprietor in the apron and baseball cap. 'It's okay. No doubt at all. The city government says they are, right?'

Perhaps the last word on the Christian relics of Oita Prefecture ought to go to the mayor of Takeda City, another city in the prefecture with some ancient stones. The same Oita Godo Shimbun newspaper reported that after the disastrous, Nagasaki-led specialist committee report on the Kunisaki relics Mayor Shudo Katsuji of Takeda was asked by his local media whether he intended to order a similar enquiry into his own town's Christian relics.

"We have no plan to investigate this town's relics," he declared. "These relics have been publicly recognised [as Christian] by both the prefectural *and* the national authorities."

News that week from the outside world was grim, even potentially catastrophic: official interest rates had gone negative, meaning the complete failure of the government's economic policy. The Bank of Japan's furious money-printing had not done anything to stimulate growth — how can you fight an ageing population? North Korea was preparing to launch a missile again. The conflict in Syria was raging on, and the refugees were still heading for Europe which was totally unprepared for the influx. And America was in the painful throes of its presidential primaries. The world was in utter turmoil.

But in Kyushu we had a grip on things: Mayor Shudo was one local politician who wasn't going to let outsiders play tricks on *his* relics. The Takeda City tourism strategy would prevail.

Japan is full of bizarre English names for businesses. The Garage Halloween sits opposite the Kifune Cafe in Kunimi on the Kunisaki Peninsula, Oita Prefecture.

Thirteen

Looking for Confucius

The day I set out to find Confucius in Kyushu was a cold Saturday, 12 March 2016, and five years since the great earthquake and tsunami destroyed the nuclear power station in Fukushima. For the past few days, NHK had been broadcasting stories about the disaster and the survivors, many of whom were still living in temporary accommodation. It was sorrowful stuff. Children who had lost parents in the tsunami told their stories. Everyone made an effort to celebrate the strength and stoicism of these people in persevering after suffering such a tragedy. But the sadness of what had happened dominated everything. Some 30,000 people or so had perished: fathers, mothers, grandparents, and most awful of all, several dozen school children.

Why the search for Confucius? Everyone knows he was a Chinese sage in ancient times. In fact if any one person in history embodies Chinese culture it is Confucius. So, what was he doing in Japan? I began studying Japanese language in 1972 as an eleven-year-old boy in Australia. I persevered with it through school and university, then went to live and work in Tokyo. Yet I had never heard of Confucius being worshipped in Japan. But he was worshipped, and still is worshipped, largely in Kyushu, and this is well hidden from view.

For me, the weekend detective, such a mystery was irresistible.

Before hitting the expressway, I stopped as usual at the Family Mart convenience store in Kafuri to buy a coffee and a newspaper. It was a new store, the

Shojima family's Family Mart having been torn down and a completely new, larger Family Mart built on the same site. It was a shock to learn that the Shojimas were not running the new store, and there was no sign of the young Miss Shojima who had so cheerfully served me until now. Had they given up the franchise, or had Family Mart just replaced them with a new franchisee?

I drove off towards Karatsu, heading for the town of Taku in Saga Prefecture where there was a Confucian temple of some sort. Being the end of winter the landscape around Itoshima was a dull pale green, the bamboo groves looking worn out and lifeless. I listened to BBC radio through my mobile phone. A panel of experts was discussing the intractable problem of North Korea, whose lunatic leader Kim Jong-Eun was that very day threatening 'pre-emptive nuclear strikes' on the South Korean and US military while they were holding joint exercises aimed at showing Kim what would happen if he started a fight. Kim predicted his own armed forces would 'reduce Seoul and Washington to ashes.' The panel of experts scoffed at this. A British professor raised the probability of the North Korean regime collapsing. Other panel members gravely concurred.

'The trouble is,' said the professor, 'we don't know when this will happen.'

This, too, brought on a chorus of agreement.

Amid the tired landscape of the mountain slopes I noticed a few plum blossoms, a hint of spring's warmth to come. The change of seasons in Japan, very much an integral part of life, always appears first in the forests.

Just as I entered the town of Taku and saw the signs for the Confucian temple the sun came out. The car park of the temple was enormous, but I found only three other cars there. It was early in the day, just on 10am. No doubt more of the Chinese sage's fans would turn up later. At a wooden building at the entrance to the temple grounds I found an older man in a woolen hat sweeping the gravel path and asked him where I could buy an entrance ticket.

'It's free,' he said proudly. 'Just go in.' He pointed to a wide lawn, the grass now brown after the winter, a grove of trees on the other side. Behind the trees the slope of a mountain rose up. 'The temple is over there,' he added.

'Thank you. Can I ask you something: why is this Confucius temple here in Taku?'

'Ah,' he said, delighted by the question. I noticed he wore an official name tag that read Tominaga. 'Let me give you a guided tour.'

I protested that this would be too much trouble for him, but Tominaga-*san* would not be deterred.

'You see,' he said, 'the fourth son of Lord Nabeshima was given the Taku district to rule over. Lord Nabeshima went to Korea with the shogun Hideyoshi and distinguished himself greatly, so Hideyoshi awarded him Taku as part of his domain. His fourth son was sent here to rule, but the locals resisted him. So he established the Confucian temple and the Togenshosha School to teach *jukyō*. After that the local people's respect for him grew.'

'This school,' I said, 'it was for the local samurai children to study Confucius' teachings?'

'Not only the samurai. Anyone was welcome, even the children of farmers! That's why he became respected by everyone.'

'Indeed? That's rare.'

'Well, he was a great man.'

'And there are some other Confucian temples in Kyushu, I understand. There's one in Nagasaki, right? And in Kumamoto. Do you have friendly relations with them?'

'Oh, well, the one in Nagasaki, that was built by Chinese people,' said Tominaga-*san* with just the tiniest hint of regret, meaning it was not a *Japanese* Confucian temple.

'And the one in Kumamoto?'

'More of a tourist attraction. Ours is three hundred years old, actually.'

'I see. Very old.'

'Yes, very old. We should go and see it.'

The temple sat deep within the grove of cypress trees. It was a pale red, the wood of its pillars and walls worn by the years. In architectural style it was Tang Dynasty like all Buddhist temples and much of Kyoto. We walked up the path to the gate and approached the main building. Various mythical creatures adorned the eaves: dragons, two jet black phoenix birds, and in the centre, right above where a worshipper would stand, a ferocious-looking devil with a row of sharp teeth but no chin or lower jaw.

'A devil?' I said.

'The chinless devil,' Tominaga-*san* replied with pride. 'It's famous. It eats the bad parts of a worshipper's heart when you pray here.'

So much for Confucianism being a secular moral code free of superstition. I thought it was Taoism that was full of ghosts, demons, and mythical creatures. It seemed unfair to Tominaga-*san* to take him to task on this point. I tossed a coin into the votive box and prayed for a moment. A small group of school children arrived with their teachers as we were leaving. I greeted one of the teachers and asked whether the children were here to study *jukyō*.

'They're training to be guides,' he replied. 'They are passionate about Confucius.'

'Wonderful.'

Tominaga-*san* looked on kindly as the children mounted the steps in front of the temple and began reciting something from green-coloured sheets of paper. He didn't seem to feel threatened at being put out of a job by the children.

We walked uphill to the Togenshosha School, a single-storey building in classical style. It was quiet, but the lights were on inside.

'So, people come here to study *jukyō*, right?' I asked.

'Well, yes,' Tominaga-*san* replied carefully. 'In old times there were many students here.'

'What about now? Is it a special school, maybe on weekends, for *jukyō* studies?'

'Sometimes.'

I got the distinct impression that things were not going well in the Confucian studies world these days. Indeed, I began to wonder whether Tominaga-*san* was himself really all that enthusiastic about Confucianism at all. As we approached the front door I heard the sound of chanting, or perhaps slow singing. It wasn't the monotonous sound of Buddhist sutras being chanted (Heaven forbid, in a Confucian school), but something else. Tominaga-*san* leant close to the window of the classroom to listen, the blinds drawn down to obscure all within.

'It's a Japanese song,' he announced with a twinge of disappointment.

'Not students reciting the Analects?'

'No. Other groups use this building now and then.'

In front of the entrance door to the building I noticed an unusual device. It was a font of water with a copper bucket suspended above it from two chains. A copper dipper with a wooden handle lay in the water.

'Ah, this is very interesting,' said Tominaga-*san*, now more enthusiastic. 'This is called a *yūza no ki*. You gradually fill the bucket with water,' — he proceeded to do this — ' and when it gets too full, about 80 percent, it tips over. See?' Sure enough the bucket tipped forwards, emptying itself back into the font below with a sudden splash. 'You see, Confucius told his disciples something.' He took a small, one-page pamphlet from a holder on the wall beside the *yūza no ki*. It was written in Japanese and read:

"One of Confucius' famous sayings in the Analects was: 'There is nobody who when fully satisfied does not topple over [become ruined]." This he taught to his pupils. Further, one pupil then asked, "Even if you are fully satisfied, is there a way of not toppling over?" Confucius replied, "Yes, there is," explaining that only modesty, humility, and making allowances for others can avoid ruin. In other words, one should work for a better society.'

Later I searched the meaning of the word *yūza*. It was a compound of two Chinese characters meaning 'soothe' and 'seat.' So the *yūza no ki* was the Soothing Seat Device. I thought briefly of interrogating Tominaga-*san* as to where was the seat on the device, but that seemed a bit unfair. With people singing Japanese songs in the Togenshosha School instead of reciting the Analects he was doing his best in difficult circumstances for Confucianism.

We walked back down the hill to the souvenir shop and udon restaurant above the car park where he insisted I accept an English-language pamphlet about Taku City and its various historical tourist attractions. I promised to make every effort to attend the festival on 18 April to commemorate Confucius. Thus satisfied, Tominaga-*san* returned to his tasks back at the temple entrance. Feeling like a coffee before I left I went into the udon restaurant adjacent to the souvenir shop where I found a young man wearing a *hachimaki* kerchief on his head behind the counter. He agreed to make me a coffee. I noticed a small advertisement above the counter for "Confucius miso".

'Confucius miso? What is that?' I asked him.

'Oh, it's on sale in the souvenir shop, not here,' he replied, giving me the impression he disapproved of anyone using the sage's name on a commercial product. He gave me the coffee and I paid him. 'We sell pottery here as well as udon,' he said and guided me to a corner of the restaurant where some bowls and cups were on display. 'Actually, I am Sōda, the potter.' He bowed.

'Really? Well, that's marvelous. You run the udon restaurant *and* make ceramics?'

'Yes. It's Karatsu-style pottery.'

I noticed a beautiful rice bowl with rich, dark chocolate-coloured glaze on the outside and a pale blue-green glaze around the rim. It was ¥800, and I decided to buy it. I had no shortage of rice bowls at home, but this would make a very decent gift for someone outside of Kyushu.

'Do you get many customers here for udon?' I asked Sōda-*san* as he wrapped the bowl for me.

'Not many. There's less interest in the Confucian temple these days.'

'Did you study *jukyō* yourself?'

'Not really. Maybe at school we studied it a little. I can't remember much, I'm sorry.'

'Well, the pottery is lovely. Congratulations.'

'Thank you very much. We do get a fair lot of customers here when the cherry blossoms are in bloom. This is one of the best places to see them around here. And the autumn colours are also pretty popular.'

'Well, keep up the pottery. I'll come back and buy some more one day.'

'Thank you very much.' He bowed in gratitude.

I returned to the souvenir shop and decided I had to buy the Confucius miso as a gift for my mother-in-law. She was not a great Confucianist, but she loved miso soup. At the cash register I asked the lady who was serving me what was so special about the Confucius miso.

'Ah, well, the local ladies make it by hand,' she replied.

'Does it taste special in some way?'

'Well, it comes to us via JA.'

'And its flavour? Some special attribute, perhaps?'

'It tastes very good. There are some other products from this area that also use the Confucius name. Would you like some sweet Confucius *manju* cakes, perhaps?'

I declined her offer. It was time to leave

Between my in-laws' shop near Hita Station and the old quarter of Mameda-machi there is a school called Kangi Primary School. My daughter Sara attended this school when she was eleven years old, living with her grandparents above the kimono shop. She much enjoyed the experience and became fluent in Japanese as a result. Being a native English speaker, Sara was an indispensable aide to the school's English teacher who, though she was proficient enough to teach reading and writing, could not put together a coherent sentence in spoken English. Sara, to the delight of her classmates (and the teacher) supplied this extra facility.

The name Kangi comes from the nearby Kangien, a private school that flourished in Hita from 1817 to 1872. Founded by the son of a prominent local merchant family, one Hirose Tanso, the Kangien was a Confucian school, as were all such schools in those days. For over twenty years I had driven or cycled past the Kangien oblivious of its role in educating people in the decades before Japan opened itself to the outside world with the Meiji Restoration. My in-laws had always spoken of the Kangien School in reverent terms.

Now, having been to the Confucius temple in Taku, I was suddenly curious about the Kangien. When I arrived in Hita my in-laws were out taking a bath at the Bara no Yu *onsen*. I decided to give my father-in-law's ancient Honda motor scooter a run, having paid to fix its punctured rear tyre myself the previous month. After a lot of effort to get it started I puttered off through the streets to the Kangien. When I arrived there, only a kilometre away, it was five o'clock in the afternoon and an elderly man was locking it up. He told me to come back the next morning but insisted on giving me a *pamfuretto*. When he couldn't find an English language pamphlet he began apologising profusely.

'It's okay. I can read the Japanese pamphlet,' I said, 'really I can.'

'I am most terribly sorry. There is no excuse for this. The English pamphlets are all locked up inside the office.'

'No, I like reading Japanese ones. There's more information in them.'

'I'm most terribly sorry,' he said, reluctantly giving me the Japanese version.

My in-laws returned from the hot spring in a cheerful mood. I was particularly concerned with my mother-in-law's health, but she seemed fine. I gave her the Confucius miso I'd bought at Taku.

'Oh? What's this?' she asked after I'd explained what it was.

'It's miso. Like, for miso soup.'

'Here, give me a look,' said my father-in-law. '*Ooh*, well, you can buy this at the Sun Live supermarket,' he concluded.

'Confucius miso? Really?'

'Confucius? What are you talking about?' he said.

'It's called that. It's on the label.'

'*Saaa*, I've never heard of that. Let's order some *gyoza* for dinner. Want a beer? I'm having one. How about some *shochu*? Go ahead, whatever you want.'

Much to my relief my mother-in-law ate plenty of *gyoza* for dinner.

The next morning I put my dirty clothes into the car, bade my in-laws farewell — I was going to Tokyo for the next few days — and drove over to the Kangien. There was a group of elderly tourists milling around in the small museum — Japanese, not Korean or Chinese — so I went alone to inspect the old school house outside. It had been rebuilt in its original style with a thatched roof and mud walls with cedar bark exterior up to chest height. Inside it was much like all the old samurai houses from the feudal era: wooden floors all shiny from years of shoeless feet on them and sliding doors in between the rooms.

In the garden there was a small bamboo grove and a cherry blossom tree. A young woman, rather overweight, was repairing a path made of white pebbles, painstakingly taking the dirty pebbles and cleaning each of them with a cloth before replacing them as part of the path. I approached her and said, 'May I assist you?'

'No, it's my job,' she replied. 'I do it on weekends.'

'I see. And you're a garden expert?'

'No, I'm not. But I like gardens. I like cleaning them up.'

'Do you usually work here at Kangien?'

'Sometimes. This garden needs a lot of work. There's too much shade so it gets dirty.'

I realised she had a mild intellectual disability. The dignity of work was important.

'Well, you're doing an excellent job here. I'm sorry I can't help you.'

'It's okay. I can finish it.'

Life is full of coincidences. Sometimes they spook you. Sometimes they charm you.

Back in Itoshima briefly, I prepared for a trip to Tokyo where I was to spend five days visiting law firms and Japanese companies with Deanna Constable, a lawyer from Sydney who was a partner in the law firm to which I was now an advisor on Japanese matters. All that week in Tokyo as we went up and down Marunouchi and Otemachi, the two blue-chip business districts near Tokyo Station I kept thinking about the Confucian temple at Taku. The mention of Lord Nabeshima and his clan, *daimyo* of the Saga domain, reminded me of a visit to the nearby town of Takeo with my wife and son and my in-laws the previous winter. Takeo is famous for its *onsen*, whose architecture was special, as is its local pottery style. The design of the buildings at the Takeo Onsen is what you might call Taisho period with a startling Chinese flourish. I was intrigued by this memory.

Why the Chinese architecture? Was it a Confucian influence? In those days the Saga domain included Nagasaki, which these days is its own prefecture. Were the Nabeshima lords trading with China and bringing in Chinese architecture?

Tatsuno Kingo was Japan's leading architect of the late Meiji and Taisho periods. He was a Kyushu man, born in 1854 and raised in Karatsu, across the bay from my house in Itoshima. Tatsuno designed not just Tokyo Station but many other important buildings of the era. After moving to Tokyo at the age of twenty-one when his Western learning school in Karatsu was closed down he began studying at the Imperial College of Engineering (later the Engineering School of Tokyo University) under the British architect Josiah Conder, who taught and practised architecture in Japan from 1877 until his death in 1920.

My acquaintance with Tatsuno Kingo and his architecture came about by virtue of one of those charming coincidences. Over two days in Tokyo and then in Kyushu, I kept running into his life and works. Between appointments on Friday morning, our final day in Tokyo, I took Deanna to a delightful little juice bar in an old building on the south side of Shimbashi Station before we walked up to Kasumigaseki. Outside the station I pointed out to her the old black steam locomotive in the station square which commemorates that first railway line from Yokohama to the capital, the one that Tatsuno Kingo rode as a young man on his first visit to Tokyo. At the end of that day Deanna and I walked back to Tokyo Station, me proudly pointing out the renovation of the station building and the beautiful copper domes on its roof. As we approached the main door of the station we noticed a line of black limousines and a few dozen government security men standing around watching the crowd that had gathered there. At first I thought it was Prime Minister Abe doing something at the station, but something about the level of security made me doubt this. Then it clicked.

'Hey, it's the Emperor,' I said with excitement. 'He must be about to come out. Let's wait and get a glimpse. It's pretty rare to see the Emperor in the flesh.'

We stayed for ten minutes but there was no sign of the emperor and

Thirteen Looking for Confucius

Tatsu Kingo, the Karatsu-born architect who studied in London then returned to Japan to design a number of glorious Western-style buildings including Tokyo Station and the Bank of Japan headquarters. He also designed the Tang-style entrance gate to the Takeo Onsen hot springs in Saga Prefecture.

empress. What a disappointment! With no time left we gave up and went off on our way, me to Haneda Airport for the flight back to Kyushu and Deanna to her hotel.

The next day I decided to go to Takeo. A month earlier in Australia my son Cail's clumsiness and haste had resulted in one of my wife's favourite rice bowls being smashed to pieces. It was a day in late summer in Melbourne, a warm February evening, and Sayuri was serving one of her spectacular dinners on the terrace overlooking our small but precious back garden. Cail was ordered to help by carrying out various bowls of rice and other dishes from the kitchen to the table on the terrace. In his haste he dropped a bowl of rice, the bowl disintegrating upon impact with the wooden floor and the fresh, steaming rice scattering everywhere. For an instant he glanced around in the hope of blaming someone else. But no such excuse was possible. Sayuri let fly with a storm of criticism. Cail apologised quickly and we cleaned up the rice, collecting the shattered fragments of the rice bowl along with the rice. I felt some sympathy for him, having myself broken a few bowls and so forth over the years.

'I bought that in Takeo,' Sayuri said sadly.

Later on she gave me a large piece of the broken bowl. 'When you get back to Kyushu, if you can, please buy me a replacement. You might have to go to Takeo to get it.'

I adore my wife and her dinners. Takeo being not that far from Itoshima, I was happy to promise that I'd do this for her. The husband of a woman from Kyushu commits a long series of misdemeanors in his wife's eyes, so any chance to earn some goodwill must be seized immediately.

When I returned to Japan a few weeks after the broken Takeo rice bowl incident, it was a fortnight before the cherry blossoms came out in bloom for the annual *hanami* or blossom-viewing season, one of the most important events in the calendar in Japan. The world was in its usual state of semi-turmoil: Donald Trump was rampaging through the Republican Party primaries (and causing tremors of fear in Japan, it should be said); Kim Jong-Eun was launching missiles into the Sea of Japan in a frenzy of protest at the US-Korean military exercises on foot in South Korea, *and* preparing to test a nuclear warhead; the Bank of Japan's negative interest rate policy was causing anguish in Japan's financial markets; and the price of handguns on the black market in Japan had doubled as the Yamaguchi-gumi, Japan's largest *yakuza* gang fractured into two rival gangs and prepared for an internecine war that looked like rivaling even the bloody *yakuza* war of the 1980s.

But all was not lost. The spring sumo tournament in Osaka began, and the senior Japanese wrestlers, including Kyushu's favourite sumo son Kotoshogiku, all started well. On the first day, much to everyone's surprise, the top two Mongolian wrestlers were defeated.

One small item in the newspaper did bother me, though. In the previous week's Diet committee sessions someone asked the head of the Cabinet Legal Bureau a disturbing question about Japan's Constitution: does the Constitution's pacifist clause, Article Nine, forbid the possession or use of nuclear weapons? The official replied, 'For the minimum necessary protection of our country, the use of various sorts of nuclear weapons is not considered forbidden by the Constitution.' Whilst correct in a strict legal sense, this was a shocking thing for an official of government to say in public. Why he didn't merely say 'We haven't ever considered this question,' was a complete mystery.

Later at a press conference Cabinet Secretary Suga — who really ran the Abe Government — was asked about this official reply and whether it was possible Japan could acquire a nuclear weapon capability. 'Absolutely impossible,' he said. Yeah, well, maybe not now, I thought when I read this. But with Obama, Trump, Hillary, and the collapse of American prestige, and with Fatty Kim threatening havoc on the Korean Peninsula, who knew what was impossible or not? Japan with its own nuclear weapons?

Takeo is another twenty kilometres or so from Taku on the road to Nagasaki. It's a small city, with a population of around 50,000 people, and if you ask anyone about it you'll probably hear about its *onsen*, and maybe about its popularity with Korean tourists who go there for what they call *olle* in Korean — mountain walking. Around Takeo there are a number of small mountains with distinct flat, rocky tops, unlike anything else in Kyushu. Quite why Takeo became an *olle* destinations for Koreans was beyond me. It turned out that Kyushu's tourism organisation had specifically reached out to Korean tourists who visit Jeju Island over in Korea (where *olle* began) and created four such destinations in Kyushu, Takeo being one of them. The organisation pays a million yen a year to Jeju Island in royalties for use of the term *olle*.

As with the visit to the Confucian temple at Taku the previous week, instead of taking the expressway all the way around Fukuoka I drove down past Karatsu and crossed the mountains where the old coal mines had once operated behind Imari. As I drove along the coast, occasionally glancing out to sea in the direction of Korea, I thought of what Tom Yates had said about the plans for an evacuation of the Korean Peninsula should war break out with North Korea. Kyushu was the logical place for foreign residents of South Korea to land in the event of an emergency evacuation. Both Karatsu and Imari had decent-sized ports, so we could expect arrivals there. Even the fishing ports in Itoshima could probably accommodate fairly large vessels. Thoughts of such an emergency reminded me that I hadn't got around to stockpiling what would be necessary if the worst happened: tinned food, rice, bottled water, batteries, gas canisters for the camp stove, and extra fuel for my car and motorbike. Thanks to Fatty Kim, survivalist necessity is something that comes to mind in Kyushu these days.

These thoughts receded once I headed inland from the coast and got well into the mountains. Another week of spring weather had advanced the cherry blossoms a bit, but it was still a good week away from the beauty of their being in full bloom. As I found my way into Takeo I was in two minds. Should I look for the museum of the Nabeshima samurai clan, or look for the pottery first? It's a rule of thumb in Kyushu to look to one's wife's needs before satisfying one's own curiosities, so I turned towards the *onsen* area where I thought Sayuri had bought the rice bowl. At the Takeo Onsen the large Chinese-style gate — the *romon*, built in 1914 — dominated the car park. I found a space for my car and went to examine the gate. It reminded me of Xian, with its huge white walls and tiled roof, the wooden structure of its roof a bright red. In Xian, because of the filthy air, the colours are the same but faded and dirty. A sign at the base of the *romon* gate said that the architect of the gate and the *onsen* buildings was none other than Tatsuno Kingo. Again! Twice in two days I had run into this man's works

Tatsuno had designed both the gate and the *onsen* buildings behind it. The latter were built in a style somewhere between feudal, Edo period Japanese design and the European style of late Meiji and Taisho, very pleasing to the eye.

I went into the *shinkan* building — the New Pavillion — and asked a lady in the souvenir shop whether there was a restaurant in the *onsen* grounds for lunch.

'No, there's not,' she said, 'but if you hurry you can get lunch down the street. There's a restaurant there, but it closes at two o'clock. I think you've still got time.'

'Two o'clock? That's pretty early to close.'

'Well, you'd better hurry,' she insisted.

I asked her whether there was pottery for sale down the street where the shops were located and showed her the fragment of the broken rice bowl.

'Yes, but you'd better hurry or you'll miss out on your lunch.'

I took heed of her advice and hurried back out through the Chinese *romon* gate, walking down the street past a group of tourists posing for a photograph in front of it. The shops seemed asleep. A few tourists wandered around in no great haste to do anything. One shop had a recruiting poster for the Self-Defense Forces and tiny model cars in the window. This had to be the sleepiest *onsen* town in Japan. I found the sole restaurant and went inside. It was completely empty. An old man emerged from the kitchen and smiled at me. I ordered the *champon* noodles, paid in advance, and sat down to watch the television which was broadcasting one of those idiotic game shows. A younger man came out from the kitchen and gave me a glass of water and a pair of chopsticks.

'It's not so busy today,' I said.

'Not busy, no,' he replied.

'Is it the quiet season now?'

'Quiet, yes.'

'I heard you close at two o'clock.'

'Ah, sometimes we do. It depends on the customers.'

'Well, the cherry blossoms will be blooming soon. Are they pretty around here?'

'I'm not sure.'

With this sort of attitude it was no wonder the *onsen* shopping street was bereft of customers.

I ate the *champon* alone and in silence. It wasn't as good as the *champon* in Hita, but that was hard to beat. At least the topping was generous. Afterwards I decided it was better to have a bath before looking for the rice bowl. Inside the *onsen* building that housed the baths the ceilings were high, everything made of lovely aged wood. I washed myself at the taps and chose the more tepid of the two baths, tepid being 42°C which was quite hot enough. The "Hot Bath" next to it was a scalding 44°C. Such heat in a bath can exhaust you, and I had an hour and a half's drive ahead of me.

Back at the souvenir shop there were now two ladies on duty. I showed them the fragment of the rice bowl and said I was looking for the same thing. This sort of particular enquiry brings delight to Japanese people. The exactitude of life in Japan brings out a sort of excitement, and this was no exception. They oohed and aahed about the fragment. Definitely it was from around here, they said. The pattern was local, no doubt about it. But which pottery made it? That was a mystery. One had to consult the right sort of person.

'You'll have to ask Mrs Nakamura,' said the older lady. 'She runs the tea shop down the street. She knows a lot about the different potteries around here.'

'Is her shop still open?' I asked.

'Oh, yes. She lives there.'

I went back down the sleepy street. It was well past two o'clock by now and I was pleased to see that, despite previous advice to the contrary, the restaurant was still open. As predicted, Mrs Nakamura was in her shop surrounded by packets of green tea and a few pieces of local pottery. She examined my fragment and then led me down the street to another shop which functioned as a tourist information kiosk as well as selling pottery. She went straight to the shelves, found what she wanted, and announced that the pottery that made Sayuri's rice bowl was called the Kōun Pottery. I wrote down its telephone number and later typed it into my car's navigation system. Before driving off I returned to the souvenir shop to thank the two ladies.

'Actually,' I said, 'you know that this place was designed by Tatsuno Kingo, the famous architect, who also designed Tokyo Station.'

'Well, that's right,' they replied. 'Amazing, isn't it?'

'And just yesterday I was there at Tokyo Station.'

'Really? Amazing.'

'And so was the Emperor.'

'The Emperor? *Araa*! Amazing!'

'I waited to see him, but I ran out of time.'

'How terrible.'

'I think he was returning from Fukushima.'

'Oh, dear. Perhaps he was. They had the *tsunami*…..'

'Well, anyway. Tell me, do many famous people come to the Takeo Onsen?'

'Oh, yes. But they come privately. Sometimes television crews come and film here.'

'Has Tsurube been here?'

They frowned. 'I don't think so. Not him, no. But other celebrities have come.'

'And the gate…..it's very Chinese in its design. Why is that, I wonder? Does Takeo have some special connection with China?'

Again they frowned. China was a troubled issue these days. 'We don't really know,' they said.

I thanked them for their help and took my leave, driving up into the mountains behind Takeo in search of the Kōun Pottery. When the navigation system announced that we had arrived at the desired location I could see nothing of any pottery, just a few farmhouses and a kindergarten. Two boys were playing baseball outside the kindergarten on a piece of flat, empty land. I stopped and asked them if they knew of the pottery. Stunned at being asked such a question by a *gaijin* in a car they looked blank.

'A pottery,' I said. 'It's called Kōun. Isn't it around here somewhere?'

'*Saaa*, we don't know,' said the younger boy who was batting.

'Okay, well, thanks. By the way, do you guys support the Hawks?'

The Softbank Hawks were Kyushu's only major league baseball team.

'Sure, we do,' the younger boy replied.

'Will they win this year?'

'Ah, maybe.'

'Are you guys going to be pro baseball players when you grow up?'

They looked nonplussed at the question.

'Well, thanks,' I said.

'*Sayonara*,' the younger boy said formally. Such good manners were a delight.

'*Sayonara*,' I replied. One had to leave a good impression as a *gaijin*.

I called the telephone number of the Kōun Pottery but nobody was home, just an answering machine on the other end that said, 'Sorry, we are not home.'

Takeo may be doing well with Korean tourists, I thought, but it's hard going for a man looking for a rare rice bowl.

An American friend, Andrew McDaniel, called to invite me to go *inoshishi* hunting in Itoshima early the next morning at 5.45am. That's when I was to meet him at the course maintenance office of Keya Golf Club where he worked as course superintendent. A cheerful fellow from Alabama, we had made friends after being introduced by Ty Takakuwa, a mutual friend who owned a golf course near Nagoya. Andrew, who had had been in Japan for over ten years, was the only foreign golf course superintendent in Japan. He had married a girl from Tokyo and spoke good Japanese.

I rose at 5am, had a coffee and a couple of *mikan* oranges to eat, and drove off in the darkness to meet him. We took his car and headed over towards the golf practice range that I often used at a place called Baba the other side of Mount Keya. Arriving at a farmhouse in the dim, pre-dawn light we found a man waiting for us dressed in overalls and a woollen hat. This was Brian Freeman, a Canadian, who was principal of the elementary school within the Fukuoka International School. I had heard about Brian from my British friend Humphrey Smith, who described him as a ferocious, Rambo sort of character who was devoted to pig hunting. When we introduced ourselves, instead of a muscle-bound, tough-talking Rambo I found Brian a soft-spoken, thoughtful fellow.

Two large hunting dogs appeared and Brian coaxed them into the back of a small van. I sat in the front passenger seat and Andrew sat in the back with the dogs. One of the dogs gently sniffed the back of my neck.

'Let's try over at Fukae first,' said Brian in his quiet way.

'You hunt with the dogs on public land?' I asked. 'I assume the land belongs to Itoshima City?'

'Not sure of that,' Brian replied. 'Maybe. Actually, most of it is privately-owned. If it's forest I go in there, just walking the dogs.' He chuckled.

'I see. And that's okay?'

'Plenty of people walk their dogs early in the morning.'

'Yeah, but you kill pigs,' said Andrew from the rear. Brian had used the dogs to clean out all but a few of the *inoshishi* on Andrew's golf course.

'Can't help it if a pig ends up in a fight with my dogs. Anyway, I have a hunting licence. It's all legal. Just as long as I do it way away from anyone's house there's no trouble.'

I began to understand. A lot of forests in the larger Itoshima area were classified as just that — forest, which could never be built on. Either that or there was no point in building anything given the poor state of the economy. As such these forests were havens for *inoshishi* that bred in great numbers and then came out to maraud the local farms. The local farmers were delighted to see someone getting rid of them. An absentee land owner who did nothing about the problem was in no position to complain.

We arrived at Fukae and drove up one of those narrow forest roads in the hills near the sea. Brian parked the van and released the dogs, both of which had leather jackets on them to protect their bodies from *inoshishi* tusks, with a GPS tracker attached to it so he could follow where they were running on his hand held GPS device. The dogs loped off into the forest in search of a scent. We hurried after them, climbing and descending a series of steep slopes. Being late winter the ground underfoot was bone dry. Soon we heard barking.

'They've got one,' said Brian and ran after them. Andrew and I did our best to keep up. When we came within sight of the dogs Brian was standing there, hands on hips. He said with disappointment, 'It's a badger. No pig.'

The dogs had caught a large *anaguma* and were vigorously pulling its dead carcass one way and another. That was one very dead *anaguma*. Brian pulled the dogs off the animal and we continued back towards the van. With all the noise of the *anaguma* fight any *inoshishi* in the vicinity would have long run away. I felt sorry for the *anaguma*, but what could you do? We drove over to the forest on Mount Keya behind Kanae's petrol station, but after half an hour with the dogs in the forest there we had no luck.

'You can go out half a dozen times and get nothing,' said Brian. This wasn't very encouraging.

'There's plenty of *inoshishi* in the forest behind Funakoshi,' I suggested. 'I thought they're all over the place in Itoshima.'

'Well, we're getting near the end of the season,' Brian said. 'There's been 1800 *inoshishi* caught in Itoshima over the past year. The numbers are down a bit by now.'

'Who keeps count?'

'Oh, the city. You get a bounty for each one. Ten-thousand yen for an *inoshishi* over a certain weight. Twenty kilograms.'

'Ten thousand yen? At that rate I'm surprised more people around here don't go out and hunt.'

'Well, I wouldn't encourage them. I like the money.'

'How do you get the bounty paid?'

'You have to take in a photograph of the dead pig and give the city the ears and tail.'

I laughed at this prospect. Someone in the Itoshima City Office had been designated as the *inoshishi* bounty clerk with the duty of accepting and filing the ears and tails of all the dead *inoshishi*. I imagined some bookish young man with thick glasses and the standard white shirt and dark tie carefully taking possession of the ears and tails and then putting them into a plastic bag with a numbered tag, or some such efficient clerical system of recording the catch. Our estate in Funakoshi was paying our own *inoshishi* catcher ¥5,000 per animal that he caught in his traps. And the man was no doubt getting an extra ¥10,000 from the city! This was too good to be true. I pondered applying for a trapping licence myself. With enough effort I could see myself earning an extra $1000 a month. The only trouble was I wasn't in a position to keep a dog. But using food bait and rabbit traps secured to the ground with cables I felt sure I could capture a few *inoshishi* every week.

It began to rain. With the time now 6.30am we decided to try one more forest over in the hills between the fishing ports of Kishi and Keya. Brian stopped at a point close to the highest point of the forest road there and released the dogs. It was dead quiet, the air still. The rain had stopped. The dogs found a scent immediately and took off up the hill from where we stood by the van. Brian watched their progress on the GPS device. Within a minute we heard frenzied barking and raced off after them. It was hard going up the hillside, but within a hundred metres we found them fighting a large, dark brown *inoshishi*, the hair on its mane standing upright as the dogs each bit into its ears.

'It's a boar, a big one,' Brian shouted. The boar was thrashing around trying to wound the dogs with its tusks.

Brian approached the boar from behind and grabbed its tail. He threw his knife in its sheath to me. 'You know where to stab it?'

'Sure,' I replied. I took out the knife. It had an eight-inch blade and a soft, comfortable rubber handle. I got up close to the boar, grabbed its mane, and plunged the knife in up to its hilt just behind the boar's right shoulder, aiming for its heart. The knife went in easily, and the boar gave a shriek of pain and went berserk, rounding on me with the dogs still attached to its ears. It came at me in a fury, but I side-stepped, and it brushed my right leg without getting a tusk into me. Needless to say, this was very exciting stuff.

I heard Andrew behind me shouting in glee, saying something like 'It's still fightin', that boar.' Unfortunately, this was true. I had not pierced its heart with the knife, and this was one very enraged boar now.

'Here, give me the knife,' said Brian. As he took it from me I noticed my right hand was covered in blood. Brian then grabbed the boar and plunged the knife into the boar in front of the shoulder. More shrieks of pain erupted and blood poured out, the dogs and the boar tumbling down the hill. They continued fighting for a few more minutes, the boar getting slower and weaker as time passed. Soon it keeled over dead.

'*Whooee!*' Andrew exclaimed. 'That was fun. '

'Pretty decent boar,' said Brian. 'Maybe eighty kilograms.'

'Let's get some photos,' I said. We propped the dead boar up on a rock and sat astride it holding its ears to keep its head up while having

An inoshishi (wild boar) I killed with a knife early one morning in a forest not far from my home in Itoshima. It had been first pinned down by Brian Freeman's hunting dogs. These inoshishi caused havoc within the Lauben Kolonie estate until the management committee finally employed an expert to trap them, thus sparing our gardens from devastation.

photos taken. This was the typical pig hunting photo you see in Bacon Busters, the pig hunting magazine that I used to read in the House of Representatives during Question Time when I was a backbencher and had time on my hands.

Brian examined the dog which, despite having the leather jacket on her, had taken a nasty wound to her front flank. He concluded it was not a serious wound. We dragged the dead boar down to the road and loaded it into the back of the van in a large plastic tray so it wouldn't bleed everywhere and mess up the van's interior. The dogs sat happily on the carcass as we drove back to Brian's house. By now it was 7am. I felt like another cup of coffee.

'Another ten-thousand yen for this one,' Brian said with a smile. 'I'm glad we got one. It wasn't looking good there for a while.'

'Well, it's been a lucky month for me so far,' I said.

On the way back the three of us talked and joked about *inoshishi*, women, life in Kyushu, and other things that men enjoy discussing. I felt mildly exhilarated by the experience. As a teenager in Australia I had done some pig sticking using dogs, though we usually hunted the feral pigs there with rifles. Once, out hunting with my friend Yasuhiro Takama, my wife's former boss at Nomura Securities in Australia, I shot a sow from behind with a .45 calibre muzzle-loader, the smoke from the black powder lingering in the cold early morning air. The heavy lead bullet split the pig almost in half, killing it immediately. Takama-*san* was deeply impressed. He called the muzzle-loader a *tanegashima*, the old Japanese word for such weapons.

I asked Brian what he was going to do with the dead boar.

'We eat what we can from them,' he replied.

'I heard of an Italian fellow out on Tsushima Island making salami from *inoshishi*,' I said.

'I've been meaning to do that myself, but the casings you can buy here in Japan are way too thin. They're for sausages. I think you need really thick casings for a salami.'

I promised to try and bring him some proper salami casings from Australia.

A couple of days after the *inoshishi* hunt I showed my parents-in-law a photo of myself sitting astride the dead boar, its bloody mouth prominent in the shot with my grinning face above it and the forest in the background.

'*Hora*! What's that?' my father-in-law exclaimed, peering at the photo on my iPhone. 'An *inoshishi*?'

'That's right,' I said.

'You shot it?'

'No. We killed it with a knife.'

'A *knife*? *Araa*!' cried my mother-in-law in horror.

'Well, guns are a little dangerous,' I said. 'We got it in Itoshima, and there are a fair few houses around there. Hunting the *inoshishi* with a knife is quieter.'

'*Araa*,' she repeated, staring at the photo.

'How did you catch it?' my father-in-law asked. 'Did you use a trap?'

'No, with dogs. Big dogs. My Canadian friend breeds them.'

'Ah, hunting dogs,' he said approvingly and laughed. 'You should bring them out here. Everyone complains about the *inoshishi*.'

'*Maaa*, you killed it with a knife,' my mother-in-law said in awe. To her, much of what I did when away from their home was in the realms of semi-fantasy.

I was surprised that my father-in-law spoke so approvingly of hunting and killing the boar. For all the time I had known him he had been a devout Buddhist. Often, he knelt down in front of the family altar in the room opposite the kitchen to recite a sutra before breakfast. This he did to pray for the souls of deceased previous generations of the family. Buddhist doctrine, in its strict form, forbids the killing of any living creature, and ever since Sayuri and I married twenty-five years ago she had warned me I was never to go hunting in Kyushu because this would greatly upset her father. She didn't object to me going hunting in Australia or America or Britain over the years, but I had always respected her admonition when in Japan — until now.

Given his amusement at seeing the photo of me and the dead boar it seemed clear that my father-in-law's attitude had changed. At heart he was a country man, having grown up deep in the mountains in the village of Amagase. He liked growing things in fields, and indeed had loved toiling away in his own vegetable field until a year ago when his back grew too painful for the task. The damage the *inoshishi* inflicted on fields locally and all over Japan was quite real, thus he now seemed to have no qualms about me going out hunting and killing them. In fact, he sounded as if he was encouraging me to do this somewhere around Hita.

For a while I daydreamed about founding a business to make *inoshishi* salami and other such charcuterie — the Kyushu Wild Salami Company, perhaps. Now that the beauty salon my mother-in-law had run for decades downstairs was closed maybe I could set up a shop there to sell the goods. We would have to find somewhere else to make the salami, the process of which was doubtless pretty messy. But the narrow area of the beauty salon was perfect for a small shop selling smoked wild pork and my Kyushu wild salami. Brian could supply the *inoshishi* meat to his heart's content.

Fourteen

The Admiral

Of all the historical facts I dug up wandering around Kyushu, perhaps the quaintest of all was finding the identity of the first Japanese person ever to see a kangaroo.

Kyushu is home to plenty of Japan's historical heroes. One could argue at length about who was the greatest, but I had two in mind — Saigō Takamori, the last of the samurai, and Admiral Tōgō Heihachiro, Japan's greatest naval hero.

Looking for Admiral Tōgō's life and legacy these days can take one to various places in and around Kyushu, and in Tokyo to the shrine dedicated to his memory in trendy Harajuku. The Tōgō Shrine is only a hundred metres along the Meiji Dori thoroughfare from Yamashita Dori, the narrow street crammed with Japanese teenagers searching for the latest weird fashions, a good few foreign tourists, and a gang of suspicious-looking Nigerians selling heaven-knows-what illicit goods or substances. It's all a far cry from Tōgō's austere conservatism, but the shrine, built in 1940, was there well before Harajuku became Japan's epicentre of teen culture.

Living in Kyushu, though, the first place I went to in search of Tōgō was the naval port city of Sasebo, which lies on the south-west coast of Kyushu around fifty miles north of Nagasaki as the crow flies. Sasebo's harbour is deep and protected by a ring of high hills, with a narrow exit to the Yellow Sea beyond. One of Tōgō's first missions as a young officer commanding his own ship was to survey the coast of Kyushu and find a suitable place for Japan's first naval base. In 1883 he chose Sasebo because of its harbour, its location close to Korea and China, and because of the nearby coalfields around Imari. Thus, what was then a small fishing village at the mouth of a minor river became Japan's key naval station. Why didn't he choose the port of Nagasaki, bigger and already long established? Probably because it was traditionally the port for foreign vessels, and a new navy needs its privacy.

Tōgō served as a teenage soldier in the two-day war between the Satsuma domain and Great Britain in 1863. By 1871, after time as a young officer on board a Satsuma warship in the battle to overthrow the shogunate, he was chosen to study in Britain along with several other Japanese students.

Tōgō spent his first months in Cambridge studying mathematics and English before moving to Plymouth where he became a naval cadet, later studying at the London Naval College and crewing aboard HMS Worcester. He proved to be an outstanding student and graduated second in his class. Historical material has it that he displayed a big appetite for bread which he usually dipped in his tea, much to the amusement of his young colleagues. On being teased and, to his fury, called "Johnny Chinaman", Tōgō responded with his fists, as any young samurai's honour would have required. To perfect his grasp of English he kept a diary in that language, and hence the story of the kangaroo.

While Tōgō was training in Britain, Japan purchased three warships there. After making a voyage on one of these British naval vessels all the way to Melbourne, Australia, he noted in his English diary that he had seen "a very strange animal." Surely, I thought, this was a kangaroo.

I drove over to Sasebo early on a Sunday morning the day after visiting Kumamoto and Aso to see the earthquake damage. It was sunny, with lovely pale purple strands of wisteria decorating some of the cedar trees on the slopes of the mountains. The fine particulate mist blowing over from China had started to shift with some helpful winds, and the sombre mood that had possessed me the day before after seeing the destruction the earthquake caused began to fade. The previous two nights I had been reading Jonathan Clements' biography of Tōgō — *Admiral Tōgō: Nelson of the East* — and had developed a respect and even an affection for Tōgō. He was, to coin a clumsy phrase, an admirable man in so many ways.

The harbour and the city of Sasebo are well concealed by the surrounding hills. Driving in on the expressway you don't see the city, apart from some unremarkable suburbs, until you emerge from a tunnel. There in front of you are the sudden and confronting shapes of the huge US Navy ships sitting at the docks in the naval base across the other side of the harbour. In an instant you go from ordinary life driving a car along an expressway to seeing raw naval power. These ships fight. Or they intimidate the enemy. You don't mess with these ships, as Admiral Tōgō's successors in the Imperial Japanese Navy discovered to their cost.

At the Japan Naval Museum, I introduced myself to the lady behind a window and asked what the entrance fee would be. 'Oh, it's free,' she cried.

Excellent, I said, adding that I was especially interested in anything about Admiral Tōgō. An older man emerged and greeted this announcement with strong approval.

'Start at the sixth floor,' he said, 'then come down floor by floor. That's how the museum is laid out.'

'Do you need an English pamphlet?' the woman asked me.

'No, Japanese will be fine,' I said. To my surprise she gave me nothing at all, merely indicating the lifts across the lobby. As instructed I ascended to the sixth floor to find that history began there and continued through the years as you descended to the second floor where the modern-day Maritime Self-Defense Force (MSDF) was explained. It was on the fifth floor that I found Admiral Tōgō and the Russo-Japanese War.

The exhibits were fine. Panels of illustrations came with the usual push-button commentaries in Japanese. At the rear of each floor there were actual uniforms, decorations, cooking utensils, and other genuine articles in glass cases. I read old newspapers — the Osaka Asahi Shimbun — reporting Tōgō's victory in the Battle of Tsushima. The Japanese text was very old-fashioned, but I congratulated myself on being able to read most of it.

Many of the Chinese characters were written in the old style which is still used in Taiwan and Hong Kong.

Back down on the ground floor I saw a small shop selling souvenirs such as caps, model ships, key rings, and so forth. I went in and bought a cap emblazoned in English with Japanese MSDF on it and a bottle of Admiral Tōgō shochu. I asked the lady minding the shop whether there was a particular Shinto shrine in Sasebo at which Japanese naval personnel went to pray before going to sea. In a fluster she picked up a telephone to consult someone on the matter. 'You'd better go to the reception office,' she said. 'They know about such things.' I went to the men's room first and then approached the reception where three people were now gathered waiting for me, one of them a man in a blue MSDF uniform. I greeted them in a formal manner.

'I wonder is there a special naval shrine in Sasebo?' I asked.

They were prepared for the question. 'There's the Old Naval Cemetery,' said the same lady who had asked me whether I needed an English pamphlet. 'You should go there.'

'It has a shrine?' Cemeteries in Japan were Buddhist.

'Indeed. But it's twenty minutes from here. Does your car have a navigation system in it?'

'Yes, I have one.'

'Well, here's the address,' she said, proudly handing me a pamphlet on the cemetery. 'Are you sure you can get there?'

'It won't be a problem,' I replied. 'May I ask you another question? Does Sasebo have some special local food I might have for lunch?'

The three of them conferred. 'Well, there's the Sasebo Burger,' said the woman. 'It's famous. There's quite a few hamburger restaurants downtown.'

'What about ramen or something Japanese?'

'Oh, there's Sasebo ramen,' said the older man with approval. 'But you'd probably enjoy that for dinner.'

'You're right,' I said. 'A hamburger is for lunch.'

The cemetery was on a hill across the other side of the harbour. I parked in the small carpark and walked into the grounds. The azaleas were in full bloom, a mass of pink and white everywhere. An old man emerged from a substantial pavilion and greeted me. 'What are you looking for?' he asked.

'Well, actually, I'm studying Admiral Tōgō Heihachirō.'

'Ha! There's his statue right there,' he said, pointing to a large bronze statue of the great man. It stood on one side of a lawn in front of a Shinto shrine, the graves on the hill behind the shrine.

'May I look around the cemetery?'

'Of course! Please go ahead. You're American, perhaps?'

'No, I'm Australian.' I introduced myself, and he did the same. His name was Kinoshita. I told him I thought Tōgō had been the first Japanese person to see a kangaroo.

'Really? Amazing. How did you know that?'

'Well, he wrote a diary, and when he visited Australia on the way back to Japan after studying in England he wrote that he saw a strange animal. That must've been a kangaroo.'

'Amazing.'

'It's not an important thing,' I said. 'He was a great man.'

'Yes, indeed. There's the statue, of course.'

Japan takes its naval history and heritage very seriously. This cemetery was one of the best kept I had ever seen. I walked around and looked at the graves for individual Japanese naval officers and a series of special monuments dedicated to specific ships lost in the various wars. The names of the crew who perished were inscribed on the monuments. The monuments for the major Japanese aircraft carriers sunk by the Americans in the Pacific War were immaculately kept, with fresh, gold lettering depicting the ships' names. There was a special monument for Japanese submarines lost in war. At the top of the hill I found a large column, maybe ten metres high, dedicated to all the naval personnel killed in the *Dai Tōa Sensō* or "Great East Asia War", the traditional name for what we — and most Japanese — call the Pacific War. According to a Japanese website, in 1942, after the attack on Pearl Harbour, there was a Cabinet meeting in Tokyo on 10 December, during which the Imperial Japanese Navy proposed the name "Pacific War" for the conflict. But the Tōjō Cabinet, dominated by the Army, insisted on "Great East Asia War" because of the fighting in China (which the Navy basically opposed). A formal announcement was then made using this name. After Japan surrendered in 1945, the US Occupation authorities under General Douglas MacArthur banned the use of "Great East Asia War" as being what they called "wartime vocabulary".

Yet here in the Old Naval Cemetery, essentially the preserve of the Japanese Navy, whether modern MSDF or the old Imperial Japanese Navy, the Tōjō Cabinet's name for the war was there on the major monument! This puzzle was explained when I returned down the hill and went to see Kinoshita-*san* in the pavilion. On the wall I noticed the Yasukuni Shrine calendar. The Yasukuni people — including the Jinja Honchō and the other nationalist groups — love using the old name for the war. I thanked Kinoshita-*san* and asked him another question.

'When Admiral Tōgō was commander of the Sasebo Naval Base where did he live? Did he have an official residence here?'

'Ah, well, let me see. Ah, wait a moment,' he said, retreating into his office where he consulted another old man who then came out to see the *gaijin* visitor. Both men began looking through some pamphlets laid out on a desk near the front door. 'Here,' said Kinoshita-*san*, 'it's on this map somewhere. It was near the *arubakaaki bashi*.'

Whatever the *arubakaaki bashi* was — *bashi* means 'bridge' in Japanese — it didn't sound like a Japanese word.

'Arubakaaki?' I said.

'Yes, it's the bridge at the *nimitsu paaku*.'

I examined the map he proferred. There was a Nimitz Park in the middle of the city, doubtless named after Admiral Chester Nimitz, commander of the US Navy in the Pacific War. And the *arubakaaki bashi* was the Alberquerque Bridge. So, in the middle of a Japanese historical naval centre there was a park named after the man who had masterminded the destruction of the Imperial Japanese Navy, killing thousands of loyal Japanese sailors? Only in Japan.

I drove back to downtown Sasebo, parked my car, and found one of the restaurants that served the famous Sasebo Burger. It was a small place and every seat was occupied, so I ordered a takeaway lunch of a burger and fries and took it to the park to eat. It turned out that Nimitz Park was an area located within the larger Sasebo Park, Nimitz Park being an area for the exclusive use of US Navy personnel and surrounded by a stout wire mesh fence. As I walked past I saw a baseball field where a women's softball match was in progress. The American women were huge, some of them bulging out of their lycra sportswear. Well, why not, I thought. No point in recruiting small, petite ladies to fight the enemy. You need strength for a war. And maybe to fight off the occasional inebriated, amorous male sailor.

Outside the wire, in Sasebo Park, I sat on a bench and ate my Sasebo Burger. A few Japanese families with children ate lunch and played together. We, the non-Americans, had our own park. Two young boys grasped the wire mesh fence and stared inside at some American men playing soccer. The scene looked odd, like something from the Occupation days. Still, the Americans inside the wire were there to safeguard our security against the Chinese communists, the North Koreans, and probably the Russians too. Though the wire fence seemed unfortunate, a degree of gratitude was due to the people inside it.

I searched the park for Admiral Tōgō's official residence as commander, but it was no longer there. The Alberquerque Bridge was there, however, a steel structure across the small Sasebo River, erected to commemorate a sister city relationship.

With no house remaining in the park there was no more of Admiral Tōgō to see in Sasebo. Driving out of the city on the elevated expressway I slowed down to have a last look at the mighty naval vessels in the harbour. Then it came to me: this was the age of ballistic missiles and nuclear weapons. If, or when, conflict with Beijing and the PLA Navy erupted, it was Sasebo that would be the enemy's first target, along with the naval base at Yokosuka near Tokyo. Chinese missiles, maybe even carrying nuclear warheads, would arc up into the atmosphere and land somewhere here in Sasebo to cripple or destroy the Japanese and US naval assets that were the only thing between the status quo and Chinese domination of North Asia. Nagasaki suffered a nuclear attack in 1945. Would the naval base and the hamburger restaurants of Sasebo one day suffer the same thing? Such speculation might seem bizarre to anyone far away, but Kyushu was right on the front line of the new Cold War. And Sasebo was the front line of that front line.

Three days later, on a humid day in Tokyo, I went to the Tōgō Shrine. Walking through the crowds of Harajuku I noticed all manner of weird haircuts among the young people and a large billboard on Meiji Dori with the English words YOU ARE (A) CULTURE. Really, I thought. You are *a* culture? You are *the* culture? Between Yamashita Dori and the shrine, a huge new shopping precinct was under construction, called Harajuku Town. Tokyo had all the new projects these days. No such project was underway in Fukuoka, probably because of the *yakuza* gangs there who make such things very expensive.

At the entrance to the Tōgō Shrine there was a row of banners on each side of the path, each carrying the Japanese word for 'victory'. Each banner had the name of its purchaser on it. The shrine was, unsurprisingly, dedicated to victory. Any victory. A few of the banners had the names of high school baseball teams on them. Fair enough. Inside the grounds there was a four-storey wedding hall with a Japanese garden and a pond in front of it. A bride and groom in traditional costume were posing for photographs by the pond. I walked past and climbed some steps through the forest that led to the actual shrine. A sign at the entrance said "VERBOTEN — No eating, drinking or smoking." To use a German word instead of the English word "Forbidden" was somehow impressive. Inside the shrine I bought an amulet for safety at sea — after all, I did have a small sailing canoe in Itoshima, and I was planning a trip out to the island of Tsushima soon — and bowed before the *honden* in honour of the admiral. Two foreign tourists, a young man and woman, wandered into the grounds of the shrine and dawdled on the gravel, looking around in wonder. The man was horribly tattooed, the garish inked images on both legs and arms and even up the back of his neck. The woman had pale pink hair. Oddly enough she hadn't mutilated herself with any visible tattoos. I heard the man say in a crude British accent, 'Well, where's lunch, then?'

Outside the shrine I noticed a small sandwich board advertising lunch at the Tōgō Café on the ground floor of the wedding hall. There was a curry lunch on special for ¥1300, which seemed very expensive, but it came with a salad and *wagyū* beef. There was also the "Tōgō Soda" for ¥640 that contained "Tōgō Honey". Sometimes Tokyo disgusts you with its crass commercial approach to things. Still, according to Jonathan Clements' book, Tōgō was plagued during his lifetime with people using his name without permission to promote products — Tōgō soap, for one — and selling his original calligraphy on the open market. To hell with it, I thought. The last thing I wanted was a Tōgō curry or a Tōgō soda. The admiral himself wouldn't have had a bar of it.

In 1905, after founding the Imperial Japanese Navy, Tōgō commanded the naval forces that defeated the Russians in the Battle of Tsushima, the body of water that lies between Kyushu and the Korean Peninsula. The war, and Japan's victory, had a profound effect on the country, and indeed on the perception of Asia around the world. The context for this war was typical of the colonial age in Asia. Tsarist Russia came to be considered a grave threat to the Asian interests of Britain, whose battle to maintain and grow its commercial and political influence in China after the Opium Wars drove much of its foreign policy. As far away as the British colonies in southern Australia, authorities built forts and acquired warships to deal with the Russian threat, frankly an absurd notion.

In a more local context, Japan was modernising rapidly and had a small but very well trained navy and army whose ferocity in battle was to surprise the world. Russia's growing dominance of Manchuria in the north-east of China posed a serious threat. Japan had only recently emerged from two centuries of feudal isolation. It was an island nation lying offshore from the Asian mainland. If hostile powers such as Russia established a strong position in north-east China and then sought to control the Korean Peninsula, Japan could be cut off and strangled, or so the Japanese came to think.

Tsushima — the Japanese island close to Korea — was the scene of Tōgō's defeat of the Russian Baltic Fleet in 1905, a conflict we call the Battle of Tsushima and the Japanese call the Battle of the Japan Sea. The car ferry to Tsushima leaves from Fukuoka's Hakata Port twice a day. It was a large vessel painted bright white with a two-tone blue stripe at the waterline. The sky was bright with sunshine when I headed to the port and the surface of the sea was calm, perfect sailing weather. In the car on the way to the port Sayuri called me to pass on the news that Aunt Tsugika had died early that morning.

'It's my mother I'm worried about,' she said. 'This will really cause her to go to pieces.'

I feared she was right. A few months back, when we all visited Aunt Tsugika in the hospital near the Harazuru Onsen, gave a clue to my mother-in-law's feelings. On the way home from the hospital she had talked in emotional tones about her older sister, recalling their childhood days as the happiest of her life. She did not want to lose her. Once on board the ferry I called my mother-in-law's mobile phone, but it was my father-in-law who answered. I asked about the funeral arrangements.

'Don't know yet. Maybe tomorrow.'

'Tomorrow? Isn't that rather quick?'

'Well, you needn't attend. Maybe it'll be later on.'

'How is *okaasan*? Pretty sad, I suppose.'

'Oh, well, sad, yes. But Tsugika was in hospital for a while, you know. It's….well, it's not a big surprise.'

This was true. But the impact on my mother-in-law's mood and wellbeing from now on was a real worry. She was inclined to become depressed at any time because she so rarely went out of her house, and the death of her older sister, no matter that it was expected, would only worsen such depression.

The ferry made solid progress across the Genkai Nada Sea. On board the passengers were a mixture of families, men on their own, men carrying fishing gear, men on a motorbike tour, and one solitary *gaijin* — me. It was the third day of Golden Week, the extended holiday at the beginning of May each year. Tsushima's population was around 40,000, so some of the passengers were surely Tsushima-born people returning to spend a few days with their parents or grandparents. On the way we stopped at Iki Island where half the passengers disembarked, allowing me to take a comfortable seat inside instead of sitting outside on the stern deck in the wind. I read the newspapers and ate two *nigiri* for lunch.

The big news of the day was a meeting in Beijing between Japan's Foreign Minister Kishida and his Chinese counterpart, the sour-faced Wang Yi. I noticed something on the television the previous night about this meeting, but it hadn't struck me as significant until I read in the newspaper that, because of the usual Chinese intransigence, the bilateral meeting was the first in four years to take place either in Japan or China. Relations had been so bad, that until now, Wang had refused to meet Kishida except at international conferences. Now, finally, the Chinese had grudgingly consented to a meeting in Beijing. And, no surprise, Wang blamed Japan for all the current difficulties in the relationship. One could only look forward to the day when Wang was arrested, purged, and banished or imprisoned as was usually the case with senior Chinese officeholders these days. He was an appalling piece of work.

I dozed off in my seat for an hour and woke to find us less than a mile from Tsushima's coast. Going outside onto the stern deck to have my first good look at the island I was surprised to see it was almost entirely mountains. The landscape was forbidding, to say the least. We docked at Izuhara Port and I drove into the small town behind it, sandwiched between steep hills. It was a typical Japanese port town, a small area of flat land fully occupied with buildings, half tourist town, half maritime industrial. Consulting a map I received from my hotel, I figured out it was a solid two-hour drive to the northernmost tip of Tsushima where the major monument to the Russo-Japanese War was located. That was too much to attempt with only four hours of daylight left.

I drove for half an hour instead to an old fort atop a mountain called Mount Himekami. The last mile or so involved a rough, single-vehicle track up the mountain through a light forest. Halfway up I passed a group of hikers descending. *Hooo!* they exclaimed when I stopped to let them pass.

'How far is it from here to the top?' I asked.

A man replied in Korean. Right, so this was the first cohort of the many Korean tourists I'd heard visit Tsushima throughout the year.

'*Kamsa hamnida*,' I replied in his language. Thank you.

At the top there was a crude carpark, the grass long. Nobody ever comes up here, it seemed to say. I walked another half mile up the track to the summit where I found a well-preserved arsenal made of sandstone blocks and red bricks, on top of which was a platform for what were once huge artillery guns. A sign with old black-and-white photos and explanatory text said there were once six 28-inch guns sited there, and indeed there was an ancient 28-inch artillery shell on a small platform to one side of the sign. The guns had been pointed out east towards the Japanese mainland so they could cover the Tsushima Strait. This fort, like twenty-three others on Tsushima, had been built in 1904 in anticipation of the war with the Russians, and abandoned in 1945 when Japan came under American occupation. I stood on top of the walls at one of the observation posts and gazed out at the Tsushima Strait where Tōgō's fleet has "crossed the T" in front of the approaching Russian fleet and destroyed his opponent's warships with relentless cannon fire from his own ships. The view was magnificent, both eastward out to sea and westward behind the fort across the island looking back towards Korea.

What puzzled me was how far out to sea the guns of Mount Himekami's fort could have fired at the Russians with any hope of hitting them. A mile? Two miles? Perhaps the guns were there to make sure that no enemy vessel could get close to Tsushima and conquer it. One thing struck me as obvious: ships can move, but island-based gun emplacements are stationary. So, in theory a battleship might steam around to avoid being hit while firing back at the enemy on land. That said, this fort had been built right on the crest of the ridge. It would have been an extraordinarily accurate shot from a ship to hit it fair and square.

I drove back to Izuhara Port at the bottom end of the island. Not far from my hotel, a small *bizinesu hoteru*, there was a collection of small restaurants and bars alongside a canal. Being much closer to Korea than to the Japanese mainland Tsushima has lots of Korean tourists — they come across by fast hydrofoil from Busan, only an hour's voyage — and I was keen to avoid any restaurant popular with the Koreans. It wasn't because I loathed them, but they tended to be raucous at night, more so even than Chinese tourists who tend to be raucous during the day. Dining out in Seoul was always fun, but Tsushima was Japan, and good Japanese food is best enjoyed without one's fellow diners getting blind drunk and shouting the place down.

I chose the nearest *izakaya* restaurant, a tired place that had an advertisement outside beside its menu seeking staff. Inside I sat by myself at the counter. The extraction fan hood over the steel hotplate was dirty, the accumulated grease never cleaned away. No wonder they needed more staff, I thought. Yet it was a comfortable place with a very local sort of atmosphere, a small flag on the counter carrying a recruiting slogan for the Self-Defense Forces. I ordered a draft beer, fried tofu, and the *okonomiyaki* special. Sitting there I read the Asashi Shimbun newspaper and listened to the conversation of the customers sitting on the *tatami* behind me. Everyone in the place was Japanese, except me. It was an ordinary, though filling meal. The draft beer, so cold that it had slivers of ice on the surface, was lovely. I left after an hour and walked around the block, checking out the bars. It was a Sunday night and most of them were closed. One restaurant had two English signs on the door and the wall beside the door:

NO KOREA
NOT ALLOWED

So much for neighbourly feelings and peaceful international relations. This animosity stemmed from the incident in 2012 when a gang of Korean thieves stole some valuable artifacts from some Shinto shrines and a Buddhist temple in the northern part of Tsushima. The Korean police caught the gang and they were duly tried and convicted in a Korean court. Then, upon a petition filed by a Korean nationalist (i.e. anti-Japanese) group, the court refused to order the return to Japan of one of the stolen artifacts — a bronze statue of Buddha — claiming it may have been pillaged from Korea some centuries ago. The Japanese were outraged at this decision and insisted that the Korean Government step in and return the statue to the temple on Tsushima. Nothing happened, and relations went downhill fast after that over other issues such as the comfort women and a disputed island in the Sea of Japan, which the Koreans call the East Sea.

The next morning, I had breakfast as soon as the buffet opened at 7am and drove off with a coffee in a small thermos, heading north to see the war monuments and the beaches that the Tsushima tourism websites said were among the best in Japan. One thing surprised me: Tsushima had no convenience stores, no Seven-Elevens, Family Marts, Lawsons. None at all. Just the odd supermarket. For a place with a population of 40,000 this was extraordinary. The rest of Japan has *kombini*, as they're called, almost everywhere you look.

The road north ran through the mountains, through a long series of tunnels. A lot of people in Japan have gotten very rich building tunnels through mountains That's why there is an identifiable group of LDP Diet members called the "Road Tribe" who spend most of their time lobbying the Ministry of Land and Transport to build more roads or tunnels in the rural parts of the country. The local construction companies who reap the benefits of this public largesse then contribute generously to the Diet members' election campaign expenses, and everyone is happy.

It took the full two hours to reach the port and town at the top of the island, a place called Hitakatsu. Along the way I passed through the villages one by one, hoping in vain to find a *kombini* to buy more coffee. With all its mountains Tsushima has very few fields under cultivation. It looked to exist on little else but commercial fishing and tourists.

Hitakatsu Port had an International Terminal for the hydrofoil that comes across from Busan twice a day. In fact, as I was driving past the International Terminal I saw a group of uniformed customs or immigration officials walking across to the terminal to start work processing the incoming Koreans. The town had a few souvenir shops and a lot of flags from various countries to emphasise its role in the international community. I passed an aged care home that had perhaps a hundred such sovereign flags on a long string out the front. I doubted there was anyone but Japanese citizens in there. But you never know. Maybe a few Koreans snuck in for some care.

The monument to the Russo-Japanese War that I was keen to see was built on a small peninsula further north of Hitakatsu, near a beach called Miuta Beach. I stopped there in the car park to use the public toilet — spotlessly clean — and strolled out onto the sand. My tourist map said that Miuta Beach had been chosen as one of Japan's "100 Most Beautiful Beaches". The honour was well deserved. It was a lovely stretch of sand with clear, aqua-blue water and a small bay dotted with outcrops of dark rocks. Above all it was tranquil. I got the feeling that very few people ever came here to enjoy it. Japanese people, like the British, are not habitual beachgoers like Californians or Australians, and their best beaches are a long way from where most people live.

As I was standing on the beach an old lady carrying a large wicker basket strapped to her back came plodding across the sand past me. I greeted her politely, but she said nothing in reply. I watched her walk to the other end of the beach and then out onto the rocks exposed by the low tide. One could only assume she was going out there to collect shellfish or edible seaweed. Two men stood at the water's edge unpacking their fishing gear, and a young Korean couple took turns to photograph each other with the bay in the background.

The Japan-Russia Friendship and Peace Monument sat on top of a hill on the other side of the bay from Miuta Beach. In fact, there were two monuments. One was a huge bronze relief depicting Admiral Tōgō and his colleagues visiting the Russian admiral Rozhestvensky in hospital in Sasebo where the Japanese had taken him to recover from his wounds. Though Tōgō made sure that such gentlemanly and chivalrous treatment was made available to his defeated enemy, Jonathan Clements wrote that Rozhestvensky complained about his treatment at the hospital, "scandalised at his poor food and dirty utensils he told them quite plainly, that 'in Russia pigs were better treated than we had been in Japan.'" So much for Russian gratitude.

The other monument was a much older stone plinth engraved with an example of Tōgō's calligraphy which I translated as "On the blessed ocean we are proud to do our duty." There was also a newer stone block engraved with the names of all the Russian and Japanese sailors who died in the battle, each written in either Russian or Japanese. A sign related the story that when a few hundred Russian sailors made it to the shore of Tsushima at Miuta after their ship sank the local farmers' wives immediately took them to a local spring to refresh themselves and thereafter gave them shelter in their homes. Those were the days.

On the way back to Izuhara, I decided to visit the temple and shrines from which the Korean gang had stolen the religious artifacts. The Kannonji Temple, which had lost the statue of Buddha, was anything but grand. It sat just off the main road in the village of Sasuna with no signs whatsoever indicating its presence. After that I somehow missed the Takuzuma Jinja, the first of the Shinto shrines that had been robbed, but the Kaijin Jinja was well marked by signs. It sat in a forest on a hill on the west coast of the island. I wandered into the grounds and began reading a sign with photographs of the shrine's treasures. The text said quite plainly that these treasures included centuries-old artifacts from various Korean dynasties. Just then a young man came up behind me. I greeted him and he stood beside me staring at the sign, or rather staring at me reading the sign. He didn't look like a tourist.

'This shrine is the major shrine on Tsushima, correct?' I asked him, which was what the sign said.

'Oh, yes. It's the major shrine.'

'And it was one of the shrines robbed in 2012?'

He laughed nervously. 'Yes, it was.'

'Robbed by a Korean gang.'

'Ah, yes.'

'I understand that the statue of Buddha has not yet been returned from Korea.'

'Correct. But two of the three artifacts were returned. *Tsuu. Tsuu,*' he added, trying to say the English word 'two.'

'Ah!' I exclaimed, feeling obliged to compliment or thank him for using an English word. 'Two?'

'Yes, two were returned,' he said in Japanese.

'Really? Well, that's a good thing. Are they here now at this shrine?'

He looked wary, as if suddenly suspicious that I might have come to steal them. 'Ah, maybe they are here. I don't know,' he said.

'Well, thank you for explaining things. I think I'll go up and look at the shrine.'

'Yes, it's up there,' he said, pointing up into the forest.

'May I ask you, here on Tsushima there are many Korean tourists. Do they sometimes come to this shrine?'

The question flummoxed him. 'Ah, I don't know. Maybe sometimes.'

I didn't feel like pressing the point. Quite probably many of the Koreans were embarrassed and dismayed by the theft of the artifacts, whatever their feelings about history. It's always a disappointment for us *gaijin* to see the Japanese and Koreans at odds with each other, especially when the real threat to peace and stability lies in Pyongyang and Beijing.

I left the shrine and drove back through the local village toward the main road. The radio was saying that the next day's weather would be bad, with heavy rain and very strong winds expected, the wave height up to five metres around Tsushima. This was alarming news given that I was booked on the afternoon ferry the next day. I decided to cut short my visit and get on that afternoon's ferry back to Fukuoka. At the terminal in Izuhara Port the lady at the ticket counter said this would be no problem. An hour later, having quickly checked out of my hotel, I was on board and sitting in a comfortable seat inside. There were not many passengers. I had some regrets leaving Tsushima early, but with the bad weather on the way there was a good chance the next day's ferry crossing would be cancelled.

Fifteen

The Earthquake

Kyushu has long been a part of Japan largely free of earthquakes, unlike Tokyo which suffered a devastating quake in 1923 which hit the city from directly underneath. This was also what happened in Kobe in 1995. These local earthquakes are especially dangerous because they bring an up-and-down shaking which wreaks more damage than a side-to-side shake. Paradoxically, perhaps, Japan's buildings, elevated expressways, roads, and pipes survive the sideways shaking well. But a large upward jolt – brought on by a geological fault slipping directly underneath – tends to bring surface buildings and infrastructure crashing down.

And in 2011 there was Fukushima. This quake came from a massive slip in a fault under the seabed, but it was the tsunami it generated that caused all the damage, especially to the nuclear power station located right there on the coast. If the large seabed fault offshore from Mount Fuji, known as the Tokai Trough, ever suffers a similar slip, the devastation along the coast between Tokyo and Nagoya, and on Shikoku's Pacific coast, hardly bears contemplating.

Kyushu has more than its fair share of active volcanoes, hot springs, and other geological oddities. Yet for centuries its many geological faults have been dormant. Typhoons batter the island every year, bringing fierce winds and torrential rain. This has been Kyushu's chief natural threat. All this changed on a day in the fortnight after the cherry blossoms bloomed in 2016. On Friday 15 April, a large earthquake struck a small town on the east side of Kumamoto City late at night, followed by another quake of magnitude 7.3 in the early hours of the following morning.

This town, called Mashiki, was the epicentre. It lies on flat land just at the edge of the foothills that lead up to Mount Aso, an active volcano. Mashiki is an ordinary part of Japan, once a collection of small farming villages and now an urban area of free-standing houses, low-storied apartment blocks, schools, shops, and local roads. Further up the slope towards Mount Aso, in the town of Minami Aso, the quake caused a series of huge landslips. Around fifty people were killed in both Mashiki and Minami Aso, most of them elderly people whose houses collapsed on them. A dozen people were buried alive in the landslips, and a student dormitory near Minami Aso belonging to a university agricultural faculty likewise collapsed, killing some of the students on the ground floor.

There had also been some serious shaking over near Beppu, particularly in the town of Yufu near the Yufuin *onsen* resorts. The expressway there was closed, pretty much cutting off Beppu and Oita City.

The whole country was shocked that an earthquake of magnitude 7.3 could occur so suddenly in an area that had never before experienced such a disaster. Such is the nature of seismology, perhaps. This was much the case with the 1995 Kobe earthquake. Around Mashiki, the damage was very severe. Railway lines and the main expressway were closed, their tracks and surfaces badly disturbed. About 20,000 people were evacuated immediately to public shelters, the evacuees too scared to remain in their houses either because they had been destroyed or for fear of aftershocks. Hundreds of people began sleeping in their cars, which led to a peculiar and unprecedented problem – economy class syndrome, or deep vein thrombosis, brought on by prolonged periods sitting still in a confined space. The first victim of this, an elderly woman, died on the following Tuesday from a thrombosis caused by sleeping in her vehicle. NHK dutifully went into overdrive on the subject, gravely excited by this new threat to life. Prime Minister Abe consented to the US military helping with the rescue efforts by ferrying in food supplies using the fleet of Osprey helicopter aircraft which had been the subject of fierce protests down in Okinawa.

Three days after the quake struck, I came back to Kyushu from overseas. In a taxi from Maebaru Station to Funakoshi, I asked the driver what the shaking was like there in Itoshima.

Fifteen   The Earthquake

'Oh, a fairly big shake, it was. Everyone felt it.'

'I thought Kyushu was free of earthquakes,' I said.

'No, we've had some big ones in the past. Four hundred years ago this area was wrecked by an earthquake.'

'Four hundred years ago?'

'Oh, indeed. It's in the historical records.'

'Well, at least we don't have any active fault lines around here in Itoshima.'

The driver was one of those many Japanese people who delight in lecturing foreigners on the fragility of life in Japan. 'Japan is full of geological faults,' he said with gravity. 'You never know when they'll shift.'

After the Friday-Saturday quakes in Kumamoto, Minami Aso, and Beppu-Yufu a series of aftershocks began, spreading into Oita Prefecture as the faults in the whole of mid-Kyushu were loosened up. This began to look dangerous. I called my parents-in-law to ask how they fared in Hita.

'Nothing at all,' said my father-in-law somewhat tersely.

'But you must've felt the shaking.'

'Ah, a little bit. But it's not a problem here. Not at all.' He seemed to imply that suffering an earthquake was some sort of moral stigma that Hita would never experience.

On the Tuesday night when I was back home in Itoshima, the tremors began again, with three occurring at a magnitude of 5 within two hours, just to the south of Kumamoto. Clearly the faults in that area had not settled down at all. Rather, they had been brought to life by the original quake. Another major quake was a real possibility. I drove to Hita to find the television and radio broadcasting nothing but post-earthquake news. At the Kanpo *onsen* there was a notice in the lobby:

"Because of the earthquake there is some cloudiness in the bath water, but it is not a cause for concern."

It was true: the water in the indoor pools was indeed cloudy. The quake had done something to shake up the tiny particles of minerals deep down in the acquifer, and the hot water that rose up to provide Kanpo with its baths was now so full of mineral content that it had lost its usual clarity. If anything, this ought to have made the baths more healthful than ever.

After taking a bath, I sat down to enjoy my usual *kabosu* juice and read the Oita Godo Shimbun. It was running page after page of stories and photos of the disaster. I studied its map of Kyushu showing where the major geological faults lay, noting with alarm that there was a cluster of faults near Kusu, not that far from Hita and under the seabed in Oita Bay. There had already been a tremor of magnitude 5.3 felt in Yufuin, the glorious *onsen* town on the way to Beppu. If the faults near Kusu and Oguni started moving in a bad way, we would likely be getting a few nasty jolts in Hita. Suddenly the focus of Japan's earthquakes wasn't Fukushima or the region north of Tokyo, it was Kyushu, and our district could well be next.

Over dinner with my parents-in-law, we discussed the possibility of a severe earthquake happening in Hita.

'I've never known earthquakes in my whole life to continue for a whole week,' said my father-in-law, shaking his head. 'No one who's alive now has ever experienced such a thing.'

'Maybe we should stock up on bottled water and canned food,' I suggested.

'Oh, I detest canned food,' he replied. 'It's bad for your health.'

'*Otoosan*,' my mother-in-law chimed in. 'We might need it. What're you on about?'

'If a bad earthquake strikes Hita we'll have to evacuate to somewhere,' I said with as much seriousness as I could muster. 'Maybe we could go to the citizens' hall. There's plenty of room inside. They hold concerts there.'

'No, we'll go to the station,' said my father-in-law.

'The station?'

'It's the highest point in the town. No doubt.'

'But we're talking about an earthquake. The station might be badly damaged.'

'It's the highest point in the town,' he repeated. 'Midway between the two rivers.'

'We'll be safe there,' said my mother-in-law.

'But why would water be a problem if there's an earthquake? It's damage to buildings that's the danger,' I said.

'An *earthquake*?' said my father-in-law. 'Oh, an earthquake.'

Fifteen   The Earthquake

One of the houses in the town of Mashiki, near Kumamoto, destroyed in the 2015 earthquake. After the 2011 tsunami and nuclear disaster in Fukushima many of Japan's geological faults were disturbed such that earthquakes have become much more frequent since then.

'Yes, like the one in Kumamoto on television. Our building could be badly damaged. I doubt there'll be a flood here.'

'Well, the station's a good place.'

Clearly, with two rivers flowing through Hita, all people like my parents-in-law could think of was the risk of flooding. I had a good look at their kitchen and what might fall on them if a quake struck when they were sitting at the *kotatsu* eating or watching television, which these days occupied most of their waking hours. At least one of the glass-fronted cabinets full of crockery could come crashing down. They found this exercise very entertaining and laughed at the notion of pots, pans, cups, and saucers raining down on them at home.

'It won't fall,' my father-in-law declared. 'Can't. Impossible.'

'I don't think it'll fall over,' my mother-in-law agreed.

'If it's a big enough quake it'll fall over,' I said.

'*Saaa*, we'll have to jump out of the way,' said my father-in-law with a laugh.

'You won't have time,' I said. 'I'll secure it to the wall with some wire.'

My father-in-law muttered something about it being a matter for the gods what happened in an earthquake.

'Well, let's try to arrange things so you don't get injured.'

'We'll go to the hospital,' my mother-in-law said confidently. She had enjoyed her time at the Chuo Hospital the previous year when she broke her leg in an *inoshishi* trap.

In Kumamoto before the quake they probably would have said the same thing. On the television there were endless stories of the evacuees in Mashiki and Minami Aso and how difficult it was for them to have lost their houses and to be living in an evacuation centre. 'People are getting so angry,' said a young mother who had spent the days stuck there with a small child. 'It's so hard to get a good sleep. We just wish it would end, but you can't go back to a house that's collapsed.'

The next morning, we had breakfast and I asked my mother-in-law to cut my hair in her salon downstairs. The salon had been shut for a year or more, but she liked doing the occasional bit of hair dressing either for me or for one of her old friends. The chairs, mirrors, shampoo bottles, scissors, and combs were all still there, many of them decades old. It was like sitting down in a hair salon from the 1970s, a rare feeling I always enjoyed. My mother-in-law, now just over eighty, took her time slowly snipping my thinning hair, muttering in her heavy dialect about the earthquake and various other matters of concern.

When she finished the haircut, I thanked her and left to visit the Lawson convenience store to buy the morning newspaper. Returning to my parents-in-law's shop I found my father-in-law now receiving a haircut, of what little hair he had left. I announced that I was leaving to head back to Itoshima via Aso and Kumamoto, where I proposed to see the earthquake damage and maybe volunteer to help for a day.

'What? You'll never get there,' my father-in-law cried. 'The roads are closed. There've been landslides over there. It's all blocked off.'

'I'll find a way to get there,' I insisted.

'Impossible. It's been on television.'

'They're still having earth tremors over there,' my mother-in-law added, scissors in hand. 'It's a terribly dangerous journey. Maybe you should reconsider.'

I thanked them for their concern and headed off. Driving through the mountains toward Oguni – home to the dairy that had Jersey milk cows originally imported from Australia – I saw with pleasure that the wisteria was in bloom – *fuji* in Japanese, though written in a different way from Mount Fuji. On the slopes of the valleys there were wisps of pale purple *fuji* in the branches of the dark green cedar trees here and there. Though rain was forecast for the afternoon it was still a warm and sunny morning.

Despite this happy start to the trip, as I got closer to Mount Aso and the area hit by the earthquake the weather turned grim. Clouds soon covered the sky and spots of rain appeared on the windshield almost as soon as I came over a saddle and saw the plume of steam rising from Mount Aso's crater. It was still very much an active volcano. Vehicles from the Ground Self-Defense Forces – as Japan's army is known – began to appear on the roads heading in the opposite direction: dark olive Humvees, four-wheel drives, and even a few armoured cars with machine-gun bullet shields on their roofs, but no weapons of course. Once or twice I passed pairs of SDF motorbikes, Kawasaki bikes painted the same colour as the SDF vehicles. Beyond doubt this was now an emergency area, though I was puzzled by the absence of any police cars. It seemed to be entirely a military response.

I followed the road through its long series of hairpin bends down into the huge caldera of Aso, the town at the base of the volcano. There were a few cracks in the road surface, but it wasn't obvious that they had been caused by the previous week's earthquake rather than the usual wear and tear caused by trucks. Near the town of Aso I noticed the SDF had set up a base at a sports park, the playing fields now crowded with military vehicles. Through the open window I heard a large helicopter and saw a twin-rotor craft in camouflage colours taking off. Soon after that I heard the radio reporting that Prime Minister Abe was visiting Aso that very morning. It was probably him and his party in the helicopter.

I stopped at a Lawson convenience store to use the toilet and buy a coffee.

Its blinds were down, a hand-written sign in the window reading, "Due to the earthquake our levels of stock are low. Please understand." Inside I found a young man and a glum woman behind the counter. The entrance to the toilet was taped off with a sign forbidding its use due to a lack of water. I asked them whether I could buy a coffee from their machine. The Lawson coffees were not bad.

'The only coffee we've got is in cans,' said the young man. 'These ones are warm.'

'There's no water,' said the woman.

'Terrible,' I replied. 'The earthquake was that bad?'

'Oh, yes,' she said. 'It damaged everything.'

'At least you've got power.'

'That comes from some Kyuden generator trucks down the road.'

'Really? Even the power has been cut off here?'

'Oh, yes.'

I bought a warm can of coffee given it was now raining outside. As I paid for it I asked the young man if there were many evacuees in the town.

'Plenty. A lot of houses were damaged,' he replied, smiling.

'I'm sorry to hear that. So those people can't stay in their homes at all?'

'No, they're all staying at the elementary school.' His smile remained.

'And all the SDF men here, what are they doing?'

'They're checking the houses. Roof tiles are broken.'

'Terrible. I suppose you can't get the usual deliveries of stock because it comes up here from Kumamoto. Does that mean the road to Kumamoto is closed?'

'Well, there's a detour. I think you can drive there.'

'Really? And despite that you can't get your usual stock?'

'They haven't got it down there, either,' said the woman. 'It comes from Fukuoka, and the expressway is closed.'

'I see. That's really bad. I hope they recover things for you soon.'

'Thank you.'

I thanked them and left. These were real people, not just faces on a television screen. They had suffered.

Fifteen   The Earthquake

Driving down the road to Kumamoto I suddenly noticed many houses had blue plastic sheeting on the roofs where the tiles had been displaced, the sheeting weighed down with small sandbags. On closer inspection I saw that many of the older houses were standing slightly askew, clearly uninhabitable in case another tremor struck the area. I drove on, seeing more and more such damaged houses in what was a semi-rural area. Then there were roadside shops with broken windows, everything abandoned. It made me recall a visit I made to Fukushima in late 2011, shocked at the devastation there from the earthquake and giant tsunami that followed it. Minami Aso, this lovely upland town in the huge, ancient caldera, had the same eerie atmosphere – destroyed by the violent forces of Nature. People had been happy here one day, going about their lives as dutiful, diligent citizens, and the next day they'd lost the very houses they lived in.

I came to a roadblock with a sign indicating a detour on the route to Kumamoto. Beyond the roadblock was the site of the huge landslip that had killed a dozen people. The SDF personnel were still searching for the bodies there. I noticed a dark olive SDF four-wheel drive vehicle parked beside the road, the two soldiers in it eating bowls of instant noodles. The vehicle had markings showing it came from Hiroshima.

Taking the detour, I listened to the BBC World Service through my iPhone. A panel of guests was discussing "gender fluidity" and the situation of feminism these days. A woman was vigorously criticising Germaine Greer, who had herself criticised Bruce/Caitlyn Jenner. Another woman, a black lady from New Orleans, said she was 'not goin' around policin' the folk.'

Maybe it was an important issue for the BBC and its taxpayers, but gender fluidity seemed a stupid notion when you see a town after an earthquake. I passed an abandoned *takoyaki* restaurant, the two giant red octopuses with smiling eyes on its roof now half falling off. The inside of the restaurant was in utter chaos. In an earthquake they say it's the state of the ground underneath that determines how hard the shaking gets. That's why some areas suffer more damage than others only a few kilometres away. Driving up the side of the caldera through more hairpin bends I noticed long brown scars through the forest where more landslips had occurred.

Soon I was over the crest and heading downhill on the road to Kumamoto with other cars and trucks. The BBC presenter – a man – was asking his panel with some urgency 'whether feminism can actually *survive* gender fluidity?' An American woman replied, 'Of course, and there's now a range of masculinities!'

Down near Kumamoto Airport I was surprised to find there was no roadblock to Mashiki. Though the town on the western outskirts of Kumamoto City had been where the quake hit hardest, all the traffic seemed to be heading directly there. Indeed, with the main expressway closed, the road through Mashiki was one of only three routes past Kumamoto that you had to take to get to the southern half of Kyushu. No wonder the logistics system was in such chaos. I crawled along through the traffic past the airport. When I reached Mashiki the full horror was there right beside the road. Houses had completely collapsed, their tiled roofs rent asunder, pieces of timber all splintered, concrete and cinderblock walls destroyed. The surface of the road was uneven, but passable. For another mile I drove through the town, past an evacuation centre with tents outside. This was ground zero, the place utterly wrecked in a few terrible seconds.

The BBC had turned its attention to the four hundredth anniversary of Shakespeare's birth – or was it his death? An American guest on the program asked, 'If Shakespeare were alive today, what would he think of Ferguson?'

This was all too much for me. I dropped my earphones and resumed listening to NHK radio which was broadcasting continuous coverage of the earthquake aftermath. I drove out of Mashiki looking for some lunch. At a Seven-Eleven store the clerk said there was no hot water to use if I bought instant noodles. Heading across the fields I entered the urban outskirts of Kumamoto City. Suddenly I found myself going along a narrow road with severely damaged houses on both sides. Further into town there was a tramway, still operating, its tracks intact only a couple of miles from the destroyed houses. I noticed a sign for a McDonalds restaurant, but it was closed. For the next half hour, I drove around the eastern part of Kumamoto looking for a fast food restaurant that was open. No such luck. They were all closed. The radio said they had lost gas and water. Embarrassed at feeling hungry I gave up the search for lunch.

NHK's two o'clock radio news bulletin reported that at an evacuee centre in Mashiki two Pakistani men had set up a curry stand and were serving a long line of evacuee customers free curry. A man evacuated from his house after the quake said the food in the centre was monotonous and he was very grateful for the curry. Police reported the arrest of a man who sneaked into a destroyed house and stole a tablet computer. One could only imagine the fury of the police who caught him, and the vigour with which they extracted his confession.

In the steady rain I drove north to where the expressway back to Fukuoka was open. It was a long slog home from there, but the rain had lifted by the time I got to Funakoshi, the air utterly still. I took a cold can of beer down to the beach and drank it slowly while watching the sun set gracefully over the island of Himeshima. Normally these moments of tranquility gave me a spiritual lift, but not tonight. The sea was part of Nature, and Nature had just delivered a terrible blow to a part of Japan I liked. Doubtless it's a sentimental failing of the human condition that we tend to dwell on Nature's beauty and marvel at our ability to dominate her, until she reminds us that we're not as clever or safe as we think we are. Life in Japan certainly teaches that.

The Japan Meteorological Bureau said they were still very concerned about the possibility of more serious quakes, and the next day a magnitude 3 tremor hit the town of Oguni over towards Hita. If that area's faults had been disturbed so badly, how soon before a really damaging quake came to Hita? And how long would the tremors continue?

Sixteen

James Bond and the Search for Kissy Suzuki

In his long career as a professional golfer, my father met many famous people along the way: American presidents Eisenhower, Bush (both), Clinton, and Obama; Hollywood actors such as Bing Crosby, Bob Hope, and Clint Eastwood; singers, comedians, champions from other sports, prime ministers, kings and queens, sumo wrestlers, and famous novelists among others. The novelist with whom he played the most golf was Ian Fleming, the creator of James Bond. Fleming had great affection for my father, and when they became friends in Britain during the 1960s he made my father promise never to read a James Bond book. 'They're really rubbish,' he said. Loyal to his promise, my father has never read one. My mother said that Fleming was the most charming man she ever met.

That Ian Fleming had a connection with Kyushu, and with the area of sea and islands that I could see from my balcony in Itoshima, was a delightful surprise. Dr Andrew Southcott MP gave me a copy of *You Only Live Twice* after we had dinner in Tokyo with Hiroshi Takaku and Shunichi Yoshida, president of Asahi Broadcasting. I didn't start reading it for a couple of weeks, but as I got through the chapters it suddenly became very interesting as Bond and his Japanese host, Tiger Tanaka, head of the Japanese spy agency, arrived in Kyushu. Years ago, I had watched the movie *You Only Live Twice*, starring my father's friend Sean Connery, but there was nothing about Kyushu in it. All the action took place around Tokyo and in Mie Prefecture. The book, however, is completely different. Bond and Tiger go to Kyushu in pursuit of the villain, Ernst Stavro Blofeld, who is disguised as a wealthy Swiss botanist living in a castle down the coast from Fukuoka.

Blofeld – Dr Shatterhand, as he called himself – had acquired an old castle and set up a garden of poisonous plants within its walls, along with a pirhana-infested pond. When I first read this, I thought of the site where Nagoya Castle once stood (written differently in Japanese from the city of Nagoya in central Japan). The Nagoya Castle in Saga Prefecture, a few miles the other side of Karatsu, was once the Shogun Hideyoshi's base as he was preparing to invade Korea. It sits on a hill overlooking the Genkai Nada Sea. Looking across Karatsu Bay from my house I could see the hills where the castle once stood. There were some large islands offshore, too.

In Fleming's book there is an island called Kuro just offshore from Blofeld's castle. Kuro is home to a community of *ama*, the women who dive for pearl oysters, abalone, and other shellfish. Bond goes to Kuro in disguise, falls in love with a beautiful *ama* girl called Kissy Suzuki – she had a brief but unpleasant career in Hollywood, hence the name Kissy – and swims across the narrow strait to penetrate the castle dressed as a ninja and assassinate Blofeld.

All this suggests that Fleming himself came to Fukuoka to survey the area to create the story for *You Only Live Twice*. He certainly came to Japan and spent a fortnight travelling with his friend Dick Hughes, who was based here as a correspondent. Hughes knew Japan well. Beyond doubt, much of the detail about Japanese culture in Fleming's book, though somewhat crude in its descriptions, would have come from Hughes, and from Fleming's own interrogation of Hughes's friends in Japan, including a few spies, police officers, and local journalists.

These days it seems only men dive for shellfish. I saw them often, both out in their boats and in the fishing ports wandering around in wetsuits. In most fishing villages in Japan you see wetsuits hanging on pegs outside the houses here and there. Women do occasionally still dive for abalone and *sazae* shellfish, and for *uni* sea urchins and *wakame* seaweed. Fleming must have seen the *ama* at Toba in Mie Prefecture diving for pearl oysters on his way to Kyushu. In the book, Bond and Tiger Tanaka travel to Toba and then take a boat from Osaka down to Beppu to enjoy the hot springs.

I suspected there were once *ama* in Itoshima, as well as other fishing ports along the Kyushu coast. What seemed obvious as I read the chapter about the island of Kuro, Bond, Kissy Suzuki, and the attack on Blofeld's castle, was the need to go and look for myself. I had a canoe and plenty of snorkelling gear, weekends on my own, and a deep curiosity about the whole affair. I had met Dick Hughes as a teenager and read his book *Foreign Devil: Thirty Years of Reporting the Far East*, with its wonderful chapter about Fleming's visit to Japan. Sayuri, had she known, would not have been too happy about it, but in the back of my mind I wondered whether a current version of Kissy Suzuki existed on one of the islands. The question was, which island was Kuro?

I thought it unlikely that Fleming would have gone all the way to the Nagoya Castle ruins. In the 1960s, when he visited, there was no expressway heading west from Fukuoka, just narrow local roads. From what was written in the novel it seemed obvious that Hughes's friends had taken Fleming on a boat trip from Fukuoka down the coast to Itoshima where he saw the beaches, the cliffs, and the small island of Himeshima which I saw every day from my house in Funakoshi. More than likely then, Himeshima was Kuro in the novel, and the coast of Itoshima around Keya was the *locus in quo* of *You Only Live Twice*, at least in the book if not the movie. What a discovery, I thought.

There was more good news ahead, and much closer to home. I had been asked by a client in Australia in the aquaculture business to help them source some machinery for processing *uni*. They were harvesting *uni* in Tasmania and processing them by hand, a very expensive way of doing things. The Japanese machinery for processing the *uni* cracked the shells open on a conveyor belt and washed the innards out so the edible part could be separated efficiently. I knew there were companies in Hokkaido that made such a machine, but I was hoping there was a manufacturer somewhere in Kyushu. On a visit to the petrol station on the way into Maebaru I began telling my favourite petrol pump girls, Kyon-*chan* and Kanae-*chan*, about the search for the *uni* cracking machinery.

'Oh, there's a device like pliers they use for that,' said Kyon-*chan*. 'One of Kanae's relatives is a fisherman who has one.'

'Yeah,' said Kanae as she put fuel into my car.

'I wonder who makes the device?' I said.

Both girls looked blank. 'Don't know,' they said in unison.

I drove into Fukuoka for an appointment, and when I returned home at the end of the day the old man on guard duty at the gate of Lauben Kolonie handed me a single sheet of paper. On it, printed in large type, was the following text:

To Thomson-*san*
From Ohkushi Fuel Ltd
Regarding *uni* shell-cracking machines
Hamaguchi Co. Ltd, Karatsu
Tel: 0955-72-5135

What a kind gesture, I thought. The girls had called the fisherman and found out the name of the *uni* pliers maker, then gone to the trouble of typing it out and delivering a note for me. In any other part of Japan, let alone other countries, they would have waited for me to come back to the petrol station to fill my car again. But not in our Itoshima. I went back a few days later after the visit to Omuta to see the coal museum (and the *yakuza* gang headquarters) to fill my car and thank the girls for their kind effort. The Hamaguchi Company in Karatsu had ceased making the pliers, but what did that matter?

'Thanks for the note, though,' I said to Kanae. She had a touch of rouge on her cheeks as usual. 'By the way, when is the *uni* harvesting season here in Kyushu?'

'Oh, well, ah….I used to go out with my grandmother to get *uni* at the beach in Lauben Kolonie. But it was a long time ago. I can't remember what month it was.'

'What? Your grandmother was an *ama*?'

'Yes, she was.'

'Really?' I was astounded. 'An *ama*? In Funakoshi?'

'Yes, she lived there. She's dead now.'

'What a pity. I would like to have met her. By the way, do you know the James Bond movies?'

'Ah…..?' said Kanae, a blank expression on her face.

'Sure,' said Kyon-*chan*. 'Like 007, right?'

'Exactly,' I said. 'One of the stories was set in Japan, and in the story the British spy James Bond fell in love with a beautiful *ama* girl called Kissy Suzuki. And in the book the *ama* girl lived somewhere here in Itoshima. Maybe out on Himeshima Island. Maybe it was your grandmother who inspired the character.'

'No!' said Kanae, laughing loudly.

'Well, look how beautiful you are! Surely that comes from your grandmother.'

The three of us had a good laugh over the matter, and I drove off wondering at the lovely coincidences of life.

It was the Sunday of Golden Week when I set off to find the Kissy Suzuki of Bond's adventure, if she were still alive and living on the island of Himeshima. Well, given that she was a fictional character I was eager to find any old lady who might have been an *ama* diving girl when she was young. That day the weather was sunny and warm with a light sea breeze blowing. I decided to ride the Honda Cub over to the ferry dock in the next port along the coast, a village called Shima Kishi, or just Kishi as the locals called it. I still had to ride the Honda another ten kilometres or so before we could take the engine apart to check the condition of the piston to see how the ester-based additive was cleaning away the accumulated sludge.

I got to the ferry dock early and rode along the coast road to the saltworks at Fukunoura and back to kill some time. A series of marathon runners wearing numbers came along the road. On the beaches near Fukunoura a few families were fishing at the water's edge. An old man in a sea kayak, clad in layers of gear to protect him from the sun, paddled right across their fishing lines, doubtless disturbing what few fish might be there to be caught.

Just as I got back to the ferry dock the Honda spluttered to a halt. I checked the petrol tank and found it empty. That problem would have to be solved upon my return from the island. Inside the waiting room for the ferry two women were selling local vegetables and other produce. The younger woman was very attractive. To my surprise she addressed me in English.

'Hello! Please buy something.'

I replied in Japanese, saying I was going out to Himeshima on the ferry and would buy something when I came back.

'Where do you come from?' she asked, again in good English.

'Ah, from Funakoshi,' I replied.

'No, no. Before that. Originally?'

'From Australia,' I confessed.

'Oh! I used to live in Brisbane. For nine years. It's so expensive in Australia!'

'No doubt about that. Japan is much cheaper.' Open borders and merging your economy with China has its downside. Japan had resisted the fool's gold of China and had low growth, an affordable standard of living, and a peaceful, tranquil society.

'Why are you going to Himeshima?' the young woman asked me. 'For fishing?'

I chuckled. 'Just to wander around. I might do some fishing there.'

'Well, don't forget to buy something when you come back, okay? '

I gave her my business card. We exchanged bows.

'I am Satoko,' she said formally. The older woman looked on with intense interest. Other ferry passengers milled around examining the vegetables. I looked at two bottles of camellia oil. They cost ¥1200 each. I asked Satoko whether the oil was edible. 'Should I use it in a salad, maybe?'

'No, you use it on your skin. Or on your hair.'

'I think sumo wrestlers use it for their hair,' I said.

This greatly impressed the older woman, whose fascination with me had her completely ignoring the other customers.

On the fifteen-minute voyage out to Himeshima I noticed that the mountains inland were enveloped in a peculiar mist. This was *kōsa*, fine yellow sand that blew across from the Gobi Desert in China in spring. NHK had taken its usual delight in warning us about the *kōsa* cloud for the past couple of nights on the weather forecast. Among the other passengers on what was a relatively small ferry I noticed two officers of the Fukuoka Prefecture Fire Brigade. They were dressed in dark blue and orange uniforms.

As we neared the island I thought more about my mission of the day. I knew nobody on Himeshima. It was very small, but how would I find the old women who were once *ama*? When we docked at the harbour I filed out behind the two fire brigade men. After pausing for a while on the wharf I walked into the village and stopped at the only shop, called the "Seagull Shop" in English. I went in and bought a can of coffee from a lively woman behind the counter. After a short walk through the wooden houses I found myself at a concrete barrier wall looking out to sea over the rocks on the edge of the island. A few vessels were out there anchored as they fished, small white sails at their sterns keeping them pointing into the wind.

On the rocks below the barrier a crow was foraging for scraps. Three cats prowled from rock to rock. An old lady wearing a bonnet pushed a wheeled trolley past me laden with newly harvested garlic plants. I greeted her, but she said nothing. She stopped a while and began methodically laying the garlic plants on top of the barrier wall to dry in the sun. In the eaves of the houses that sat along the foreshore strings of pale brown onions hung there drying. The wind blew in from the southwest, from the direction of Sasebo and the Genkai nuclear power plant. I thought of the possibility of a North Korean attack with nuclear-tipped missiles. We wouldn't be in good shape if this wind blew on the day of the attack. The fallout would come our way and kill us.

When I walked back towards the Seagull Shop the fire brigade officers had assembled a group of local women, who were all dressed in a dark blue uniform with the name HIMESHIMA on their backs in English and in Japanese. The men were drilling them in fire-fighting techniques. They had fire hoses rolled up. Two pairs of women at a time took turns in rolling the hoses out and then carefully rolling them up again, using metre-long pieces of wood with slots in them to roll the hoses up neatly. The older women in the group, stouter of body and no doubt veterans of this drill, were much better at it than the younger women. As the younger women took their turn at the drill, one older woman broke away from the group watching and gave them some close-up advice. The two men laughed. At the end of the drill the two men hefted the coiled hoses and hurled them forward, using a bowling ball action, the hoses snaking out in rapid succession. The assembled women clapped and said, 'Wonderful!'

Two or three older men on bicycles passed slowly by, ignoring the drill. A sea eagle hovered above everything, its huge wings extended majestically. Next the fire brigade instructors began the second part of the drill – how to attach the metal nozzle to the fire hoses.

I ate a couple of *onigiri* rice balls as I watched, then wandered back to the Seagull Shop to buy an ice cream and use the men's room. The lady running the shop smiled at me as she took my money.

'May I ask you,' I said, 'in olden times were there *ama* ladies on the island who dived for shellfish?'

The lady pursed her lips and said, 'Well, there were times when a man would row the boat out and the wife would dive for the shellfish. But that's so long ago. We don't do that anymore.'

'Of course. But there are some very old ladies on the island.'

'Oh, yes. Our grandmother is ninety-four.'

'And was she once an *ama*?'

'Oh. I don't know.'

'Well, I'd be honoured to meet her and ask about it. Is she in good health these days?'

'Her hearing isn't too good, but otherwise she's in good shape.'

I introduced myself with a business card and explained that I was writing a book about Kyushu. The lady said her name was Yoshimura. I told her the story about Ian Fleming and *You Only Live Twice*, which greatly amused her.

'Is your husband a fisherman?' I asked.

'Oh, he dives a bit.'

'Really? For shellfish and *wakame*?'

'Only shellfish. *Wakame*? Mmm, there's only two people on the island who do that nowadays. It's not really worth it.'

'And your grandmother? Would she agree to an interview with me? I don't mean to trouble her…..'

'Well, she's asleep now.'

'I see. If I came back again with an appointment to see her?'

'Oh, of course. Just call in advance. Ask for Yoshimura. There's only one Yoshimura, me.'

I agreed to come back again after making an appointment.

Sunset over Himeshima Island, offshore from my home in Itoshima. Research suggests strongly that Ian Fleming visited the island before writing the James Bond novel set in Japan, You Only Live Twice. The movie starring Sean Connery used a different setting for Bond disguising himself as a Japanese fisherman and falling in love with an ama diving girl named Kissy Suzuki. My visit to Himeshima in search of an ageing ama lady led to some interesting discoveries about fishing life before the age of boat engines.

The next ferry back to Kishi left at two-fifteen. While I was waiting for it I did some fishing from the wharf but to no avail. A sense of lethargy seemed to have settled over the harbour. Nearby a dozen other anglers sat on the concrete barrier above the wharf. Nobody seemed to be catching anything. One man had erected a pyramid-shaped tent. Some crows attacked the rubbish bins along the wharf. Overhead a squadron of sea eagles vigorously chased each other through the air above the harbour. The sun shone on the water, and small waves made the strings of buoys around the aquaculture pens bob gently. An hour later, as I boarded the ferry with two dozen other passengers, I overheard a few of the anglers in conversation.

'Did you catch anything?' one man asked another.

'Not a thing. *Tsuri-tsuri bōzu!*' the other man replied, using the phrase "bald-headed fisherman", meaning a zero catch.

The ferry had a television set which was showing people in France preparing for the French presidential election. Marine Le Pen appeared at a campaign rally yelling warnings about France being overrun with foreigners.

I looked at the news of the day on my iPhone. UNESCO had just approved the listing of the sacred Shinto island of Okinoshima, a place where no women could set foot for religious reasons. I wondered how this would go down in the politically correct world of the UN. But the UNESCO inspection committee had given its approval. After all, Saudi Arabia was a member of the UN Human Rights Committee. Anything was possible. The North Korean crisis had reached a stalemate as China began threatening sanctions against Pyongyang, leading to an exchange of newspaper criticism between the two countries. I read a website in which an American professor of business studies commented on Donald Trump's negotiation strategy, calling him "the most game-theoretical president ever". An office lady in Yamaguchi died after taking only four days off work in six months, the media declaring that it was probably a case of *karōshi* or overwork. China asked the United States to fire Admiral Harry Harris, commander of the US Navy in the Pacific region, accusing him of stoking tensions with North Korea.

Once back at the Kishi ferry dock, I called a taxi and returned with my Toyota to fetch the Honda Cub. I wandered into the waiting room and bought a bag of peas, some bamboo shoots, and a jar of local honey. Satoko said she might need a lawyer one day so she might call me. I asked her whether she lived in Itoshima.

'Yes, I live in Kuka.'

'That's almost part of Funakoshi, just along the road.'

'Sure. Next place.'

'What sort of work do you do on weekdays?'

'I'm a housewife. I have a three-year-old daughter.'

'Does your husband work in Fukuoka?'

'Ah, no. He's on a boat.'

'He's a fisherman?'

'No. It's a ship. It's…..ah, it goes to Tokyo.'

'A freighter? *Kamotsusen*.'

'Yes. That's it. He's away for six weeks at a time. I might need a lawyer.'

'I don't think so,' I said, feeling sorry for the absent ship's captain, if that's what he was. 'Anyway, I'm retired, and I was a foreign lawyer, not a *bengoshi*.'

'Well, thanks for talking to me,' she said wistfully.

Rain came two days later, with strong winds in the afternoon. It blew away all the remaining *kōsa*, leaving the Itoshima area suddenly blessed with crisp, clean air. When the sun came out around four o'clock it bathed the mountains in a glorious light. By six o'clock I was on the way home, awed by the sight of it all. Such evenings were rare. After lunch that day I had come back from the city and dropped in to see Andrew McDaniel at Keya Golf Club. I wanted to put some of my client's ester-based lubricant additive into one or two of his turf-cutting machines. After leaving his maintenance shed I drove back to Funakoshi and stopped at the Matsuo Barber Shop. Dr Goto, one of my fellow residents at Lauben Kolonie, had strongly recommended Barber Matsuo. 'He knows everything about this area,' the doctor said with certainty.

This indeed proved the case. Matsuo-*san* was probably in his seventies, a kindly man who wore a red necktie when cutting his clients' hair. I introduced myself and explained that Dr Goto had recommended him.

'Ah, how very kind of him. I taught him to play tennis.'

'Really? Tennis?'

'Oh, yes. He loves the game. He drives a convertible BMW, too.'

'That's him. I understand he's a famous surgeon.'

'Oh, indeed. A brain surgeon.'

We got down to business after he showed me a sheet of various hairstyles, insisting that I choose one. I said it was up to him, just that I wanted an orthodox haircut, nothing fancy. 'I'm not some movie star,' I said. He examined the back of my head for a while, uttering a series of grunts and sucking his teeth.

'Right,' he said. 'I know how to proceed. It's true I haven't had a foreign customer before, but I'll do my best.'

I warned him that my hair was probably not in good shape because of my frequent swimming in the sea.

'You swim?'

'Fairly often. There might be a lot of salt in my hair. I like swimming in winter, too. It's good for your health.'

'*Maaa*, I suppose it is. Not many people around here swim in the sea.'

'Really? But we have such nice beaches.'

'*Saaa*, the fishermen don't swim.'

' Except those who dive for shellfish or *wakame*.'

'True. But that's work, not swimming for fun. But you know, in recent years a lot of tropical fish suddenly appeared in the sea around here, and they ate a lot of seaweed, which is the food for the *sazae* shellfish. So the numbers of *sazae* declined a lot.'

'I'm sorry to hear that.'

'Sometimes they get decent sized *sazae* out on Himeshima. You see them in the fish markets from time to time. But elsewhere it's no good.'

'Tell me, many years ago were there many *ama* women in these fishing villages?'

'Of course. *Ama* were everywhere. The women could dive deeper than the men. They used to get all the abalone.'

'Why could they dive deeper?'

'Something to do with their lungs and the size of their bodies.'

'Do you know any women who used to be *ama*?'

Matsuo-*san* laughed. 'No, I don't think so. I only cut men's hair.'

We fell to discussing the Itoshima area in general. He said the history of the place went back more than a thousand years.

'You see, the bay here was always a place of refuge in bad weather. And there was a lot of contact with Korea and China, right here. Also, the bay was once a place where the *wakō* lived. They were a sort of Japanese pirate who used to raid Korea. They stole a lot of Buddha statues and so forth and brought them back to Japan.' He laughed. 'Then the Koreans went to Tsushima and stole them back!'

I told him I'd been to Tsushima a year ago to investigate the Russo-Japanese War.

'You went to Tsushima? *Maaa.*'

'Yes, on a ferry. Tsushima was bigger than I expected.'

'Really? I've never been there. Fancy that, you a foreigner have been to Tsushima…..'

After the haircut he insisted on serving me a cup of coffee at the cash register. I gave him a business card, which he filed away under "Lauben Kolonie" in a tattered book. 'You know,' he said, 'I don't know everyone's name among my clients, including many of the guys from Lauben. But I always remember the look of their hair. That's what a barber does. There's some sportsmen there. I don't know what they do, but I know their hair.'

I found some useful articles about *ama* on the internet, including pieces by Alanna Schuback on jezebel.com and Amy Chyan on mashable.com. Both articles covered the *ama* who live in the Toba region in central Honshu. Other pieces carried old black-and-white photographs of *ama* wearing only a loincloth, as was the custom in the really old days. These days the *ama* wear black wetsuits and masks. What struck me as odd was that none of them seemed to use a snorkel.

The descriptions of the *ama* lifestyle put emphasis on the sisterhood aspect of their lives and work. Some *ama* had special huts where they gathered before or after diving. Another aspect was the advanced age of some *ama*. That they kept diving into their eighties was remarkable. In a financial sense their diving provided them with an independent income. They didn't have to depend on their husbands for money, doubtless an attractive prospect in fishing villages which, like farming, were and remain a largely masculine world. For that matter a man married to an *ama* was probably grateful for the extra income in the family.

Although Japan's fishing industry – at least in the villages – has considerable political clout within the LDP and the bureaucracy, the industry does not attract anything like the level of subsidies and trade protection that agriculture enjoys. This is probably due to the far greater numbers of farmers than fishermen. In the Sunny supermarket near my home in Itoshima I could buy salmon from Russia or Chile any day of the week. In fact, I thought the foreign salmon tasted better than the Japanese salmon. For the average fishing boat owner in Japan life was no picnic. During my haircut Matsuo-*san* had given me a brief lesson on the finances of these boat owners.

'You see, there are two types of fishing with nets. One type requires only one vessel. They cast it out and catch certain fish. The other type requires two vessels, in which they spread the net out between them and drag it through the ocean. So, the cost of this type of fishing is double. For two vessels the rough cost of fuel for one voyage is ¥400,000. Just to pay that, they must catch ¥400,000 worth of fish. Then they need to catch more to pay their labour costs. It's a rather risky venture at any time. They don't go out when there's a north wind.'

'Why is that?'

'I think it's because of the ocean currents that flow to the north.'

I didn't understand this but decided to avoid a discussion of the intricacies of ocean fishing with him.

'People say the price of fish is steadily falling,' I remarked. 'I suppose that makes it all the harder to make a profit.'

'Our population is falling, so the fish price goes down,' said Matsuo-*san*.

'According to the statistics, yes, but there seem to be plenty of children around here.'

'It's true. Husbands are home early. Not like in the cities. It's expensive to raise children there.'

'True enough.'

'Out on the islands it's bad. The young people won't stay. Fishing life is not what they want.'

I got up early that Sunday morning, around six-thirty, having enjoyed a deep sleep after a long drive back to Itoshima from Miyazaki, way down at the bottom of Kyushu, via Hita where I'd stopped at my in-laws' home to pick up some frozen sardines. I turned on the television to see an emergency broadcast on NHK: North Korea had launched a missile an hour before. The NHK anchors were saying the missile had landed somewhere in the Sea of Japan. Well, so what, I thought. That was always the case. Though with things now in a state of unusual tension because of Donald Trump's heavy pressure on Kim Jong-Eun – along with pressure from Beijing – any missile launch was now a different matter. I fixed myself some breakfast and sat down at the table to watch Prime Minister Abe give an impromptu press conference. Abe said the missile launch was "a grave threat to Japan's security" and that his government was "certainly not going to tolerate it." Oh, terrific. Not *tolerate* it? Meaning exactly what? As usual nobody was going to do anything apart from pass some useless resolution in the UN Security Council. And that would have precisely zero effect on Kim.

The weather forecast was for sunny skies and mild winds all day. I cleaned the house and worked on revising my book's manuscript for a couple of hours before heading off to the Himeshima ferry dock at Kishi. On the way I stopped at my local convenience store, the Nakamura-ya, where I bought a can of hot coffee and the Nikkei newspaper. The lead story that Sunday was about Toyota investing in a project to build "flying cars". Heaven help us, I thought. With Japan's ageing population did we really need elderly drivers flying through the air? Driving on the roads they were doing enough damage ramming into shop fronts and mowing down pedestrians.

I reached Himeshima around noon. It was Mother's Day, so from the wharf I called my wife and then my mother before setting off in search of the *ama* lady. At the Seagull Shop I was surprised to find Mrs Yoshimura absent. I bought some instant noodles for lunch and ate them on the shop's terrace, washed down with a can of Asahi Super Dry beer. The lady on duty – Mrs Suda – kindly called the Yoshimuras and explained that a *gaijin* had arrived to see grandmother Masae. She hung up and asked me to wait a half hour until her shift ended. Then she would guide me to the Yoshimuras' house. I went off and sat on the edge of the wharf, enjoying the sunshine. A sea eagle took an inordinate interest in my presence, hovering close overhead.

I returned to the shop. Mrs Suda greeted me with more enthusiasm now. She was a cheerful woman, and I got the impression she was now very pleased to be escorting the visiting *gaijin* writer. We chatted as we walked slowly through the narrow alleys between the wooden houses.

'I suppose the fishing here changes with the seasons,' I remarked. 'Do they catch different fish at various times of the year?'

'Oh, I'm not sure,' said Mrs Suda. 'My family aren't fishermen. I think they're catching snapper right now.'

The Yoshimuras' house sat right on the foreshore facing the sea. I entered the house to find Mrs Yoshimura smiling nervously. She urged me to come inside. I noticed she had dyed her hair light brown. I produced a bottle of plum wine I'd brought as a gift. Sitting at a low table on the floor inside was her mother-in-law, Masae, a neat, aged woman with grey hair and a well-lined face. I bowed low and introduced myself, apologising for the trouble of visiting them out of the blue.

'*Obaasan* doesn't hear too well,' said Mrs Yoshimura. 'He's from Australia,' she shouted into her mother-in-law's ear.

Mrs Masae Yoshimura, the oldest resident of Himeshima Island, who, though amused by the story of James Bond, turned out not to be Kissy Suzuki.

'Oh? How about that?' said Masae.

I asked them what the population of Himeshima had been fifty years ago.

'Sixty households,' said Masae.

'That's around two hundred people,' said Mrs Yoshimura.

'The same as today,' I said. 'Quite something, that. In fifty years the island hasn't lost anyone.'

'*Maaa.* Well, maybe.'

'And *Obaasan*, may I ask, were you born on Himeshima?' I asked.

'Oh, yes. I've been here all my life.'

'You got married here, to an island man?'

'Yes, I did. I went to the primary school here.'

'And in the really old days, before the fishing boats had engines, how did you get the fish to the mainland?'

'Oh. Well, Yoshisaburo would take it all in his boat to Kafuri port. And others, too. You see, in those days there were only three boats of a size that could do that. Everyone else had only rowboats.'

'Did the big boats have sails?'

This puzzled her. Mrs Yoshimura shouted more questions, speaking in a heavy dialect, but Masae kept insisting that the island had very few large boats.

'What's your secret of long life?' I asked her.

'Oh, I don't eat much. Just *hara hachibu*,' she replied, using a phrase that meant filling the stomach only eighty percent.

'I suppose you eat a lot of fish.'

'Not really. I like beef. Sukiyaki especially.'

'Really? Beef?'

Mrs Yoshimura nodded. 'She eats a lot of beef.'

'It tastes better than fish,' said Masae with a giggle. 'And don't eat oily food. No good.'

'Do you like watching television?'

'I like historical dramas.'

'What about baseball or sumo?'

'She loves sumo,' said Mrs Yoshimura.

Sixteen James Bond and the Search for Kissy Suzuki

*Kanae Kuwano, the petrol pump girl whose grandmother
was an ama-san or shellfish diver at Funakoshi*

'The tournament starts today,' said Masae, vigorously tapping the newspaper on the table. 'I read the television column every day.'

'No spectacles?'

'Not me. I can read it okay.'

'And the diving in the old days,' I said. 'When you were an *ama*. How was that?'

'Me? Oh, no. In the old days, only the men did the diving.'

'What?..... I thought you were an *ama*.'

Mrs Yoshimura looked embarrassed. 'Actually, there were no *ama* here on Himeshima. It was only the men.'

So much for James Bond and Kissy Suzuki.

'We women waded out among the rocks and picked up shellfish using *hakome*,' said Masae. A *hakome* was a wooden box with a pane of glass used to peer underwater, a crude mask of sorts.

'I see,' I said. 'I thought you were an *ama* in the old days. Were there *ama* on the mainland in Itoshima?'

'Oh, I wouldn't know,' she said, shaking her head. 'I've always lived on the island. I don't know about anything else. Just here.'

Back at Funakoshi later that day I went to the beach for a beer and a swim before dinner. It was another tranquil evening, the sun slowly setting over Himeshima in the distance. This time, however, the feeling was different. It was no longer just that island out there. Now I knew people who lived there. I'd been in their house. Ian Fleming may well have seen Himeshima and the cliffs along the coast of the mainland opposite to imagine Bond's adventure in Japan, but the *ama* of his novel had never existed on Himeshima. They did exist elsewhere somewhere around the coast of Itoshima, but not as he had written. Never mind. Fleming was my father's friend and a vastly entertaining writer. The experience of having chatted with ninety-four-year-old Masae Yoshimura who had been a young woman on Himeshima in the 1940s was satisfaction itself. Kissy Suzuki did not live there.

Seventeen

Japan's Gettysburg

Few people outside Japan know that there was once a two-day war between Britain's Royal Navy and the samurai domain of Satsuma in the south of Kyushu, known as the Anglo-Satsuma War of August 1863. This war, if you could call it that, does feature briefly in the Japanese school history curriculum, but there's not much common knowledge about it these days. In Kagoshima though, the modern name of the old Satsuma domain, the war is very much a part of local lore, and along with the arrival of American Commodore Matthew Perry and his steam-powered warships off Edo (Tokyo) in 1853 and 1854, it is probably the key conflict between feudal Japan and the West that prompted Japan to shake off the old ways and modernise itself. Satsuma, by dint of the anger and sense of urgency among the local samurai, became the key driver of this enormous change in Asia's history.

The Satsuma samurai, led by the redoubtable Saigō Takamori and the wily politician Okubo Toshimichi, mobilised with other disaffected domains in the south-west of Japan and overthrew the feudal regime of the shoguns. They restored the Emperor Meiji to the head of government and embarked on a vigorous program of modernisation — essentially Westernising the country — which created the Japan we see today. But all did not go well in the beginning. Many samurai in Kyushu resented the changes. A decade after the shoguns were replaced the samurai rebelled. A civil war broke out in Kyushu, and for a few months it seemed as if Japan's modernisation would end in bloody failure.

Saigo Takamori, the last of the great samurai. Saigo led an uprising against the modernising Meiji Government in 1877 in a futile effort to preserve samurai privileges, a rebellion that culminated in his death in Kagoshima. No figure in Japanese history is more revered.

One of the key reforms of the Meiji Government was the abolition of the samurai class and its feudal privileges such as the exclusive right to wear swords and the annual rice stipend each samurai family received at the expense of the farmers and the common townspeople. The Satsuma domain largely ignored the edict ending the stipend system as part of its resistance to the building of a powerful, centralised government. By now Kagoshima Prefecture, the Satsuma leaders also ignored the imposition of a national land tax designed to break up the old domain land ownership structure and give private ownership to the farmers.

What sparked the rebellion of former samurai in Kyushu was the order in 1876 banning anyone except soldiers and policemen from carrying swords. Then, when samurai rice stipends were converted into thirty-year bonds paying 5 to 7% interest and reducing incomes by a third, all hell broke loose. Around two hundred samurai stormed Kumamoto Castle, killing the garrison commander and the prefectural governor. These rebels called themselves the Shinpūren or "League of the Divine Wind". The Meiji Government forces, armed with rifles and cannon, swiftly overcame the samurai who refused to fight with anything but swords and spears.

All over Kyushu the rebellion simmered for a few months. Then, when the Tokyo authorities sent a ship to Kagoshima to seize the city's arsenal, the students in the traditional samurai schools erupted in fury. In January 1877, they raided the arsenal and removed all its ammunition. Saigō, the senior figure in Kagoshima, was away hunting in the mountains. At first he was ambivalent about supporting the uprising in Kagoshima, and was quoted as saying something like 'Well, that's done it now.' But, when rumors spread that the government in Tokyo was plotting to assassinate him — probably a falsehood, extracted from a government spy under torture — he returned from the mountains and took leadership of the rebels. Thus, the die was cast and there was no going back.

Saigō formally announced that he would go to Tokyo and confront the government. He had an army of twelve thousand samurai, a reasonable supply of rifles and artillery pieces, but little in the way of logistical support. The imperial troops had ships, telegraph communications, and behind them the full power of Japan's central government. It was never going to end in anything but defeat for Saigō's forces.

The rebels marched north from Kagoshima to attack Kumamoto Castle. After a long fight they retreated, and a key battle took place north of Kumamoto at a pass called Tabaruzaka. Here the rebels held off the imperial troops for three weeks, each side losing four thousand men in the pouring rain. Eventually the imperial forces prevailed, and Saigō began a long retreat through the mountains of southern Kyushu.

Around the time I was about to head down to Kagoshima to look into Saigō Takamori, Okubo Toshimichi and the rest of the Satsuma legend, President Obama came to Hiroshima after attending the G7 Summit at Iseshima. The weather was warm, being late May, and the wheat and barley in the fields around Funakoshi ready for harvest so that rice could be planted. Prime Minister Abe was all over the television greeting his fellow G7 leaders such as Angela Merkel and David Cameron and escorting Obama to the ceremony in Hiroshima's Peace Park. Obama made a long speech about "death falling from the sky" and so forth. He made no overt apology for Harry Truman's decision to drop the bomb on Hiroshima. Yet his constant stress on America being the only country ever to have used a nuclear weapon in a war left nobody in much doubt about what he thought of Truman's decision.

NHK and the rest of the Japanese media made a huge fuss about Obama being the only serving American president to visit Hiroshima, but without an apology, there seemed little to the event beyond the president's words. And there was little mention in the media of the years leading up to the bomb being dropped in August 1945 and what had happened to bring it about.

I listened to various American radio stations all that week on my iPhone. I heard a lot about the Pacific War and why Truman made the decision to use the bombs on Hiroshima and Nagasaki. Much was said about the Allied forces having to land in Kyushu if the bombs not been used, bringing the war to an end, and how many deaths and casualties that would have meant. Where would the US Navy choose to land? Down in Kagoshima

Okubo Toshimichi, the Meiji era statesman who created Japan's modern form of government post-1868. Okubo grew up in Kagoshima with Saigo Takamori. They were colleagues in the Meiji Government until Saigo joined the samurai rebellion in Kyushu and led it against Okubo's government forces. Saigo died in the final battle, and Okubo was assassinated in Tokyo some time later by dissident samurai. A monument stands on the site of the assassination across the road from the New Otani Hotel in Tokyo.

somewhere? Maybe, though the geography of Kagoshima Prefecture would have made moving further into Kyushu very difficult. You needed beaches for a start. If they had destroyed all the airfields in Kyushu first, the Americans would probably have chosen a place from where they could move quickly inland to gain control of Kyushu. That would mean northern Kyushu, and even the beaches of Itoshima.

The American talk show hosts were in full flight on the matter:

'The fanatical Japanese people were even sharpening bamboo spears in readiness to fight our troops…..Women and children were being trained to fight guerilla-style……..Hundreds of thousands would have died had we not dropped those bombs…..'

This was more or less true. Local governments were at that time carrying out regular citizen drills in hand-to-hand fighting, more as a propaganda exercise than as preparation for a final stand against the enemy. By that time, mid-1945, most people knew the war was lost, but there were plenty of fanatics in the military government who were prepared to fight to the last man, woman, and child. Obama didn't come all the way to Hiroshima to deal with historical facts. He came to make his usual cosmic speech, be lionised, and then to fly home to Washington. History does have a power over us, and views will always differ. The survivors of Hiroshima's atom bomb felt better for Obama having visited, and that's perhaps the best that could be said of the whole event.

Elsewhere I noticed an odd story in the weekly magazine *Shukan Bunshun* that I always bought when travelling somewhere by plane or train. Mainoumi, a former sumo wrestler famous for his small stature and now a regular sumo commentator, had joined the nationalist political group, the Nippon Kaigi. *Shukan Bunshun* was highly amused. Was the failure of Japanese sumo wrestlers to overcome the Mongolian wrestlers somehow related to reform of the Japanese Constitution, that being the Nippon Kaigi's *raison d'etre*? they wondered.

"Well, I joined because my teacher is in it," Mainoumi was quoted as saying. "I don't know much about all that stuff, but if my teacher's in it then I suppose it must be a good outfit. I joined because of that."

All political groups love it when a celebrity joins up. Publicity is good for the cause, though the Nippon Kaigi doesn't hold press conferences or issue public statements. Ninety percent of sumo wrestlers are probably very conservative men. After all, sumo itself embodies tradition and the spirit of Shinto, as well as having strong echoes of *bushido*. I wondered how many other former *rikishi* like Mainoumi were Nippon Kaigi members.

I headed south for Kagoshima, centre of the old domain of Satsuma, whose samurai had changed the course of history. Two of those men in particular had caught my imagination: Saigo, the last of the samurai, and Okubo, the Bismarck of Asia. Driving down to Kagoshima you get a strong sense of the isolation of the Satsuma domain. At the bottom end of Kumamoto Prefecture, south of the town of Minamata, the expressway suddenly veers into the mountains and enters a tunnel. What follows is a whole series of tunnels as you travel through a huge belt of mountains, some of them very high. Between the tunnels you look out the car window to see deep valleys with no houses at the bottom. Finally, you emerge into a lovely upland plateau, a place called Hitoyoshi. Then there are more mountains until eventually you reach Kirishima near the top of Kagoshima Bay. Kagoshima Prefecture, the old domain of Satsuma, is cut off or protected by all these mountains.

I got there late on a Friday afternoon in mid-March. President Park Geun-hye of South Korea had been dismissed from office by a court in Seoul that morning and all the news bulletins were full of this momentous news. The court ordered a presidential election be held within sixty days, and it seemed almost certain that a left-wing candidate would win. The South Korean left-wingers were very anti-Japanese, and they were likely to oppose a tough line against North Korea, exactly the opposite of what we wanted in Japan. Relations between Japan and Korea under the prickly President Park had been bad, but they looked like getting even worse under her successor.

Before dinner I strolled over to the Kajiyamachi District, just across the Kōtsuki River from my hotel. This small precinct, perhaps a square half-mile in area, was the birthplace of half a dozen extraordinary men who went on to create Japan from 1860 onwards, Saigō and Okubō the two most famous among them. On a bridge where the city's trams and cars cross the river there was a huge bronze statue of Okubō, inscribed with one of his noteworthy sayings: "Government must be pure and clear." Okubō, with his trademark muttonchop whiskers and beard and wearing a Victorian era frock coat, stood there towering over the passers-by.

Back at the hotel I noticed an odd English translation on the floor directory in the elevator. On the third floor one could find something called "Dear Professor God". The Japanese phrase on the directory suggested a Shinto shrine used for weddings, but Dear Professor God? Was it Kagoshima's isolation, I wondered, that might account for this strange phrase.

I'd been to Kagoshima before, including my first visit as a teenager, but I didn't know the city well. Though only four hours drive from Fukuoka I hadn't had reason to travel down here for any work purpose. Now, though, I felt I had to have a good look at Saigō Takamori down here, right in his hometown, and to a lesser extent Okubō Toshimichi. A student of history must, of course, read about great men in books to understand what they did for their countries, but visiting their birthplaces adds a greater depth to such understanding. Can you really understand George Washington and Thomas Jefferson without visiting Mount Vernon and Monticello in Virginia? No, you can't. Likewise, if you want to understand the Meiji Restoration — and for that matter the modern history of Asia — it's no good merely wandering around Tokyo or Kyoto. You must go all the way down to Kagoshima.

Kagoshima is immensely proud of its history. The number and quality of its museums is testimony to this fact, and Saigō Takamori is the star of all. In Kajiyamachi you find the Isshin Furusatokan Museum, which concentrates on the Meiji Restoration and the part the Satsuma men played in bringing it about. I walked into the place as soon as it opened at nine o'clock on the Saturday morning and was intrigued to observe a pair of Saigō's underpants among the many exhibits. Likewise, it was a pleasure to note that the sign on the men's toilet showed the silhouette of a man wearing a top hat, just as the Meiji leaders did after they adopted Western-style dress after 1868. It could've been Abraham Lincoln or William Gladstone.

Say the name Saigō Takamori to any Japanese these days and you'll get a smile of admiration. Saigō, the gutsy samurai with a death wish who died fighting the government he had risked his life to establish, Japan's favourite rebel. He was a man of natural frugality who wore a simple cotton kimono and straw sandals to Cabinet meetings when other ministers wore English-style frock coats and leather shoes. He went from exile on a barren island south of Kagoshima to command the military forces that overthrew the shogunate and restored the emperor to political power — the Meiji Restoration of 1868. Thereafter he accepted control of the new government in Tokyo while the best and brightest of Japan's new crop of leaders spent two years travelling the world to gain a first-hand understanding of how industry, government, and education worked in the West. During the delegation's absence Saigō did not seize power for himself as a new shogun. When they returned, rather than let them know that he was still in charge, he resumed his role as one among equals.

An entire day can be spent in the museums of Kagoshima, along with a visit to Shiroyama, the hill where Saigō and the remnants of his army made their last stand. But I was on the trail of Saigō the man that day, so I decided to leave the Furusatokan museum and go to the great man's grave and the Shinto shrine dedicated to him, the Nanshū Shrine.

That day was 11 March (2012?), the sixth anniversary of the Fukushima earthquake, *tsunami*, and nuclear disaster. Some 18,446 people had perished that day, 120,000 were still unable to return to their homes, and the media was fretting that the country had basically forgotten about them. All this was a long way from Kagoshima.

The Nanshū Shrine and the cemetery beside it sat on a hill a few miles from Shiroyama where Saigō and the last rebels met their end. After being mortally wounded in the battle Saigō was ritually decapitated by a retainer, and his head was never found. His grave sits in the front and centre of the cemetery, in which are buried the others who fell in what is called in English the Satsuma Rebellion. In Japanese it's called the *Seinan Sensō* or South-Western War. In the grounds of the shrine there is a wall inscribed with the names of all the samurai who died fighting with Saigō. Plainly, far from any regret about the rebellion, Kagoshima is defiantly proud of its fallen heroes.

All Shinto shrines sell amulets for good luck, and being a shrine dedicated to such an illustrious figure it seemed appropriate to buy a Saigo amulet. That said, Saigo, although a great man, had not exactly been blessed with a lot of good luck in his life. The office that sold the amulets was unoccupied except for a black cat with white spots on its belly who lay on its back sunning itself on the ground in front. It was a beautiful day, no clouds in the sky, and from the top of the hill the mighty volcano Sakurajima loomed large across the bay. That morning the volcano was quiet, no smoke, ash or steam rising from its crater. A while later the priest emerged to greet me.

'I'd like to buy a Saigo Takamori amulet,' I said.

'By all means,' he said, sliding the window open.

I chose a small amulet and a cloth towel decorated with Saigō's calligraphy, the characters meaning "Respect Heaven, Love the People."

I thanked him and said, 'May I ask you, are there descendants of Saigō Takamori living in Japan these days?'

'Oh, yes. There's about a thousand of them.'

'Really? Do they celebrate Saigō every year?'

'Indeed. They have a gathering. I gave a speech to them last year.'

'And here at the shrine, do you have a Saigō festival of some sort?'

'Of course. On 24th September.'

'The anniversary of his death.'

'Exactly.'

'I understand that in every Kagoshima school there's a picture of Saigō above the blackboard in the classrooms.' I had seen this a few years ago in a Japanese movie set in Kagoshima.

The priest chuckled. 'There used to be. But not these days.'

'Oh? Why did they remove his photo?'

'It's not a photo. It was just a portrait. There were no photos taken of Saigō Takamori.'

'Well, it seems a shame to remove his portrait from the schools.'

'Mmm,' he said, clearly in agreement but unwilling to say more.

I walked back down the hill in front of the shrine to my car, which I'd parked at a convenience store. On the street I noticed an English conversation school called Lindy Lizard's English House. Lindy *Lizard*? Along with Dear Professor God this town had a special way with the English language.

Fighting in the Satsuma Rebellion began not down south near Kagoshima but in Kumamoto, halfway up the western side of Kyushu. Saigō led his troops in an attack on the government garrison based at the Kumamoto Castle. After a fortnight of fighting the garrison was still holding out, so most of the samurai troops, around 7,000 of them, headed north along the road to Fukuoka to confront the government forces on their way to put down the rebellion. North of Kumamoto City the land is flat for thirty kilometres or so before changing into steep hills and gullies just before the next range of mountains rears up. It was here, at a place called Tabaruzaka, that Japan experienced its Gettysburg. This was the key battle that decided the civil war. Saigo and his samurai were defeated.

Bear in mind that the Meiji Government was just a decade old. Okubō and the modernisers had pushed through radical reforms causing a lot of unease, and the samurai were in open revolt. Indeed, had all the samurai in Kyushu joined forces with Saigō and the Satsuma rebels, the Meiji Government would probably have lost control of much of south-western Japan and thereafter might well have disintegrated as confidence in its authority evaporated.

I drove to Tabaruzaka early on the Sunday morning after staying the night in Kumamoto, where I'd eaten a satisfying meal of *baniku* or horse-meat cuisine, Kumamoto's signature dish. The Tabaruzaka Museum opened at nine o'clock, and as the first visitor that day *and* being a foreigner, my appearance caused both shock and delight among the staff at the ticket office. A man gave me four or five different pamphlets, one in English, and a smiling woman in her early sixties insisted on accompanying me to explain each exhibit. At first, I found her presence irritating, but she was kind and softly spoken, and she was very knowledgeable about the rebellion. I let her talk as she wished and listened carefully.

'The important thing to understand here is that the government forces were very well supplied,' she said. 'They had ships to bring them food and ammunition from Tokyo, and they had the telegraph.'

'Telegraph?' Indeed, in a couple of ancient black-and-white photographs of the battlefield you could see the telegraph poles along a road. 'Communications support,' I said.

'Oh, yes. They could report back to the government every day.'

'And where was Saigō during the battle? Was he involved in the fighting himself?'

'No, he wasn't here. He was in Kumamoto.'

'I see. Maybe the samurai would've won if he'd been here.'

'Saaa....'

'Japan's history would've been very different.'

'Well, yes. But the Satsuma forces had inferior guns. They were muzzle-loaders from the American Civil War, from the southern forces. The government troops had Schneider rifles that used cartridges. They could fire much faster than the Satsuma force's rifles.'

As a keen shooter myself I was impressed with her knowledge of firearms. In the past I'd owned two muzzle loaders, a percussion cap one and a flintlock Kentucky rifle. You wouldn't want to fight a battle with such weapons.

'So the Satsuma people bought their rifles from America?' I asked.

'Yes. Interesting, isn't it?'

Maybe the Satsuma authorities should have given this purchase more consideration, I thought. The Confederacy lost. Buying their muzzle loaders was hardly a recipe for success. Maybe the muzzle loaders were all there was to buy on the market.

One display showed a comparison between the clothing and food that both sides had available to them. The government forces wore warmer clothes and had beef to eat, while the samurai wore thinner, cotton garments and had no beef, only fish, rice, and pickled vegetables.

'I noticed back down the road there is a cemetery for the Satsuma dead,' I said. 'It's not far away from here.'

'Yes, it's there. You know, the government soldiers who died were buried individually with their names on them. But the Satsuma dead were buried all together, in groups of bodies with no names. Later on, many people came up here from Satsuma to exhume the bodies and take them home to Kagoshima. Mothers were able to identify their sons because they themselves wove the clothes the men wore. So that's how the mothers knew which body was their son. They could recognise the pattern in the cloth.'

What a grim tale, I thought, but who wouldn't want to find their dead child and see them buried properly?

Eighteen

The Challenge of Air-Conditioning

Early in the summer of 2015 I spent a month away from Kyushu, travelling with my parents in Scotland and then spending a fortnight in Melbourne with my wife and children. I left Fukuoka in mid-June, just as *tsuyu*, the rainy season, was starting. *Tsuyu* is one of those annual rituals of life in Japan, providing comfort that the seasonal cycle is, as the gods decree, an immutable fact of our existence on these islands. The rain is occasional and in general light, but the humidity steadily rises, and you must prepare for it. Much more rain falls in September when the typhoons begin, but *tsuyu* is the "official" rainy season.

Before I left for Scotland, Sayuri came for a visit, attacking the house in Funakoshi with mops, brooms, and all the other cleaning gear she could find. She turned what I thought a tidy if dusty abode into something to marvel at. The devotion of Japanese women to domestic hygiene is a confronting and embarrassing thing for we *gaijin* husbands. At the GooDay store in Kafuri she bought a dozen small boxes that absorb moisture — called *mizutori* boxes — and placed them in my clothing cupboards to deal with the forthcoming humidity. This, she said, would reduce the incidence of mould. Because the house was half surrounded by a dense forest of sub-tropical trees the moisture in the air inside the house could be intense.

'If you use the air-conditioning the moisture is reduced,' she explained, 'but when you go away you won't be leaving it on for weeks, will you?'

Lecturing me on such elementary facts was a source of great satisfaction for her. Imagine having a husband who already knew such things!

The previous year I hadn't used any *mizutori* boxes, and the mould on my clothes, on the wooden surfaces of the furniture, and on the leather surfaces of two briefcases had been dreadful. Sayuri hadn't seen it, but foolishly I'd mentioned the disaster and been severely reprimanded for my ignorance and neglect. And for the extra cost of dry-cleaning the mould-infested jackets, suits, and trousers.

The fortnight in Scotland was something of an emotional trip. My mother, at 82, was in fine shape, but my father was frail, the Parkinsons Disease relentlessly reducing his mobility and clouding his memory. He had built his career and reputation as a professional golfer in Scotland and northern England in the 1950s, and he loved the place dearly. Scotland was special. It was in our blood.

It was fun being there, a bit like being in Kyushu. You're far away from the national capital, you've got decent cities that aren't crowded, and the rural landscape is unscarred and generally beautiful. Spending time with my parents was more valuable than anything as they got older and less able to handle everything by themselves.

The big difference between Kyushu and Scotland, though, was the scale of threats in the UK, being so close to Europe and its jihadi infiltration. In Japan we had the menace of North Korea and its missiles, but the terrorist attacks in France, and the threat of such things happening in Britain was something of a shock to experience first-hand rather than through the media from a great distance. One day in St Andrews, I played golf with an American man. He looked at me oddly when I said I lived in Japan.

'Japan? You *live* there?'

'I do,' I replied. 'It's safe. You can say that.'

'Oh, yeah. I read in the media they don't have immigration, so no Muslims, right?'

'Well, very, very few. We do have earthquakes, though.'

'Hey, I'll take the earthquakes any day,' he said with a laugh.

When I returned to Kyushu it was boiling hot. The temperature was 35°C when I arrived at Maebaru Station and got into a taxi. The driver grinned as we discussed the heat.

'No rain,' he said. 'And none forecast for a week or more. How about that?'

The very hot weather — *mōsho* in Japanese — was a major source of semi-panicked news on NHK. On the evening television news there were images of people in Tokyo, Kyoto, and Osaka sweltering in the heat, the news anchors solemnly warning the nation that a lot more heat was on the way and that many lives were at stake. As if we didn't know! The micro-authoritarianism of government and NHK combined would seize on anything to keep us under their mind control.

Down at the beach the sea was warm now, and it was nearly the jellyfish season. These were small creatures that could give you a fair sting if you ran into them. Most Japanese people bathe in long sleeves and ankle-length tights to avoid getting a suntan, and the jellyfish make this sort of swimming garment a necessity by early August. That was still two weeks away, and, unlike everyone else, I swam bare-chested in just a pair of shorts.

Early one morning I was sitting under the roof at the beach enjoying a coffee when an elderly man emerged from the water covered head-to-toe in protective clothing, a mask pushed up on his forehead. He trudged up the sand to where I was sitting. We greeted each other, and I remarked that the water was quite clear.

'Oh, yes, it's clear. The weather's been good lately. But you have to look out for the jellyfish.'

'Their numbers increase after Obon, right?' I replied. 'Mid-August is when people stop swimming.'

'Well, the jellyfish are here already. But the big ones don't hurt you. It's the small ones that sting.'

'You're very well prepared with that swimsuit and mask.'

'Ah, but I got stung this morning,' he said, glad to report this triumph of Nature over mankind. 'Right here,' he said, pointing to his cheek, the only uncovered part of his body.

'Really? On the face? How terrible.'

'They're out there,' he said, staring at the sea.

'Put some vinegar on the sting,' I suggested. 'We should keep a bottle here at all times for jellyfish stings.'

'Mmm,' he said, unsure of whether to agree with this lone *gaijin*.

Soon it was time to drive to Hita to see my parents-in-law and pay whatever taxes I owed at the city office. Hita is often the hottest place in Japan in summer because it sits in a bowl-shaped valley that traps the heat. Sayuri had told me that work was scheduled to repair the air-conditioning in my in-law's kitchen where they spent most of the day. I called on the Thursday and my father-in-law answered.

'I hear you're getting new air-conditioning in the kitchen,' I said.

'No. No air-conditioning. It's hot,' he replied.

'But in this terrible heat you really need it. Sayuri says it's going to be fixed this weekend.'

'*Saaa*, it's really hot. But we've got a fan.'

'Don't worry, you'll have air-conditioning by the weekend. How is *okaasan?* Is she okay? How's her health?'

'She's at the day care.'

'Is her health okay?'

'Well, it's hot, you know.'

This was about all I was going to get out of him on the phone. Later that day my mother-in-law called me to ask if I was coming to Hita that night. No, I said. Sunday was more likely. I'll wait until the air-conditioning is restored, I said. She laughed and said that was sensible.

'But it works in the spare bedroom,' she added, hoping that would be enough to tempt me to rush to Hita that night. My visits were a welcome interruption to life with my father-in-law in the stifling heat. I felt sorry for her, but I had work to do in Fukuoka and the thought of Hita in 35°C heat without air-conditioning in the kitchen was too much.

'I promise I'll come on Sunday,' I said.

Friday and Saturday were baking hot with little wind and not the slightest hint of rain. NHK continued its dire warnings of heat stress. At night the temperature inside my house fell to a comfortable 24°C with the air-conditioning going, allowing for a good sleep. I went to the Orange Golf practice range and hit balls under a fan for an hour each day using my hickory set. It was sweaty work and required regular gulps of a cold drink every few minutes. I loved the therapeutic rhythm of golf practice. At night I cooked and ate cold noodle dishes topped with smoked chicken pieces or *nattō* mixed with beaten raw eggs, with plenty of cold beer or *sake* to slake my thirst.

On Saturday night, the television weather forecast predicted rain for Hokkaido and Okinawa. At a maximum temperature for Sunday of 37°C, the hottest place in all of Japan would be…..Hita! For a while I thought no, I can't go. I'll wait until Monday. It'd be too much at 37°C. But loyalty got the better of me. I had solemnly promised my mother-in-law. I stopped off in Fukuoka to have lunch with Tom and Susan Yates to discuss the appalling state of the world, which was our usual topic of conversation. With China's clumsy aggression in the South China Sea and now its regular joint exercises with the Russians, it was only a matter of time before things would 'go over the edge,' as I put it. The sad thing was that Tom's time as Consul-General in Kyushu was to end in a few months' time. I would miss his company very much, his old-fashioned conservatism and dedication to the consular task.

'I really hope we have a Korean crisis while you're still here,' I said. 'You deserve it. I can't think of anyone better to be in charge.'

Tom was circumspect, saying nothing in reply. Clearly, he wanted to stay on in Kyushu longer, but the Department's decisions on personnel movements were not open to appeal. He didn't know what his next post was going to be.

After lunch I drove off in the heat, heading for the hottest place in Japan. As I came off the expressway and drove into Hita the thermometer on my car dashboard showed 38°C. Inside my in-law's kitchen the temperature was 35C. Every window was open. My mother-in-law appeared, a weary smile on her face.

'Ah, Andrew, you're back! Where've you been? It's a month since we saw you. Oh, dear, it's so hot.'

'The air-conditioning's been fixed, right? Aren't you using it?'

Just then my father-in-law appeared wearing a singlet and shorts. 'It doesn't work,' he said.

'I've opened all the windows and doors to let the breeze come in,' said my mother-in-law.

'But surely the air-conditioning works.'

'No, it's not going,' said my father-in-law.

Then suddenly I noticed. It wasn't the old system that had been repaired; it was a brand new unit installed high on the wall, made by Hitachi. I saw a remote control lying on the table over the *kotatsu*. I grabbed it and began trying to get the air-conditioning started. It was a simple task. In a few seconds it was blowing out ice-cold air.

'*Ara!*' cried my mother-in-law. 'It's working!'

'It'll be too cold,' said my father-in-law.

'But it's 35 degrees in here,' I said. 'The temperature will come down very quickly. It'll be very comfortable.' I went and closed all the windows and doors.

'How did you get it started?' my mother-in-law asked.

I showed her how to operate the remote control, indicating the start and stop buttons.

'Isn't that wonderful,' she said. 'It actually works.'

'Well, it was installed just yesterday. How come you weren't using it?'

'Oh, *Otoosan* doesn't get these machine things.'

'I do so,' my father-in-law protested. 'The fellow never explained it properly. I couldn't understand what he was saying.'

'He explained everything,' my mother-in-law replied. 'You just don't get these things. Always the same….'

'It was….well, he was in a hurry. Nobody could've understood him.'

I drove them to Amagase to the Bara no Yu *onsen* for a bath. To bathe in a hot spring on a day when the temperature was 38°C weather might seem an act of madness, but in fact it was refreshing. The temperature of the bath water wasn't as hot as usual, which made it bearable. On the drive back to Hita I noticed some serious rain clouds on the horizon and remarked that we would likely have some *yūdachi* or evening showers.

Eighteen The Challenge of Air-Conditioning

'Nope, no chance of that,' said my father-in-law from the passenger seat. He didn't like being a passenger, but in my car, he had no choice.

'Why's that?' The storm is over near Kurume. It might come to Hita.'

'We won't have showers. It's certain.'

He was right. The rain clouds moved elsewhere and it remained hot, even after sundown. Not for nothing was Hita Japan's hottest place.

We went out for dinner to Takaraya where my father-in-law got drunk pretty quickly. It must have been the heat, I thought. I did my best to get the meal over as soon as possible and get him out of the restaurant where he had begun shouting at the waitresses. When we got home I retired early. The air conditioning unit in the spare bedroom was too cold, the temperature of the remote control stuck on 22°C, which forced me to switch it off and on every hour or two during the night. But at least it was cool enough to sleep. In the morning I found my in-laws in the kitchen just after seven o'clock, the windows open and, of course, the air conditioner not yet switched on. The thermometer showed 30°C inside already. My father-in-law looked guilty when he saw me glancing up at the air conditioner on the wall.

'Well, put it on, then,' he said. I closed the windows and started the unit using the remote control, then went and had a shower. When I returned to the kitchen I found him standing on the tatami gazing up at the air conditioner.

'I can't see what temperature it is,' he complained. 'It's just blowing out cold air. What temperature is it?'

'It's on the remote control,' I replied, showing him the digital display. I had a feeling it was my mother-in-law to whom fell the task of starting and stopping the air conditioner, my father-in-law boycotting the remote control because of what he claimed was an inadequate explanation from the technician who installed it.

'Oh? How about that?' he said, peering at the temperature display.

'You can adjust it up and down with these buttons,' I said. 'But leave it on 22°C. That'll get the room temperature to around 25°C.'

'Really? That's very cold. I could die.'

'Oh, nonsense, *Otoosan*,' said my mother-in-law from where she was preparing breakfast near the sink. 'Do what Andrew says. He knows all about the air conditioner.'

'I'll catch a cold. They're dangerous, these things,' he grumbled.

He sat down and began complaining about a lack of butter for his toast, which was already smeared with a lot of mayonnaise. Then he applied some blueberry jam to the mayonnaise. My mother-in-law saw this and cried, 'You can't mix the jam and the mayonnaise!'

'Well, I did,' said my father-in-law with satisfaction. 'No butter.'

On Monday night I was back at the beach at Lauben Kolonie, surprised to be quite alone. All the weekend bathers had gone. It was a Monday, sure, but because of the lovely sunset I'd expected one or two of the permanent residents like me to be there. Not so. I drank a can of beer slowly and smoked my pipe as I gazed out to sea listening to Tubular Bells on my iPhone. The south-western sky was overcast, the clouds obscuring the sun. Suddenly, however, a hole in the clouds appeared, allowing the sun's rays to hit the sea surface directly in front of Himeshima Island, creating a bright orange glow on the water. The orange glow stayed there for a full five minutes, the tranquil scene something of exquisite beauty. Why was I, a lone *gaijin*, there by myself to enjoy it?

I swam in the warm waters, no jellyfish to sting me, tempted to strip completely naked like I did in the off seasons when nobody at all was around and exult in the solitary joy of it all.

Nineteen

Preparing For War

On Father's Day, Sunday 4 September 2016, a typhoon came up from east of Okinawa and approached Kyushu from the south, making landfall at Shimabara in Nagasaki Prefecture. NHK was calling it a 'strong typhoon,' but it was only half the size of the very large typhoon that struck Iwate Prefecture and Hokkaido a week before. On Saturday night the typhoon's predicted path had it hitting Itoshima and Fukuoka Prefecture directly late on Sunday night, with winds of 125 km/hour, gusting to 200 km/hour and rainfall to 200 mm. To put this into perspective, a normal summer storm would bring around 20 to 40 mm of rain. We were going to be very, very wet. That much was obvious. The path of any typhoon is difficult to forecast accurately, but the chance of this one heading out to sea towards Korea and sparing us the full brunt was slim.

On Saturday afternoon in humid weather I went to the Orange Golf practice range and hit balls for an hour with my hickory set. I'd become pretty good with these antique clubs, and Fujiya-*san*, the owner of the range, loved seeing me there with them. He said my swing had 'a lovely flavour.' The feeling of hitting a dead straight ball with century-old clubs was quite special.

At sunset I went down to the beach again and drank a can of Yebisu beer before having a swim. The sun, a bright orange orb, slowly descended into a bank of dark cloud on the horizon, casting a bright yellow light upon the sea surface. Despite the approach of the typhoon there was no wind at all. In the shallows I noticed a small stingray, something I'd never seen before at our beach. Alone on the eve of Father's Day I ate a dinner

A typical Japanese hot spring or onsen with an outdoor bath, similar to the Bara no Yu onsen in Amagase village to which I took my parents-in-law every time I returned to Hita.

of *jidori* chicken, *nattō* mixed with raw egg, and a small bowl of delicious boiled Kyushu white rice.

The typhoon slowed its pace such that it was now going to hit Fukuoka on Monday morning rather than Sunday night. Father's Day would turn wet in the afternoon, and the worst of the gale force winds would arrive around dawn on Monday. I called Andrew McDaniel and we discussed the effect of the typhoon on his golf course.

'Gonna be wet, that's for sure,' he said in his Alabama drawl.

'And windy.'

'Probably. But it's turf out there. Trees are small.'

'Will the course be closed?'

'I doubt it. There's always someone who'll play, whatever the weather. Japanese love their golf. Hell, they'll all just get wet, I reckon.'

That weekend, Japan was otherwise at ease. Prime Minister Abe had just had a meeting with Vladimir Putin in Vladivostock, Putin making soothing noises about visiting Japan in December to discuss the conclusion of a peace treaty. At the end of the Pacific War Josef Stalin seized a group of islands to the north-west of Hokkaido — which the Russians call the Southern Kuriles, and Japan calls the Northern Territories. This made a formal peace treaty impossible. Since the war it's been a basic tenet of Japanese foreign policy that return of these islands is a precondition for any such treaty and the economic benefits to Russia in the form of Japanese investment in Russia's Far East. These days the islands are populated with plenty of Russians, and the last thing an ultra-nationalist like Putin would do was hand them back to Japan in exchange for money, no matter how broke Russia was in an age of low oil prices.

Yet the Japanese had to keep trying. Part of the reason for engaging with Putin was to keep the Russian leader aware of the benefits of not siding too closely with China in its disputes with Japan (and almost everyone else). One could be forgiven for feeling a degree of scepticism about this notion.

Other news that week included the increasing incidence of bear attacks on people in Honshu, some of these attacks not all that far from Tokyo. Because of the declining population in the mountain towns and villages the number of bears was rising for want of locals hunting them. But, it seemed, the bears didn't have it all their own way. The Japan Times joyfully reported an incident in which a bear attacked a 63-year-old man in Gunma Prefecture. The man, one Atsushi Aoki, was a fifth-degree black belt karate champion. After the bear bit and clawed him Aoki-*san* punched and kicked his attacker as hard as he could. 'I had the chance to hit its eyes,' he told TBS television. 'So I destroyed its right eye, and the bear turned its back and fled.' He added, 'It was hard to look at it without losing presence of mind. Since I have some experience, I was able to deal with the situation to a certain extent.' The Gunma police praised Aoki for driving himself calmly to hospital after the attack, but they warned others venturing into the local mountains not to try and emulate the karate champion's efforts.

This, I thought, was a wonderful metaphor for how to deal with aggressive behaviour like that on display in the South and East China Seas. Two weeks previously I had gone to Sydney to spend an hour with Julie Bishop, Australia's Foreign Minister. She and I had been good friends as junior

MPs, and it was always a delight to see her in the news doing a fine job. All the reporting in Japan about the continuing fantasy of Abenomics and negative interest rates didn't seem to be reflected at all in the global English-language media. This, I felt, was a bigger problem than people outside Japan realised. Japan was getting weaker, and a sudden reversal in interest rates would bring on a severe financial crisis like the post-Bubble bank collapses of the mid-1990s. With Japan on its knees financially, Xi Jinping and his military forces might well choose this moment to do something really aggressive such as seizing one of the Senkaku Islands. Would, or could, Japan respond with military action if its government was transfixed by the collapse of banks and insurance companies?

I explained all this to Julie and her Asian affairs advisor, the young Dr John Lee. They had not heard such facts before from the embassy in Tokyo and seemed keen to hear more. Julie was appropriately circumspect about Chinese aggression, but she did let go one thing that I found quite alarming. The US Administration (except for one or two White House officials) was not really interested in problems in Asia. In other words, we were quite on our own in handling Beijing's increasingly dangerous conduct. If she had said, 'Look, don't worry. Soon we will all join together to confront Beijing and bring this aggression to a stop, like we did with Putin,' then I would've been greatly reassured. But she didn't. Instead she looked despondent.

Back in Japan I gave this encounter a lot of thought. I was reading a book about the Battle of The Atlantic and was astonished to learn how close Hitler came to choking off Britain's supply of food and oil, largely due to a failure in Washington to appreciate the scale of the threat and join in the battle. There was a lot of anti-British sentiment in America in those days, not unlike the subtle hostility to Japan and Korea these days.

Now, here in North Asia, relations with Beijing continued to deteriorate. Xi and the PLA were sending more of their ships into the territorial waters around the Senkakus as every week passed. The Japanese media — except the right-wing papers like the semi-hysterical Sankei — were reporting this without stridency, but it was an undeniable and alarming fact. Beijing was escalating things once again, and while Japan stuck rigidly to the diplomatic choreography of formal protests and Coast Guard interdiction, the day when a real clash happened seemed to be approaching ever more quickly.

What would this do to life in Kyushu? It was difficult to imagine. If NHK suddenly reported that an exchange of fire between Japanese and Chinese naval vessels had occurred, how would everyone react? Panic buying of petrol and food? Maybe so. Before things escalated into a general war one could imagine a global effort at the UN and so forth to stop the conflict from growing, but would the Chinese comply? Everyone would be urging them to avoid doing even worse things, such as launching a massive cyber-attack on Japan's vital infrastructure. Why would they back down? After all, they had a veto in the UN Security Council. And would the North Koreans come to China's assistance and launch missiles right at Japan's nuclear power stations or even Japan's cities? Would they use nuclear warheads on the missiles?

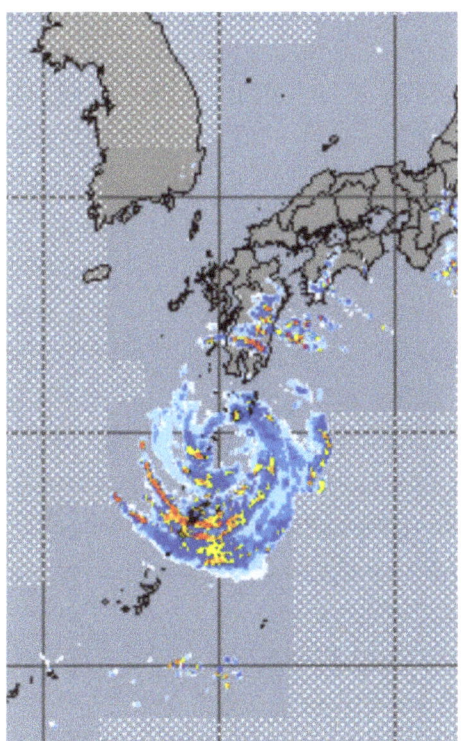

The weather radar map showing a typhoon approaching Kyushu. Every year Japan is battered by typhoons, Kyushu and Okinawa in particular. Yet the rain that comes with them is what fills Kyushu's deep basins of water, source of the island's thousands of hot mineral springs.

For those of us on the front line, so to speak, would it not make perfect sense to hurry to the local petrol station and fill our cars, then hurry to the supermarket to buy canned food and whatever else we might need to sustain ourselves if things did escalate beyond a naval skirmish? An outbreak of war on the seas between Kyushu and Taiwan…..unthinkable, perhaps. But what you see is too often what you get, unless some greater force intervenes.

What greater force? America?

If things did escalate into a war I supposed I'd be stranded in Kyushu for some time. The electricity supply would be a key issue in such an emergency. If the Chinese disabled the grid, even partially, then we would be in mortal trouble. Everyday life would become very hard indeed. The government would place severe restrictions on vital supplies such as fuel and a lot of food. Hardly believing what I was doing, I decided to take action in advance. I drove to Kafuri and at the GooDay store bought a twenty litre fuel tank. At the Sunny supermarket nextdoor to GooDay I bought fifteen kilograms of rice and, absurdly, a four litre plastic bottle of *shochu*. I didn't bother to buy the fifty cans of tuna I'd imagined I'd be needing. That could be done on the next shopping trip. I also bought an extra twelve cannisters of butane gas for the camp stove I used in my kitchen.

On the way home at the Ohkushi petrol station I filled my car and asked Kanae to fill the 20 litre fuel tank, telling her I was about to acquire a 50cc Honda scooter for use around Funakoshi and wanted to fill it at home. This was more or less true. My father-in-law had given me his ancient Honda 50cc scooter and I had taken it to be repaired, given its atrocious condition. In extreme circumstances I imagined leaving Itoshima and driving back to Hita to wait until the evacuation to Australia became possible. Hita would be safe, and I would be more or less comfortable living with my parents-in-law, eating rice and tuna and whatever vegetables we could buy locally. In the worst case we might have to move further south to get away from any danger around Fukuoka, especially if the Genkai nuclear power station was destroyed and was belching out radiation across the north coast of Kyushu where Itoshima and Fukuoka sat.

Yet a full-scale conflict between China and Japan — and perhaps the

United States — would likely have severe consequences for major cities such as Tokyo and Osaka. Kyushu might well be much safer. We had plenty of food and water. Even if the electricity grid was disabled it would be a much easier place to live and get around. The major cities with their concentrated populations might be a living hell as food and fuel dwindled.

In Kyushu there would always be a supply of basic protein, whether from fish or wild boar or deer. The chokepoint might be carbohydrates: bread or grain or rice. Grain would be useless without a way to make flour, so it made sense to build up as large a stock of rice as possible. At a daily ration of 300 grams, a five-kilogram bag of rice would last sixteen days. So, two bags would be needed for each month. If I were to live with my parents-in-law, a six-month supply would be thirty-six bags or 180 kilograms. No doubt they would eat less than me, but a little extra would come in handy. A six-month supply of protein was a bigger problem. Alcohol, too, was worth considering. It could be bartered for other things. One litre of *shochu* a week would be reasonable personal consumption, so that meant 26 litres for six months, or around seven of the large four litre plastic bottles. With some yeast on hand we could even brew our own crude *sake* in winter.

This whole exercise seemed too bizarre for words. Yet every bit of news suggested that Xi Jinping and his team were not afraid of a conflict; that they were calculating that China would emerge in better shape than their foes and that this would leave them masters of all Asia, no matter how badly the region and the world had been trashed. Hitler was, in his day, much the same. Where Hitler saw the world as determined to suppress Germany, my own experience of life in China between 2009 and 2011 left me certain that Xi positively believed the same about China and the world these days: that, as ridiculous as it seemed, everyone was out to keep China weak and at bay. That was why he had declared it his mission to take control of the region.

The question then was, would the region allow this to happen? South-East Asia, Australia, New Zealand…..forget it. No one had the power to stop Xi. It would fall to America and Japan. Maybe, given Japan's inherent military strength and population, Xi would decide it was easier pickings to take control of the South China Sea and all of South-East Asia. But that

Preparing for a chemical weapons attack from North Korea. During the year leading up to the Pyeongchang Winter Olympics the atmosphere became increasingly tense as Kim Jong-Un sent missiles into the Sea of Japan and twice over Hokkaido in the far north. The Japanese Government was cautious about not alarming the population too much, but when missiles strike drills began to be held I became concerned enough to buy a gas mask and stock up on extra fuel and food. Kim's charm offensive in early 2018 eased the tension, but the outcome of the proposed summit with Donald Trump was anything but assured, the threat of Kim's weapons of mass destruction still on foot.

wouldn't be so easy. The US Navy had a huge presence in Japan, its home in Asia. To keep the Americans out of the South China Sea, Xi would have to destroy or disable those US bases in Japan first, at Sasebo in Kyushu and Yokosuka near Tokyo, much as Japan attacked Pearl Harbour to try and take control of the Pacific Ocean at the end of 1941. Some sort of attack on Sasebo would surely be an integral part of Beijing's strategy for winning the initial conflict. That meant a full-on attack on Kyushu. The disruption of vital infrastructure — electricity, gas, communications, transport, and so forth — would be unavoidable.

At one point I drove into Fukuoka to have lunch with my Swiss friends, Aldo and Joelle Bloise. We usually had lunch at a pizza restaurant in Fujisaki, but on Mondays it was closed, so we met at a Japanese restaurant in Nishijin called Ootoya. It served cheap but generous meals. Being the day of the typhoon — which proved to be nothing more than an hour or two of strong winds — the schools were closed, and they had their four-year-old son Matteo with them. I liked Aldo and Joelle a lot, and I had given Aldo some work building an English language website for one of my clients.

Over lunch I felt the need to unburden myself of my worries about the situation with China. I explained what I had done in buying the extra fuel and rice. Joelle blanched.

'So, we're to go to the mountains and make a farm?' she exclaimed.

No need for that, I replied, embarrassed at having alarmed her. Aldo rubbed his head and muttered a series of vague concerns.

'It's not looking good,' I said, 'but you can rest assured Japan will cope with it all.'

'Oh, that's great,' said Joelle with sarcasm. 'Where would we go?'

They did not own a car. In fact, Aldo had never held a drivers licence. He and Joelle rode bicycles everywhere.

'In the worst case I would come and get you in my car,' I said.

'But it's not big enough for all of us.'

'Yes, it is. It's got a roof rack, too. Look, this is not likely to happen, but I'm just telling you what I've done to prepare.'

'Well, thanks,' she muttered. I felt bad. She was a mother with a lovely little boy to worry about. I decided to keep these things to myself from now on.

That evening we learned that North Korea had launched yet another salvo of missiles into the Sea of Japan. This was now something that happened almost every month. Was I completely mad to be stockpiling fuel and food, or was I being negligent in not buying more? Wars in North Asia have a habit of starting with a surprise attack. Maybe the current tensions were the only warning we would get. Maybe we would wake up in a month's time to learn on the early morning news that North Korea and China had launched a pre-emptive attack on us in tandem.

Despite the vague misgivings I had about stockpiling food and fuel I wasn't entirely alone in thinking about taking preemptive action. On 21 August, Reuters reported that the German Government planned to tell

Swiss friends Aldo and Joelle Bloise with their son Matteo. After the tsunami and the Fukushima nuclear disaster in March, 2011, the family quickly left Tokyo and settled in Fukuoka. I took cruel delight in talking about the chances of war with North Korea or China in front of Joelle, but we remained close friends as often happens with fellow gaijin in Japan.

its citizens to stockpile ten days' supply of food and water as a civil defence strategy. This was the first time since the Cold War that such a measure would be taken and was driven more by fears of a major terrorist attack than a military clash with Russia. In Japan it was a fact of history that the 1973 oil shock set off a wave of panic buying of toilet paper, doubtless attributable to the cultural penchant for very high standards of personal hygiene. Shortages of toilet paper also occurred after the 2011 earthquake and Fukushima nuclear disaster.

I decided to put this on my shopping list. That said, at Lauben Kolonie we had the sea to bathe in to maintain personal hygiene after a bowel movement.

For a few days I did nothing except buy a single pack of eight toilet rolls and a selection of tinned food to try out — sardines, tuna, and *yakitori* chicken. When I opened the tin of *yakitori* I found chunks of cooked chicken in a jelly. It smelled exactly like cat or dog food, but I picked out a single chunk of chicken with chopsticks and had to admit it tasted very good. I mixed the tinned *yakitori* with a bowl of raw egg and *nattō*, mixed in a capful of *kabosu*-flavoured soy sauce, and enjoyed a very nice dinner with some steamed rice to go along with it and some *shochu* to wash it down. If this was to be the standard meal after conflict with China broke out, then I was confident I would eat reasonably well. The next step was to buy around five hundred tins of food to accompany my supplies of rice and *shochu*.

I began to relax as the G20 Summit in Hangzhou ended. Obama's humiliation at the hands of Xi Jinping was bad, yes, and Xi's solemn declaration that China would "unswervingly" pursue its illegal island-building in the South China Sea was worse. But Obama would soon be gone and maybe the next American president would somehow put an end to the threat that Xi posed to all of us. Then, on a Friday morning, came the news that North Korea had carried out a nuclear test of what was thought to be a ten-kiloton bomb. Worse, experts were saying that the seismic blast signature suggested that the North Koreans had succeeded in reducing the size of the bomb, perhaps not yet to the small size required for a missile warhead, but progress toward that end nonetheless.

Japan, I thought, was the target of these missiles, not Seoul or continental America. The bases at Sasebo and Yokosuka that constituted the key threat to North Korea and China would be the first missile targets, beyond any doubt.

Japan has a fair number of native monkeys, but they're not something you tend to see outside dedicated monkey parks or certain wild locations in Hokkaido or the Tōhoku area at the top of Honshu. National Geographic and other such magazines from time to time carry photos of Japanese monkeys playing in the snow or enjoying an *onsen* somewhere, but I had never heard any friend or acquaintance in Japan say they had, or intended, to take a trip to see the "snow monkeys." Monkeys are accepted as a rare but generally harmless fact of life for those very few people who choose to live in such remote places.

Our village of Funakoshi was not a remote place. It was only thirty minutes drive from the centre of Fukuoka City. We had our share of *inoshishi*, *anaguma*, spiders, sea eagles, and various insects, hardly surprising given the plentiful forest behind the fishing village and within the boundaries of Lauben Kolonie. But it was not as if we were living in some empty wilderness in Hokkaido or Tōhoku.

Yet one Thursday morning around eight o'clock as I left home to drive into the city to do battle with the Tenjinmachi branch of the Fukuoka Bank, where I maintained an account for Pie Face Japan, I came around a bend maybe fifty metres from my house and saw a brownish animal on the road in front of my car. At first I thought it was an *anaguma*, or maybe an *inoshishi*, but in an instant I recognised it for what it was — a large monkey. It paused for a moment and then leapt into the forest above the road in the direction of my house.

A monkey! A bloody monkey! A *saru*!

It wasn't enough to have become rid of the *inoshishi* — maybe — but now we had a monkey invasion. Kim Jong-Eun's missiles and nuclear tests were a far-off though fearful enough threat, and being typhoon season we

Nineteen Preparing For War

A newspaper image of Kim Jong-un's sister, Kim Yo-jong. The Japanese media speculated at length about Kim Yo-jong, especially when she attended the Winter Olympics in 2018. Some reported that she is the brains behind the Kim regime these days and is responsible for maintaining the cult of personality that surrounds her brother. The conservative media pointed to her as the key figure in brutal measures such as the assassination of Kim Jong-nam, her half-brother whom the Chinese Government was thought to be warehousing in case the need arose to remove Kim Jong-un from power.

were in for a series of regular batterings from gale force winds and torrential rain, but now there was another challenge to face. Like the beginnings of the *inoshishi* problem I had a feeling that the monkey problem — the *saru no mondai* as it later came to be called in talks with the estate staff– would take a long time to solve.

An hour later from my desk in my client D1 Chemical's office I decided to make some calls about the monkey. (The encounter that morning with the bank had ended in failure when I filled out a pension form incorrectly and quit the branch to retreat to my client's office for the rest of the day.) First, I called the office at Lauben Kolonie to report the monkey sighting to Toya-*san*.

'It's your old friend Thomson here,' I began.

'Oi, Thomson-*san*!' Toya cried. 'What's up?'

'Well, I know you face a lot of difficulties looking after things on the estate, but I'm sorry to inform you of one more.'

'Oh? What's that?'

'This morning, around eight o'clock, I saw a large monkey on the road. There's no doubt. It was a monkey.'

'Aaaah….'

'It ran away into the forest. No mistake. It was a monkey, not an *inoshishi*. We've been invaded.'

'Aaaah. Well, actually, we've had three reports this morning about this monkey.'

'Really? So it's true. A monkey.'

'Yes, a monkey.'

'It was quite big. An adult, I think.'

'I know. A few people saw it.'

'How many monkeys have come into the estate?'

'We don't know,' said Toya. 'But it looks like there's a few of them in the forest behind the fishing village.'

'Can we trap them like we did with the *inoshishi*?'

'Saaaa…..'

'Well, I'll call the Itoshima City office to report it.'

'You should do that. Definitely.'

'I don't have any weapons to use, but we should consider the strongest possible measures.'

'Ha! I thought you were more worried about the North Koreans and the Chinese.'

'Oh, I am,' I said. 'But monkeys can carry diseases. Maybe the North Koreans sent this monkey in.'

Toya found this very amusing. A cheerful brand of pessimism was his usual mood as general manager of the estate, and I enjoyed the conversations with him about problems such as *inoshishi*, North Korea, China, and now monkeys. The next call I made was to the Itoshima City office.

'Ah, my name is Thomson. I live in Funakoshi, and I'm calling to report a monkey.'

'A monkey?' said the lady operator.

'Oh, yes. A monkey. It seems like a problem, you know, so I feel obliged to inform the Itoshima City office.'

Nineteen   Preparing For War

A troop carrier of the Ground Self-Defense Forces on manoeuvre in Oita Prefecture. Whenever tensions with China or North Korea increased such vehicles were a frequent sight along Kyushu's expressways, a signal that a military clash in our region was more than a theoretical possibility.

'Understood. I'll connect you to the Agriculture & Fisheries Department.'
A young girl came on the line next.
'I'm calling from Funakoshi,' I said. 'There's a monkey problem here. It's a bit of a worry, so I thought I'd ask for some advice about how to deal with invading monkeys.'
'Oh. Well, first, keep your distance from any monkey. They can bite you.'
'Really? Can the city do anything to catch them?'
'*Saaaa.* It's a problem.'

'Yes, it is a problem. I'm thinking of setting a trap for the monkeys.'

'Oh, you need a licence to do that.'

'Like for trapping *inoshishi*?'

'Yes. Harmful animals and birds can be trapped only by people with a licence to do so.'

'I thought so. Can you send a person to trap the monkeys?'

'I will report your complaint. But please don't do anything without a licence.'

'Well, these monkeys are a real problem. They carry all sorts of diseases. We could be infected.'

'Well, keep away from them at all costs.'

'Yes, but I live here. What do I do if the monkeys come close to my house? I feel like I should kill them.'

'Oh, please avoid doing so. A licence is required.'

'Well, okay. But I'd be grateful for some action from your department. I know that monkeys are clever and it's difficult to catch them in a trap, but the infectious diseases they carry are a big concern out here.'

'I see. It's a problem I will report to the department chief.'

For a moment I considered raising the notion of legal liability for any monkey bite, but the girl was doing her best and there was nothing worse than a troublesome *gaijin* abusing a diligent municipal officer.

'Well, I appreciate your help,' I said. 'We've dealt with the *inoshishi* problem out here, and the monkeys are a part of Nature, but as long as you're aware of the problem I suppose that's fine.'

I went back to China for a two-day visit in late October on the way back to Kyushu from Australia, to a city called Zhongshan, which lies between Guangzhou and Macao. Travelling with a friend from Melbourne, Michael Beer, we went to visit a Chinese company with ambitions to list itself on the Australian Stock Exchange. Though a very old city, dating back to the Sung Dynasty, Zhongshan now was just another boring Chinese urban expanse of apartments, offices, and factories. Its people spoke Cantonese. Driving around the streets I noticed that unlike Beijing there were very few Party banners strung up with the latest propaganda slogans on them.

The company we visited was in the business of selling luxury foods both through its website and a network of franchised retail stores. The owner of the company was a man called Jackie. He spoke little English. One of his staff, a young man who called himself Ayer, spoke a little more English, but not enough for a coherent business discussion. As a result, I spent the two days doing all the translating as well as offering vague legal advice from time to time. This greatly tested my Mandarin skills, and though I quickly regained a degree of fluency in the language I found myself exhausted at the end of each day.

We battled through a series of business meetings in which we laboriously explained the requirements of a stock exchange listing and the concept of continuous disclosure, and we went out by car to inspect some of the the company's retail stores in Zhongshan and then paid a visit to the museum at Dr Sun Yat-sen's ancestral home just outside Zhongshan. The tollways were good, and every so often I saw clusters of cranes at the construction sites of new apartment developments. Though the pace of the economy had

A scene from Korean television news shown in Japan at the time Kim Jong-Un was threatening to hit the US base on Guam with a nuclear ballistic missile. The flight path from North Korea to Guam is right over my house near Fukuoka.

slowed, China was still doing its best to grow. Guangdong Province was the wealthiest part of China, and it showed. On the streets of Zhongshan there were plenty of foreign cars: Mercedes-Benz, Porsche, Audi, Toyota, Nissan, BMW, and Lexus, but no American cars.

On that first day in Zhongshan we had our initial meeting with Jackie in the morning, followed by lunch in the company's restaurant on the ground floor of their office building. The lunch was a series of exotic dishes designed to impress Michael and me with the company's capacity for selling such rare and expensive foods. We duly expressed our admiration and our confidence in the company's future. But by mid-afternoon, after another meeting with Jackie and his senior staff, I began to feel sick. We returned to the hotel for *xuixi* — rest — in preparation for a formal dinner that night.

I slept for an hour in my hotel room, but upon getting up at around five-thirty in the afternoon I didn't feel any better. I dreaded the idea of a banquet, but because I had to do so much translating for Michael and Jackie there was no way I could stay in the hotel room and avoid my duty. After all, they were proposing to appoint me as a director of the company's subsidiary in Australia and, given the shaky position of my client Pie Face, I felt the need for another source of fee income. So, I dragged myself downstairs and went off with Michael and Raymond, Jackie's manager for anything-to-do-with-foreigners, to the same room in the same restaurant for dinner.

I drank a little beer in the hope that it would somehow improve my stomach — it was a Lowenbrau beer — but I couldn't bring myself to eat more than a few morsels. I didn't want to cause embarrassment by attributing my upset stomach to the food served at lunch, so I made up a story about mistakenly drinking some tap water in the hotel room.

'Oh, tap water is very bad,' Jackie said immediately. 'We never drink it. Only bottled water.'

'I won't repeat the mistake,' I said. 'My stomach is very uncomfortable, but it'll be fine by tomorrow morning.'

'Ah!' cried Michael, busy drinking toasts of *bai jiu* white spirit with Raymond across the table amid much shouting. 'We have to go to *karaoke* after this.' He didn't want his translator suddenly disappearing.

'I think I'll have an early night,' I said.

'No! No!' all the Chinese cried. 'You're coming with us!'

My stomach felt all the worse for hearing this.

At the *karaoke* salon Michael began singing Beatles songs at an excruciatingly loud level. Jackie was late arriving, leaving me at the mercy of a solidly drunk Raymond who kept shoving his cellphone in my face. The cellphone had an app that translated his spoken Chinese phrases into incoherent English, which he thought was fantastic. Finally, I brushed the cellphone aside and hurried out of the room in the midst of the cacophony of Michael's singing. Raymond staggered out after me and insisted on seeing me to the car where young Ayer was waiting. Soon enough I was back in the empty lobby of the hotel, much relieved to be free of the drinking and the noise. I slept like a log.

In the morning, now feeling much better, I showered, got dressed, and opened the door to go down to breakfast. On the floor outside my room I noticed something on the carpet. It looked like a leaf, but on closer inspection it turned out to be a small turd.

So, welcome back to China. The message the turd conveyed was crystal clear — you foreigners are not wanted here. One more night in this ghastly place, I thought, and I'll be back in Kyushu.

While in Zhongshan it struck me that China really was rich in places like this. Yet everything the leaders in Beijing did in their foreign policy was putting this wealth at risk. Or was it? Confronting America and Japan on the oceans, building military bases on artificial islands, and pursuing aggressive diplomacy almost everywhere seemed likely to bring on a clash and end in either disastrous military conflict or a regime of painful economic sanctions. Yet, except for Japan, everyone else was giving in to Beijing. Some, such as the gangster president of the Philippines, Rodrigo Duterte, had even gone over to Beijing's side, another landmark in Barack Obama's foreign policy ineptitude. The Chinese leaders had a lot to lose, or so it seemed. Yet they were playing against a very weak opponent in Washington.

When I arrived back in Kyushu, Duterte was in Tokyo after having visited Beijing where he poured scorn on America. Prime Minister Abe hosted him with a constant smile, promising all sorts of economic gifts. Duterte made a few more anti-American remarks but toed the Japanese line in proclaiming his support for the rule of law in the South China Sea, diplomatic code for "China is in the wrong." No one really believed Duterte was genuine, but at least he said what Abe wanted to hear in public. It was crystal clear what was going on here: another small, poor country cadging money from wealthy Japan. Duterte was just shopping around for money from both China and Japan, playing one off against the other. That said, he really did hate Obama's guts. For as long as he was in office the Philippines would not lift a finger to help restrain Beijing. If anything, Duterte was going to kick out all US military forces from his country and quite likely invite the Chinese to replace them.

In the South China Sea, all was lost. That this would embolden Beijing — and probably Pyongyang as well — was obvious. As I had feared, things in the East China Sea around the Senkakus would probably now get much worse. Donald Trump was pretty well finished in the imminent presidential election, so it would all fall to Hillary Clinton and her team to decide our fate. During the election campaign she had said nothing much about the security situation in Asia.

But if Hillary had the guts to confront Xi Jinping and his military, would Xi really risk the huge economic damage to places such as Zhongshan that a military clash with America would bring? Yes, I thought, he would. From a Western perspective, a business or economic perspective, such reckless policy is hard to conceive. But the Chinese Communist Party does not think like that. In the West a bad economy does damage to an incumbent party. But in totalitarian China, the Party has always found strength in times of crisis. *Duo nan, xing bang*, goes the expression in Mandarin: many difficulties strengthen the nation. The terrible mistake we business-focused democrats were making was that Xi valued a better life for the Chinese people. I was convinced that in fact he thought the opposite. Just like Adolf Hitler.

Twenty

Elections

A few miles offshore from my home in Funakoshi on the coast of Itoshima there was an island called Himeshima. The two Chinese characters in its name mean "Princess Island". It's a small island with a population of 75 people who live off fishing. I had been out there twice — once catching the ferry and staying the night in a small *minshuku* inn, and once sailing out there in my boat to spend time snorkeling among the rocks that surround the island.

One night, while staying with my parents-in-law in Hita, I was watching the local Oita prefectural news on the television when I heard the announcer mention an island called Himeshima. The name of this island came up on the screen, and I noticed it was written with the same Chinese characters as the island near my home in Itoshima. That seemed odd. Why would the Oita prefectural news be discussing an island offshore in Fukuoka Prefecture?

The answer, of course, was that Oita Prefecture had an island with the same name. It lay off the Kunisaki Peninsula. This eastern side of Kyushu is not well visited and isn't exactly a place of spectacular scenery or any red-hot action these days. In feudal times it was different: a busy place, being the embarkation point for samurai lords and their retinues taking a boat through the Inland Sea to Kyoto and on to Edo where the shogun lived. With the end of the feudal era and the advent of Western-style ships all the samurai, and later ordinary people, began leaving from their local ports, be they Kagoshima, Nagasaki, Kumamoto, or Hakata. Eastern Kyushu lost its traffic and slowly faded from prominence.

I searched the web for information about the Himeshima Island in Oita. It was not all that far from Hita, and it looked like the perfect place for a day trip on the Vulcan. Somehow, in searching for material about Himeshima, I came across an article written by a former Japan correspondent for The New York Times. The New York Times? How was it that this obscure island had made the international media? According to the article, written in 2009 by Martin Fackler, the island's politics were unusual.

"If Marxism had ever produced a functional, prosperous society, it might have looked something like this tiny southern Japanese island," he wrote. The island had not had an election for mayor since 1955, the two mayors since then being a father and then his son. Everyone on the island had the right to work at the island's administrative office part-time under a work-sharing scheme, and its *kuruma ebi* or tiger prawn farms were collectively owned by the residents.

"Himeshima is North Korea, just a livable version," Fackler quoted an island resident as remarking.

Apart from the political situation on the island I was keen to know what its two thousand residents did for an income apart from tiger prawn farming. The other noteworthy thing about the island was its unique summer festival which featured a *kitsune odori* or fox dance, in which the island's women and children dress as foxes and perform a special religious dance. I was keen to meet some of these foxy women and wondered whether, rather than a day trip, it might be worth staying the night on Himeshima. Who knew what foxy female-related things might happen after a few drinks at night.

I rode the Vulcan all the way to the port where the Himeshima ferry docked, bought a ticket, and waited to drive the bike on board. The other passengers almost all came off a bus to join me: a group of farmers and their wives on some day trip. One old man stared at the Vulcan for a while.

'It's big,' he said.

'Yes, it's certainly big,' I replied.

'What are you doing?' he asked, using fairly rough language.

'I'm going out to Himeshima on the ferry, and I plan to ride around the island.'

This notion astonished him. 'Why would you do that?'

'Tourism, I suppose.'

'Tourism? Hmm,' he grunted and shuffled away to tell his fellow travellers about the *gaijin*, his huge motorbike, and his absurd idea of visiting Himeshima. It wasn't the normal pleasant exchange one has in rural Japan. I had a sense the old man was suffering a touch of dementia.

The voyage out to the island took only twenty minutes, and the terminal on the island seemed very big for such a small place. Two storeys high, it seemed another example of Japan's political establishment pouring taxpayers' funds into distant rural towns to shore up the conservative vote. One could tut-tut about this from an economic standpoint, yet to do the opposite — to spend most of the taxpayers' money in the cities where the bulk of the population lived and leave the countryside to decay — would leave Japan, and the world, in a bad state. Japanese culture exists side-by-side with Nature, and with farming and fishing. The culture also exists in the cities, but it is nourished from the mountains, the flat plains covered in rice fields, the coasts, and these islands.

On this first visit to Himeshima, I rode around the island on the Vulcan, feeling conspicuous on such a large motorbike. I went to the lighthouse, the unusual *onsen* whose water turned brown on exposure to the air, and looked at the main town and the three other tiny hamlets. I had a lunch of tiger prawn *soba* in a restaurant run by three attractive women, but they weren't much interested in a foxy conversation with me, so I took the ferry back to the mainland and rode all the way back to Hita.

In October a political bombshell hit Oita's Himeshima Island: for the first time in sixty-one years there would be a contested election for the position of mayor. Someone had dared to challenge the 73-year-old incumbent mayor, Mr Akio Fujimoto, who had been elected unopposed eight times in a row. The Oita Godo Shimbun splashed the story on its front page with the headline UNPRECEDENTED ELECTION CAMPAIGN — FIRST MAYORAL ELECTION ON HIMESHIMA IN 61 YEARS.

The challenger was 67-year-old Mr Toshikazu Fujimoto, who had been born on Himeshima before leaving to pursue a career with the national broadcaster NHK. Challenger Fujimoto had been back living on the island in retirement for two years before deciding to launch a political career.

'I'm a complete election novice,' he told the newspaper.

'Well, if my opponent does start an election campaign I'll have to respond,' said Mayor Fujimoto. 'Otherwise people will say "He's full of himself."'

Because Himeshima was so small with so few roads there was doubt about whether campaign cars should be used. Mayor Fujimoto expressed grave concern at the nuisance such vehicles would cause if the candidates drove around blaring out campaign speeches and slogans, as was the custom in Japanese elections. This seemed an obvious ruse to limit the challenger's campaign against him. Further, there were no boards erected on the island for campaign posters to be displayed, a further blow to the challenger. With only 1,958 people eligible to vote in the election, the campaigning would not be so much a matter of public messages as person-to-person persuasion.

'I will campaign in a way that suits the island,' the challenger told the newspaper. 'I have to make it understood that there's a need for reform and that re-election of the incumbent will be damaging.'

An island resident was quoted as saying, 'The result will be decided by blood ties and local relationships.'

In other words, the challenger had no hope.

Having read the article I decided to go back to Himeshima and see what this election was all about. As a keen observer of politics anywhere it was an irresistible visit. On a Thursday in early November we had a public holiday — Culture Day — so without much else in mind I thought it would make a decent day trip. I had my father-in-law's ancient 50cc Honda motor scooter, which I decided to take to Himeshima. On the Wednesday night I loaded it into the back of my Toyota Landcruiser in preparation for the trip from Itoshima. Riding it around Himeshima would be fun, I thought.

I rose at 6am the next day to make an early start. Things began badly when the Toyota refused to start. The battery was dead, so I unloaded the scooter around 7am and rode down to the Ohkushi petrol station in the hope they might have a new battery.

The owner, Mr Ohkushi — Kanae's boss — took my request very seriously.

'*Saa*, a Toyota Landcruiser? Well, I don't have any batteries for that big a car. You'll have to go to the Nafco store to get it. Make sure the size is right. It's no good trying to use a battery that's too small.' He examined a manual of some sort. 'See, you need a size 70. I've only got a 40. And make sure you buy a Japanese battery. The foreign ones — Korean or Chinese — are no good. It has to be a Japanese one.'

'Like a Yuasa?'

'Yes. Or another Japanese one. Understand?' I had the distinct impression that he thought I would — as a *gaijin* — be partial to buying foreign batteries. Nothing could be further from the truth.

'I promise I will definitely buy a Japanese battery,' I replied.

Two hours later I rode down to the GooDay store, which was closer than its rival Nafco, and bought a Hitachi battery.

It took only two and a half hours to reach the Himeshima ferry at the tiny port of Imi on the coast of the Kunisaki Peninsula. Himeshima lay a few miles offshore. I unloaded the scooter from the Toyota in the car park, rolling it down a wooden plank. At the ticket office inside the terminal I asked for a return ticket for one adult and a 50cc scooter. The prices for vehicles were graded according to the size of the engine, and a 50cc scooter cost ¥210 each way.

'You can buy a return ticket for yourself,' said the lady behind the glass, 'but for the scooter you can only buy a one-way ticket.'

'Really?' I said. This sounded very odd. I couldn't remember it being like this when I took the Vulcan to Himeshima. 'Then how do I bring the scooter back? Is the scooter ticket valid for both ways?'

'Oh, no. You have to buy another ticket for it on the island. You go into the terminal there and buy it. Not here.'

'With respect, that sounds a strange way of doing things.'

'Well, you'll need another ticket for the scooter,' she said, ignoring my criticism. 'Make sure you don't lose your own return ticket.'

'I understand. Thank you.'

There weren't many passengers on board, and it was fun to ride the scooter into the hold of the ferry and park it on one side where the helmeted crew went to great lengths to tie it down securely. On the voyage over I noticed another ferry coming back to the mainland. For an island with only two thousand or so residents and one fishing port this seemed rather extravagant: two large car ferries and two very decent terminals. The very cheap cost of the tickets meant that the whole ferry operation must have run at a steep loss, financed no doubt by the prefectural government. Why, I wondered, as an Oita Prefecture taxpayer, did this small island have such unusual political muscle?

Once on the island I went straight into the ferry terminal, all two storeys of it, to buy the return ticket for my scooter as instructed.

'Which departure do you want?' asked the lady on duty.

'The four-thirty ferry, please.'

'Come back at three-twenty. That's when we start selling tickets for the four-thirty ferry,' she said.

I might have known. 'Surely you could sell a ticket now?' I asked.

'It's impossible. Come back at three-twenty.'

North Korea.

Himeshima describes itself as a "geo park" because of its rare geological features, which include a certain type of black obsidian rock that is only found on one cliff face on the island. According to a tourist sign this rock was highly valued for decorative jewellery in the feudal period and was "sold to Nagasaki at that time". According to a website I read, the rock was valued well before that: in prehistoric times it was used to make blades and arrow heads, some of which had been found in various prehistoric sites around Western Japan.

The island was only seven kilometres long. I took off on the scooter to visit the eastern end where the lighthouse sat on a promontory. Halfway there in a valley where some rice fields lay brown after the harvest I noticed what looked like a group of people standing around dressed in colourful costumes. It was Culture Day. Maybe they were performing some sort of rare Shinto ritual like the fox dance. I stopped the scooter to have a closer look, only to find the people in the field were actually a group of life-size dolls. Later enquiry by phone to the island's tourist office revealed these were *kakashi* dolls, a kind of scarecrow doll representing a god of rice fields. Nobody was present but me, and the whole scene had a mysterious, rather ghostly feel about it. I had never seen life-size dolls in Japan before, except there on Himeshima. A website from Kyoto about dolls I read later had it that "People appreciate *kakashi* and present sacrifices at the altar." What sort of sacrifices?

The roads were quiet, and I came back to the port on a narrow but recently resurfaced asphalt road that ran along the water's edge. Here and there tiny hamlets of a few houses each sat nestled into gullies in the side of the hill. Back at the ferry terminal I noticed a tourist information office across the road that doubled as a café, with a menu on a sandwich board outside and a banner that said in English "Let's have a break." Why not? I parked the scooter across the road and went inside to find two women talking to each other behind the counter. They greeted me politely, visibly relieved to hear me speak Japanese. I ordered a coffee and a vanilla ice-cream. The younger woman disappeared behind a curtain to prepare my order. The other woman, wearing a severe expression and a bit overweight, regarded me carefully as she took my money.

'Where are you from?' she asked.

'From Hita,' I replied.

'Hita?'

'I am originally from Australia. But I live in Hita these days.' This was not entirely true given my Itoshima house, but I did pay tax in Hita.

'Hita? You came on that scooter, right? All the way from Hita on a scooter?'

I laughed. 'No, I brought the scooter in my car. I just rode it onto the ferry to use it here on the island.'

She produced a rueful smile. 'You brought the scooter by car from Hita, so you could ride it on Himeshima?' Her expression was clear: only a *gaijin* would do such an extraordinary thing.

'Sure. I like riding scooters. And I'm testing a special oil additive in it.' This last explanation was lost on her.

The younger woman, whose teeth were in dire need of some serious orthodontic work, brought the coffee and the ice cream.

'So, Australia, eh?' said the overweight woman, whom I thought of as a housewife. 'There used to be an Australian man who lived here for a while. He married a local.'

'Really? How extraordinary.'

'Oh, yes. He was the first *gaijin* here ever.'

'And many people from here have been to Australia because of him,' said the woman with the bad teeth. 'He taught English conversation.'

'Amazing,' I said. 'Was that his only job here? He didn't work in the fishing industry, or in the prawn farms?'

They laughed. 'No, that would be impossible,' said the housewife. 'He just taught English here.'

Did any other *gaijin* come to live here after him?'

'No,' they said. 'It's an island,' added the younger woman as if this were a disqualifying condition.

'Anyway, how come you live in Hita?' asked the housewife.

'I married a woman from there.'

They nodded in unison. Why else would a *gaijin* live in the countryside?

'But she went back to Australia. I stayed here.'

They found this highly amusing. 'You stayed in Hita?' exclaimed the housewife.

'Well, on weekdays I live and work in Fukuoka, in Itoshima. But on weekends I usually come back to Hita. This is my second visit to Himeshima. I hear you have an election soon.'

'Yes, next Sunday,' said the housewife.

'It's the first election in many years, right?'

'Yes.' Neither woman seemed enthusiastic about the topic.

'And both candidates have the same name — Fujimoto, right?'

*My Kawasaki 900cc Vulcan Classic,
a bike that carried me far and wide over Kyushu.*

'Yes.'

'Are they related?'

'Oh, no,' said the housewife.

'A lot of people on the island have that name,' said the younger woman. 'But they're not necessarily family relations.'

'And the challenger, does he have any chance of winning the election?' I asked.

'*Saaa*, nobody knows,' they chorused.

'Well, Japan is a democracy,' I remarked. They didn't seem too impressed with this observation. 'I notice there are no election posters anywhere,' I continued.

'No, we don't have that sort of thing here,' said the housewife approvingly.

'What about broadcast cars?'

'Yes, they're using cars,' said the younger woman, who seemed more comfortable with the notion of an election.

I drank the coffee and ate the ice-cream, which was excellent. We changed the subject and chatted about the weather and the seasons.

'Recently there was a big earthquake in Kumamoto, and a fair bit of shaking in Oita. Did you feel the shaking here?' I asked them.

'Not really,' said the younger woman. 'We don't get earthquakes around here.'

'Well, that's what the people in Kumamoto thought,' I said. 'Do you have *tsunami* drills?'

'Of course,' said the housewife. 'Everyone has them if you live near the sea.'

'I'm sure Himeshima will be safe,' I said.

As I left the café the housewife also left, carrying some shopping. I offered her a lift on the scooter, and she laughed at the idea. 'Your husband might be angry if he saw you on a scooter with a *gaijin*,' I said. She shook her head immediately. I got the strong impression her husband would be unwise to express any objection to her conduct.

'Is the mayor going to win the election?' I asked her.

'Of course,' she replied.

During our conversation the women had urged me to go over to the island's school to see the local Culture Festival — this being Culture Day — so I rode the scooter through the streets of the town according to their directions. In a tiny park in front of the school I found a television news crew sitting on a bench. A young woman with them smiled at me and we struck up a conversation.

'What material are you gathering here?' I asked her. 'Culture Day?'

'Well, actually we came to get material about the election,' she replied.

'Me, too. Well, sort of. I'm not a journalist, just a tourist. Who's going to win, the mayor or the challenger?'

'Oh, it's not clear. We don't know.'

'Until the election nobody knows.'

'That's true.'

'Would you like to interview me about it?'

'Ah…..I don't know.'

'I can offer some opinions on democracy in Japan. After all, Himeshima has been mentioned in the New York Times. It's world famous.'

'*Saaa…..*'

I gave up and went over to the school auditorium from which the sound of singing could be heard. Inside around two hundred people were sitting listening to a series of local men and women singing *enka* ballads on a stage, just like the Sunday noontime television program *Nodo Jiman* in which NHK goes out to local towns and holds a singing competition. Some of the participants are terrible, but some are very good. I entered the lobby of the auditorium where a man gave me a single page program and urged me to go inside. I did so and stayed about fifteen minutes listening to the singing, then left on the scooter. There didn't seem anywhere else to go but the port. Across the road from the ferry terminal I found a large bronze statue sitting within a small, well-landscaped park. It was a statue of the current mayor's father, Mr Kumao Fujimoto, who had served as mayor of Himeshima for twenty-nine years and was always elected unopposed. Beside the statue was a stone plinth carrying a commentary about this man.

"Mr Kumao Fujimoto was a great man, born on Himeshima," it began.

"He was a heroic figure in the whole of Oita Prefecture." The commentary went on to explain that he had worked in Manchuria as a young man and had returned to Himeshima at the age of thirty-four when "the war ended in misfortune." Thereafter he selflessly devoted himself to the welfare and prosperity of the island, rising to serve as chairman of the Inland Sea Area Fishing Industry Committee and as a member of the National Fishing Ports Inspection Committee. He was chairman, too, of the Oita Prefecture Fishing Cooperative, and a strong supporter of the great Eiichi Nishimura, Deputy President of the Liberal Democratic Party. No wonder Himeshima had such an oversized ferry service and such good roads. "Residents of the prefecture thought of Mayor Fujimoto and Eiichi Nishimura as one and the same person," proclaimed the commentary.

With such an illustrious *pater* it would be astonishing if his son, the current Mayor Akio Fujimoto, lost the forthcoming election. The only matter of interest would be how many votes the challenger would pick up.

At the front of the park was a huge block of the obsidian rock for which Himeshima was famous. I wandered across the road to a souvenir shop and began inspecting the items on sale, looking for some obsidian rock ornament. Two older ladies who ran the shop greeted me cautiously. I told them I was keen to buy a souvenir, and did they have something made from the famous obsidian rock?

'Oh, you speak such good Japanese!' said one of the ladies.

'It's not so good. But what about the famous rock? I'd love to buy an ornament of some sort.'

'Oh, no, you can't do that. If you take a piece of the rock you'll be fined,' one of them said severely.

'Fined? But I want to buy a souvenir. I'm not going to steal any rocks.'

'Oh, no. It's forbidden. Perhaps you'd like to buy something to eat.'

'Well, maybe,' I said. I began looking at the various preserved seaweeds and the frozen tiger prawns in a freezer cabinet. Nothing really took my fancy, but I saw some jars of *iwanori*, the pulverised *nori* seaweed you put on boiled rice. I loved *iwanori* and as it happened had none in my fridge at that time.

The phallic shrine at Port Imi on the Kunisaki Peninsula in Oita Prefecture where the ferry crosses to Himeshima Island. Certain strands of folk Shinto worship such symbols as a fertility rite.

'I'll take the *iwanori*,' I said.

'You'll definitely like it,' said one of the women.

'It's made here on Himeshima?'

'Oh, yes.'

'I understand you have an election coming soon.'

'Yes,' they said, suddenly cautious.

'Who will win? The mayor or the challenger?'

'*Saaa*, we don't know,' they said in unison.

'Well, there's a big statue of the mayor's father over there,' I said, pointing to the park across the street. 'Surely the mayor will win.'

'Yes, he will,' said the woman who packed up my *iwanori*.

'I've been going around the island today and I saw a lot of prawn farms,' I said. 'I heard they are all communally owned. Is that really true?'

'Well, the farms belong to a joint stock company.'

'Really? Who are the shareholders of this company?'

'Ah, we are.'

'All the island residents?'

'Yes.'

'I see. And what if someone comes to live on Himeshima? Do they get shares in the company?'

'Ah, we're not sure about that. Wouldn't you like to buy some frozen prawns? They're very tasty.'

'Thank you, but I'll just take the *iwanori*.'

'Oh, what a pity.'

'Well, I'm riding a scooter. The frozen prawns would thaw out.'

But these women, being shareholders of the prawn farming company, were not to be deterred. 'We can send them to your house frozen.'

'Next time, I promise. Maybe I can place an order by telephone next week,' I said, edging out of the shop. It was twenty past three, so I rode the scooter the hundred yards or so to the ferry terminal and filled in the form to buy the return ticket for the scooter. One of the spaces on the form asked for my age. I couldn't help but ask the lady on duty at the ticket window why this was necessary.

'Well, it's on the form,' she said, accepting my money.
'But is it really necessary to know my age?'
'I don't know.'

There didn't seem much point in pursuing the matter. Next time I thought I'd enter a false age in protest. I would claim to be a hundred years old, like Prince Mikasa who had died that week.

On the return voyage the late afternoon sun illuminated the mountains on the mainland in a series of misty silhouettes, giving them a mysterious appearance. Small coastal ships were visible on the horizon. On the television inside the cabin Kei Nishikori was battling some European opponent on a tennis court somewhere. The passengers stared at the television with vacant, weary expressions. There was probably not one tennis court in the entire district. In the car park at Port Imi I got the scooter back into the Toyota and drove off to see the Imi Betsugu Shrine, which sat just behind the port area. It was recommended on a website I'd found dealing with the Kunisaki Peninsula. This Shinto shrine was said to be famous in the district and of course very old. Within the grounds there was a small separate shrine containing a perfectly formed stone phallus, decorated with a sacred straw rope — a fertility god. I hesitated before it, feeling it would not be proper to offer a prayer. After all, I had two children already. This was a shrine for young people, I decided, not a hundred-year-old scooter tourist.

The only time I got to see the mayor of Himeshima and his challenger was on a television broadcast the morning after the election. I had gone up to Tokyo for a few days of meetings with law firms and the election on Himeshima had made the NHK morning news bulletin which I sat watching in my hotel room while eating breakfast. In the report Mayor Akio Fujimoto came across as confident but inarticulate, wearing the usual *hachimaki* headband with his name on it and a broad paper sash, also with him name on it, over his suit. As if anyone on the island didn't know his name!

Challenger Toshikazu Fujimoto was, by contrast, fresh and well-spoken. This, I thought, did not bode well for his chances. The NHK reporter explained that around ten percent of the islanders were employed in the administrative office at any one time under the work-sharing arrangement. The population was shrinking, and the fishing industry was in decline. Three residents were interviewed, one lady expressing fears that the campaign 'could become ferocious.' An elderly man grumbled that things were bad on the island and that 'there's collusion going on.'

The final scene of the report showed Mayor Fujimoto raising his hands in a *banzai* salute of victory. He had won the election with 1,122 votes to Challenger Fujimoto's 512.

Meanwhile another political bombshell struck Japan — over in America Donald Trump won the presidential election. The shock this caused in Japan was no less than anywhere else in the world and very quickly turned to mild panic in the media. Japanese people have always regarded America as a country where the most unusual things happen in all walks of life. But Donald Trump? It had been assumed as a complete certainty that Hillary Clinton would win and become the next US President.

So, think again, as they say.

Trump? The only presidential candidate who had ever questioned the value of the US-Japan alliance? The man who had blithely suggested that Japan (and Korea) build nuclear weapons to defend themselves? The man who peremptorily threw the whole TPP trade agreement into the lake, an agreement that Prime Minister Abe and the LDP were *that very week* ramming through the Diet? How could he…..?

Abe was good on his feet. He called Trump immediately and had what was described as "a warm conversation." I was delighted at Trump's victory, but I thought when you have "a warm conversation" with a New York real estate mogul get ready to be put on the rack. As Mao once said of the Kuomintang, "When the fox seems friendly, put another lock on the chicken coop."

The problem for Abe, and Japan, was that Trump seemed to have formed his view of Japan in the late 1980s during what was called the Bubble

Economy. This was a period of rampant speculation in Japanese assets and absurdly easy money, a time when Mitsubishi Estate bought the Rockefeller Center in Manhattan. Trump was just then emerging as a real estate developer in New York, and quite likely he took severe umbrage at these Asian intruders outbidding him for sites with their easy money. Japan went broke when the bubble burst in the early 1990s, but Trump never forgot. Now it was *him* in charge of things, and Japan would have to submit to *his* wishes.

NHK was fair in its post-election coverage. Now that the broadcaster had conservative leadership under Chairman Momii it was hardly going to be expressing regret at Hilary's defeat. The early hope among many in Japan was that Trump's fierce anti-China rhetoric during the campaign would mean he would end up on Japan's side in all the disputes with Beijing. Moreover, Trump seemed unusually friendly with Vladimir Putin, and Abe was doing his best to forge some sort of understanding with Putin and — unlikely as it was — get some or all of the islands north of Hokkaido back from the Russians. Was it possible, the Sankei Shimbun asked, that a new US-Japan-Russia friendship could come about?

The Sankei Shimbun is Japan's most right-wing daily newspaper. One inkling of conservative thought in Japan surfaced in a front-page opinion piece the day after Trump's election victory.

"So what if Donald Trump walks away from the US-Japan alliance?" the editorial committee member wrote. "That might be a good thing. It would force the Government to acquire our own aircraft carriers so we can actually defend ourselves."

Well, yes, I thought as I read the column. Japan could indeed build its own carriers. The heavy industry companies would be delighted. I felt sure Trump would applaud this, too. Better than American taxpayers footing the bill for more naval assets in the Pacific. China was building its own carriers. Why shouldn't Japan do so? Burden sharing had to mean more than just writing cheques and sending them to the US Department of Defense.

At home in Lauben Kolonie everyone was preparing for the fall of the autumn leaves. Yamashita-*san* and his boys had persuaded the management committee to acquire a vacuum truck to save on labour costs. One day I heard the truck driving around making a huge noise. The hot summer weather had lasted longer than usual, and the leaves were late in turning brown and falling to the ground. Yet the vacuum truck drove along our roads doing nothing but fanning a huge cloud of dust. I found Toya-*san* driving along behind the truck in his car to observe its performance. That's what senior managers in Japan do. I noticed he had dyed his hair a dark grey.

'Oi, Thomson-*san*!' he cried.

'You've dyed your hair,' I said.

'Only a little.'

'Amazing. You look younger.'

'As if.'

'No leaves yet.'

'Soon,' he said, nodding sagely. 'It's going to get cold next week.'

'Well, I hope the machine works okay,' I said, pointing at the leaf vacuum truck ahead which was still making an incredible noise and throwing up a typhoon of dust.

'It's fine,' said Toya-*san*. 'Saves us money.'

'That's good. I'm going back to Australia for a month.'

Toya-*san* looked pained. 'A month? That's a long time.'

'Things to do, you know. My wife's coming back with me in December.'

'Great.'

'I suppose so. How about Trump, eh?'

'Oh, Trump. Scary.'

'He'll be okay.'

'Really?'

'Sure. He plays a lot of golf. Golfers aren't dangerous.'

'I don't know.....'

Down at the Ohkushi petrol station I filled my Toyota and spent a few minutes bantering with Kanae.

'I'm going away for a month,' I said. 'I won't see your smiling face for weeks. It's terrible.'

She laughed. 'You'll be okay.'

'Well, I have to go. Business, you know.'

'I suppose so.'

'What did you think of Donald Trump winning the election in America?'

She looked utterly puzzled. 'Trump.....Oh, well.....'

'He's going to be the next American President.'

'*Saaaa*, he probably is.'

'Well, we have to deal with China and North Korea.'

'Really?'

'Well, maybe. When do you start working Sundays at the oyster huts?'

'I'm going to wait a month before starting. It's too soon now.'

The geopolitical consequences of Trump's election, needless to say, were a long way from the thoughts of a petrol pump girl in Itoshima. But I had a feeling that such isolation was going to change.

Winter came, and in late December, just in time for New Year, I was back in Kyushu with Sayuri and Cail. Sara, the young adult, had other travel plans: Central America with her friends. As usual Sayuri took to cleaning the house at Lauben Kolonie with more than the usual vigour. A sort of mania possessed her. Clothes were removed from drawers, examined, and a torrent of criticism came my way for allowing various insects to eat holes in my sweaters or for spots of mould from the summer's humidity to remain on coats or trousers. All up, I was declared totally incapable of managing life in a place as wild as Funakoshi, an irresponsible fool who plainly didn't recognise the importance of the fight against domestic turpitude.

And this was only in Funakoshi. When we drove to Hita and she took her first look at her parents' state of affairs she became, to put it mildly, very concerned. It was true that the house in Hita was not all that clean and tidy. Moreover, my parents-in-law's continued deterioration was obvious. Sayuri gave them the necessary chastisement, which, perhaps unreasonably, caused me no small upset. I reacted poorly by treating her with coldness and suppressed anger. If she wanted her parents to change their behaviour, I thought, there was a better way to do it: gentle, continuous persuasion. Using strident words only provoked them into resisting, which led to more quarrelling. My mother-in-law often retired to her bedroom to escape the criticism. She was frail now and her memory loss was worsening. My father-in-law reacted stubbornly to Sayuri's broadsides, sitting at the *kotatsu* with the heater off, rugged up in four layers of wool and grumbling in a low voice about the unfairness of his daughter's criticism.

I thought my parents-in-law had a grip on how they lived, but Sayuri was right. Somehow or other they had to adapt to their gradual lack of ability to manage their lives, and a vigorous chastisement was probably the best way to achieve this result. That said, there was no way in their dotage they would ever meet her standards of hygiene or eat perfectly balanced meals. Yes, their mental faculties were poor and steadily worsening, but they had a geriatric care worker from the Hita City Office — called a *herupaa* (helper) — visit them three days a week to see to adequate food and so forth. More than this, my mother-in-law spent three days a week in a day care centre for elderly people, which did her a world of good. Sometimes she was completely lucid, but more often she was in a state of mild dementia, regularly asking the same questions and forgetting what she was told. Much of Japan was in this situation, and you could see before your eyes where the tax revenues were being necessarily spent.

For the past couple of years, the number of car crashes involving elderly drivers (mostly men) had steadily risen, and lately there had been some terrible accidents in which small children had been killed by drivers with dementia. Public concern about this threat of elderly, incompetent drivers grew rapidly, and my brother-in-law Hidenori made the decision to sell my father-in-law's Toyota Prius, leaving the old man with no means of transport apart from his bicycle and buses or trains. It was a sad but necessary measure to take. His daily drives to the Bara no Yu *onsen* in Amagase were becoming too great a risk. Sooner or later there would be an accident and some elderly pedestrian — or, horror of all, a small child — might be killed. Under Japanese social norms responsibility for the accident would have partly fallen on Hidenori ('You knew he was a dangerous driver, but you did nothing!'). Such wide apportioning of blame is common in Japan, far beyond the boundaries of common law or civil law notions of legal liability.

Otoosan took the confiscation of his car with dignity. He knew well enough himself that his driving was dangerous. Hidenori had even had a new bath installed in their home, one that was easier to get in and out of for elderly people. But — and this became a focus of Sayuri's anger — my parents-in-law, after a full month without the car and the daily trips to the *onsen*, had yet to use the new bath. My mother-in-law had a bath at the day care home three times a week, and my father-in-law was down to maybe two baths a week by taking a taxi to the Kanpo *onsen*. Even I could not defend such behaviour. With us back in Hita, though, we were able to drive them to either Bara no Yu or another *onsen* every day, and they were utterly delighted. The new bath at home…..Well, you can lead a horse to water, as they say in English. Japanese has no such proverb, but the one perhaps closest in meaning is *uma no mimi ni nembutsu* — reciting Buddhist sutras into a horse's ear — which means taking a useless measure.

The four days and nights spent in Hita that winter were, apart from the remonstrating between Sayuri and her parents, a pure delight. It was the annual ritual of it all that I really enjoyed. On *oomisoka* or New Year's Eve Hidenori arrived with the special New Year food — *osechi ryori* — which you eat for brunch on New Year's Day. On New Year's Eve we stayed up until midnight eating, drinking, and watching the NHK singing contest on television. In the morning we all went to the Ohara Jinja for *hatsumōde*, the first prayers of the year. It was very crowded in the grounds of the shrine. My parents-in-law enjoyed it, though we had to keep a wary eye on my mother-in-law whose presence of mind was so poor that she was liable to wander away and get lost in the crowd.

I wondered whether this would be the last New Year we would spend at the family home in Hita. It was a miserable thought that due to my parents-in-law's poor health they would in the coming year have to move into an aged care home such that after my twenty-five years of marriage to Sayuri the annual ritual of *shōgatsu* in Hita would come to an end.

My fears of the looming military crisis in our region ratcheted up another notch as spring came upon Japan. North Korea launched four missiles simultaneously a week into March. It happened early on a Monday morning as I was flying back to Kyushu from China. The missiles flew 1000 kilometres and landed in the Sea of Japan offshore from Akita Prefecture. Had they been aimed at Kyushu they would have struck Fukuoka, or northern Nagasaki Prefecture. The North Koreans jubilantly announced that the missile launch was a drill for striking American military bases in Japan: Yokosuka near Tokyo, Iwakuni near Hiroshima, and Sasebo near my home.

As mad as Kim Jong-Eun seemed, this was an obvious strategy. He probably didn't yet have an ICBM that could reach the American mainland, but he was demonstrating a clear ability to strike his enemy where some of its most potent assets were to be found — in Japan.

Abe and Trump made the expected noises of outrage, but what could they do to stop the worst happening? They talked in elliptical terms about military retaliation against Kim. This was hardly going to stop him, I thought. The US began deploying an advanced anti-missile system in South Korea, much to the fury of Beijing, but some reports had it that the North Koreans were not so stupid. They had perfected a technique of launching their missiles at an unusually high angle so the trajectory on return to Earth was much steeper, making them harder to intercept and destroy.

Kim had succeeded in assassinating his half-brother Kim Jong-Nam in Kuala Lumpur Airport in mid-February, using VX nerve gas to kill him. Kim Jong-Nam had been warehoused by the Chinese in Macao, perhaps to become the new leader of North Korea if the Chinese were to mount a coup against Kim Jong-Eun. This was altogether a reasonable possibility. After all, Kim's reckless behaviour had led to the Americans deploying their most potent anti-missile system right on China's doorstep. Beyond doubt, there were plenty of people in Beijing saying, 'This fat little shit has to go.' Or worse.

In Kyushu we sat back and watched things steadily deteriorate. Obama, whose pacifism encouraged every evildoer in the world to escalate their misdeeds without any restraint, was gone. Now we had Donald Trump as our protector.

Twenty-one

The Stones of Miyazaki

Down at the bottom end of Kyushu between Kagoshima and Oita Prefectures lies Miyazaki Prefecture. This large, mountainous region faces the Pacific Ocean and every year takes a ferocious beating from typhoons. I'd read somewhere that Miyazaki is Japan's poorest prefecture measured by average income. It doesn't look especially poverty-stricken. It's just that no great industry of any sort has taken root there. Inland its mountains are sparsely populated. The rest of the prefecture is pretty much devoted to agriculture. But it does have Japan's best surf beach, at Hyuga, and it certainly has Japan's oddest-looking monument — the Miyazaki Peace Tower.

This enormous stone structure hit the national news briefly in March 2015 when an unusual woman Diet member uttered a vastly politically incorrect phrase when asking a question of the Minister for Finance, our old Kyushu friend Aso Tarō. The Peace Tower, as it is called these days, was built in 1940. As an article in The Japan Times by Hiroshi Motomura described it:

> "A monument in the city of Miyazaki built to glorify Imperial Japan's occupation of Asian nations and later rededicated as the city's Peace Tower has been a source of local discomfort for decades.
>
> In 1965, authorities restored an Imperial-era slogan on the 36-meter stone tower, despite opposition from critics who felt it sent the wrong message.
>
> The four-character phrase is "Hakko Ichiu" (Eight Corners of

the World Under One Roof). The slogan was used by the Imperial Japanese military as it sought to create 'a new world of human fraternity under the Japanese emperor.' The tower was built in 1940 to commemorate the 2,600th anniversary of the ascension of Emperor Jimmu, the nation's first emperor.

Made of stones from around the Japanese empire, it was used to rally people's fighting spirit in World War II but was later scorned as a symbol of that ill-fated venture. It eventually survived as a symbol of peace."

Reading this article at the time I resolved to go and see the Miyazaki Peace Tower one day. It took me two years to get there, but one fine Saturday in March 2017, the morning after I had returned to Kyushu from Tokyo, I set out early in the morning and drove all the way down to Miyazaki. The tower was visible from a couple of miles away, jutting skywards from the top of a hill at the back of the city, not far from the Miyazaki Jinja, dedicated to the nation's first emperor, Jimmu. It was built of dark stone and looked very like something from Angkor Wat. From its hilltop position it dominated the landscape of what is otherwise a lovely expanse of forested parkland.

I wandered into the park, finding a broad lawn in front of the tower. Two small girls were playing around a bench by the entrance. One of them, a chubby child wearing serious spectacles, looked at me and said, '*Harō.*'

'Hello,' I replied cheerfully in English. Both girls stared at me boldly. Kyushu women are not easily intimidated. I switched to Japanese and asked, 'Where are you from? Miyazaki?'

'No,' the serious girl replied. 'From Kobayashi.' This town was a half hour away inland.

'Kobayashi? Wonderful place,' I said.

They smiled but said nothing more.

'I hope you enjoy your visit to Miyazaki,' I added.

'*Hai*,' they said slowly.

The four characters of the phrase *hakko ichi-u* appeared on the front of the tower, very obvious to anyone looking at it. The main tower sits on a huge plinth, on each corner of which are helmeted warrior figures carrying shields and swords, their faces and armour rather Middle Eastern. These figures are anything but samurai-like, and not exactly symbols of peace, one could well say. I walked up to the base of the tower and then descended the front steps to find a group of three people standing on the path directly in front of the tower. One by one they stood on a flat, square stone and clapped twice, bowing their heads in prayer.

In the carpark right by the entrance to the park I saw a small van open at the back, selling food. A sign by the van advertised "corn and hot dogs." It was two o'clock, and despite having actually eaten a small hot dog at a service area on the side of the expressway halfway down to Miyazaki I was still hungry. I approached the van and found an old woman and a young woman inside.

'May I order a piece of corn?' I asked the old lady.

'Oh, of course,' she replied cheerfully. 'And a hot dog? They're delicious. Been on television.'

'Well, forgive me but I'll just have the corn. Maybe I'll buy a hotdog next time I come.'

Behind the old woman the young woman was eating something, a white face mask hanging from one ear as she ate.

'I wonder, may I ask you, is the tower some sort of Shinto shrine?' I asked.

'Oh, no.'

'I noticed some people clapping in front of it.'

'Ha! That's just to make an echo. If you clap hard enough it echoes back at you.'

'It's not religious in any way?'

'Oh, no, not at all.' She thrust a piece of boiled corn into a small oven toaster, having basted it with a thin savoury sauce first. 'Are you sure you wouldn't like a hotdog? They're famous.'

'Ah, I wish I could. But it's two o'clock and I had something to eat around noon. A piece of corn would be just right.'

'Ara.'

'Have you been here serving food for long?'

'Forty-seven years. Continuously.'

'Really? Congratulations, what a long time. Is your daughter going to carry on the business?' I asked, indicating the young women behind.

' I doubt it. But I'm still healthy. I'm not ready to retire.'

I introduced myself formally and handed the old woman a business card, saying I came from Fukuoka.

'Oh, dear. Aren't people in such a terrible hurry up there! It's so frantic, people running around at a terrible pace. Here in Miyazaki we take things easy. *Nombiri*, you know.'

'Well, Fukuoka seems pretty *nombiri* compared to Tokyo. I was in Tokyo only yesterday. The trains are packed like sardine cans. It's inhuman,' I said, recalling my awful journey from Shinagawa Station to Haneda Airport the previous evening on the Keisei Line.

'How terrible! Tokyo…..'

'Have you been there recently?'

'No. Why would I? Too busy here. Did you say you're from Kumamoto? Awful what happened to them with the earthquake and all that.'

'No, I'm from Fukuoka.'

'Oh. Well, they got it bad in Kumamoto. We felt sorry for them.'

I decided to tackle the tricky issue of *hakko ichi-u*.

'On the Peace Tower there are four large Chinese characters. I can't understand what they mean. Could you explain them to me, please?'

The old woman laughed. 'They're very old,' she said.

'Like classical Japanese?'

'Maybe.'

' There's an eight, and a one, and two others. What do they mean all together?'

'*Saaa….*'

'I'm sorry to ask you such a difficult question. My Japanese is not so good.'

'No, you speak wonderful Japanese!'

'Well, it could do with some improvement.'

'There you are,' she said, handing me the corn wrapped in a piece of paper.

Twenty-one The Stones of Miyazaki

Across the road from the Miyazaki Peace Tower lies the Miyazaki Jinja, a Shinto shrine dedicated to Japan's war dead. In the small museum within the shrine grounds there is an exhibit of memorabilia from Papua New Guinea and the Pacific, including this photograph of the remains of a Japanese soldier on the island of Bouganville. After the war a few Japanese went back to these battle grounds to gather the bones of the fallen soldiers for repatriation to Japan. This activity was well portrayed in the book by Charles Happell entitled 'The Bone Man of Kokoda.'

The sauce was dripping out one end. 'It's a pity you didn't have a hotdog. People come from a long way to eat them..'

Inside the van I noticed some photos of a pretty woman and an autograph. 'Is that a famous actress or singer?' I asked.

'She's from Taiwan,' said the old woman. 'Plenty of people from there come to Miyazaki.'

'And they like the Peace Tower?'

'They generally come to swim at the beach, or play golf.'

I thanked both women and went off to my car to eat the corn. It was fresh and crisp, the sauce just right, even if it did drip onto my trousers.

Later I searched the internet in Japanese for more about the Peace Tower. The Wikipedia entry was interesting reading. The tower was a project strongly promoted by the governor of Miyazaki in 1940, one Aikawa Katsuroku, as a measure to celebrate the 2,600[th] anniversary of Emperor Jimmu and expand the presence of the Miyazaki Jinja, the Shinto shrine dedicated to him. Aikawa seems to have chosen the *hakko ichi-u* slogan as a patriotic gesture, hardly surprising for anyone holding public office at that time. Prince Takamatsu, brother of Emperor Hirohito, attended the ceremony to dedicate the tower. According to the Wikipedia entry the stone statues I had noticed on each corner of the great plinth are not all warriors. Each one represents in turn a warrior, an artisan, a farmer, and a fisherman.

In 1946, the Occupation authorities banned the use of the phrase *hakko ichi-u* and ordered it removed from the tower, along with the warrior figure. Inside the tower a calligraphy scroll written by Prince Takamatsu and carrying the *hakko ichi-u* characters was secretly removed by local officials and hidden in a vault at the nearby Miyazaki Jinja. In 1957, the tower was formally renamed the Peace Tower. For a while it was used for rock climbing practice.

Then in 1962, well after the Occupation had ended, the warrior figure was restored to the tower and the *hakko ichi-u* characters were reinscribed on its front. Leftist politicians and labor unions furiously protested, but the chairman of the prefectural tourism association, Mr Iwakiri Shotaro, is recorded as sternly replying, "It's a work of art, and restoring it to its original state is only natural."

Such is the history of this — frankly speaking — unattractive monument. Walking around the park I found a sign that read: "Peace monument is made of stone gathered from all over the world in 1940. It is 37m high."

Was this true? I wondered.

A more considered report on the incident appeared on the Livedoor blog website. The Nanking "citizens group" was actually the Nanking Anti-Japanese War Museum. The Livedoor blogger reported a man in the

A Japanese soldier's helmet recovered in Papua New Guinea in 1977 on display in the museum at the Miyazaki Jinja shrine.

Miyazaki Prefectural Government as saying, "It's true that it [the tower] was built during wartime. But until now we've had no protests from China, Taiwan, Korea, or North Korea. It's been seventy years since the war, and this protest is the first one."

A man living close to the tower was quoted as saying, "Construction of the tower was a regional effort carried out by the prefectural government of Miyazaki at the time. It's doubtful that there's any direct link with the Japanese Government such that it's a symbol of some sort of 'invasion war'. Many people were engaged in the construction of the tower as a sort of gesture of respect, and many elderly people have a strong feeling about it. After the war, that's why we changed the name to 'The Tower of Peace.' There is no talk of tearing it down. It's a healthy thing."

Livedoor further reported that the demand for the return of the stones did not come directly from China. Instead it came from a Japan-China friendship group within the prefecture, which was "just passing on a request from China." This group claimed that part of the stone of the tomb of the founder of modern China, Sun Yat-sen, was used in the tower, and that it is regarded as a symbol of invasion in China. "It is embarrassing for Japan that such things exist. We started exchanging with Nanjing organizations about three years ago and we decided to seek return of stones to Miyazaki Prefecture after discussing it with them."

Did the Imperial Japanese Army deliberately take stones from Sun Yat-sen's tomb in Nanking and gleefully send them back to Japan to be part of the tower? This sounds very much like Chinese Communist Party propaganda, which a naïve group of left-wing Japanese people might easily swallow. Who knew what's true in all this? It was all rather depressing.

The following day I had to attend a vintage car rally in Bungo Takada over on the Kunisaki Peninsula, and I hadn't seen my parents-in-law for a week, so I decided to go to Hita that night instead of going back to Fukuoka. It looked like a long and wearying drive back from Miyazaki. The last time I'd been down this way the road back to Oita Prefecture was a local road that hugged the coast. There were some wonderful views of small islands and plenty of charming little fishing ports — local Kyushu at its best — but it took an awfully long time. I braced myself for what appeared to be a six-hour journey. Instead I discovered the wonders of Abenomics — a new expressway that ran all the way from Miyazaki to Oita. Oh, the beauty of printed money! It was only a two-lane expressway with passing lanes every few miles, but it sure made the trip easy. More to the point, starting from Fukuoka one could now circumnavigate Kyushu entirely by expressway. A new era had dawned.

When I reached my parents-in-law's home in Hita it was six o'clock in the evening and the air was very cold. In their kitchen the heater was not switched on and both of them wore heavy sweaters.

'Shouldn't we use the heater?' I suggested. The thermometer showed it was only twelve degrees inside.

'We're fine,' said my father-in-law. 'I'll go out and get some sashimi.' On the table there was already a plate of dark red *basashi*, his beloved horse sashimi.

Once he had gone off to the supermarket I began looking for the remote control for the air conditioner/heater, the *remokon* in Japanese.

'Where is it?' I asked my mother-in-law.

'It's…..it's lost,' she said, smiling with embarrassment.

'Lost? Surely not. It never leaves the kitchen.'

'We've looked for it, but…..'

'How many days have you not been using the heater?'

'Oh, dear. Well, we're okay…..you know…..the…..the…..what is it?'

'The *remokon*. For the heater.'

'Oh, yes. Well, we just can't find it.'

'It must be here,' I said, searching the floor. It was cluttered with various books, newspapers, bills, medicine, and everything else that an elderly couple felt the need to keep handy.

'Have you had a bath?' my mother-in-law suddenly asked. 'Perhaps I should fill the bath for you. I'm sure you'd enjoy a bath.'

'No need. I'll have a shower after dinner. We have to find the *remokon* to get the heater going. It's only twelve degrees in here.'

'I think you should have a bath.'

Sure enough the *remokon* emerged, cannily hidden under some books. By the time my father-in-law came back with the red snapper *sashimi* the kitchen was more or less warm.

It's hard to say which of Alan Booth's two books is the better one: The Roads to Sata or Looking for the Lost. Both are written in the same style. There's a mixture of history, descriptions of the landscape, Booth's opinions on things in Japan, and his quirky interactions with local Japanese people, particularly the many semi-fruitless conversations one enjoys in rural Japan. Because he insisted on walking everywhere he went, one gets a real sense of the physical effort he put into the journeys and the consequent pain and exhaustion he endured. Among my favourite chapters was one called Local Heroes in the second section of Looking for the Lost, titled Saigo's Last March. This chapter deals with a time midway through Booth's walk along the mountain trail in Miyazaki and Kagoshima where he stayed in the village of Mikado and then walked onwards to the villages of Shiromi and Murasho. The chapter includes a classic piece of writing on the notion of the hero in Japan. Booth wrote:

> "In the West a hero is presented to a young mind in the hope that he or she will inspire imitation. Japanese heroes, on the other hand, are meant to be admired from as safe and uninvolving a distance as possible. The question of imitating them, if it arose, would likely be laughed at.
>
> Indeed, it often seems as though they are selected for their status precisely because they represent everything that Japanese society teaches it members to avoid. They are not models; they are cautionary examples, and sometimes they are scapegoats. In a conformist nation, they are misfits and sore thumbs; among a materialistic people they pursue impossible dreams."

I found this analysis more or less true. It may not have applied to

Admiral Tōgō, but it certainly applied to Saigō Takamori. Conformity in Japan is the essence of social life and too much of business life. It was conformity that killed off Japan's once-dominant electronics industry, a conformity that discourages radical thinking and hence the development of new generation products. In car manufacturing Toyota is still dominant, but the company's severe commitment to perfection in its manufacturing activity tends to obscure an equally strong will to experiment with new materials, new fuels, and new ideas about what a motor car should be. Somewhere within Toyota there must be heroes of technology who do the radical, non-conformist thinking.

I decided to go and have a look at the villages mentioned in the Local Heroes chapter, hoping to find someone who actually met Alan Booth when he passed through the area in the early 1990s. Upon arriving in Mikado, Booth, soaking wet from a typhoon, found refuge at an inn called the called Nango Ryokan. I found the Nango Ryokan on my Google map and looked up its telephone number. When I called a man answered crisply.

'*Moshi, moshi,*' I began. 'My name is Thomson. I'm calling from Fukuoka to enquire about making a reservation.'

'Ahh!' cried the man.

'I'd like to stay one night, on Thursday.'

'Ah! It's a public holiday, you know.'

'Indeed it is. I thought I'd drive down and visit the mountains of Miyazaki. I'm very interested in Saigō Takamori.'

'Well, you can't stay here, I'm afraid. We're full on Thursday, *and* on Friday.'

'I'm sorry to hear that,' I said. 'I'll rethink my travel plans and call again sometime.'

This was a severe disappointment. It's true it was Golden Week, a period of around a week that included three public holidays in a row, plus a full weekend. Many people took the entire week off and either went overseas or travelled within Japan. Instead of driving to Mikado and looking for another *ryokan* I spent the Thursday at the Lauben Kolonie beach with Aldo and Joelle, their son Matteo, and their friends Ziv and Chika and their son Ori. Ziv was a tall, good-humoured Israeli who smoked electronic cigarettes. On the Friday I regained my enthusiasm for Miyazaki and decided to go down there on Saturday. The returning traffic on Sunday heading back north to Fukuoka would probably be terrible, but I didn't care. I called the Nango Ryokan again and a lady answered.

'I'm calling to make a reservation for tomorrow,' I began. 'I'm on my own.'

'Oh, tomorrow we're closed!' she cried. 'And on Sunday.'

'Well, maybe I'll try next weekend if' — I said, but the lady abruptly hung up on me. These Miyazaki innkeepers were a difficult bunch. Why would they close the *ryokan* during Golden Week? Obviously to have a holiday themselves. But one would think a village such as Mikado was hardly overrun with visitors outside times like Golden Week, Obon, or New Year. Why did the Nango Ryokan have to deliver me a second snub by closing on the weekend? The whole trip would have to wait another week.

Breakfast with my parents-in-law had, over the years, settled into an expected routine. I would arrange my timing to appear in the kitchen around ten minutes after they had dressed and gone downstairs to begin organising something to eat. We would greet each other, remark on the weather, and get down to the business of feeding ourselves. My mother-in-law would put two pieces of bread in the toaster, fuss about in the fridge, and entirely forget about making coffee. This task usually fell to me. I would plug in the hot water pot and look for the coffee plunger. Toast would soon appear on the table, but I would re-insert my piece into the toaster to give it a little more colour.

'But it'll be burnt!' my mother-in-law would protest.

'No, I'll see to it,' I would reply. Occasionally I'd get distracted and the toast would suffer a slight burning, which I actually liked.

'*Ara!*' my other-in-law would exclaim at the carbon on the toast. 'Scrape it off. It'll hurt you.'

This particular Friday morning there was no jam in the fridge. Quite where the jam had gone was a mystery because only my mother-in-law ever used it, and even then, in small amounts. I spread some margarine on my toast and cut it in half. The water was near boiling now, so I looked for the ground coffee to put into the plunger. My mother-in-law had a jar of instant coffee in hand and was spooning it into two cups, one for me and one for my father-in-law. I took the jar from her and peered inside. Oh, dear. She had mixed the ground up coffee with the instant coffee. As she poured water into the two cups a scum of ground coffee appeared on the surface in each.

'I'm not sure you should mix the ground coffee with the instant,' I said gently.

'Looks bad,' said my father-in-law gruffly.

'Oh, dear. Well…..ah, there you go,' said my mother-in-law. She poured in some milk and gave us the coffee.

My father-in-law was busy slicing pieces of a banana to put on his toast. He lifted the toast to take a bite and spilled some of the banana slices into his lap. This didn't deter him from continuing to attack the toast. He picked up the banana slices and replaced them on the half-eaten toast.

I sipped my coffee, swallowing the scum of ground coffee. As much as I was reluctant to admit it, my mother-in-law's mental condition was steadily deteriorating.

The early morning television news was ablaze with warnings of heavy rain on the way. Northern Kyushu would get 180mm, and southern Kyushu 200mm. That was a lot of rain. Floods were on the cards, said the weather forecaster with gravity. In Hiroshima, a police station had been robbed of a large amount of cash from its administrative section. This was thought to be an inside job. Then there was a tornado warning for the Goto Islands offshore of Nagasaki.

'Oh, floods,' my father-in-law grunted. 'Where are you going today?' he asked me.

'To Miyazaki,' I replied, glancing up from the iPhone on which I was reading the foreign news. Donald Trump had just fired James Comey, the FBI Director. The Democrats said Richard Nixon was back.

'*Saaa*, it's going to be wet down there,' he said with glee.

'*Ara*, Miyazaki?' my mother-in-law sighed. 'Why?'

'I'm looking for Saigō Takamori,' I replied.

'Hah!' my father-in-law laughed. He said no more. The banana slices on his toast required more diligent scrutiny.

'Are you coming back tonight?' my mother-in-law asked hopefully.

'Not a chance,' said my father-in-law. 'Miyazaki.….It's a long way. You'd better go there via Tsuetate. Better than the expressway.'

I agreed. Driving there on local roads would be more fun than speeding all the way there on an expressway. And so it proved. The rain was forecast to start falling in the afternoon, and the morning's drive up and across the great Aso caldera was a delight. I stopped at a convenience store in Aso when a bowel movement became necessary, but the toilets were all occupied by local workmen. I bought a coffee and drove on. Shortly after I turned off onto the road to Takamori and Takachiho I noticed a young foreign man by the side of the road with a rucksack trying to hitch a ride. Ashamed of myself I drove right past him. He looked unwashed, but why didn't I give him a lift? Maybe he could have caught a bus, I thought.

The road between Aso and Takamori wound up high into the peaks and then descended into a beautiful forest. In late spring it was one of the most scenic places in Kyushu, I thought. I saw two draught horses grazing in a pasture with some *wagyū* cattle. In a tiny hamlet a young woman was placing fresh flowers on the family grave beside some vegetable fields. On the radio, NHK was reporting the confirmation by the Senate of the new US Trade Representative, Robert Lighthizer. He was quoted as saying that Japan's agricultural protectionism was "the number one target". Just then I passed two small *wagyū* farms, the cattle peacefully munching on their special feed inside very old wooden sheds. Trump and Lighthizer are after you guys, I thought. Pity help these small producers.

I reached the town of Takachiho, home to a very sacred Shinto shrine. In Alan Booth's book *Looking for The Lost* he had stopped for the night in a nearby village called Hinokage where the locals had taken him to see an old tin mine once operated by an English mining engineer called Hans Hunter. An English-style clubhouse had been built for the British staff and their Japanese management colleagues. Hinokage Town had restored the clubhouse, now called the Eikokukan (English Hall is the best translation), and made it open for public inspection. Booth had been charmed by this piece of Englishness way up in the Kyushu mountains, so as a gentlemen's club member myself I felt obliged to visit it. After using the men's room at a *michi no eki* market near the bridge over Hinokage I turned up a road that followed a river into the steep valley. It had to be the narrowest, most winding road in Kyushu.

The road ran so deep into the mountains and in such a narrow valley that the only radio station I could get was NHK 2, an educational station for the most. There was an Italian lesson being broadcast, the text of the day being about Roman history. The Japanese host patiently repeated the translations of what the Italian man was saying. I drove another twenty minutes and the lesson turned to German. A woman began counting something in German. Japan had thirty million square kilometres of territory? The Japanese host explained that in German they don't count in units of ten-thousand like we Japanese.

It took forty minutes to reach the Eikokukan, which sat high on a hill in a forest of maple trees, a single-storey, wooden building coloured dark brown. Around it the peaks of the surrounding hills were very high. At the door a telephone sat inside a perspex box with instructions to call for help to be let inside.

An old lady drove up in a few minutes and accepted my ¥300 before unlocking the door. We introduced ourselves. Her name was Mrs Sago. Inside there were rooms with various exhibits of mining equipment and some large photographs of Hans Hunter and the various British and Japanese managers of the mine. The highlight was a video on a television set of old black-and-white film of the 1930s, showing foreign children riding around on bicycles and Hans Hunter in fine costume.

'He was a great man,' I said to Mrs Sago. Her sister lived in Hita, married to the owner of the Kawanami Gumi construction company.

'Oh, he had many interests outside of his business,' she said. 'He loved fishing in the rivers and golf.'

'Golf? Did he play here in Kyushu?'

'I don't know. But it says something about golf in English in here,' she said, showing me into another room. 'I'm afraid I can't read it.'

The text on a large caption below a photograph of Hunter explained a lot about his life. In fact, he was half Japanese, born in Kobe of a Japanese mother and an Irish father. At birth he was named Hanta Hansaburo but changed his name to Hans Hunter when sent to school in England, where he later graduated as a mining engineer. It seems he made quite a pile from his investments in tin and copper mines in Kyushu. The text said he was devoted to golf and that he had been one of the founders of the early golf clubs in Tokyo and Kobe such as Hodogaya, Koganei, and Hirono. I was thrilled to read this. As the only foreign committee member of the Japan Golf Association I saw this man as my logical predecessor. I wondered what had happened to him during the Pacific War and where he was buried.

As I was leaving I asked Mrs Sago whether she was at the Eikokukan every day should any friends of mine come in the future.

'Oh, pretty much,' she said. 'But its's the accommodation down the hill that we really do up here. Hikers and fishermen come and stay. A couple from Yokohama have come to manage everything. They're on a three-year contract. They work hard. I'm here most of the time.'

On the drive back down the narrow road it began to rain steadily. The language lesson had now lapsed into English. An American-accented man said in an incredulous tone, 'Leo has volunteered to be in charge of composting.' Then more: 'Please don't leave your garbage here......Empty...... Empty.....An *empty* house.....'

I was now heading for the Nango Ryokan in the village of Mikado, quite a distance away. This entailed a drive back through Takachiho and then into the mountains where Saigō and his rebellious samurai had fled from the better-armed government forces pursuing them. These mountains were not small. The road soon became a *rindō* or forest road, a single lane winding upwards through dark cypress forests. I ascended this way for perhaps a half hour until I reached the Iiboshi Pass, at a height of 1,037 metres above sea level according to a post. Rain was now falling heavily, and the mist was thick. Six appalling, huge wind turbines stood on the ridge above me, their giant propellers turning slowly. I got out of the car with an umbrella to take a pee and saw an old stone monument that marked Saigō's passage in 1877. Names of the people who had donated money to erect the monument were inscribed at its base. By now NHK 2 was giving French lessons, a woman talking about Japanese people in French. Nothing is more likely to catch people's attention in Japan than a foreigner talking about Japanese people and their fascinating characteristics.

Beyond doubt, the road up to Iiboshi Pass was formidable. That Saigō and his samurai, *and* Alan Booth, had walked up here in the August rains was really something to admire. I had the luxury of a Toyota Landcruiser.

Down the other side of the pass I ran into a road construction project. A cheerful young woman with a fat, round face dressed in heavy wet weather gear and a white helmet apologised profusely that I would have to wait for thirty minutes before proceeding further.

'What's going on?' I asked her. 'An accident or something?'

'No, they're removing trees from the road,' she explained. 'I'm most terribly sorry.'

Thirty minutes later I drove on and eventually arrived in Mikado. The rain was now pelting down. I rushed into the foyer of the Nango Ryokan, put my umbrella in the stand, and found a young man and a middle-aged woman there to greet me. Yes, I was Thomson who had reserved a room. They were nonchalant about my arrival, and the woman showed me upstairs to a typical tatami room. The walls were old, the carpet in the hallway stained with spots here and there.

'Have a bath,' the woman said. 'Dinner is at six-thirty.'

In the small bathroom on the ground floor I found a young man in the bath. He had a large tattoo on his upper arm, but it wasn't a *yakuza* tattoo. I soaped myself at the taps and he soon quit the bath, leaving me to soak in the hot water alone. Back in my room upstairs I had a quiet glass of *shochū* with warm water and watched the local Miyazaki news on television. A young woman was talking about a charity for children living in poverty. She received donations of food and drove around distributing them to poor single mothers. Outside my window a bright green Japanese maple spread its branches, the rain dripping off them and down into a tiny garden below. So, this is where Alan Booth stayed, I thought.

At dinner on the ground floor I sat alone at a Western-style table in a room with paper sliding doors, a television set before me with the NHK news on. It was a generous meal of tempura, grilled river fish, and a small chili-flavoured *nabe* hotpot heated by a round candle underneath. The middle-aged woman brought in a plate of semi-frozen sliced *wagyū* beef. A few moments later the doors slid open again and in came the *okami-san*, the proprietress Mrs Sakamoto.

'I hear you're interested in Saigō Takamori,' she said with a smile.

After formally introducing myself I explained that I was equally interested in the author Alan Booth, who had stayed here sometime around 1990.

'Oh, you know about him?' she exclaimed.

'Indeed. I'm following in his footsteps according to his book. That's why I came to stay at your *ryokan*.'

'*Maaa*. No one has ever done that before. Amazing.'

'Well, it's a very good book. He made a tremendous effort. Do you remember him?'

'Oh, yes,' she said. 'But in fact, we didn't know he was a famous man until one day we saw on television that he had died. We were shocked. It's quite something that you've come to visit because of him. My husband knows more about him, I should say.' She left with a polite bow.

A few moments later a man entered the room. I leapt up and introduced myself with a business card, assuming he was Mr Sakamoto. The man accepted the card happily and then sat down at the other table in the room. Far from being Mr Sakamoto he was just another guest. I felt stupid, but we began a friendly conversation as we ate dinner. He told me he was on holiday looking for *suiseki*, ornamental rocks.

'It's my hobby. I go all over Japan searching for good *suiseki*. Even up to Hokkaido.'

I expressed my admiration. 'And you find them where, in the ground?'

'Oh, in riverbanks or by the sea. You look for ones with some white crystal in them. Often they're displayed along with bonsai. Actually, there are some really good ones at the port of Moji.'

Mrs Sakamoto returned with bowls of hot soba instead of rice.

'As regards Saigō,' she said, 'he actually stayed the night at a house up the road. He didn't stay here. Our *ryokan* is only a hundred years old.'

The television news predicted tornadoes in Miyazaki tomorrow.

I drank my *shochū* after finishing the soba and made excuses for going to bed early. The futon on the tatami floor was anything but soft, but I didn't mind. This was not an expensive place to stay (it cost me a mere ¥7,300). I read a few pages of Booth's book and then went to sleep to the sound of the rain outside.

At breakfast the same man appeared and gave me two magazines about *suiseki* and a business card. He was Mr Tanida Junichiro from Kumamoto. A pretty young girl with hair dyed almost blond served us bowls of rice and *miso* soup. After breakfast I checked out and met the real Mr Sakamoto.

'So you know about Alan Booth? Amazing,' he said.

'Well, I've read his book a few times. He made a great effort walking around Japan, and he stayed here.'

'Oh, yes, I recall it still now. A huge *gaijin* appeared suddenly one rainy night, soaking wet and carrying a rucksack. We gave him the best room. He was researching Saigō Takamori. Actually, a weekly magazine called Walk Walk Japan serialised his diaries about the walk. And I think he wrote an article for an airline magazine.'

I asked him if he'd ever seen the Booth book.

'No, we've never seen it. But if we did our grandson could read it. He attends the American School in Tokyo.'

'Really? How is that?'

'Our daughter married a man who was transferred to his company's office in London for some years.'

It was then I realised the incongruity of it all: they didn't have a copy of Booth's book. I retrieved my own copy and said I wanted to donate it to the *ryokan*. If any foreign guests came they should read it. I marked the pages that mentioned the Nango Ryokan and wrote an inscription dedicated to Alan Booth's memory.

'Please keep it for your grandson,' I said, handing it to Mr Sakamoto. He thanked me gravely and accepted the book. 'Actually, Booth stopped at a liquor shop in Mikado and had an argument with an old lady,' I added.

'Oh, yes, he did,' said Mr Sakamoto, laughing.

'I wonder, is the liquor shop still there?'

'Indeed. It's called Takeda. The old lady used to run it, but not now.'

I thanked him for everything, and he gave me a printed article about Saigō.

Outside I made my farewells. Mrs Sakamoto and the young girl came out to see me off, bowing as I drove away. I stopped at the Takeda Liquor Store and bought a bottle of local *shochū*. A well made-up lady of around fifty served me. She insisted I also buy a bottle of plum wine. I explained the story about Alan Booth visiting the store around 1990.

'He met an older lady here and drank some beer. There was something of a disagreement when he asked for a glass.'

The lady laughed. 'We wouldn't give anyone a cup here,' she said. 'It's just not done.'

I said I'd heard the old lady had passed away.

'Not at all. She's ninety-seven, in the hospital.'

'Really? Well, maybe she won't remember the *gaijin* that asked for the glass.'

'Oh, she might. I'll ask her.'

'He stayed at the Nango Ryokan that night. He was sort of famous. A British author.'

'*Maaa*,' said the woman.

Despite the dire warnings of tornadoes and rain from NHK, the air was perfectly still. The forests on the sides of the mountain slopes had an extraordinary clarity and colour, small puffs of cloud and mist drifting among the ridges. I drove down to the coastal city of Hyuga, famous for its surf beaches. The river alongside the road was a brown, foaming mass of flowing water from the previous night's rain. NHK radio was now prattling on about a North Korean diplomat saying talks with the Trump Administration were possible "under the right conditions." As if, I thought.

At the surf beach the carpark was half full of exhausted surfers, the beach a wide expanse of brown sand with some half-decent waves on the sea surface. A dozen surfers were out there bobbing up and down, some of them catching a wave now and then. One man in the carpark had silver hair like mine. I drove up the coast and found a par three golf course where I played nine holes on my own with my hickory clubs. In America Louis Oosthuizen, the man with the most beautifully slow swing in the world, was leading the USPGA Tour tournament of the week.

Afterword

It was the forty-fifth anniversary of Okinawa being handed back to the Japanese Government by the US Occupation authorities. Naturally a lot of Okinawans used the occasion to stage protest marches against the remaining American military forces stationed in Okinawa. NHK and the other mainstream media played it down, Okinawa and its deep-seated discontent being an embarrassing issue for Japan. Prime Minister Abe and his government were rushing about on account of another North Korean missile launch early on Sunday morning. The missile was said to be a new type, apparently capable of reaching Hawaii. Elsewhere on that Monday morning, however, the country was quiet.

After two years of visiting parts of Kyushu and writing about it I had done enough. That said, there were a good few things I'd not included in the book, *onsens* for one. Kyushu is blessed with hundreds of these delightful hot springs, and while I had visited plenty of them I hadn't felt the need to write a special chapter about them. Someone else could do that, I thought. Another topic I had not dealt with adequately was Kyushu's fishing industry. It was very hard to get to know the fishermen and their communities, and although I was living right next to a working fishing port at Funakoshi I didn't really have a *madoguchi* or 'window' into the community such that I could write about it with any authority.

Kyushu is different from the rest of Japan, though not in any obvious way. Its history as the nearest part of what you might call mainland Japan (that is, excluding Okinawa) to the rest of the world, beginning with Korea and China, made it the historical *madoguchi* into Japan for all the Chinese and later Western culture that made the country what it is today. Kyushu people know this, yet they don't go around proclaiming it. In fact, one thing I discovered was that few people in Kyushu identify as *Kyushu* people. They are far more likely to identify with the city of prefecture in which they live. Few Kyushu people living in Tokyo or Osaka will be heard to say 'I'm from Kyushu.' They will say, 'I'm from Kumamoto' or 'I grew up in Fukuoka.' After all, there is no Government of Kyushu.

For the foreigner, however, the idea of Kyushu seems more distinct. It's an island, and on a map it looks to be separate from Honshu and the rest of Japan. If your Japanese language is good enough you can discern the various dialects spoken around Kyushu, the Kagoshima dialect being the most difficult to understand.

Looking at its modern history, say, going back a hundred and fifty years or so, I learned that what unified Japan as a modern nation was the political movement born in and pushed forward largely from Kagoshima. This movement resulted in the overthrow of the shogun and the restoration to political power of the Emperor Meiji in 1868. Once this was achieved Kagoshima, and much of Kyushu, slowly faded into obscurity. Except for the samurai rebellion in Kumamoto and Kagoshima in 1877, Kyushu as a distinct part of Japan became a redundant notion.

I've lived in Kyushu for six years now. Whenever I go up to Osaka or Tokyo – especially Tokyo – I find I'm appalled by the crowds there, and by the sheer density of everything. How, I ask myself, do people put up with it? How did Japan allow these cities to grow so big? Wouldn't it be better to spread some of the wealth, population, and development to other parts of Japan? But it never happened, and it never will. In fact one reason Tokyo and Osaka are so big is the abundance of flat land in each region. Back in 2011, when the tsunami destroyed the Fukushima nuclear power station, there was talk in the early days after the disaster of Tokyo having to be evacuated should the radiation leaking from the reactors get beyond control. But evacuate to where? In Kyushu there's a good deal of flat land around Fukuoka and Kumamoto, but it's not that much.

Now, though, Japan's population is shrinking. The effects of this are glaringly apparent in rural Kyushu where the mountain villages and small coastal towns are visibly emptying of people. Houses sit abandoned, and the quiet streets are populated almost entirely with old people. Elderly farmers drive around dangerously in their light trucks. The only young people you see are those working in convenience stores and other shops. The men and women on traffic duty at the many road construction sites are pensioners, standing there for hours stopping cars with a red flag or waving them through with a white one. The rural economy is kept afloat by these largely useless construction projects, financed by the money-printing of a government in hopeless, chronic deficit.

In writing about Kyushu, another topic I neglected was its many islands. I did visit and write about two islands called Himeshima, and also Tsushima over close to Korea. But I didn't spend any time writing about the lovely Yakushima south of Kagoshima or the Goto Islands offshore of Nagasaki, the latter home to many of Japan's Hidden Christians and partly the scene of Martin Scorsese's movie Silence. Nor did I visit Iki Island between Fukuoka and Tsushima, an island I could see on the horizon from my home on a clear day. I hope readers will find the time and the curiosity to fill in these blanks.

Most foreign visitors to Japan have a good look at Tokyo, Kyoto, and often Hiroshima. These days a lot of foreign tourists go up to Hokkaido to enjoy some of the world's best ski resorts. But few of the nearly twenty million foreign visitors every year make it down to Kyushu. This is a pity. Kyushu has no traffic jams, few earth tremors, the occasional typhoon, and as many Japanese people will attest, the best food in the country. For anyone with a thought of actually coming to live in Japan, Kyushu can't be beaten for sheer quality of life. There isn't much work down here for a foreign resident, but after a little while in these parts you will find the rest of the world very difficult to endure.

www.ingramcontent.com/pod-product-compliance
Lightning Source LLC
Chambersburg PA
CBHW042117300426
44117CB00021B/2978